The History of the
VIETNAM WAR

The History of the VIETNAM WAR

Author: Charles T. Kamps Jr.

Temple Press/Aerospace

Published by
Temple Press/Aerospace
an imprint of the Hamlyn Publishing Group Limited
a division of the Octopus Publishing Group
Michelin House, 81 Fulham Road
London SW3 6RB
and distributed for them by Octopus Distribution Services Limited
Rushden, Northamptonshire NN10 9RZ

Produced by Chris Bishop
Aerospace Publishing Limited
179 Dalling Road
London W6 0ES

Printed by Mandarin Offset Hong Kong

First published in 1988

ISBN 0-600-55783-9

DEDICATION

This book is dedicated to the Americans of my generation who served in Southeast Asia – the living and the dead.

Acknowledgements

I would like to recognize the valuable assistance of Capt. Shelby L. Stanton, who helped me through the ambiguous order of battle information – such as it exists – regarding the South Vietnamese, Cambodian, Thai, and Laotian armies. We spent hours talking on many subjects dealing with the war, and his guidance was irreplaceable. Thanks are also in order for two of my colleagues at the BDM Corporation, David C. Isby and Col. Guy M. Lubold Jr. (Ret.), who respectively provided declassified intelligence sources and weapons information so useful in writing the text. I would also like to acknowledge the contribution of Chuck Emerson, who made his personal references available to me for the project. Last, but not least, my thanks go out to Judy Van Benthuysen of the Navy Office of Information at the Pentagon, and Gwen Rich of the Naval Aviation History branch, for providing important items on very short notice. Any errors are my responsibility alone.

Burke, Virginia
30 April 1988

Contents

CHAPTER ONE

INTO THE ABYSS

Officers commanding the French Paratroopers at Dien Bien Phu meet to discuss their precarious position. Without the massive resources that the United States were later to bring into play, the French suffered a grievous military defeat.

The tragedy of Southeast Asia over the three decades after World War II is comfortably distant for most Americans. Veterans and Vietnamese refugees remain the living reminders of the most divisive period of US history since the Civil War. For the South Vietnamese, Cambodians and Laotians, however, it was a long, slow and agonizing end to a way of life, marked by death and desolation at every turn.

Vietnam's past is a history of constant struggle. Historically the ancient foe was China, but in the mid nineteenth century France expanded its colonial empire into Indochina and within two decades had gained a stranglehold on Vietnam, Laos and Cambodia. French language, education (of a sort), and Roman Catholicism were introduced, and were embraced by the native elite, so that articulate opposition to French colonial rule was almost non-existant. France's defeat at German hands in 1940 changed everything. The Vichy regime acquiesced to Japanese occupation of French Indochina, and that weakness in turn sparked a native resistance movement that would change the region completely within thirty years.

During the remainder of World War II the Vietnamese Communist Party's Viet Minh resistance group rose to prominence under the political leadership of Ho Chi Minh and the military prowess of Vo Nguyen Giap. With funds and supplies from the US Office of Strategic Services, the Viet Minh waged a guerrilla war against both the Japanese *and* the

EARLY DAYS

The United States began to funnel aid into South Vietnam as early as 1955. Military assistance took the form of equipment and advice. When North Vietnam declared that the political struggle with the South was now a military struggle, it was inevitable that the Americans in Vietnam would be sucked into the ensuing war. At first, the advisors remained just that, but with the inauguration of President Kennedy in 1961 a rapid US build up commenced. In 1962 the MACV (Military Assistance Command Vietnam) was set up. US Army helicopters were the first to see action.

South Vietnamese Navy recruits train under US instructors at San Diego. During the course of the war all RVN forces were gradually recast along American lines.

Left: The 57th Helicopter Company was among the first American units into Vietnam. This .30 caliber door gunner is seen aboard one of the company's CH-21s at Tan Son Nhut in February 1963.

Vichy French. At war's end in 1945 the Vietnamese Communists, as the strongest faction in the power vacuum after the Japanese defeat, stepped forward to take up the reins of government. During the ensuing confusion, France, liberated and smarting from the humiliation of its lacklustre performance in World War II, moved to restore its colonial relationship with Indochina.

French colonial policy

The post-war period was generally marked by the Western Allies' release of their former colonies. Initially, France stood alone in contrast to this movement, and found little support for her high-handedness, except from the United States, which ironically turned a deaf ear toward Ho Chi Minh's pleas for assistance in ridding Indochina of French colonialism. The reason was the American fear of a monolithic Communist bloc, directed from Moscow; a single-minded threat to all democratic nations. In fact, at the outbreak of the Korean War in 1950, the Trumand administration fully expected a co-ordinated Soviet attack to occur in Europe. The myth of the Communist monolith effectively prohibited the United States from supporting national liberation movements during the remainder of the Cold War

French Paratroopers jump from their transports and descend into the Tonkin jungles. Before long, they would be involved in a fierce and ultimately losing fight with the Viet Minh.

Left: A US advisor with an ARVN patrol. Officially non-combatants, the few US troops in the early days of the Vietnam conflict made conspicuous targets because of their size.

Above: In addition to advisors, American aid to the Republic of Vietnam took the form of military equipment. This M113 of the 4th Mechanized Rifle Squadron was in action in 1963.

Below: The Piasecki H-21 helicopter was the mainstay of early Army aviation in Vietnam. This example is seen in a tribal village, where advisors were establishing relations.

Victorious communist troops over-run a French strong point at Dien Bien Phu. The Viet Minh victory was complete; before long the French would have left and a new phase of the war begun.

period – a reversal of traditional American policy.

In the face of heavy French reinforcements the Viet Minh melted into the jungles and mountains to organize a protracted guerrilla war. In order to gain support the French granted nominal independence to Vietnam in 1948, under the titular emperor, Bao Dai. Ho Chi Minh countered by forming a shadow government which received immediate recognition and supplies from Moscow and Peking. The French, still recovering from World War II, found difficulty in meeting the rising requirements of the war. They relied heavily on indigenous and colonial troops for manpower, and on the Americans for financial assistance. Sources variously estimate the United States' contribution as between 50 and 75 percent of the total cost of French war effort.

By the time Dwight Eisenhower was inaugurated as President of the United States in 1953, the French/"Free" Vietnamese position had deteriorated considerably. Large sections of the northern part of Vietnam were in Communist hands, and supplies flowed freely over the Chinese border. In the context of the ongoing Korean War, and the tension between Taiwan and China, Vietnam remained in the mould of East/West confrontation. Eisenhower sent supplies and money to the pro-Western forces, but refused to commit troops, other than as advisors.

Dien Bien Phu

In a desperate bid to break the Viet Minh position in the north and cut their approach to Laos, General Henri Navarre committed nearly 16,000 French and Colonial troops to the defense of an air strip which was overlooked by surrounding hills at a place called Dien Bien Phu. Early in 1954, this position was fortified and reinforced in the hope that the Viet Minh would be shattered against the French defenses. This strategy, in effect taking the low ground and daring the enemy to come in from all sides, was based on a massive underestimate of General Giap and his forces, especially their ability to overcome natural obstacles and place artillery on the heights dominating Dien Bien Phu. Not only did Giap succeed in this endeavor, but he also moved large numbers of anti-aircraft guns into the area, to upset French air support and resupply – the only method available to replenish the surrounded garrison.

Viet Minh forces amounted to five divisions and

THE VIET CONG

The most difficult part of the war for American soldiers trained to fight a conventional war was knowing just who the enemy was. The North Vietnamese Army was one thing, but how could you identify a Viet Cong guerrilla? During the day he was a farmer, or a Saigon taxi driver, or even the little girl who cleaned your hootch every day. Even those who hated the communists might be helping them. The Viet Cong had no compunction about recruiting by terror, or holding a family hostage to the good behaviour of one of the members. About the only way you could be certain of a Viet Cong suspect would be to find them actually in possession of weapons.

Above: A VC agent discovered on a junk at the mouth of the Cua Tieu river in the Mekong Delta in February 1967. She was ferrying medical supplies to a mainland VC field hospital.

Below: Two VC suspects being held on a riverine patrol boat. The detainee on the right was later proved to be VC; the other had an RVN ID card issued to government supporters.

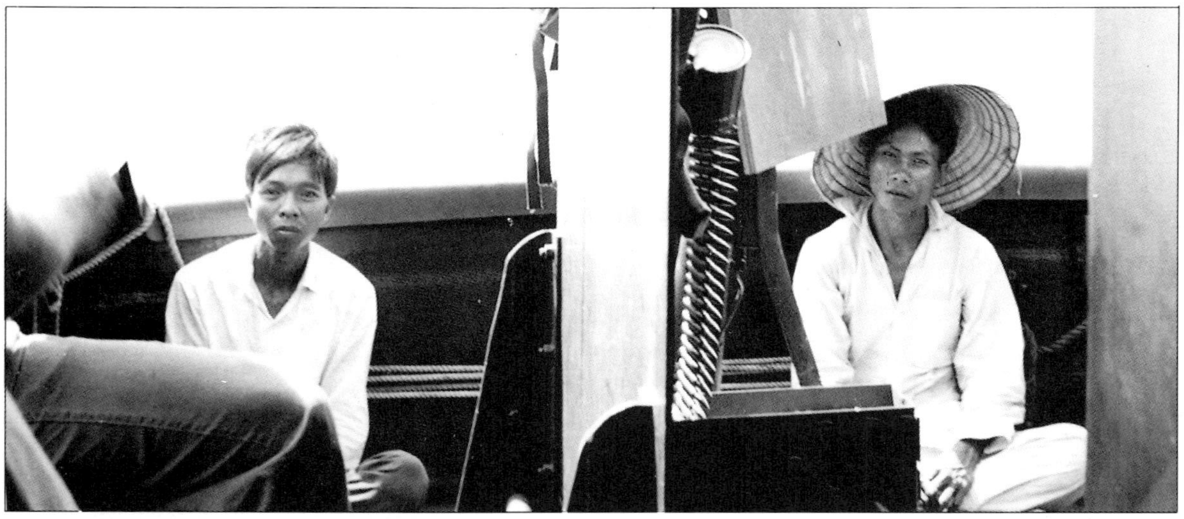

Below: Korean troops question two suspected VC in 1967. The Koreans were fiercely anti-communist; the prisoners' chances of survival after successful interrogation would be slim.

"I've always thought the Vietcong were a kind of scraggly bunch. They sure surprised me. Their mortar fire was extremely accurate. We got hit all over the place. I've never seen anybody better camouflaged. Once somebody yelled 'There they go!' and all I could see were seven bushes running along the paddy wall about 50 yards away"

Right: A typical South Vietnamese peasant, and cigar. The NVA intelligence agency CRA recruited, by propaganda and blackmail, a huge network of ordinary people as informers.

outnumbered the French by five to one. One by one the French outposts fell to heavy artillery and fanatical infantry assaults. It became obvious that the shrinking perimeter could not be held, and that American assistance would not be forthcoming. In early May of 1954 the last French bastions fell and the survivors were taken prisoner. The blow to France was psychologically overwhelming and negotiations began in earnest to end the war. By the 20th of July 1954, the interested parties signed an agreement in Geneva, Switzerland, to end hostilities in Indochina. Further, unsigned, agreements recognized a defacto temporary partition of Vietnam along the 17th parallel and advocated a Vietnam-wide election to decide the long-term fate of the country.

After the ceasefire agreement hundreds of thousands of refugees streamed north or south according to their political outlook. North Vietnam solidified under Ho's Communist regime, while South Vietnam's premiership fell to Ngo Dinh Diem, a powerful politician and a member of the Roman Catholic elite. Diem immediately faced challenges to his

President Ngo Dinh Diem receives Major General Matthew K. Deichelmann in 1958. Although corrupt, Diem was the most powerful politician in the south of Vietnam.

leadership, including coup attempts and reaction from opposing political parties, Buddhists, and strong-willed members of his own family. In 1955, Diem defeated Bao Dai for the presidency of South Vietnam in a rigged election, while Ho Chi Minh consolidated his power in the north by exterminating the remaining landowners. In 1956 the French evacuated the last of their troops from South Vietnam, and by 1957 Ho felt strong enough to unleash approximately 6,000 guerrillas who had stayed behind in the south. He counted on Diem's foot-dragging over agrarian reform as a basis for popular support of an insurgency like those Ho had previously mounted against the Japanese and the French.

Guerrilla country

South Vietnam's physical situation favored insurgent methods of operation. Its long western frontier bordered on Cambodia and Laos, nations were ostensibly neutral during the war but in fact served as sanctuaries for Communist forces and conduits for their supplies. Within South Vietnam the terrain was also friendly to guerrillas: the highland areas of the I and II Corps zones consist mainly of heavy canopied jungle over a mountainous spine, with some grassy plateau. The road net was poor or non-existent and off-road travel was slow and difficult. Ground air observation was very limited, with consequent degradation of indirect (artillery) fire and close air support. The highlands were sparsely populated by scattered mountain tribes which were not ethnic Vietnamese, and were often at odds with the Saigon government. The coastal lowland areas contained most of the north-south road net and were comparatively heavily populated, being suitable for rice farming and fishing. Visibility was generally good, as were conditions for air operations during the summer. Most of the southern part of South Vietnam (III and IV Corps zones) consists of the "Delta" region – the rice bowl of Indochina. This heavily populated area contained many long-time Viet Minh (later Viet Cong) strongholds. Roads were generally unsatisfactory because the extensive waterways formed the primary transportation net, though conditions in the Delta were generally favorable for air and helicopter operations.

Battle-hardened North

By the mid-1950s, the North Vietnamese Army (NVA) emerged from the war against the French, a tough, battle-hardened force with a winning record. The regular field force consisted of six veteran infantry divisions (304th, 308th, 312th, 316th, 320th and 325th), an artillery reserve (351st Heavy Division), and over 20 independent infantry regiments. The South Vietnamese Army (ARVN) declined in strength after the 1954 armistice, and was subsequently rebuilt, with the assistance of US advisors, between 1957 and 1959. By the later date it had three corps headquarters and a total of seven infantry divisions, an airborne group (5 battalions), four armored cavalry battalions with obsolete M-24 light tanks and M-8 armored cars, and eight separate artillery battalions. The ARVN did not have to face regular NVA troops initially, but only the guerrilla cadres in the Mekong Delta region. At first the ARVN proved adequate to the task, but it was often sidetracked to suppress Diem's political opponents and other dissident factions. Similarly, the NVA was put to work in the north to eradicate lingering pockets of resistance to the Communist regime.

Rise of the Viet Cong

By 1958, Ho Chi Minh began to reinforce the Vietnamese Communists (Viet Cong or VC) in the Mekong Delta area and coordinate their guerrilla campaign. By the next year, VC guerrillas increased their activities in the Central Highlands and in Tay

RANCH HAND

A programme initiated in Southeast Asia during January 1962 was to raise perhaps the most heated controversy in years to come, and one that still continues today. Under the programme name 'Ranch Hand', converted Fairchild UC-123 Provider transports sprayed large amounts of defoliant agents on selected areas of jungle, in order to deny the Viet Cong its cover, and in some instances to deny them foodstuffs.

***Above:** A Fairchild UC-123B sprays defoliant over the South Vietnamese jungle. For a short while the 'Ranch Hand' detachment flew with South Vietnamese markings.*

***Below:** Three UC-123Ks spray against the setting sun. This version of the Provider featured an auxiliary turbojet under each wing to augment its payload-carrying ability.*

***Right:** Standard transport Providers are seen prior to departing on a 'woods-burning' mission into the Boi Loi area in 1965. Later attempts used B-52 bombers.*

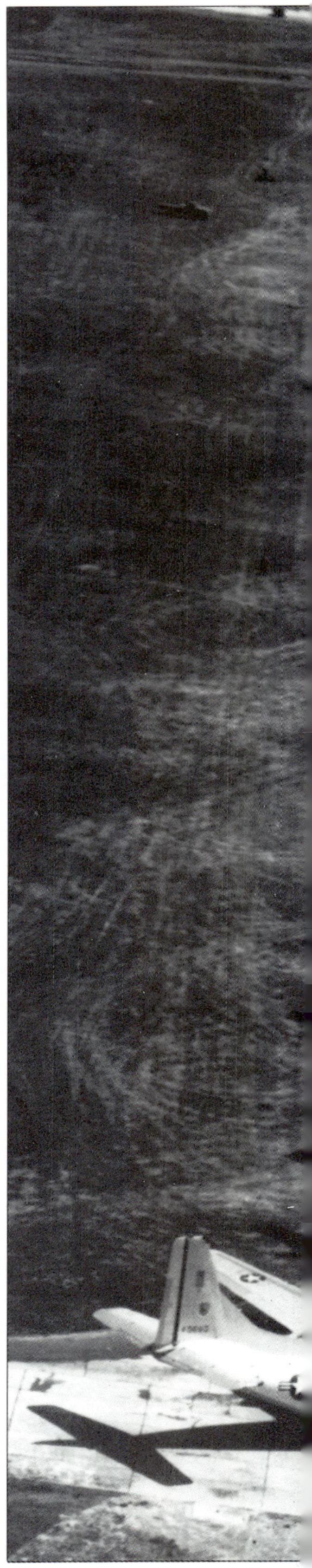

Ninh Province, close to South Vietnam's capital, Saigon. To support operations in the south, the NVA formed the 559th Transportation Group – the controlling authority for what would be known as the "Ho Chi Minh Trail". During 1959 it became obvious to the US Central Intelligence Agency that the infiltration of NVA cadre and supplies into the south was increasing rapidly. Likewise, VC political assassinations of South Vietnamese government officials showed a dramatic increase. Also, for the first time, VC units were conducting large-scale ambushes of ARVN units and decimating them. To match the increased level of Communist activity, the US enlarged its contingent of military advisors in South Vietnam from an average of about 650 during 1954-1959 to 900 in 1960.

US plans

The American military establishment had considered US reinforcement of South Vietnam as far back as 1952 – mainly in conventional terms. During the French struggle a plan was put forward to insert up to eight US divisions, but the ongoing Korean War, the mood of the American population, and the need for a strategic reserve effectively ruled out any such commitment.

After partition, US Army planners anticipated a regular NVA invasion, such as had taken place in Korea, and drew up contingency plans to reinforce South Vietnam with the US 1st and 25th Infantry Divisions, the 101st Airborne division, and the 3rd Marine Division. The object would be to hold enclaves which would support the defense of areas vital to South Vietnam's survival: Da Nang, Qui Nhon, Nha Trang, Vung Tau, Bien Hoa, and the airport at Tan Son Nhut. A decade later these locations would indeed serve as centers for US military activity. The envisioned conventional invasions didn't materialize, but Viet Cong guerrilla pressure posed an equally menacing threat to the Saigon government. During 1960 the NVA infiltrated about 4,500 hard-core cadre into the south, and established the National Liberation Front (NLF) as the shadow government for the Communists in South Vietnam. In reality the NLF was a deception which was wholly controlled by the North Vietnamese.

The election of John F. Kennedy to the United States presidency in November of 1960 brought a heightened interest in Vietnam and a new direction to American policy there. Kennedy was a supporter of counterinsurgency concepts and a champion of

> **The ARVN was either unable or unwilling or unable to clear the Boi Loi Woods by mounting a conventional ground operation. We tried to substitute a technological solution for manpower – using defoliants to strip the leaves from the trees and deny the Viet Cong its use as a hiding place. We began spraying in January 1964, and in one month delivered 83,000 gallons of herbicides**

Above: With four UC-123s flying in a stepped trail formation, area coverage was impressive.

Below: Operating at slow speeds and low altitude made the UC-123s vulnerable to groundfire. Escorting F-4 Phantoms attempted to keep the VC gunners' heads down.

President Eisenhower, seen during an Asian tour in 1960, had been presented with plans for US military intervention in Vietnam as far back as 1952.

the US Army's Special Forces, who donned their famous green berets during his administration.

Special Forces A detachments were placed on temporary duty in Vietnam from the 1st Special Forces Group on Okinawa and from the 5th and 7th Special Forces Groups at Fort Bragg, North Carolina. By December 1963 Special Forces detachments, working through counterpart Vietnamese Special Forces units, had trained and armed 18,000 men as strike force troops and 43,376 as hamlet militia, the new name for village defenders. (1)

He was convinced that political and economic reform and a US advisory/support effort, could turn the tide in South Vietnam. In 1961, Kennedy moved to aid the ARVN by funding a 30,000-man increase in its strength.

On 11 December 1961 the United States aircraft carrier USS *Card* docked in downtown Saigon with 32 U.S. Army H-21 helicopters and 400 men. The 57th Transportation Company (Light Helicopter) from Fort Lewis, Wash., and the 8th Transportation Company (Light Helicopter) from Fort Bragg, N.C., had arrived in Southeast Asia. This event had a two-fold significance: it was the first major symbol of United States combat power in Vietnam: and, it was the beginning of a new era of airmobility in the United States Army.

Just twelve days later these helicopters were committed into the first airmobile combat action in Vietnam, Operation CHOPPER. Approximately 1,000 Vietnamese paratroopers were airlifted into a suspected Viet Cong headquarters about ten miles west of the Vietnamese capital. The paratroopers captured an elusive underground radio transmitter after meeting only slight resistance from a surprised enemy. Major George D. Hardesty, Jr. of the 8th Transportation Company and Major Robert J. Dillard of the 57th could report that their units had performed outstandingly under their baptism of fire. (2)

US build-up

US advisors and support troops (mainly helicopter transport units) continued to build, and reached a total of 16,300 by the end of 1963. To direct the increased effort, the US Military Assistance Advisory Group was replaced in 1962 by a larger headquarters, Military Assistance Command Vietnam (MACV), under General Paul Harkins of the US Army.

US Air Force "support" missions expanded into flying reconnaissance sorties, air commando ground attack missions, and Operation Ranch Hand, defoliation sweeps with herbicides.

A South Vietnamese Air Force (VNAF) H-34 helicopter equipped with a HIDAL spray system flew the first defoliation test mission in South Vietnam along a road north of Kontum on August 10, 1961. Exactly two weeks later, a VNAF C-47 flew the first fixed-wing spray mission. Both missions dispersed the herbicide Dinoxol. President Diem personally selected the target for the C-47 mission on August 24. It consisted of a four-kilometer stretch of Route 13 about 80 km north of Saigon near the village of Chon Thanh. The Special Aerial Spray Flight provided the spray equipment used in the VNAF C-47 and also sent TSgt Leon O. Roe to South Vietnam to assemble and install it. Capt. Mario D. Cadori, an experienced spray pilot formerly assigned to the SASF but at that time serving in the Pacific Air Forces (PACAF) area, was sent to train the South Vietnamese pilots who flew this and other C-47 test missions in low-altitude spray techniques. Although American evaluations of the results of this particular test were disappointing, President Diem was reportedly impressed by the overall results of the tests. He remained thereafter a staunch supporter of the defoliation program. (3)

US Army helicopters, reinforced by some US Marine helicopters, began to conduct combat air assaults with ARVN infantry units. In general however, the Viet Cong remained elusive and continued guerrilla operations at a low level – concentrating in battalion-size units when necessary. President Diem's government proved incapable of dealing effectively with either the Viet Cong or with its own internal problems. The ARVN grew in size but not in efficiency or leadership. The Strategic Hamlet program, which displaced the population, concentrating villagers into fortified areas, did nothing for security and alienated the peasants, who had strong attachments to their ancestral land. Real governmental and economic reform seemed stalled, and the Buddhist majority population faced continued harassment.

Diem is killed

By early October of 1963, South Vietnamese general officers had planned a coup to unseat Diem,

Above: An American volunteer helps with a childrens party in a Saigon hospital.

Below: The villagers moved to protected hamlets often did not see that they would be safe from the VC, just that they had been torn from their ancestral homes.

HEARTS AND MINDS

There is only one way of winning a guerrilla war, and that is by denying insurrectionists the support of the people. You can either physically cut the villagers off from contact with the enemy, or you can endeavour to make their life more pleasant than the enemy can. There was some success along these lines in Vietnam. MACV was helped in its aim by the Viet Cong technique of terrorizing supplies and volunteers out of reluctant villages. Indeed, some of the Viet Cong themselves were induced to change sides, where they become known as Kit Carson Scouts and proved most valuable.

and had informed US officials of their intentions. President Kennedy made no move to discourage the plotters. On November 2nd the generals seized the presidential palace and took Diem prisoner. He was quickly murdered and control of the government passed to General Duong Van Minh and his Revolutionary Military Committee. Kennedy, who would himself die from an assassin's bullet twenty days later in Dallas, Texas, was shocked by Diem's violent end. Thrust into the presidency, Vice President Lyndon Johnson carried on with what he assumed to be Kennedy's intentions for continued American support for South Vietnam.

The view from Hanoi

During 1964, the North Vietnamese and the Americans evaluated the situation in South Vietnam. Ho Chi Minh, at that time, was convinced that continued or increased US assistance would doom the Viet Cong to ultimate failure. On this basis he prepared the NVA for a more active role, including the infiltration of regular combat units into the south. This would have probably been inevitable in any case however, because Hanoi's perception of the war from the start was one of a reunification effort – not the establishment of an independent Communist South Vietnam.

The first US Army units into Vietnam were helicopter units, supporting the operations of the Republic's army. The pilots soon found themselves in combat.

The view from Washington was equally pessimistic. The Viet Cong appeared to be successful in spite of the presence of 23,000 US support personnel and massive aid programs. ARVN battalions began to be defeated on a disturbingly regular basis. Nor did the Saigon government inspire any confidence. In January, General Minh was ousted by Major General Nguyen Khanh, who promptly purged the ARVN's corps and divisional commands, leading to further demoralization.

Domino theory

In June, General Maxwell D. Taylor replaced Henry Cabot Lodge as US Ambassador to South Vietnam, and General William C. Westmoreland replaced Harkins as MACV commander. Westmoreland's personality would dominate the US Army's participation for virtually the remainder of American involvement in the war. "Westy" quickly proved accomodating to President Johnson's perceptions about the war. At this time Johnson was

Above: Kit Carson Scouts were former Viet Cong who had been won over to the Free World forces. They were vital links in the struggle for the hearts and minds of the people. Here one of the ex-communists working with the 11th Cavalry checks ID cards in the village of Hung Loc.

Above: Green Berets distribute medicine among Vietnamese children, part of a wide range of programs that included engineering, advice on agriculture, and education.

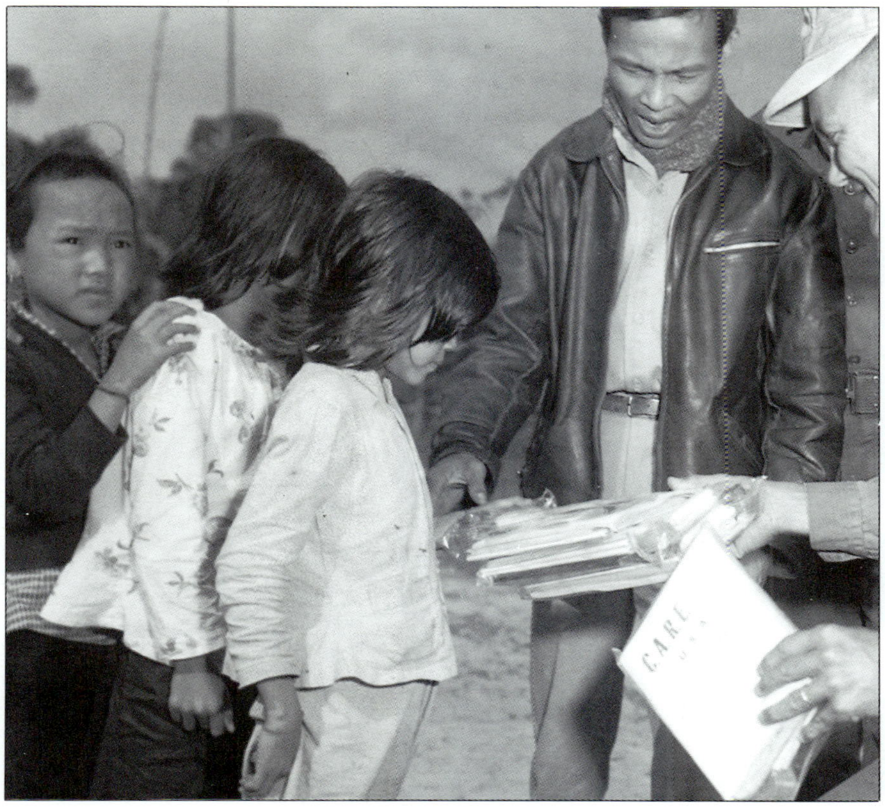

Right: Children of Phong Bac school receive explanatory literature issued by the Co-operative for American Relief Everywhere, in 1965.

Below: A US Marine and a Kit Carson Scout in an operation near Da Nang, 1970. The KC Scouts' inside information on VC movements, supply caches and camps proved invaluable.

expounding the so-called "Domino Theory" – that the fall of South Vietnam would trigger the fall of Cambodia and Laos (and maybe more), and cause irreparable damage to the US position in Asia – while the Central Intelligence Agency was telling him that this was not necessarily the case because of the strong US presence in the insular West Pacific nations. In fact, a rational assessment of US policy would have revealed that South Vietnam and Indo-china were not and never could be vital to American interests.

The South falters

During July, further lacklustre performance on the part of the ARVN reinforced the American perception that South Vietnam was about to collapse. At Chuong Thien, the Viet Cong executed a masterful battle plan, which would become a standard formula

In 1964 the pilot of an Air Force reconnaissance plane could only watch the Viet Cong in the act of torching a Montagnard village.

for success. By attacking an ARVN outpost, the VC drew out an ARVN relief force which they ambushed en route. The ARVN suffered 200 casualties and lost 100 weapons in this one engagement. Later that month the VC, led by NVA regulars and Red Chinese advisors, succeeded in overrunning Cai Be in Dinh Tuong Province, slaughtering South Vietnamese local troops, women, and children. With Viet Cong forces country-wide estimated at over 30,000 main force regulars and over 75,000 local force VC, the situation looked grave.

Incident in the Tonkin Gulf

Then, in August, came the incident which would set in motion full US anticipation in the war. For the better part of the year, the US Navy had been engaged in covert actions in support of Operations Plan 34A. These included reconnaissance flights over Laos and electronic surveillance of North Vietnam by ships in the Gulf of Tonkin. On August 2nd the destroyer USS *Maddox*, carrying out surveillance in the Gulf, was unsuccessfully attacked by North Vietnamese torpedo boats. Gunfire from the *Maddox* and F-8 jets from the carrier *Ticonderoga* drove off the attackers. On the evening of the 4th, the *Maddox*, in company with another destroyer, *Turner Joy*, reported another North Vietnamese attack. There are grave doubts that this attack ever took place. By the time the situation was clarified, President Johnson had already authorized air strikes against North Vietnam in retaliation for the "second" attack. On the afternoon of the 5th, aircraft from the carriers *Constellation* and *Ticonderoga* attacked North Vietnamese naval bases and oil storage installations at Hongay, Loc Ghao, Phuc Loi and Quang Khe. Lyndon Johnson had served notice that the United States was entering the shooting war.

THE PEOPLE'S WAR

Vietnam is a land of many tribes and peoples, and some who opposed the Viet Cong were not much better disposed to the Saigon government. Nevertheless, they would be ferocious fighters in defence of their homes. Supplied with US equipment, a number of organizations came into being. The Self-defence Corps was renamed Popular Forces in 1964. Civilian Irregular Defence Groups operated alongside US Special Forces in remote areas. Regional Forces were more military, being used to defend military and strategic installations, unlike the Popular Forces who were local.

***Right:** A South Vietnamese Self Defense Corps patrol assembles, October 1962. In 1964 these volunteers were reorganized and renamed Popular Forces.*

Above: US Marines and ARVN Popular Forces return fire on a sniper while on patrol south of Quang Tri City in August 1968. The PF's local knowledge could be invaluable to US forces: these troops were part of Combined Action Group 4.

Right: The crew of a fishing boat is covered by a member of the RVN Junk Force armed with a Thompson .45 SMG while the ship is searched for supplies and arms destined for the Viet Cong, in May 1962. By 1973 such volunteer forces were largely supplanted by the 42,000-man-strong RVN Navy.

Right: Montagnard troops prepare for a patrol against the Viet Cong in 1963. Wicker baskets were used as capacious backpacks. Montagnards were first recruited into the war in 1961 as Civilian Irregular Defense Groups (CIDGs) by US Special Forces, to halt NVA and VC infiltration in the Central Highlands. CIDGs fought well with US advisers, but a long-standing hostility to the Vietnamese led to two revolts against the RVN government. Today, Montagnards continue the guerrilla war against communism.

Right: Veteran anti-communist fighter Le Van A attends a class in hamlet defense with other Popular Forces members in 1970. While the PF were village-based, Regional Forces defended isolated strategic outposts in the countryside such as bridges and ferries.

Left: Volunteers for the PF march off for a 13-week training course at the ARVN's National Training Center. After 1964 all volunteer forces were integrated into the ARVN command.

"A handful of Americans and Nung tribesmen made a last stand at the Special Forces camp in the A Shau, but the irregulars went over to the Viet Cong and turned their guns on us. Most of the survivors were rescued, but if I could get my hands on that Chung Wei (the top Vietnamese officer in the camp) I'd kill him!"

PF Volunteers are transported in a US Navy PBR to their night ambush position along the Vinh Te Canal.

CHAPTER TWO

COMMITMENT

1964-1965

A crewman maintains his CH-21 Shawnee watched by uncomprehending peasants. It would not be long before every South Vietnamese would be familiar with the sight of American helicopters.

The most important result of the attack on the *Maddox* was the passage of the Tonkin Gulf Resolution by the US Congress. This law gave the President carte blanche to take steps necessary to protect US interests in Southeast Asia. In the years to come it would serve as Lyndon Johnson's tool for conducting the war without reference to Congress. That notwithstanding, throughout America's period of active involvement there always seemed to be a Congressional majority which approved the military budget. This would indicate that on the Congressional scale of priorities, where getting re-elected comes first, there was a perception of voter support for, or at least acquiescence with, the war. Even at this early date there were clouds on the horizon, however. In September of 1964 the Berkeley campus saw the first large student demonstration against the war.

In South Vietnam the search for a stable government continued. Minh was demoted by the Military Revolutionary Council, which installed General Nguyen Khanh as the new president. Buddhist reaction was swift and violent. Catholic reaction was even worse – an attempted coup by Generals Lam Van Phat and Duong Van Duc, which was finally defeated by threatened air attacks from Air Vice Marshal Nguyen Cao Ky. Khanh's government was short lived however, as he resigned the premiership the next month in favor of former Saigon mayor Tran Van Huong. The Saigon government's internal strife provided an opportunity for several Montangnard tribes in the Central Highlands to strike at ARVN outposts in September. US advisors, training and supporting both sides, had to intervene to calm the situation.

Late in December another coup, lead this time by Generals Khanh and Thieu and Air Vice Marshal

The Brinks Hotel in Saigon was used by the US Armed Forces Vietnam as officers billets. On Christmas Eve 1964, Viet Cong terrorists exploded a car bomb in the garage under the hotel, killing two Americans and injuring 107 people.

Ky, set up an Armed Forces Council which at first supported the Huong government but wanted to keep a lid on rising Buddhist aspirations. At the end of January 1965, in a reversal of position, the Armed Forces Council abolished the Huong government and placed executive power in the hands of General Khanh. Khanh, in turn, gave the premiership to Dr. Phan Juy Quat in mid-February, with instructions to form a consensus government. By the end of the month, Khanh himself was unseated as commander of South Vietnam's armed forces by his own Council, and General Thieu assumed the position of power behind the throne.

US politics

In the US presidential campaign which led to the November 1964 election, the Republican challenger, Senator Barry Goldwater of Arizona, tried to present the case of Vietnam in a forthright manner to the electorate. As a Major General in the US Air Force Reserve, Goldwater had military expertise and very definite opinions about the conduct of the war. President Johnson, adopting a policy of emphasizing his social reform programs (the so-called "Great Society") and deliberately downplaying the increasing US involvement in the war, successfully

WAR AT SEA

In August 1964 the destroyer USS Maddox was operating in the waters of the Gulf of Tonkin when it came under attack from North Vietnamese torpedo-boats. Even though the active US involvement in combat operations in South East Asia was precipitated by naval actions, the power of the US Navy ensured that such events did not recur. Nevertheless, the Navy was far from inactive.

An Amphibious Task Force heading for Yokosuka leaves the Gulf of Tonkin in company with the guided missile destroyer USS Parsons (DDG-33) and the Carrier USS Bonhomme Richard (CVA-31).

Top Left: The North Vietnamese had a number of fast patrol craft such as these Chinese-built 'Shanghai II' class boats, but they had little effect on the War.

Above: PGM patrol craft were built specifically for supply to U.S. Allies. This PGM of the RVN is at anchor near its base at Binh Ba.

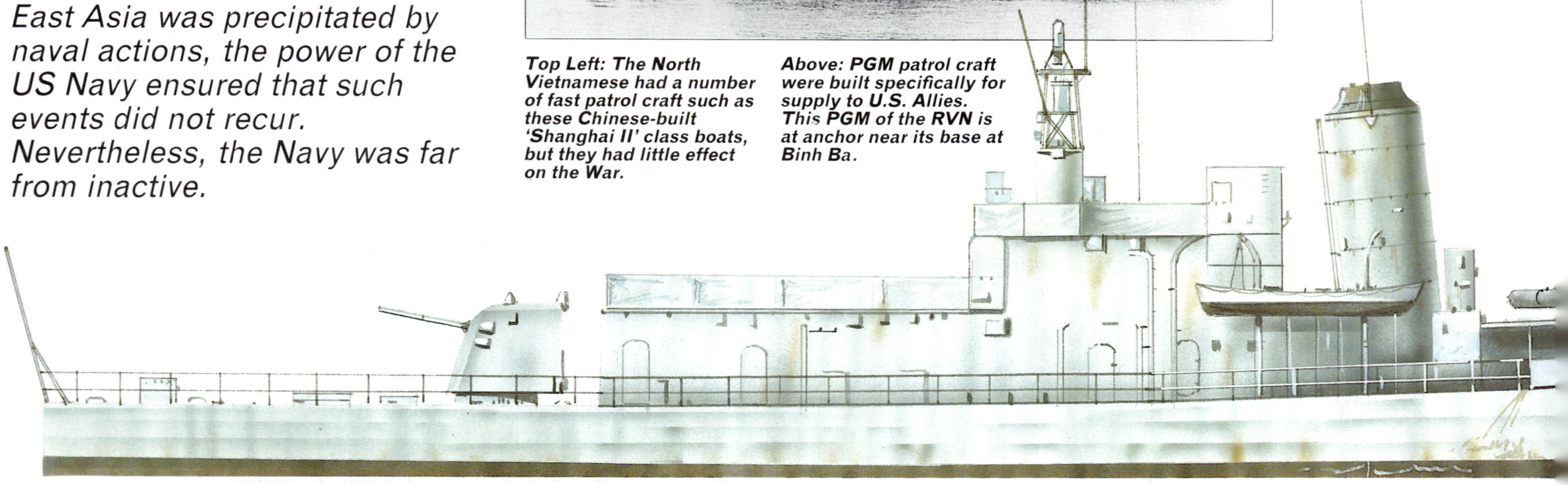

A hostile Vietnamese torpedo boat is seen from the deck of the USS Maddox. The attack on the Maddox as she steamed through international waters signalled the start of US military action in Vietnam.

branded Goldwater a warmonger in the public eye. Johnson won by a landslide, and those who voted for him in the belief that the war would not expand were sorely disappointed.

Viet Cong successes

During November 1964 a reported 1,370 VC and NVA were killed and a further 370 taken prisoner. In mid-December however, ARVN battlefield reverses resulted in 620 South Vietnamese dead and missing in a single week – the highest one-week losses up to that time. Before the end of the month, the Viet Cong scored another propaganda victory by setting off a car bomb outside the Brink Hotel, used as US officer accommodation in Saigon, killing two and wounding 65.

The old, colonial style building had been taken over as a US Army officers' billet and was replete with all the little pleasures that we brought with us to war, including a shoeshine stand, a small PX selling nylons, makeup and cosmetics to our all-male force, and a dining area nicknamed "the Pit." Prices being low everywhere, most of the men preferred to eat up the street where several joints offered hamburgers and other amenities.

On the afternoon of 24 December, tinsel hung from the ceiling in the dining area and a plastic Christmas tree was alight in a corner. With Army officer-advisors preparing to celebrate Christmas Eve, a Viet Cong sapper on a bicycle hurled a 250-lb (113-kg) *plastique* charge into the place and the Brink Hotel exploded, throwing flames and debris out into the street and collapsing upon itself.

We didn't know it then, of course, but following Lyndon Johnson's re-election the previous month, Ambassador Maxwell Taylor had urged that there be swift and powerful retaliation against North Vietnam for any such VC provocation.

It didn't happen this time, however. The latest South Vietnamese government under General Nguyen Khanh, was in turmoil seeking to cope with protests by Buddhist agitators, and was in no condition to participate in a credible joint response. The Brinks bombing came and went. (1)

The Viet Cong capped their successes in 1964 by seizing Binh Gia, south of Saigon, and holding it temporarily against a regimental-size ARVN heliborne counterattack. Characteristically, the Viet Cong ambushed ARVN Rangers moving to the scene and decimated them. For the cost of about 120 of their own, the Viet Cong inflicted 500 casualties on the hapless ARVN, including 200 dead.

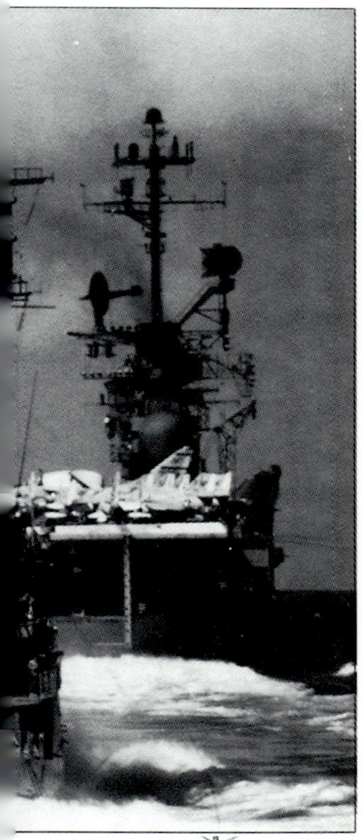

"People like me should be at sea. They should be on destroyers. What else? On destroyers, the Captain know who you are, you can talk to him man to man. Besides, I like to hear them big guns talk"

The 'Essex' class carrier USS Intrepid had a long and varied career. Hit several times by Kamikazes in the Second World War, she survived to complete three tours of duty off Vietnam.

USS Maddox was an Allen M. Sumner class destroyer completed in 1944. Modernized in the 1950s, the Maddox came under North Vietnamese attack in the 1964 Tonkin Gulf Incident, accelerating the American involvement in SE Asia.

On November 1st, 1964 the VC attacked the Bien Hoa air base, causing damage to 26 US and South Vietnamese aircraft. Normally such an incident would have triggered retaliation, but Lyndon Johnson, trying to play down the war in the days before the presidential election, simply ignored the attack. Similarly, in keeping with Johnson's policy of "low key" war, no news was released about escalation of the US air effort in Laos from reconnaissance to attack missions, known as Operation Barrel Roll, which began in December of 1964.

The Viet Cong kicked off their 1965 campaign with several simultaneous strikes against US support facilities in early February. The most serious of these was an attack on the compound at Camp Holloway, near Pleiku in the Central Highlands, which killed eight Americans, wounded 126, and damaged or destroyed 25 aircraft.

It was 2 a.m. on the morning of Feb. 7, only hours after Kosygin had assured a cheering crowd in Hanoi that Russia would "not remain indifferent" if "acts of war" were carried out against North Vietnam, that Sp/5 Jesse A. Pyle of Marina, Calif., noticed dark shadows moving near the perimeter wire 100 yards from the U.S. Army headquarters at Pleiku in Vietnam's central highlands. Pyle opened fire. It was the last act of his life. The shadows, materializing into Communist Viet Cong guerrrillas, fatally wounded Pyle with their grenades. But his quick action had awakened the men located inside the compound. As a result, the Viet Cong were forced to set off their explosive charges – which were improvised from beer cans wrapped in bamboo cord – prematurely or not at all.

Four miles away at Camp Holloway, a U.S. helicopter base, the Viet Cong had better luck.

Only two hours after the so-called cease-fire ended at midnight, two squads of Viet Cong rushed out of the high grass, cut through a double apron of barbed wire without being seen by guards, began blowing up parked helicopters and light reconnaissance planes with satchel charges. At the same time guerrillas hiding in a hamlet 1,000 yds. from the camp poured 55 rounds from 81-mm mortars smack into the compound where 400 U.S. advisers lived. They were right on target. Fifty-two billets were damaged, including some totally destroyed. Within 15 minutes, the guerrillas pulled back, covering their retreat with recoilless rifles and rifle grenades. Seven Americans died, more than 100 were wounded, and nearly a score of aircraft was damaged or destroyed. (2)

CH-21s of the US Army ferry Vietnamese Marines from Moc Hoa, 45 miles west of Saigon towards a suspected Viet Cong position. By 1964 the helicopters and their bases had become prime guerrilla targets.

They followed up their success two days later with an attack on the US base at Qui Nhon, killing 23 Americans in a barracks explosion. By this time the US estimated that about 20,000 hard-core guerrillas had infiltrated from North Vietnam, and the Saigon government only controlled 40 per cent of its own country. General Westmoreland requested, and got, US Marines to help secure US base areas from Viet

THE ARVN

Naturally, the Army of the Republic of Vietnam was numerically the strongest of the forces fighting for the survival of their country. Well equipped by the United States, it wielded considerable political influence, but on the battlefield it was not always successful. The individual ARVN soldier could fight as well as the next man, but too often he was betrayed by incompetent or corrupt leadership. Nevertheless, when the North mounted a full scale invasion in 1972, the South Vietnamese Army (admittedly helped by massive US air support) threw back the NVA with heavy losses.

Above: In 1963, the most obvious US aid to the Vietnamese Army was in providing helicopter support. They were often used to carry wounded, and here a soldier is being rushed to an aircraft.

Left: Cambodian mercenaries in Vietnamese service line up before an airlift into action. Centuries of emnity between the peoples of South East Asia meant that there were always volunteers willing to fight.

Below: Members of the ARVN 10th Division operating with troops from the US 11th Armored Cavalry Regiment.

In the highlands a patrol of the 9th ARVN Division moves up a trail. By this time the process of Vietnamization was in full swing.

Left: November 1970. By this time, ARVNs were armed and organized along US Army lines. This ARVN Ranger is on a patrol in the central part of II Corps.

Above: ARVN Rangers are airlifted into Cambodia in US Army helicopters. Vietnamese troops made up the bulk of the forces crossing the border in 1970.

Below: Hunkered down behind the turret of an M41 light tank, South Vietnamese troops open fire with a .50 cal Browning machine gun.

The M41 Walker Bulldog first saw combat in Korea, and has been supplied to more than 20 armies around the world. In Vietnam, its influential presence in many elections led to it being nicknamed the 'Voting Machine'.

VIETNAM LEADERS

North Vietnam had an advantage in the long struggle with the South in its continuity of leadership. Ho Chi Minh headed the Vietnamese communist party from before the Second World War till his death, and the same Generals who had defeated the French were the masterminds behind the Northern advances which ended the war. By contrast, Saigon had a variety of rulers. Some led the country for long periods until assassination or exile forced them out. Corruption was rife, and the army was always a force to be reckoned with in domestic politics.

Above: Ho represents Vietnam at a congress in Moscow, 1922. Ho Chi Minh was an alias, meaning 'He who enlightens'.

Below: Ho (centre) and General Vo Nguyen Giap (right) with Chinese advisers during the Viet Minh's war against France.

"You know when he's in charge. You can feel him there. Yet Giap has had no formal training. He said himself that the only military academy he'd been to was the bush"

Left: Ho Chi Minh in the 1940s when, with US assistance, he organized resistance to the Japanese invasion of Indo China.

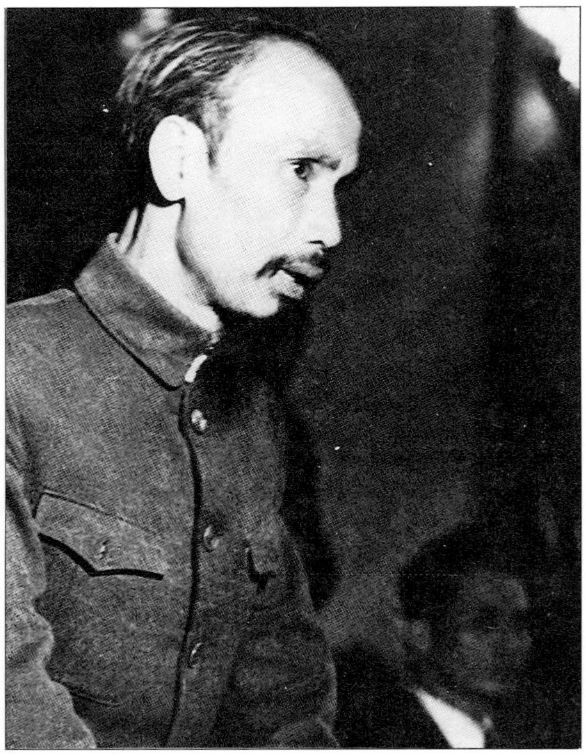

Cong attack. On March 8th, 1965 elements of the 3,500-man 9th Marine Brigade landed at Da Nang to establish a defensive perimeter around the air base there. Within two days the Marines would experience their first fire fights with the Viet Cong. From this modest beginning the US would increase its effort over the next three years until over half a million men were employed.

In retaliation for the Viet Cong attack on Camp Holloway, President Johnson authorized a strike against the guerilla barracks at Dong Hoi in North Vietnam.

Unanimous: At 7:45 p.m. in Washington, President Johnson and his National Security Council met around the coffin-shaped table in the White House Cabinet Room. Also present were Senate Majority Leader Mike Mansfield and House Speaker John McCormack. The meeting lasted 75 minutes. Its unanimous decision: reprisal.

The orders had long been cut. No fewer than three U.S. aircraft carriers – the Ranger, Coral Sea, and Hancock – were on station in the South China Sea. At 3 p.m. Sunday, Vietnam time – exactly thirteen hours after the Pleiku assault – U.S. Navy jets were on course for predetermined targets in North Vietnam. Bad weather turned back many of the planes, but 49 A-4 Skyhawks and F-8 Crusaders from the Coral Sea and Hancock got through to paste Dong Hoi, a guerrilla training garrison 40 miles north of the 17th parallel border between North and South Vietnam, with rockets and bombs. One A-4 was shot down. The pilot, Lt. Edward A. Dickson, of Wyoming, Pa., was seen parachuting toward the water, but a search failed to locate him. (3)

In response to the Viet Cong Qui Nhon attack, further strikes (Flaming Dart II) were authorized against Chap Le Barracks and Chan Hoa Barracks in North Vietnam on the 11th. These involved 160 sorties by the US Navy and Air Force, along with the South Vietnamese Air Force, and resulted in the loss of three carrier-based jets to groundfire. In quick response, the Soviet Union began delivery of SA-2 Guideline surface-to-air missiles (SAMs) by the end of the month.

In the study for further air options, one wargame (Sigma II) conducted by the Defense Department in 1964, had not been optimistic about the outcome of a bombing campaign against the North. Nevertheless, on February 13th, 1965 President Johnson approved the implementation of Operation Rolling Thunder, the controversial bombing campaign designed "to put a slow squeeze" on North Vietnam with the object of bringing Ho Chi Minh to the bargaining table. Additionally, US aircraft began undertaking close air support missions in aid of the ARVN, without the participation of South Vietnamese Air Force planes. On March 2nd, Rolling Thunder got under way when the South Vietnamese Air Force struck the Quan Khe naval base and the US Air Force hit the Xom Bong ammunition depot in North Vietnam, in raids involving 104 US and 19 South Vietnamese planes. Six aircraft were lost in the attacks. At the same time, Barrel Roll operations picked up against the Ho Chi Minh Trail in Laos.

THE US AIR FORCE AND VIETNAM 1961-1968

In 1964, the US Air Force was probably the most powerful instrument of war that had ever existed in the history of the world. It had the capacity to bring nuclear or conventional destruction to any corner of the globe in amounts that made World War II campaigns pale in comparison. The cigar-chewing Chief of Staff, General Curtis LeMay, was credited with saying that he could bomb North Vietnam back to the Stone Age. This, however, was not to be, and the

Left: President Ngo Dinh Diem was assassinated by the RVN military in 1962 after violent unrest. The US knew of the plot beforehand but did nothing.

Below: Ex-Vice President and Prime Minister of the Republic of Vietnam, Air Vice Marshal Nguyen Cao Ky departs his defeated country on April 29, 1975.

Below: President Nguyen Van Thieu. He enacted long-overdue civil reforms but these did him no good in the face of the North Vietnamese Army.

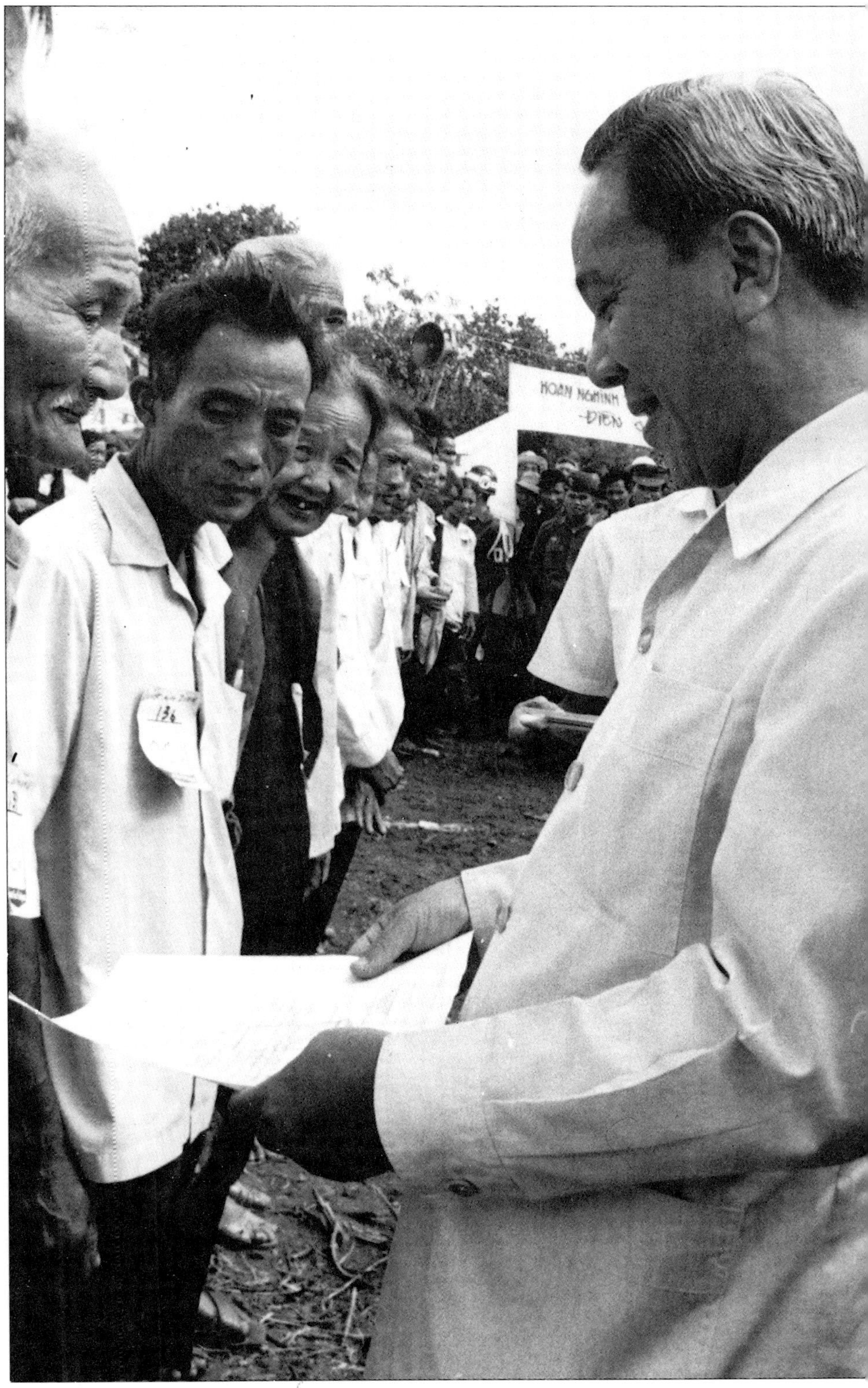

history of the USAF in Vietnam was fated to be one of a mis-used service and lost opportunities.

The Air Force's involvement in Vietnam began seriously in 1961. At first its participation was mainly in the areas of training and covert operations with "Air Commando" squadrons, flying old prop-driven aircraft like the A-1 and the B-26. Later, a miscellany of jet aircraft rotated through South Vietnam's major air bases to undertake tentative reconnaissance, bombing, and air defense missions (i.e., the RF-101, the B-57, and the F-104). Barrel Roll armed recon missions over Laos were carried out by Navy and Air Force units throughout 1964, but were deliberately kept small and low key. The reprisal strikes for Viet Cong attacks on US destroyers and bases in 1964, Pierce Arrow and Flaming Dart, were not considered very effective by anyone in the US military hierarchy.

Attacking the North

The Joint Chiefs of Staff, who from the outset looked on the Air Force as an excellent form of leverage against North Vietnam, proposed to deploy a further 325 combat planes to the theater (including 30 B-52s) by shifting nine Air Force squadrons and adding a fourth Navy carrier to the Western Pacific.

A Navy Phantom from VF 21 releases its bombs over a suspected Viet Cong position. Based on USS Midway, the squadron was in action over Vietnam from the spring of 1965.

Targets on the "JCS List," which included all priority military, transportation and industrial installations in North Vietnam, were to be struck as part of a massive and swiftly-delivered bombing campaign. President Johnson and his civilian advisors saw things differently however. They envisioned the Rolling Thunder program as "a systematic but restrained air offensive against selected military and economic targets in carefully delimited areas of North Vietnam." As ludicrous as it may seem, Rolling Thunder missions were chosen from lists forwarded from C-in-C Pacific to the Secretary of Defense by President Johnson and a group of *civilian* advisors at Tuesday luncheons at the White House!

The result of the self-imposed restrictions of Rolling Thunder was that large "sanctuary" areas were created which insulated 80 per cent of North Vietnam's industry and 75 per cent of its population. For the most part, these areas included everything within 30 nautical miles of the Chinese border or Hanoi, and within 10 miles of the port of Haiphong. Otherwise, most significant targets could be attacked, with the utmost care being taken to avoid hitting populated areas. In spite of North Vietnamese propaganda to the contrary, precautions were

IN-COUNTRY AIR WAR

Tactical airpower was introduced to South Vietnam by the Air Commandos of the 'Farm Gate' detachment. Flying elderly prop aircraft they at first 'advised' the South Vietnamese before the escalation of the conflict allowed open US Air Force participation. From then on a full range of jet aircraft were brought to bear against the Viet Cong. In-country operations were not carried out with the sophistication of those against the North or the Trail.

Above: A Douglas A-1E Skyraider strafes a South Vietnamese hamlet in a diving attack.

Above: A napalm-armed Douglas B-26 Invader, part of the 'Farm Gate' detachment of Air Commandos.

Right: The effects of napalm are graphically illustrated by this A-1E attacking a hamlet sheltering VC guerillas.

Below: Another fearsome weapon employed from A-1s was the phosphorus bomb, whose dramatic effect is shown here.

"Hell, with the Skyraider we can put our ordnance within 50-foot tolerances. We can stay in the air for five or six hours at a time, and operate when the weather's not good enough for jets. The way I see it, Jets are every day, but this big hog with the fan out front, that's unique"

A North Vietnamese quadruple 14.5 mm AA gun fires on raiding US aircraft. Before the end of the war Hanoi was to have the most formidable defense against air attack the world had seen.

taken and civilian casualties were minimized. In addition to the frustrating sanctuaries, air operations were hampered by weather conditions during the Northeast Monsoon (December to mid-May), during which aircraft were limited by cloud cover to approaches at 4,000 to 6,000 feet – prime targets for air defence guns.

Rolling Thunder

In the beginning, Rolling Thunder missions were divided between attacks on fixed targets and armed reconnaissance flights. As fewer fixed targets were left outside of the sanctuaries, armed reconnaissance missions assumed more importance. They would be assigned route segments along transportation lines and have authority to attack any legitimate targets which appeared. By the end of 1965, twice as many sorties were devoted to armed reconnaissance as to fixed targets. To facilitate operations, the "Route Package" system was devised, dividing the map of North Vietnam up into Route Package Areas (1, 2, 3, 4, 5, 6A and 6B) assigned to the commanders of the

Above: The sun glints off rice paddies as this A-1E heads home after a strike in the Ca Mau peninsula.

Below: Air defence for South Vietnam was handled by Convair F-102A Delta Daggers of the 509th FIS.

Above: Martin B-57s patrol the Mekong Delta. These were the first jet bombers deployed to the theatre.

Below: The 13th TBS of the 35th TFW flew this B-57 on in-country bombing raids from Phan Rang AB.

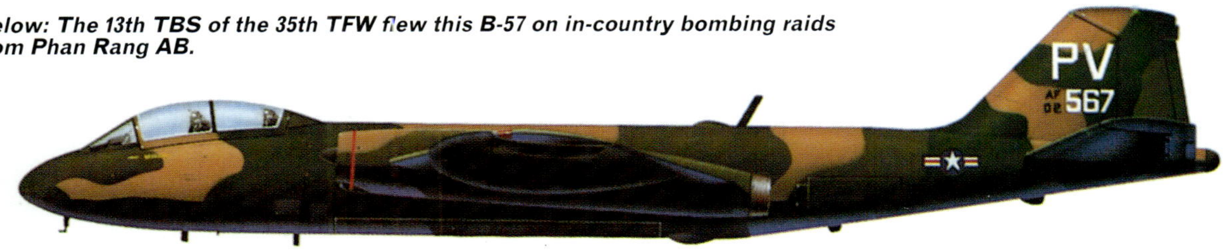

US Pacific Fleet, the US Pacific Air Forces, and US MACV for coordination purposes.

Normally, bombing missions over the north were undertaken by tactical fighter wings (TFWs), each of which had two to five squadrons of 18 to 24 planes. Early tactical missions would employ squadron or wing-size attacks, composed of flights of four aircraft each. Three quarters of the Air Force's Rolling Thunder missions were carried out by two wings of F-105 Thunderchief ("Thud") fighter-bombersa based in Thailand: the 355th TFW at Takhli and the 388th TFW at Korat. The F-105 was originally designed for the nuclear strike role, but turned out to be the most adaptable aircraft available at the beginning of the war. Other aircraft used initially, the B-57 and the F-100, were relegated to support roles or missions within South Vietnam. Escorting the "Thuds" were F-4 Phantoms, mainly from the 8th TFW at Ubon, Thailand, and the 366th TFW, based in South Vietnam. The F-4s would carry bombs as well, and jettison them if air-to-air combat was imminent. Electronic support was provided by the EC-121 airborne radar picket and the EB-66 electronic warfare platform. F-100 (later F-105F) "Wild Weasel" air defense suppression fighters took on SAM launcher sites with radar-homing Shrike air-to-surface missiles. Reconnaissance support, to assess air defense threats and post-mission damage, was provided by RF-101s, and later by RF-4Cs of the 432nd Tactical Reconnaissance Wing from Udorn in Thailand. Distances and bomb loads made it necessary to use air-to-air refueling, provided by the Strategic Air Command's KC-135 Stratotankers.

Bombs from USAF F-105s strike the runway at Kep airfield, 38 miles from Hanoi. The Thunderchiefs of the 355th Tactical Fighter Wing flew out of Takhli AB, Thailand.

If US air services could be faulted severely for anything, it was lack of air-to-air combat training at the beginning of the war. With an emphasis on ordnance delivery, dog fighting was initially neglected, leading to some nasty surprises. The North Vietnamese Air Force had about four squadrons of MiG-15 and MiG-17 fighters at the outset, supplemented by a squadron of MiG-21s in mid-1965. While US pilots eventually recovered and gained the upper hand, by the end of Rolling Thunder the kill ratio of North Vietnamese planes downed to US planes downed was only 2.5 to 1, a far cry from the 12 to 1 ratio inflicted on the North Koreans in 1950-53.

Surface-to-air missiles (SAMs) proved to be another matter. While anti-aircraft guns claimed most US aircraft losses, SAMs imposed further operational restrictions and forced the US to adopt sophisticated countermeasures. Between March and October 1965, the Soviets set up three SA-2 Guideline SAM regiments at Hanoi, Thanh Hoa and Haiphong. Each regiment had four battalions, and in all there were 32 identified launch sites by the end of the year. These shot down five US jets and four reconnaissance drones between July and October. The increasing efficiency of the SAM system gave impetus to the "Wild Weasel" air defense suppression program.

By the end of 1965, a certain measurable effect had been produced by Rolling Thunder. Because the sanctuary areas shielded half of North Vietnam's port capacity (which received 80 per cent of its military imports) and 60 per cent of its petroleum storage and electric power facilities, the overall impact of the air offensive was small however. Although between 1965 and 1968 an estimated 750,000 North Vietnamese were diverted from their normal jobs to cope with the bombing effort (damage repair, casualty replacement, construction, transportation, and air defense), this loss was offset by an addition of 720,000 people to the labor force through the population growth and the loan of 40,000 Chinese personnel to help with transport maintenance.

Viet Cong structures erupt into flames following an attack by A-1 Skyraiders. The size of the explosion indicates ammunition touched off in the attack.

Bombing continues

After a month-long bombing pause in January 1966, Rolling Thunder resumed its torpid pace in spite of military recommendations to enlarge the scope of operations to include closing North Vietnamese ports and destroying their oil storage and transportation system. To the Johnson administration, the "carrot" seemed more important than the "stick" in the bombing campaign. Secretary of Defense Robert McNamara, who should have presented the viewpoint of the military, was the first to ignore the advice of the service chiefs. As a result, less than 20 per cent of the militarily important targets in northeast North Vietnam were hit during the 1966 campaign.

In 1967 some allowances were made to permit certain strikes within the Hanoi sanctuary area against power generating facilities. These raids cut North Vietnamese production by perhaps 50 per cent. Communist propaganda played up the issue of civilian casualties, to which the Johnson administrative was overly sensitive. In fact, half of the pre-war population of Hanoi had been evacuated and the remaining half were engaged in essential war work. Nevertheless, Johnson's civilian staff endorsed the idea of a shift in the air effort towards the interdiction of supply routes from North Vietnam through Laos to South Vietnam. The difficulty of intercepting

NIGHT INTERDICTION

Viet Cong operations in the south were highly successful thanks to tactics, terrain and, above all, a steady and regular supply of weapons and equipment from the North. Most of this came at night through a maze of tracks in the Laotian jungle, and the US Air Force spent much effort on stemming this never ending tide. Due to the nature of the problem, many highly sophisticated weapon systems were used against the truck traffic, employing the latest night sensors to spot the widely spread targets beneath several layers of jungle canopy, and destroy them with pinpoint weapons.

Left: Two Fairchild Providers were converted to NC-123K status for programme 'Black Spot'. Fitted with nose radar and a chin turret with infra-red and low light level sensors, the 'Black Spot' aircraft detected trucks moving on the Trail and then bombed them.

Below: A much modified nose with laser designator, IR and TV sensors allowed the Martin B-57G 'Tropic Moon III' to achieve great accuracy with laser-guided bombs against Trail traffic. This aircraft is from the 13th Tactical Bomber Squadron, based at Ubon in Thailand.

For missions at night there were few better than the Martin B-57B Canberra, serving from the early days of the war with the 8th and 13th TBS. Good navigational aids allowed accurate attacks with a heavy weapons load. Bombs were carried under the wings and on a rotating internal bay.

The Douglas Invader was re-introduced into the war zone in the shape of the A-26K, used for night counter-insurgency missions along the Trail. Used by the 606th and 609th Special Operations Squadrons, the Invaders flew from Nakhon Phanom. This example carries bombs with fuze extenders and napalm canisters.

A Skyraider makes a firing pass on burning Viet Cong positions. Although old, the propellor driven A-1 proved ideal for the counter-insurgency style of war found in the south.

supplies scattered along hundreds of miles of jungle trails, as opposed to the relative ease of destroying them concentrated at the docks of Haiphong, made no difference to the non-professional advisors.

The 1968 Tet Offensive, though a military defeat for the Communists, was a propaganda victory. In the wake of media reports and anti-war protests the Johnson White House reeked of defeatism. The opportunity to use massive air attacks to retaliate against North Vietnam was allowed to pass. At the end of March, Johnson suspended bombing north of the 20th parallel, and shortly afterwards, north of the 19th parallel. On November 1st a complete bombing halt was announced – a major concession with no reciprocity on the part of the North Vietnamese. The primary objective of Rolling Thunder, to bring the North Vietnamese to peace negotiations, had failed completely. They had simply learned to adapt to intrusion by US warplanes, and began to gain some leverage through the capture of downed American aircrew.

In South Vietnam, the USAF operated from 12 principal air bases and a number of subsidiary fields. Close air support missions in aid of units in contact, and interdictory missions against suspected enemy locations were the primary activities. About a

“We’ll get intelligence reports that the Cong are likely to bring some goods down one of her supply routes. So we go after them, zipping up and down the trail with our lights off, scopemen studying every inch of the ground below us as though it was day. As soon as we see something, we wheel round and go in with cannon, rockets or bombs”

Above: One of the principal types employed by both day and night against the Trail was the Douglas A-1 Skyraider. With a good weapons load and long loiter, the ‘Spad’ flew rescue escort missions in addition to interdiction sorties.

Below: Introducing a sophisticated nav/attack system, the General Dynamics F-111A had an inauspicious start to its combat career in Southeast Asia, losing several aircraft in a short space of time. They were used over the Trail, and also flew ‘up North’.

quarter of the "in-country missions" were flown by the South Vietnamese Air Force. The air support system consisted of tactical air control elements with major Army units, and ground (or airborne) forward air controllers ("FACs") to guide attacking aircraft. Missions were either "preplanned" or "immediate," and sortie allocations were controlled at headquarters level. The Air Force naturally preferred to control all air assets in country. The Marine Corps, on the other hand, jealously guarded its air/ground task force concept which dedicated Marine Air units to supporting Marine units on the ground. The controversy came to a head in 1968, during the siege of Khe Sanh, when the Marines were forced to submit to a single theater air manager.

In-country missions

The 3rd, 12th, 31st, 35th and 37th Tactical Fighter Wings, flying from a variety of bases in South Vietnam, operated F-100 and F-4 series fighters in the ground support role. The 14th, 56th, and later 633rd Special Operations Wings (originally called Air Commando Wings), flew AC-47 and AC-119 fixed wing gunships and A-1 prop fighters in the close air support and trail interdiction roles, with

Bombs from a B-52 Stratofortress of Strategic Air Command fall towards suspected Viet Cong concentrations about 56 miles northwest of Saigon.

the 315th Air Commando Wing specialized in defoliation spray operations with its C-123s. Three Tactical Airlift Wings (314th, 374th, 463rd) and a number of attached squadrons operated C-130 transports for resupply and troop movement, while one (483rd) employed former Army C-7s in the same roles.

SAC and the B-52

From June 1965, the Strategic Air Command (SAC) played an active part in the air war with its B-52 Stratofortresses. With internal and external modifications, the ordnance load of the B-52 was increased from 27 to 108 bombs, for tactical support of troops. Code named Arc Light, the tactical B-52 program allowed for drops within 1,000 meters of "friendlies." The advantages of the B-52 included its high-altitude silent approach, tremendous bomb capacity, and ability to operate in all weather – especially after the introduction of the "Combat Skyspot" ground radar control system in 1966. The chief disadvantage was the comparative lack of responsiveness due to the long distances from B-52 bases to Vietnam. B-52s operated from Andersen AFB, Guam, under the command of the 3rd Air Division and its 4133rd Bomb Wing (Provisional), and from Kadena, Okinawa, under the 4252nd Strategic Wing. In mid-1966 the 4258th Strategic Wing formed at U-Tapao, Thailand, bringing B-52s closer to the action. B-52s provided awesome firepower in tight situations such as the siege of Khe Sanh. A three-plane "cell" of B-52s could blanket a three square kilometer area with high explosives – a feat which would require the attention of 60 tactical fighter-bombers.

FORWARD AIR CONTROL

For fast-moving aircraft, hitting a small moving target buried beneath the jungle canopy was often not possible, so US forces employed forward air control (FAC) aircraft. The pilots were experienced in tactical techniques, and flew over the same patch so that they knew the terrain intimately. With this knowledge, and the slow flying aircraft they flew, they could spot and track targets, often marking them with smoke rockets for the strike aircraft to aim at.

This Cessna O-2A displays the typical weapons load carried by this type on FAC missions. For suppressive fire two 7.62-mm machine gun pods are carried, with smoke rockets for marking targets.

Below: A collection of Cessna O-2s line up at Nakhon Phanom (and one O-1). This base was the centre for attacks against the Trail, and the 0-2s painted black were for night FAC duties (one of the most hazardous).

Left: Two O-2A 'Ducks' are seen at a forward operating location in South Vietnam. The extra glazed panel on the starboard side allowed the pilot improved vision from the left-hand seat, particularly underneath him.

Below: One of the more unusual types found in Vietnam was the Grumman TF-9J Cougar, used by the Marine Corps for fast-mover FAC duties. TA-4 Skyhawks were also used in this role.

Left: *FAC missions often involved extremely low flying to dodge guns. Even flying below the treeline was common, as demonstrated here by this fearless O-1 Bird Dog pilot.*

Right: *A Cessna O-1 dives in towards its target. White phosphorus 'Willie Pete' rockets will be fired to mark the target for the strike aircraft.*

Below: *Fastest and best-armed of the regular FAC aircraft was the North American OV-10A Bronco, used in this role by the Air Force (illustrated) and the Marine Corps. Rockets are being launched by this aircraft.*

Left: *A Bird Dog flies low over B-52 bomb craters. FAC duties sometimes involved providing battle damage assessment after such raids.*

Above: *FAC flying was a dangerous task, and it is a credit to this breed of men that two Medals of Honor were awarded posthumously to FACs.*

CHAPTER THREE

FIRST BLOOD 1965

Marines patrol a bamboo thicket somewhere near Da Nang. The heavy M14 rifle was not really suitable for the tropics, and was to be replaced by the lightweight M16

After the decision to commit American troops was made, things happened quickly – but not as quickly as the military would have liked. During the period of increasing US involvement, no one had the foresight to fund improvements to South Vietnam's logistical and transportation system in anticipation of increased US aid or the eventual commitment of US troops – although contingency plans existed for both. With South Vietnam's meager port capacity the results were predictable: ships waited over a month to unload, units ran dangerously low on ammunition and other supplies. Lots of engineer construction support, port reception units and the like were required to sustain a buildup of American troops. In effect, the US rushed units to Vietnam about as fast as logistics would allow, and to support the commitment, Johnson authorized an increase in the draft from a monthly total of 17,000 in mid-year up to 36,000 by October. By the end of the year, the

Army had 116,800 men in Vietnam, and the Marines had 38,200.

The 3rd Marine Regiment arrived in March, the first ground combat unit in Vietnam.

They were the vanguard of a 3,500-man force, the first marines since Korea to hit the beaches in a combat zone.

The U.S. decision to send in combat units had been weighed for weeks. Only after it became evident that the big Danang airbase in the northern tier of South Viet Nam was critically threatened, did Defense Secretary Robert McNamara recommend sending in two reinforced Marine battalions and a squadron of 24 helicopters. By then, at least twelve Viet Cong battalions – roughly 6,000 men – were in the Danang area; they launched an attack at Mieubong, only three miles away, the day before the marines landed.

The marines were shot at once during the landing, when a Viet Cong rifleman hit the wing of a C-130 Hercules transport as it approached Danang with a load of marines from camps on Okinawa. But no real damage was done.

Half of the marines landed by ship. Scarcely 24 hours after the orders to move came from Washington, a Navy destroyer and four transports hove to in the foam-flecked bay half a mile off Nam O Beach north of Danang, renamed "Red Beach Two" by the marines. A dozen LVTs (landing vehicles, tracked) were lowered from the transports and nosed toward the beach carrying 1,400 men of the 9th Marine Expeditionary Brigade.

It took just 65 minutes to put 1,400 marines ashore with rifles, machine guns, rocket and grenade launchers. At Danang, the brigade's other battalion came in the easy way – by air from Okinawa. Both battalions came prepared for heavy combat: they had 105-mm. howitzers, M-48 medium tanks, 106-mm. recoilless rifles. (1)

The 3,500 Marines had put to sea in March in the feverish post-monsoon weather, aboard the vessels *Mount McKinley*, *Henrico*, *Union* and *Vancouver*. These four ships of Amphibious Task Force 76 took six weeks to reach the Vietnam coast and spent the last few days pitching up and down in vile seas.

Enter the Marines

It was the end of a small and distant guerrilla war which had seemed romantic and a little dangerous but not very important. The sight of regular Marines storming ashore was played across TV screens in America and no one believed – nor should they have – that the Marines were in Vietnam solely to protect American airfields. They were going into combat, Americans were advisors no longer.

They were reinforced in May by the 4th Marines, at the same time that the Army dispatched its elite 173rd Airborne Brigade from Okinawa to Bien Hoa and Vung Tau. In July the 3rd Marine Division was completed with the arrival of the 9th Marines, and concentrated in I Corps. The 1st Marine Division began arriving in August with the deployment of the 7th Marines. All USMC troops came under command of III Marine Amphibious Force, and all were based out of the northern coastal areas around Da Nang, Phu Bai and Chu Lai.

The Army's 1st Infantry Division sent its 2nd Brigade to Vietnam in July and its 1st and 3rd Brigades in October. The reinforced 1st Brigade of the 101st Airborne Division was dispatched in August. Supporting brigade-size units which deployed during the year included the 12th Combat Aviation Group (September), the 23rd Artillery Group (November), and the 17th Combat Aviation Group (December). In late May the 1st Battalion of the Royal Australian Regiment came to Vietnam and was placed under command of the US Army until a larger Australian task force arrived. It served with the 173rd Airborne Brigade.

BASES

With little in the way of conventional front lines, the Vietnam War was a war of bases and operations from those bases. Some were towns in themselves, with all modern conveniences for the thousands of service men and civilians who worked there. Others were small fortified points used to observe enemy movements, manned by a few Americans and larger numbers of local volunteers. Combat units would move from location to location, setting up their various bases wherever they came to rest. A new combat base involved everything from digging trenches and laying a PSP landing strip to putting up the officer's club.

Above: An OV-1 Bird Dog, used for reconnaissance and forward air control, lands for refueling at Coa Lanh. The base has a 'portable' airstrip of aluminium matting, tough enough to take even the heaviest of airborne traffic for minimum cost.

Marine Otters unload at Dong Ha. The huge influx of materiel into Vietnam called for full-scale waterfront facilities.

Part of the tropospheric scatter radio antennae that linked US commanders in-country with Thailand bases and Washington.

A relay station for FM radio communications. These lonely outposts were easy targets – hence the heavy defences.

When the first units of the 101st Airborne Division arrived in Vietnam, they found some old friends already there. General Westmoreland had commanded the Division in the 1950s, and Ambassador Maxwell D. Taylor had commanded the 101st during World War II.

The Australian approach to the tactics of the Viet Nam war was honed in jungle warfare against the Japanese in World War II and the Communists in Malaya. Their credo: avoid trails, avoid villages, avoid resupply; slide into the jungle like a snake and hide, then terrorize the enemy at will. "Fortunately, we've trained and equipped ourselves for such a war as this in Southeast Asia for years," says Brigadier O. D. Jackson, commander of the First Australian Task Force in Viet Nam. Whereas U.S. commanders resupply their units every other day in the field, the Aussies slide into "the deep green" prepared to go it alone for a week at a time – and manage to pack ten pounds less per man than the G.I.s.

The Aussie patience and tenacity is near legendary. One eleven-man patrol tracked a single Viet Cong sniper silently through dense jungle for 14 hours before it caught and killed him. In their 14-month stint in force in Viet Nam, the Aussies count 146 killed and 192 wounded Viet Cong, to 24 killed and 132 wounded Australians. The total of enemy casualties is probably far too low for the damage the Aussies have done, because of their own stiff accounting standards. No enemy dead is ever claimed unless an Aussie can walk up and put his foot on the body; no wounded counts unless he can be trailed 300 yards, with blood seen all the way.

The Aussies allow no Vietnamese inside their com-

"Cam Ranh Bay cost more than $100 million to build. It's got 70 miles of road, a jet airfield, a port handling ocean freighters and one of the Army's largest supply depots. It's so safe that LBJ has paid two visits here"

Above: US Army helicopters are serviced at a floating base, the converted US Navy seaplane tender USNS Corpus Christie Bay. The ship provided a secure base close to active combat zones.

Khe Sanh, initially one of a series of defensive bases near the border with Laos, used as a supply staging post in 1971.

Qui Nhon, one of the first US air bases established in Viet Nam. A VC attack here in early 1965 helped escalate the war.

The mile-long runway at Qui Nhon, capable of handling all military air traffic short of a B-52 bomber.

M113 IN ACTION

The M113 APC was one of the classic symbols of the Vietnam War. Designed in the 1950s, it was fast, mobile and offered the crew protection against the small-arms fire which was the main threat from the Viet Cong. Entering production in the 1960s, it was in service with the South Vietnamese very soon after its adoption by the US Army. Indeed, the M113 first saw combat in 1962 with the armoured companies of the Vietnamese 7th and 21st Infantry Divisions. When US combat troops entered the conflict, they brought the by now ubiquitous M113. Possibly the most well known variant was the Armored Cavalry Assault Vehicle (ACAV), an M113 with extra guns.

Right: an M113 in ACAV format – with armored shielding for the .50 calibre machine gun and two side-mounted M-60s

Below: an unexpected pleasure – an American Red Cross 'Doughnut Dollie' adorns an M113 of 11th Armored Cavalry

Marine combat units were the first to be deployed, beginning operations around Da Nang. At that time the Marines were still armed with M14 rifles, and rarely wore helmets.

pounds, an inhospitality justified, they feel, on security grounds. Going into the jungle, they rarely wear helmets, strip the insignia from their uniforms. The average Viet Cong, they snort, is really "no jungle fighter; he uses trails, paths and villages. We don't. But you have to go out into the jungle to trap him. That's when we meet him on our terms instead of his."

The mainspring of the 1,700-man Australian contingent in Vietnam, the "Fighting First" Battalion of the Royal Australian Regiment is currently attached to the U.S. 173rd Airborne Brigade and, like the Airborne, its primary mission is to guard the Bien Hoa air base north of Saigon. Since their arrival in Vietnam last summer, however, the "diggers" of the First Battalion have carried out no fewer than nineteen major operations. And this January, the Aussies pulled off the biggest intelligence coup of the war. During a sweep through the notorious Hon Triangle, they uncovered a vast complex of tunnels, burrowed 60 feet deep in places, which turned out to be the Viet Cong's headquarters for the entire Saigon area. Beside capturing a big arms cache, including five brand-new Chinese Communist anti-aircraft guns, the Aussies discovered 6,000 documents giving names and addresses of important Viet Cong agents. Remarked one U.S. intelligence official of the Australian find: "It will take months for the VC to repair the damage to their organization."

One reason for the Aussies' notable success in Vietnam is the fact that they have had more than a generation of experience fighting guerrilla-style wars. Before going to Vietnam, the Fighting First, which saw action in the jungles of Borneo against the Japanese in World War II, spent twelve years helping the British put down Communist insurgency in Malaya. And some of the Australian NCO's and officers now serving in Vietnam are veterans of that campaign. (2)

By far the most controversial formation to go to Vietnam in 1965 was the 1st Cavalry Division (Airmobile). Organized by order of the Secretary of Defense, the division was assembled and rushed to the combat theater in record time. The normal stumbling blocks within the Army bureaucracy were not allowed to hinder the project, which was turned over to Army Aviation luminaries with a strict deadline. The airmobile concept was untried in battle, but the 1st Cavalry Division immediately set the pace for the rest of the Army. The division arrived in Vietnam in September with three brigades and its own aviation group (the 11th). The 1st Brigade was parachute qualified when it deployed, but eventually lost that additional role.

The Republic of Korea (South Korea) also sent

Above: The M113 is the world's most widely produced armored vehicle. One of the earliest users was the Army of the Republic of Vietnam.

Above: the M113's .50 Browning in action – accurate enough to hit a man at up to 500 metres and a vehicle at 800 metres

Right: M113s riding close together through the brush to maintain contact and be able to give covering fire if needed

Left: An M113 ACAV ready for combat. The trim vane (a plate at the front of the M113 used for keeping the nose up when in water) has been extended and filled with sandbags for protection against mines.

"Muffled by the rain, the Australian armored personnel carriers crept over the hills undetected by the VC and opened up with their .50-cal machine guns, cutting down 25 Reds with the first volley"

units to aid South Vietnam beginning in 1965. The ROK 2nd "Blue Dragon" Marine Brigade arrived in October, along with the Capital "Tiger" Division's Cavalry Regiment. The division's 1st Regiment deployed in November, and took up positions with the rest of the ROK contingent in defense of the central coast area. Although the "ROKs" earned a reputation as tough troops, they were heavy-handed with the local population and on the higher levels the relationship with US forces was strained because of the Korean commander's feeling that he was equal in position to the MACV commander.

Surging into the area in the early morning, hours before the Viet Cong normally expect such operations to occur, a platoon of South Korean troops quickly spread through the village, searching for documents, weapons and able-bodied men of an age to serve in the guerrilla forces. The village chief – known to be a member of the Viet Cong movement – was found hiding in a large earthen pot and was led off at the end of a rope for questioning. The rest of the villagers were ordered to pack up whatever they could carry and proceed to a

August 1965, and Australians rendezvous with US Army helicopters for return to Bien Hoa air base. They have just completed a five day patrol in Viet Cong infested country.

M16 IN ACTION

One of the classic weapons of the Vietnam war, the M16 was introduced to supplement the heavy high powered M14 rifle in US service. Light in weight and firing a high-velocity small calibre bullet, by 1967 it had become the standard Vietnam rifle. Early problems were plagued by stoppages, but a change to the cartridge propellant and more care in cleaning stopped the fouling which had caused it. It is accurate enough at battlefield ranges, and the smaller cartridge allows individual soldiers to carry more rounds of ammunition.

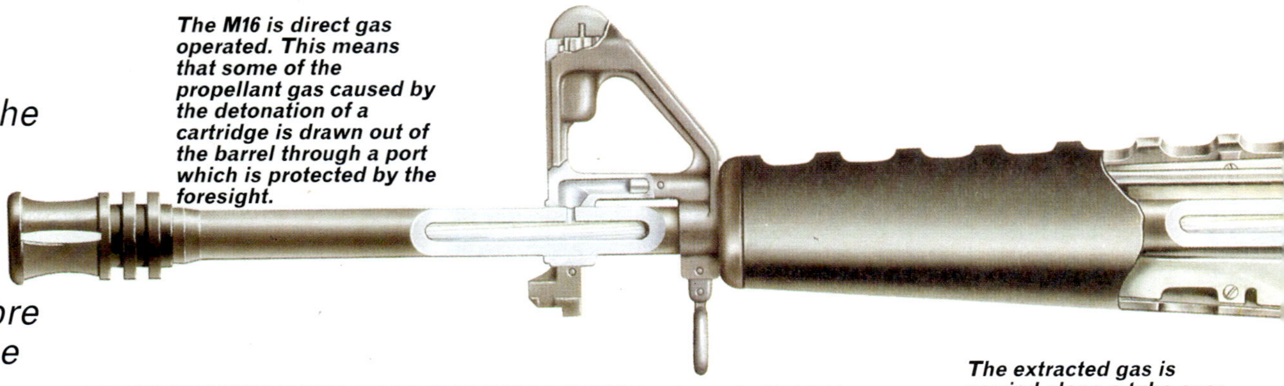

The M16 is direct gas operated. This means that some of the propellant gas caused by the detonation of a cartridge is drawn out of the barrel through a port which is protected by the foresight.

The extracted gas is carried along a tube over the barrel to the bolt, driving it back and working the action. The gas tube and barrel get very hot, so they are enclosed in a plastic hand guard.

An early M16 A1 is seen with an XM148 grenade launcher attached. The USAF were amongst the first to deploy the M16 to Vietnam, but before long the rifle had become one of the War's commonest sights.

Below: A squad leader of 1/4 Marines dashes to hand out ammo under fire. The M16's .223 calibre ammo was half the weight of the M14's 7.62mm round, but no less effective

Below: Three Marines cool off crossing a stream, M16s easily held on the shoulder with one hand. Furnished with plastic stocks, the unloaded rifle weighs less than 6lb

"refugee camp."

All this went off without a shot being fired, and before long the bustling, tough-looking Koreans were heading off down the road toward the next Viet Cong village. Along with the rest of their outfit, the crack Tiger Division, they were sweeping southward to link up with the White Horse Division in the biggest all-Korean operation of the Vietnamese war. Rejoicing in the code name *Oh Jak Kyo* ("the meeting of two stars"), the operation had as its objective the liberation of areas adjoining South Vietnam's vital Highway 1 from Viet Cong control.

As usual, however, the Viet Cong were giving the Koreans a wide berth. Back in February, a large North Vietnamese force made the error of engaging a company of Koreans at close quarters. In the bloodbath that followed, the heavily outnumbered Koreans handed the North Vietnamese a savage mauling, killing 243 and putting the survivors to flight.

That was the largest and last major collision between the North Vietnamese and the Koreans. For their part, the North Vietnamese have been content to keep their distance ever since.

The 49,500 Korean soldiers stationed in South Vietnam constitute the largest anti-Communist force fighting with the Americansa and South Vietnamese in South Vietnam. The Koreans have a formidable reputation, it is universally agreed. Their tactics, according to both Vietnamese and Americans go like this:

When they are shot at, or when a mine explodes among their soldiers, they march into the nearest hamlet and make an example of the first Vietnamese they find. The lesson is simple: if you allow someone to shoot at us or plant mines in our path, this is what happens to you. This strategy obviously helps the Koreans protect themselves, but it does little towards winning the charts and minds of the people.

If the Koreans were to go home, there would be an obvious void in allied manpower in the coastal highlands. But more than one American adviser in the area would welcome their departure as a change for the better. (3)

In April, elements of the regular NVA 325th Division were discovered in South Vietnam. The Communists were on the march, and by year's end had infiltrated some 36,000 NVA regulars into the south. In May the Viet Cong captured Song Be in Phuoc Long Province and held it for seven hours, withdrawing in the face of an ARVN counterattack assisted by US air power. Later that month the Viet Cong destroyed an ARVN battalion in I Corps' Quang Ngai Province, another near Pleiku in the Central Highlands in early June, and yet another (in II Corps) in mid-June, confirming American

CH-34 helicopters land a Marine patrol somewhere near Da Nang. The arrival of the 3rd Marine Regiment in 1965 and its employment in combat changed the

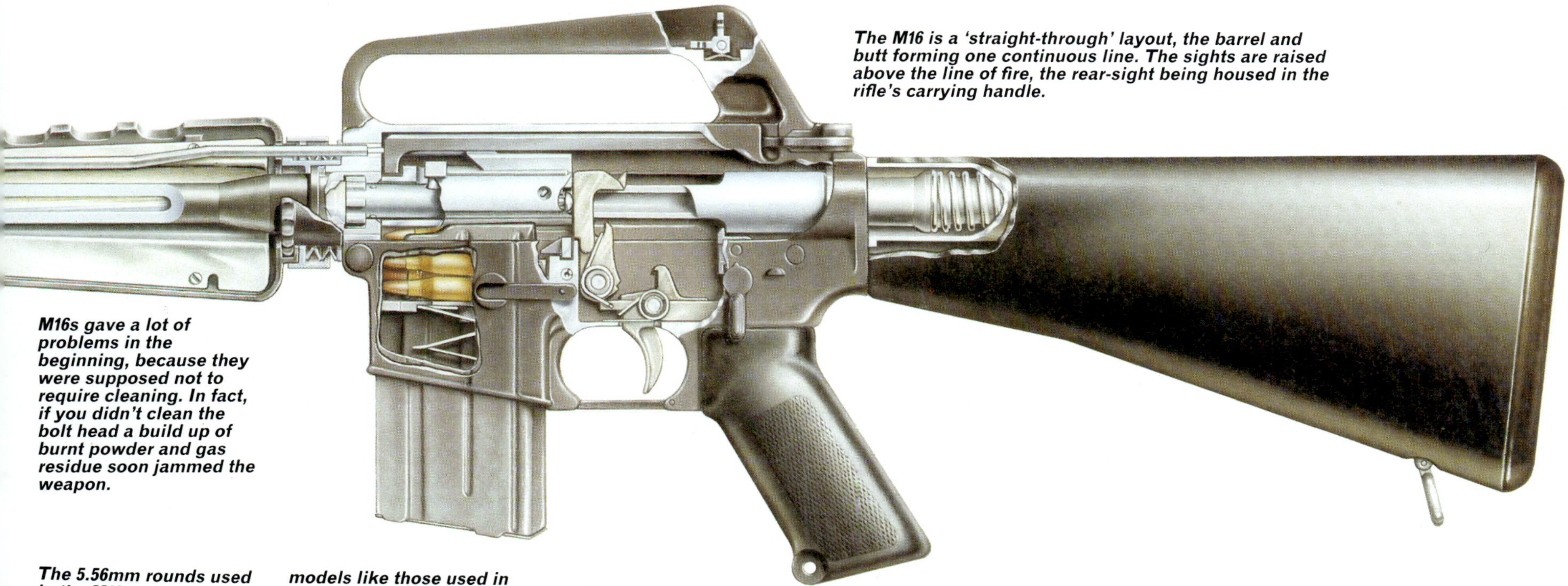

The M16 is a 'straight-through' layout, the barrel and butt forming one continuous line. The sights are raised above the line of fire, the rear-sight being housed in the rifle's carrying handle.

M16s gave a lot of problems in the beginning, because they were supposed not to require cleaning. In fact, if you didn't clean the bolt head a build up of burnt powder and gas residue soon jammed the weapon.

The 5.56mm rounds used in the M16 weigh much less than the older 7.62mm NATO round, so soldiers could carry more ammunition. Early models like those used in Vietnam were fitted with 20-round box magazines, though they have usually been replaced by 30-round boxes today.

The M16 has a thumb-operated fire-selector lever immediately above the pistol grip. The three positions are:- forward to engage the safety; upwards (as illustrated) for semi-auto or single-shot fire; and to the rear for fully automatic fire.

Below: The light weight and easy handling of the M16 were very different from the heavy M14 which preceded it. The new weapon was much more suitable for the new kind of helicopter-mobile war in Vietnam.

whole nature of American involvement in the war.

opinion that the South Vietnamese were in serious trouble. To top things off, Premier Quat resigned under pressure, leaving the government to General Thieu, who appointed Air Vice-Marshal Ky to the premiership.

The US Marines' first major operation in I Corps was Operation Starlight in Quang Ngai Province. Between August 18th and August 21st, 1965, the reinforced 7th Marines 5,500 strong, conducted a three-pronged land, airmobile, and amphibious assault against the 2,000-strong 1st Viet Cong Regiment on the Van Tuong peninsula south of Chu Lai.

> Striking at dawn on Aug. 18, the first wave of marines from the attack transport Talladega stormed ashore and moved due west, cutting off the guerrillas' escape route south. A second force of marines had already marched overland from Chu Lai the night before and set up a blocking position across the north edge of the peninsula. Completing the encirclement, a third wave was helicoptered into three landing zones – dubbed red, white and blue – on the western fringes of the 9-square-mile battle zone. Plans called for the marines flown into the western landing zone to join forces with those moving from the sea and smash the enemy against the northern anvil of the blocking force – or else drive them into the sea.
>
> From the outset, the Americans ran into stiff resistance. Concealed in deep hillside bunkers and a honeycomb of tunnels, the Viet Cong poured out a blistering hail of small-arms fire, mortars and grenades. Communist fire shot up more than a dozen helicopters. Before long, the marine commander was forced to call in a reserve force waiting off shore on the aircraft carrier Iwo Jima.
>
> But despite mounting casualties, the marines pushed ahead, flushing the guerrillas out of their hiding places. Within five hours, the amphibious companies and the heliborne troops linked forces, and the trap was set. At that, a group of more than 100 Viet Cong tried to escape to the sea, but the ships of the Seventh Fleet, stationed a few hundred yards away, opened up with their big guns and wiped out almost the entire guerrilla force as it swarmed down a cliff toward waiting sampans. Still another group of guerrillas was trapped in a valley and destroyed by air strikes.
>
> The marines suffered their worst casualties around landing zone blue, where H company of the Second Battalion, Fourth Marine Regiment, was under almost continuous enemy fire from early morning until six that night. (4)

At a cost of some 45 Marine casualties, at least 964 VC were killed, and their regiment was rendered ineffective for months.

The 1st Cavalry Division (Airmobile), received its baptism of fire in Pleiku Province (II Corps) during the Ia Drang Valley campaign (*Operation Silver Bayonet*) between October 23rd and November 20. In response to an NVA attack on the Plei Me Special Forces Camp, the "Cav" deployed for the first battle test of "airmobility." A North Vietnamese divisional group consisting of the 32nd, 33rd and 66th NVA Regiments provided stiff opposition, but finally had to retreat into neighboring Cambodia. The most famous engagement of the campaign involved LTC

Bell UH-1 'Huey' helicopters land a force of cavalry in a rice paddy. The Air Cavalry concept was a crucial part of US Army operations in Vietnam, and in general proved very successful.

Harold Moore's 1st Battalion 7th Cavalry (the organizational descendants of Custer) in what appeared to be a replay of the Little Big Horn at Landing Zone (LZ) X-Ray.

No sooner had the 1st Battalion rushed from its choppers in the landing zone than the shooting began.

Struggling to set up a perimeter near the base of a hill, the 2nd Platoon of B Company found itself under such severe shelling from mortars that it was soon forced up a fingerlike slope – apart from the rest of the battalion and in the very midst of the enemy.

For 26 hours the fight raged on as Communist crossfire kept the little band pinned down. When the remnants of the 2nd Platoon were finally rescued and brought back to safety, they were dazed and jabbering, but still had discipline.

The main battalion force soon had an even larger tragedy on its hands. At dawn, two platoons of C Company manning X Ray's southeast corner fanned out on patrol. The Communists cunningly sniped and retreated ahead of them, then sprang an ambush from the flanks and rear. Simultaneously a direct Red onslaught smashed head-on at the main C Company positions back at the landing zone, diverting both attention and possible aid to the two trapped platoons. Both were virtually annihilated. When relief forces arrived, they found several G.I.s who had been taken prisoner, later shot with their feet tied. One was left hanging head down from a tree.

Four days and nights the battle around X Ray raged, while a remarkable concatenation of American firepower kept the estimated two attacking North Vietnamese battalions at bay. The 1st Air Cav's artillerymen poured more than 8,000 rounds into the area, firing so fast that their barrels often glowed red with heat. By day and night, tactical air pounded the enemy, and for the first time, in a series of ten raids, the giant B-52s from Guam were used in tactical support, blasting suspected enemy concentrations in the lowering mountains around X Ray. (5)

Fortunately the Cavalry held on at LZ X-Ray and won the day. Total American losses were 79 killed and 121 wounded, while 634 NVA bodies were counted. Perhaps the worst incident of the campaign for the US was actually the battle for LZ Albany,

AIR ASSAULT

The rapid development of the helicopter in the 1950s and its unique abilities allowed the US Army to evolve an entirely new kind of formation in the early 1960s. Using large numbers of helicopters a division could make an airborne assault and sieze control of large areas of territory in a very short space of time. The 11th Air Assault Division (Test) at Fort Benning proved the concept. It was considered ideal for Vietnam operations, so the 11th, renamed 1st Cavalry Division (Airmobile) became the first complete US Army unit to arrive in country. In spite of the vulnerability of the helicopter to ground fire, the Cavalry proved to be one of the most effective outfits in Vietnam.

"After swarms of low flying jets had softened up the landing zone with rockets and machine-gun fire, wave after wave of helicopters fluttered in over the treetops, landing and disgorging thousands of US infantrymen. In the very middle of the zone, the sky was alive with paratroopers, and from the outskirts of the zone thousands more US and ARVN troops closed in. Operation Junction City, the biggest US offensive of the war to date, was under way"

Above: One of the most enduring symbols of America's War in South East Asia, the UH-1 was the major type used in air assaults. The sight of a flock of Hueys in close formation was common, and the larger the gaggle the more likely it was that a Cavalry operation was going in.

Left: Helicopters are probably the quickest way of getting infantry into action there is. Racing from the helicopter and off the landing zone, troops can be in action immediately even in the enemy's back yard.

Above: Early days, and a gunner sits by the open door of an UH-1. As air-cavalry tactics evolved, it became clear that an M14 rifle would not be anything like enough firepower when making helicopter assaults, and the Hueys soon began to sprout machine-guns.

Helicopters can land troops on hilltops, 'taking the high ground' in one simple step. Unfortunately, if an enemy is on the spot already, the helicopters, and the troops they land, are vulnerable.

Right: The Marines were quick to see the advantage of air-borne assaults. Helicopters gave them an opportunity to avoid heavily defended coastlines by going over them. The technique known as 'Vertical Envelopment' revolutionized amphibious warfare.

where the 2nd Battalion 7th Cavalry was caught in a march column and lost 151 dead, 121 wounded and 4 missing, while killing 403 NVA.

> Wednesday morning, X Ray proudly theirs, "the First Team" split into two units and moved on. For one unit, some 500 men from the 5th and 7th Regiments, it was a move toward near disaster. Barely three miles north of X Ray, the long column crossed the Ia Drang River. There lay two North Vietnamese soldiers sleeping in the grass, a sure sign that more trouble was not far away. It wasn't. Suddenly from all sides came a deadly hail of gunfire. The enemy seemed to be everywhere – slung in trees, dug into anthills, crouching behind bushes. It was a classic horseshoe trap, the fields of fire obviously meshed in perfect ambush.
>
> As the U.S. force scattered and took cover, a Communist battalion sliced through its middle, cutting the Americans into two isolated halves. "After that," said an officer later, "it was man-to-man, hand-to-hand fighting between two very well-disciplined and very determined outfits." Though artillery and air support were soon on the way, and reinforcements were rushed from Pleiku (where many were abruptly called out of a memorial service for their dead at Chu Pong), Ia Drang quickly succeeded Chu Pong as the costliest U.S. battle of the war in human lives. (6)

Overall, in killed and wounded, the 1st Cavalry Division lost almost a quarter of its strength during Silver Bayonet, although most of the wounded were eventually returned to duty. The NVA body count totaled 1,771, with many more probable kills, but more important, the NVA drive to cut South Vietnam in half through the Central Highlands had been stopped.

Some 1,350 US servicemen lost their lives during 1965, as well as 11,100 ARVN. In addition the Army lost 114 helicopters. Most of these (72) were operational losses, with the remaining 42 being shot down by ground fire. The Marines lost 47 helicopters and 16 fixed-wing planes. Twenty of the helicopters were destroyed in ground attacks against airfields, 15 were downed by ground fire, and the remaining 12 were operational losses. Most of the fixed-wing losses were operational (10), with the others due to ground fire (4) and airbase attacks (2).

A 15 aircraft strike at a small North Vietnamese village left the military compound which was the target completely obliterated, while the village itself was untouched.

Rolling Thunder

Rolling Thunder air operations got under way in March with several raids involving over 100 aircraft, and many smaller operations. In April, major raids were mounted against rail lines and critical bridges in North Vietnam and US air casualties rose. One of the targets was the infamous Than Hoa railroad and highway bridge, which would survive attempts to destroy it for nearly seven years. Even at this early date, the CIA's assessment was that US bombing efforts would have to be much stronger to have any effect on the Hanoi government. The lacklustre pace of Rolling Thunder continued in spite of this warning, and in spite of the call by Congressional leaders for the bombing of Hanoi and Haiphong.

April also saw the arrival of Marine fighter

ARC LIGHT

One of the most controversial aspects of the war in Southeast Asia was the use of Boeing B-52s in the conventional bombing role. First flying missions in the war zone in 1965, the B-52 raids (code named 'Arc Light') were often targetted against empty jungle, the reaction times to intelligence being such that the enemy had often slipped away hours before. Nevertheless, operations in set-pieces such as the relief of Khe Sanh and the 'Linebacker II' campaign were highly successful.

Above: June 1965 saw the first 'Arc Light' missions, against VC positions in South Vietnam. On one of these missions is this Boeing B-52F.

Above: A B-52 releases its load during early 'Arc Light' operations in 1965.

Below: These are the devastating effects of a B-52 strike. Often the target was uninhabited jungle, the guerrillas having moved on.

Below: B-52s lost their silver colour in favour of a three-tone tactical colour scheme.

Above: Base defence was particularly important as B-52s were a high value weapon.

Below: Groundcrew worked long shifts to prepare the B-52s for their missions.

"No fewer than ten B-52 raids thundered across the Iron Triangle as Operation Cedar Falls got under way, and the 1st Infantry Division moved in. The whole place looked as though it had been put into a waffle iron!"

Above: 'Arc Light' missions required a large fleet of tankers, which matched the numbers of bombers on roughly a one-for-one basis on missions.

Left: B-52s deployed to U-Tapao in Thailand late in the war, this drastically cutting the flight time to targets in the theatre.

Below: This famous B-52D was the only one of its kind to bear a 'shark's mouth'. It flew from Kadena on many 'Arc Light' missions, and is configured with the 'Big Belly' conversion and wing pylons.

RIVER BOAT WAR

The special demands of the riverine war in Vietnam saw a wide variety of craft in use. 'Game Warden' was the operation to patrol the waters of the Mekong and the Rung Sat swamp, between the Delta and Saigon. Craft used included elderly boats originally used by the French against the Viet Minh. Many US Navy landing craft were converted to Armored Troop Carriers, a number undergoing further transformation and becoming heavily armed Monitors. Other types included Command and Control Boats, Assault Support Patrol Boats and Combat Salvage Boats. Smaller craft were used by the US Navy's SEALs, and Coastal PCF 'Swift' boats could be seen in the larger waterways.

Above: Monitors were the waterborne equivalent in Vietnam of the tank. Each carried a 40mm cannon forward, an 81mm mortar and 20mm cannon aft as well as .50 calibre machine guns.

Left: The only craft specially designed by the US Navy for riverine warfare was the Assault Support Patrol Boat (ASPB).

Right: Light, small, outboard-driven skimmers like this were handy for moving small patrols in the narrowest waterways of the Mekong labyrinth.

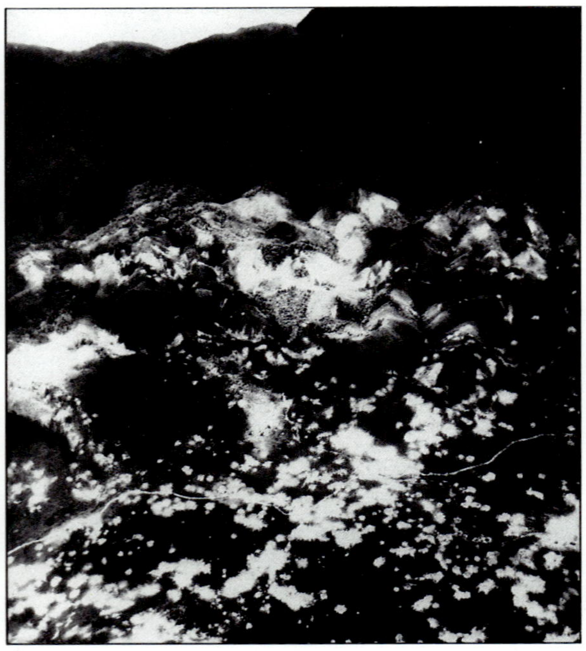

B-52 strikes against Viet Cong supply routes through the A Shau valley create a moon-like landscape. When well directed, B-52 bombing was devastating to the enemy beneath.

bombers at Da Nang, reinforcing the USMC helicopter units already in country. By the end of the year there were two fixed-wing Marine Air Groups (MAGs) in South Vietnam, MAGs 11 and 12, and two helicopter groups, MAGs 16 and 36. The Marine air base at Chu Lai resembled a fleet carrier, being equipped with arrestor wires and eventually a catapult! Built by Navy "Seabees", Chu Lai was in operation within 23 days.

In May an accident at Bien Hoa damaged more than 40 aircraft of the USAF and the VNAF, and left 126 casualties in its wake. On 17 June, the first B-52 *Arc Light* strikes were conducted from Guam. The inaugural mission, in which 27 B-52s attacked the Viet Cong in Binh Duong Province, resulted in a collision as the crews were not used to formation flying.

The raid on the Iron Triangle and its aftermath made plain just how difficult it is to measure the immediate results of the B-52 attacks. No one knows for certain, but most U.S. military men are convinced that the mammoth bombers kill very few Viet Cong. They are also inclined to believe that after an initial period of demoralization induced by the raids, the Viet Cong have now found it possible to cope with the bombings by reducing the size of their units and reverting to guerrilla fundamentals.

The B-52 partisans, in turn, argue that this is precisely the point of the raids. In at least two instances, they claim, B-52 attacks forced the guerrillas to disperse large forces which they had massed in preparation for major assaults. Beyond that, large caches of Viet Cong food and arms have been captured by ground units following up the attacks. "The bombings," a Pentagon spokesman says, "deny the Viet Cong sanctuary, even if for a short time, and eventually force them out of these hideouts."

Problems: The Viet Cong themselves have admitted that the B-52s have created "concrete difficulties" for them, but they scoff at the idea that the raids will have any significant effect on the course of the war. This, of course, may be whistling in the dark, but to some U.S. military men, it seems entirely possible that the Viet Cong are right. (7)

During the last week in July, Air Force F-4s took their first loss from SA-2 SAMs in a raid northwest of the Hanoi restricted zone. In a retaliatory strike several days later, F-105s bombed the SAM site but suffered five losses from North Vietnamese anti-aircraft guns in the process. In mid-August the SAMs downed their second US plane, a Navy A-4.

By the end of the year the total of Air Force and Navy sorties devoted to Rolling Thunder reached

Adapted from an Armored Troop Carrier, the Combat Salvage Boat was used to recover damaged 'Sea Lord' craft. 'Sea Lord' raids were combined operations into the rivers of the Ca Mau peninsula.

When we catch the guerrilla on the water, here in the Rung Sat special zone, he's in our element. His may be the dark and the jungle, but if he ventures onto ours, we're gonna get him

Above: USS Benewah, the afloat base for the Mobile Riverine Force in the Mekong, with ATCs and Monitors tied up alongside.

Below: A US Navy inshore patrol craft (PCF) returns to its afloat base from patrol on the Cua Lon river, with an underwater demolition team.

Above: A French-built 'commandament' or command boat, belonging to the South Vietnamese Navy, moves down a Mekong Delta canal on a joint US-RVN operation in 1967.

The US Navy maintained a strong presence off the Vietnamese coast. Older carriers such as USS Intrepid played a major part in the operations against the North.

55,000. In all, the USAF lost 224 fixed-wing aircraft during 1965. Of these, 66 were due to operational causes and the remaining 158 were in combat. The greatest number of combat losses (139) came from enemy ground fire, while 5 were downed by SAMs and 3 by enemy MiGs. A further 11 planes were destroyed by Viet Cong attacks against air bases.

Naval operations

The US Navy's Operation Market Time began in April with a modest commitment of six radar picket destroyers to patrol South Vietnam's coastline. The operation was designed to prevent sea-borne resupply of the Viet Cong. The next month, Navy destroyers joined in fire support operations of troops in South Vietnam's coastal areas for the first time.

Throughout most of 1965 the Navy kept six carriers in the Western Pacific for operations in Southeast Asia, usually four modern large-deck carriers and two older types. In November a nuclear-powered task force consisting of the carrier Enterprise and escorts arrived, the first nuclear ships ever to see combat. Navy fixed-wing aviation suffered 125 aircraft losses in 1965 – 98 in combat and 27 operational losses. Enemy air defense fire caused 91 losses, while SAMs accounted for 6 planes and MiGs the remaining one.

THE US ARMY IN VIETNAM

Any study of the US Army's performance in Vietnam must begin at the top and work down, starting with the strategy – or lack of it – by which the war was conducted. Prior to 1965, various contingency plans allowed for US troop involvement in conventional settings, and later for the establishment of "enclaves" protecting US bases. From these, it was envisioned, the ARVN could move out and defeat the Viet Cong. In the event, the ARVN did so poorly (losing nearly a battalion a week) that by 1965 the South Vietnamese government actually controlled less than 40 per cent of its country. Thus the US felt compelled to take a more active role in engaging the Viet Cong. During the Kennedy administration the emphasis had been on counterinsurgency warfare – Green Berets, rural development, internal reforms, etc. – for the purpose of "nation building" along American lines.

By 1965 the situation had changed. Not only did internal South Vietnamese problems throw the "nation building" strategy off course, but the nature of the enemy offensive was vastly different to a home-grown "insurgency." Various counterinsur-

PATROLLING

Vietnam was many different wars rolled into one. The pilot returning to his carrier after a mission over the North was a part of the war, as was the supply clerk at Cam Ranh Bay. But the ordinary grunt had the worst of it. Patrolling, looking for the enemy, listening for every sound. You might be carried in a helicopter or in an APC but when you got down to it most of your travel was on foot. In the dry season you choked in dust, in the wet season you sank to your waist in glutinous mud. And at the end of the day, the only prospect was more of the same.

Left: A grunt humps the PRC-25 radio telephone, the standard infantry radio used in Vietnam. Known as the 'Prick'-25, the unit was heavy and unwieldy, and was unloved by those who had to carry it into combat.

Above: Troops of 3d Bn, the 5th Marines, wade through 5-feet-high elephant grass in the downdraught from a helicopter during Operation Meade River in November 1968. In two hours, 75 aircraft inserted 3,500 fighting men.

gency experts, like Sir Robert Thompson, were called in to impart lessons learned from the British experience in putting down the Communists in Malaya. The position in Vietnam, however, was at odds with that in Malaya. While the British could virtually seal off Malaya from outside interference, Vietnam had a long border which served as a conduit for enemy supplies and reinforcements. The British had an easier task in identifying Communist Terrorists, who were ethnic Chinese for the most part, but the Americans enjoyed no such luxury in Vietnam. In addition the Malayan population was amenable to various government relocation and control schemes, while the Vietnamese had an ancestral attachment to their land and resisted government interference.

In recent years, two theories have been advanced by US Army scholars about American strategy and tactics in Vietnam. One holds that the Army paid only lip service to pacification and population protection, and went off chasing NVA regulars to no purpose. The result, it is maintained, was that America lost the support of the people because the Viet Cong took over at night when US soldiers left. The other school holds that the US government failed to recognize that it was in a full-scale war with North Vietnam, and lost because it did not do all it could to defeat North Vietnam in military terms. There is an element of truth in both.

In retrospect, the United States did not concentrate its efforts sufficiently in either area to be decisive. To be sure, the US Army could have made things a lot easier on itself by adopting something like the Marine Corps' Combined Action Program, which attached a USMC squad to each South Vietnamese Popular Forces platoon. Such measures would have won the war in the villages, which the North Vietnamese maintain was so important in getting the US out of Vietnam. To a large extent though, the Tet Offensive of 1968 and the CORDS program effectively exposed the Viet Cong infrastructure and took it out of the war. Had Vietnam been nothing but an internal guerrilla war, the counterinsurgency approach would have been enough, but the introduction of North Vietnamese regulars changed the equation.

Conventional forces succeed

In the end, it was not an internal guerrilla movement or the failure to win the hearts and minds of the people which defeated South Vietnam, but a massive conventional assault by North Vietnamese regular divisions supported by tanks and heavy artillery.

The US Forces in Vietnam were fighting a war they had not trained for in some of the most difficult terrain in the world. Even so, the few troops who saw action usually acquitted themselves well.

"You might only move 3000 meters in a day; if you had definite intelligence on an enemy presence in the area then even that figure would be reduced so you could concentrate on searching in silence"

Above: *1st Cavalry Division actions in 1968 included the relief of Khe Sanh, but most of the year 'Search and Destroy' was the norm. This squad from the 2nd Battalion, 7th Cavalry is on patrol in Quang Tri Province.*

Left: *Armored personnel carriers and tanks from 3d Tank Bn, 3d Marine Division, patrol near Quang Tri in January 1969. Armored patrols were effective here against NVA units waging conventional campaigns against US troops.*

Right: *Soldiers of the 198th Infantry Brigade on patrol in August 1970. Water, food, clothing, poncho, binoculars, ammunition, an entrenching tool and an M-16 are all vital equipment for surviving days on end in the hostile bush.*

The enemy was North Vietnam, and as long as it could operate according to the artificial rules set by the Johnson administration, there was never any hope of defeating it. American military leaders certainly *knew* the right thing to do.

Strategy and Statistics

From the first, Admiral U. S. Grant Sharp (CINCPAC) wanted to cut off North Vietnam by naval mining and execute a massive bombing offensive. General Westmoreland's staff proposed a plan in early 1966 to cut the northern part of the Ho Chi Minh trail by landing the 1st Cavalry Division in Laos by airmobile assault and bringing the 3rd Marine Division along Route 9 to Tchepone, Laos. These moves were to have been complemented by a 4th Infantry Division attack westward from Pleiku, and an ARVN 1st Airborne Division attack westward from A Shau. Another plan in early 1968 envisioned a three-division assault (2 US, 1 ARVN) on Tchepone, to link up with another US division deployed from Thailand with Royal Thai and Laotian forces. General Bruce Palmer suggests that the DMZ area could have been beefed up with 5 divisions (2 US, 2 ROK, 1 ARVN), allowing an additional 3 US divisions to drive into Laos as far as the Thai border. Of course there was always the option of a limited, or unlimited, invasion of North Vietnam, as most NVA troops were eventually deployed in South Vietnam.

President Johnson, however, would deny all requests to carry the war to a successful conclusion by expanding the scope of operations. The object was not to win the war, but to keep South Vietnam from losing it. With such restraints, any attempt at a meaningful strategy was useless. Strangely, not a single general or flag officer in the US services offered his resignation in protest to the "no win" policy of the Johnson administration. Instead, the hapless Westmoreland and his subordinates turned to the non-strategy of attrition. Statistics became the measure of success for American military leaders. For the Army, the body count was paramount. Whether the bodies counted were enemy soldiers or unfortunate civilians sometimes didn't matter. There was also a degree of inflation that went along with the body count, such as the 1st Division's "count pieces and add 10 per cent", and other local variations. According to historian Guenter Lewy, one commander of the 9th Division exerted so much pressure for a high body count that he irrepairably damaged relations with the villagers in his division area. For the other services the statistics of sorties flown, tons of ordnance delivered, shells fired, etc. chronicled their participation – whether or not they made any real contribution toward ending the war.

The one year tour

Within the Army itself, things were not well and got decidedly worse. The post-World War II Army, living in the shadow of a doctrine of nuclear retaliation (to be carried out by the Air Force and Navy), went through several organizational changes which ultimately destroyed any regimental esprit de corps. Units deploying to Vietnam at least had the advantage of having trained together in the States, but the ill-considered individual replacement policy and one-year tour of duty eliminated all but minimal cohesion in combat units. The policy provided for a continuous turnover of personnel in Vietnam by rotating enlisted men through a 12-month assignment with a unit and then returning them home. Officers had a similar program except that they would serve six months in a combat unit and six months in a staff assignment. The result was that just when a man got to "know the ropes", he would go home and be replaced by a green conscript. This has prompted many observers to comment that the US didn't fight a ten-year war in Vietnam – it fought a one-year war ten times.

To a largely careerist officer corps, the Army's personnel policies were not necessarily detrimental, but facilitated "ticket punching". While providing for a minimum of combat risk, they allowed for a maximum of "command slots" and medals. Promotions came quickly, with one year advancement from second lieutenant to first lieutenant, and another year to captain – placing very junior officers with a woeful lack of experience in charge of companies (a major's position in the British Army). Without playing down the many truly heroic acts performed in Vietnam, there was a good deal of inflation and bargaining for decorations as well. Command tours were short enough so that each officer had to work hard to make his presence felt in order to get a desirable grade on his efficiency report. An unfortunate platoon leader in contact with the enemy could be getting instructions on the radio from not only his company commander, but his battalion, brigade, and even division commanders, hovering overhead in helicopters.

Good and bad

While in Vietnam, units did gain reputations based on their performance, or at least on initial impressions after their first few actions. The top rated US division was the 1st Cavalry Division (Airmobile), which was used as a country-wide fire brigade – being deployed to the most critical areas. Also in the "excellent" category were the 11th Armored Cavalry Regiment, the 1st Brigade of the 101st Airborn Division, and the 173rd Airborne Brigade. In the last case, as Anthony Herbert's book, *Soldier*, points out, even a fine unit can be mishandled. The Army's "good" units included the 1st and 25th Infantry Divisions, and the 1st Brigade of the 5th Infantry Division (Mech). Falling into the fair category were the 4th and 9th Infantry Divisions, the remainder of the 101st Airborne Division, the 3rd Brigade of the 82nd Airborne Division, and the 199th Light Infantry Brigade. The only really poor unit was the Americal Division (11th, 196th, 198th Brigades). A couple of representative incidents are worth mentioning in this regard. The 11th Light Infantry Brigade, which had some units described by historian Shelby Stanton as "little better than organized bands of thugs", was the outfit of Lt. William Calley, perpetrator of the isolated (but not unique) My Lai massacre in 1968. The 196th Light Infantry Brigade disproved Westmoreland's assertion that the US never lost an engagement larger than company level. Its most notorious "bug out" (to use a Korean War phrase) was at the Kham Duc CIDG Camp in May of 1968, where a task force from the 1-46 Infantry, the 2-1 Infantry, and their supporting artillery, ignominiously fled from the 1st VC Regiment, throwing Vietnamese dependents off helicopters at gunpoint and abandoning seven 105mm howitzers, fifteen 81mm mortars and fifteen trucks.

Decline of an army

As time went on, especially after the 1969 announcement of US withdrawals, the Army in Vietnam declined. President Johnson's earlier decision to fight the war with draftees rather than with mobilized National Guardsmen and Army Reservists (who were collecting paychecks for such a contingency), assured that the soldiery would be unenthusiastic at the very least. Combat refusals and "search and avoid" tactics began to appear in some combat units, and drug use, racial fights, and "fragging" of unpopular officers also occurred – though more often in rear echelon units. Through self-imposed logistical and administrative overhead, the fraction of American forces in Vietnam who actually went on active operations to engage the enemy was very small indeed. On a good day *perhaps* 10,000 of the 442,000 soldiers and marines in country at the peak might be in the field. The wonder is that the Army performed as well as it did.

SEARCHING FOR CHARLIE

Without uniforms, it is difficult to tell a Viet Cong fighter from a loyal South Vietnamese (especially when the 'loyal' Vietnamese is a VC sympathizer). The only way to prove it is to find equipment, food supplies or weapons in the suspect's hut or catch them sneaking out at night with a Kalashnikov in his (or her) hand. Search and Destroy missions would go through hamlets with a fine tooth comb. If suspicious gear was found, it was often easier to burn down the whole hut than to drag a hundred pounds of rice back to base and the inevitable paperwork. If weapons were found however, the Vietnamese would have to face some rigorous questioning.

Above: A Navy SEAL commando enters a village in the Mekong Delta in September 1967, seeking hidden VC installations.

Below: A member of the 9th Infantry Division passes a flaming hootch during an operation in April 1968.

"Methodically they searched the house, poking bamboo stakes into walls and into the ground to detect hiding spots and escape tunnels. They soon dragged a number of young men out of a hidden compartment and hustled them off for interrogation. The young lady informant – out of sight – identified those with VC connections"

Above: Elements of 7th Cavalry work their way cautiously through a Bong Son village during Operation Masher, 1966

Below: Search and destroy – a member of 3d Marine Division watches as a hootch, containing enemy supplies, burns

CHAPTER FOUR

BUILD-UP

1966

Marines of G Company, 4th Marines, 3rd Marine Division fight their way up a slope near the demilitarized zone during Operation Hastings. Lasting for most of July 1966, the Marines along with the ARVNs and the Vietnamese Marines accounted for over 800 NVA regulars.

During 1966 the 1st Marine Division came up to full strength with the arrival of its 1st Marines in January and the 5th Marines in May. The Army's 25th Infantry Division brought in its three brigades – 3rd, 2nd and 1st – in January, February and May respectively. Stationed in Hawaii in peacetime, the 25th ironically had more mechanized units than other divisions which deployed to Vietnam. Reinforcements from the continental US included the 4th and 9th Infantry Divisions. The 4th dispatched its 2nd Brigade in August and followed up with the rest of the division in October. The 9th Division was configured for "riverine" warfare in the Mekong Delta area, and one of its brigades, the 3rd, arrived in December. The remainder of the 9th would not come on line until 1967.

Various non-divisional formations boosted US strength during 1966 as well, including the 52nd Artillery Group (June), 196th Light Infantry Brigade (September), 54th Artillery Group (October), 199th Light Infantry Brigade (December), and the elite 11th Armored Cavalry Regiment (September). At year's end there were 239,400 US soldiers and 69,200 marines in Vietnam, virtually double the numbers of December 1965.

Free World Forces

The South Koreans brought their Capital Division up to strength in 1966 with the arrival of its 26th Regiment. They also deployed the 9th "White Horse" Division, with its 28th Regiment arriving in

September, followed by the 29th and 30th Regiments in October. The Australian and New Zealand contingent was large enough to form a brigade headquarters of its own in April, known as 1st Australian Task Force.

Australian tactics and techniques differ sharply from those used by the more conventionally oriented Americans. While the American GI, for example, usually carries only one canteen of water, the Australian digger carries four plus enough rations to last two or three days. Eschewing heavy steel helmets in the steamy jungle, the Aussies wear light bush hats. They carry less ammunition than the Americans and fire an average of only 60 rounds from their rifles for every 100 expended by the U S soldier. Most important, when on an operation, the Australians keep on the move in order to throw off the enemy and, unlike Americans, would never dream of taking a break for a telltale cigarette.

A large part of the Aussies' effectiveness is attributable to their training methods. Because of its small size, the 27,000-man Australian Army trains exclusively for the one kind of war it is most likely to face, guerrilla conflict in the swamps and jungles of Asia. In fact, American soldiers in Vietnam often joke that the Aussies are such good jungle fighters that the VC never seem able to find them – and they can never find the VC. To which one Australian major says: "I suppose there is a tiny grain of truth there . . . But I should add that we've run into more bloody booby traps than there are flies in Canberra." (1)

The ARVN combat forces expanded during the year with the creation of the 18th Division in the III Corps Zone around the area of Xuan Loc. This, however, didn't come close to making up for the 90,000 ARVN troops that had deserted during 1965. By the end of 1966 there were an estimated 45,000 NVA regulars and 230,000 full- and part-time VC guerrillas in South Vietnam, even accounting for the 20,000 "Chieu Hoi" Communist defectors who came over to the government during the year.

Members of a Korean weapons platoon cross a stream in Vietnam. Koreans were among the toughest troops around.

From January 24th until February 21st, 1966 the US Army and Marines conducted a coordinated offensive in Binh Dinh Province. The Marines' Task Force Delta, engaged in Operation Double Eagle, moved south from I Corps to join the 1st Cavalry Division, the ARVN, and South Korean units which were carrying out Operation Masher (renamed White Wing) and Operation Thang Phong II (ARVN) in the II Corps area. The joint operation yielded 2,389 Communist casualties, most of them from the 325th NVA Division.

Far and away the most important operation was White Wing, led by 1st Air Cav Colonel Hal G. Moore, 43, a lean, laconic Kentuckian who earned a battlefield promotion at bloody Ia Drang last November. In that

AUSTRALIANS

Australia sent advisors to Vietnam from 1962, and from 1965 deployed combat troops. The 1st Australian Task Force usually consisted of two infantry battalions with armour, artillery (including a New Zealand battery), a squadron of the Special Air Service, logistics, signals and other support. The Royal Australian Air Force's contribution to the war was a squadron of Canberra bombers, which flew 11,963 sorties for the loss of only two aircraft. Over 7,500 Australians were serving in Vietnam by 1969, when the government began to withdraw them.

Above: A Huey of the Royal Australian Air Force at an LZ in Nui Thi Va, 1970.

Below: The Australians' hefty but accurate semi-auto 7.62 FN (L1A1) rifle goes into action.

Above: Members of the 8th Royal Australian Regiment on patrol near the Song Rai River in April 1970.

Above: Expert jungle fighters on foot, the Australians also engaged in large-scale armoured sweeps to flush out the VC.

"No enemy dead is ever claimed unless an Aussie can walk up and put his foot on the body; no wounded claim counts unless he can be trailed for 300 yards, with blood seen all the way"

Left: Professionals at war. The Australians were heirs to two generations of jungle warfare; most were regular soldiers.

***Left:** Fording a stream near **Ben Cat**, 1970. After a number of combined operations with **US** and **ARVN** forces early in the war, the Australian Task Force in Vietnam took over its own area of operations, fighting with the support of a contingent New Zealand gunners.*

***Right:** Searching **Hoa Long** village, April 1970. The Australian presence in Vietnam grew from a group of 25 jungle warfare advisors in 1962 to a peak of over 8,000 combat and support troops in 1967.*

***Below:** In-country training with both the **FN** and **M16** for members of 7 **Bn**, **Royal Australian Regiment**. Nine battalions – rotated after a year's tour as units, not individual soldiers – of the regiment saw service in Vietnam.*

***Left:** RAAF Hueys en route to an extraction. The Australian airmobility and heliborne tactics were developed and adapted from **US** experience.*

***Right above:** An M60 gun team in position – with back-up from M-79 grenades lying ready for use.*

***Right below:** Setting up a Claymore mine for a night ambush in **Nui Dat**, 1970. Australian ground tactics were often based on counter-insurgency techniques rather than those of conventional infantry warfare, with small units moving with the utmost stealth against the terrain, to avoid contact with the enemy until an advantage was completely secured.*

HIGHLAND WAR

Away from the Mekong Delta Vietnam is a mountainous country. The Central Highlands rise to over 8,000 feet in places, much being covered in jungle. During the War, arms from the North were filtered off the main Ho Chi Minh Trail along infiltration routes through the hills to the heavily populated coastal plain. To interrupt the supplies American troops would be landed on a hilltop LZ, patrol down into the valley and up to another hilltop to be picked up. Even the fittest of troops might take an entire day to fight their way through a mile of jungle.

Above: A US infantryman prepares to destroy a banana grove. In the Central Highlands, away from major supply routes, the Viet Cong survived by growing many of the traditional Montagnard crops.

Above: Marine CH-46 Sea Knight helicopters ferry 'leather-necks' of the 4th Marines, 3d Marine Div, into the DMZ near the Ben Hai River in September 1968. The mountainous areas of the DMZ were infested with NVA units, to counter whose activities the US established a series of fire support bases along Route 9 – among them, Khe Sanh. Large-scale movement in the area was virtually restricted to heliborne operations.

fight, he held together a single infantry battalion surrounded by three battalions of North Vietnamese regulars. This time he was the aggressor, leading the largest allied force of the war: five infantry battalions, four artillery battalions, plus a team of combat engineers and a troop of aerial reconnaissance men, all riding the helicopters of the most mobile force warfare has ever known. (2)

The enemy was waiting. Almost at once five choppers were shot down. "We're in a hornets' nest!" radioed Captain John Fesmire. Soon, both his mortar platoon leader and radio operator were killed, his company was scattered to the north of the helidrop zone, and a rescue company sent to his assistance was pinned down by crossfire as well. One of Fesmire's lieutenants, his right leg smashed by machine gun bullets, propped himself against a sand dune and, with his back to the battle, called in artillery fire by the sound of the exploding shells. The sergeant who had taken over the weapons platoon was trapped near a machine gun nest. He had his mortar tube – but no base plate, no plotting board, no aiming stakes, no forward observer. With only six rounds of ammunition, he watched five explode harmlessly some distance from the target. Then he lifted his last round, kissed it, and fired. It leveled the machine gunners' hut.

Cavalry in action

It was nearly 24 hours before the defenders of LZ-4 were relieved and White Wing took flight. Choppers dropped fresh troops to roll up the flank of the Viet Cong firing on LZ-4 from the southwest, while still another batalion was lifted into a blocking position to the north. As the units began to link up, Colonel Moore, Armalite rifle at the ready, joined his men, spent most of the rest of the week slogging it out beside them. The circle began to close, leaving only escape to the west open to the enemy – and Moore had a solution for that. In an astonishing demonstration of the 1st Air Cav's mobility, 24 105-mm howitzers were sling-loaded under twin-turbine Chinook helicopters at Dog and lifted to the northwest corner of the valley in little over an hour. There they were able not only to cover all the allied troops in action, but also to lay a curtain of fire across any attempt by the enemy to slip away.

At one point during Operation Masher, 300 men of the Seventh Cavalry were pinned down for more than 24 hours by enemy machine gunners in a narrow strip of sand at the An Thai landing zone. "Every time you raised your head," said Lt. Col. Robert McDade, the battalion commander, "it was zap, zap, zap! The dirt really flew." As a drenching rain fell through the night, the Americans took cover behind the raised gravestones of an old cemetery. Working under a murderous hail of Communist fire, Sgt. Reid Pike, 23, of Albuquerque, N.M., calmly fashioned a transmitter from the parts of two damaged radios and managed to call for help. When a convoy of helicopters arrived the next morning, the men made a mad dash for the landing zone – all, that is, except the dozens of poncho-shrouded casualties who lay in the muddy ooze of shallow trenches.

Despite such casualties, the allied offensive proved highly effective. One South Vietnamese regiment alone killed 352 guerrillas, and a South Korean unit claimed another 75. In fact, by the weekend – by which time an entire division of U.S. troops had been committed to the battle – the body count of enemy dead had reached well over 1,100. And out of the four enemy regiments that once held unopposed control of the rice-rich area, two had been seriously crippled and put out of action. (3)

Operations in the I Corps area got under way near the city of Quang Ngai with the US Marine Operation Utah and ARVN Operation Lien Ket 26. Over

Helicopters made it easier to get around the mountains, but dense forest and steep slopes made it difficult to find landing zones. Sometimes troops were delivered by Hueys hovering by the side of a hill.

"We're goin' up that hill. We're gonna get ourselves Hill 875 for Thanksgiving Day. Ain't that nice? You'll need a gas mask. We're gonna use Tear Gas on them bunkers."

Artillery supporting the Americal Division fire from their base outside Chu Lai. Although on the coast, they are firing into the foothills of Annamese mountains which reach almost to the sea at this point.

Above: An area of the Central Highlands near Pleiku, the forest scarred and smoking after a massive B-52 attack using incendiary bombs in March 1966. The Central Highlands were a key objective for the enemy.

Above: An M-113 APC ACAV leads an M-48 tank as the 10th Cavalry patrol the jungle near An Khe, 1971. Armor was of limited effectiveness in the heavily forested terrain of much of the Central Highlands.

the 4 days to March 8th, 632 NVA and Viet Cong troops were killed. Later that month the NVA attacked the ARVN outpost at An Hoa, Quang Ngai Province, but were driven off when the Marine Operation Texas (ARVN Operation Lien Ket 28) advanced with one ARVN airborne and two Marine battalions and pushed the Communists out, killing 405 between the 20th and 24th of March. US forces suffered a setback that month as well, when the NVA overran the A Shau Special Forces Camp on the Laotian border, bagging 5 of the 17 Americans and 228 of the 400 South Vietnamese in the garrison.

ARVN mutiny

The A Shau Valley became an important staging area for the NVA. At the same time a major crisis developed in I Corps – the generals in Saigon *voted* to relieve the I Corps commander (General Thi), who had a considerable number of supporters. Demonstrations broke out in the north, and the dependable 1st ARVN Division split in mutiny. Premier Ky sent ARVN paratroopers and marines to restore order, and after some confused fighting, government control returned by mid-June.

Paratroopers parade on the anniversary of the foundation of the Vietnamese Airborne. It was with elite troops such as these that Premier Ky put down Buddhist and army risings in 1966.

Only in the last dark days of dictator Ngo Dinh Diem had South Vietnam teetered so perilously close to total anarchy. All last week in the northern city of Da Nang, war crackled in the littered streets. It was nasty, confusing, bloody: ragged house-to-house fighting between elite troops loyal to Premier Nguyen Cao Ky and dissident soldiers and Buddhists. Government tanks splattered the city's sprawling Buddhist pagodas with .50-caliber bursts, and supporting Sky-raiders sent 250-pound fragmentation bombs whistling down on similar dissident strongholds.

In one strafing attack by the planes, nine U.S. Marines were wounded; and an unidentified barrage of mortar fire crumped across the American airfield at Da Nang, causing two more American casualties. Clearing the deck for possible defensive action, the U.S. evacuated its aircraft from Da Nang and the 20,000-man Marine amphibious force was put on full alert – raising the awesome specter that the U.S. might be dragged into the war within a war. (4)

The summer of 1966 saw the 9th Marines at another An Hoa (Quang Nam Province), conducting security for an industrial area under the code name Operation Macon. The long campaign (July 4th to October 27th) cost the VC Doc Lap Battalion 507 known dead. Further operations were undertaken in Quang Nam and Quang Tin Provinces

Artillery near Qui Nonh provides support to the 1st Cavalry Division during Operation Irving, in October 1966.

under the code names Colorado (US) and Lien Ket 52 (ARVN). Lasting from August 6th to August 21st, these operations netted another 674 Communist casualties. At the same time, the NVA 324B Division stepped up operations in Quang Tri Province along the DMZ. In a month-long effort, the US and South Vietnamese Marines and the ARVN launched Operation Hastings/Deckhouse II against the division, killing 882 NVA troops between July 7th and August 3rd.

It is terrible terrain for fighting. The jungle trees and vines that cover the razorback ridges and ravines of the Annamese cordillera make military movement difficult. Bombs explode harmlessly on the thick jungle canopy. But it is here, in Quang Tri Province, where North Vietnamese regulars lately have come pouring across the undefended 17th parallel, that U.S. marines ran into their most savage battle of the war.

The North Vietnamese plan, U.S. intelligence believes, was to take control of the province of Quang Tri, then possibly attack some of the larger towns in the area. But before the North Vietnamese even began to roll, the Americans struck. In a massive helicopter lift, some 8,000 leathernecks and 3,000 South Vietnamese soldiers were moved into the rugged hills in an operation code-named Operation Hastings. It was a

M60: THE PIG

One evocative image from Vietnam involves a GI peering through the jungle, draped in ammunition belts and cradling a machine gun. The gun is always the M60. Inspired by the magnificent MG42 general purpose machine gun used by the Germans in World War Two, the M60 was not initially a success. It was not easy to change the barrel quickly, and with a weight of more than 23 pounds, it came to be known as 'The Pig'. But in experienced hands the M60 was a deadly weapon, providing the bulk of platoon level fire support.

Above: An M60 gunner aboard a Navy PBR keeps watch during operations in the Saigon River. The M60 armed everything from air cushion craft to helicopters during the war.

Below: The M60 general purpose machine gun fires the standard 7.62mm NATO round. The feed mechanism was developed from that of the German MG42.

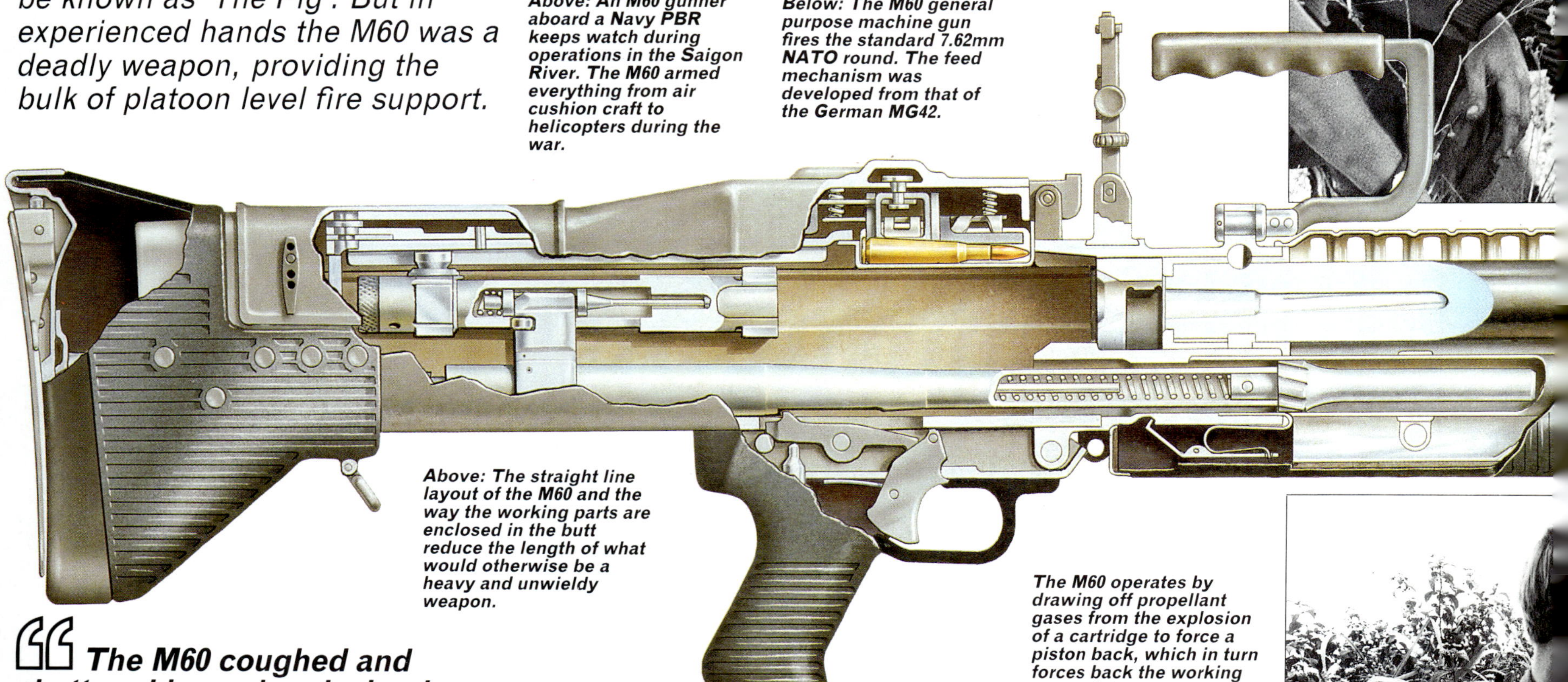

Above: The straight line layout of the M60 and the way the working parts are enclosed in the butt reduce the length of what would otherwise be a heavy and unwieldy weapon.

The M60 operates by drawing off propellant gases from the explosion of a cartridge to force a piston back, which in turn forces back the working parts of the gun.

With a cyclic firing rate of 550 rounds per minute, an experienced gunner can use the M60's large trigger to pop off single shots or short bursts without the need of a selector lever.

"The M60 coughed and chattered in my hands, louder than the beat of the rotors. The NVA were prone, trying to shoot back. I fired short, careful bursts along a line through center of the column"

daring move, but the North Vietnamese, dug into the densely covered slopes, fought back fiercely and well.

By the end of last week, the marines had lost almost 200 men killed in the two weeks of Operation Hastings, one of the heaviest tolls of the war for U.S. fighting men. But the enemy had lost even more heavily, with possibly as many as 1,600 dead. As a result, the North Vietnamese, who may well have been planning a large-scale attack, pulled back into the mountains to lick their wounds, while American B-52s blasted away at their positions – the first time the U.S. has bombed the demilitarized border zone. (5)

Following Hastings, the 3rd Marine Division left a battalion to monitor the area between Con Thien and Gio Linh. This drew out further NVA and a consequent renewed campaign by the 3rd Marine Division, dubbed Operation Prairie. During this operation (August 3rd, 1966 to January 31, 1967) the 324B Division suffered another 1,397 dead.

II Corps

US Army operations in the II Corps Tactical Zone started with support for the ARVN 47th Regiment's effort to secure rice-growing areas in Phu Yen Province. Under the title Operation Van Buren, the elite 1st Brigade of the 101st Airborne Division and the South Korean 2nd "Blue Dragon" Marine Brigade killed 679 Viet Cong and NVA soldiers from January 19th to February 21st. That summer the 101st's 1st Brigade pushed out into Kontum Province for another major operation (Hawthorne) in conjunction with the ARVN (Operation Dan Tang 61). This joint undertaking yielded another 531 Communist casualties.

Operation Paul Revere

In II Corps' Pleiku Province, the US 25th Infantry Division's 3rd Brigade took up screening positions along the Cambodian border (Operation Paul Revere) along with the ARVN (Operation Than Phong 14) and killed 546 NVA between the 10th of May and the end of July. The 1st Cavalry Division, still active in II Corps, initiated another offensive in Pleiku Province, Operation Paul Revere II, which cost the NVA 809 dead during the month of August. From mid-October to the end of December, Operation Paul Revere IV kept up the pressure in the border areas of Pleiku. The involved brigades of the 25th Infantry and 1st Cavalry Divisions were joined by the reinforcing 4th Infantry Division in this effort, and the result was another 977 Communist casualties.

Though it has been one of the biggest and longest sweeps of the Vietnamese war, Operation Paul Revere has not been a particularly spectacular one. In contrast with some recent encounters – such as Operation Hastings in which almost 200 U.S. marines and perhaps as many as 1,600 of the enemy were killed in nearly four weeks of intense action – Paul Revere has accounted for only 786 enemy dead in the 87 days since it began. And for the thousands of GI's involved in Paul Revere, their dogged pursuit of the North Vietnamese 32nd Regiment has become frustrating.

Part of the trouble has been that the monsoon rains have made U.S. air surveillance and reinforcement efforts a very chancy affair. Just how serious a difficulty this can be was shown last week when a platoon of the First Air Cavalry found itself surrounded by North Vietnamese shortly after a seemingly uneventful landing in the jungles of South Vietnam's central highlands.

Immediately after the platoon's helicopters took off, the weather closed in, making reinforcement impossible. Then the North Vietnamese opened up, killing both the platoon commander and his first sergeant.

By the time 45 minutes had elapsed, the platoon's radio had been captured, ending all contact with the outside.

Finally, a few members of the platoon managed to get off the landing zone into heavy cover. As they

Above: Gun-cleaning fluid in his helmet band, a sergeant of the 173d Airborne defends his perimeter near Dak To, 1967.

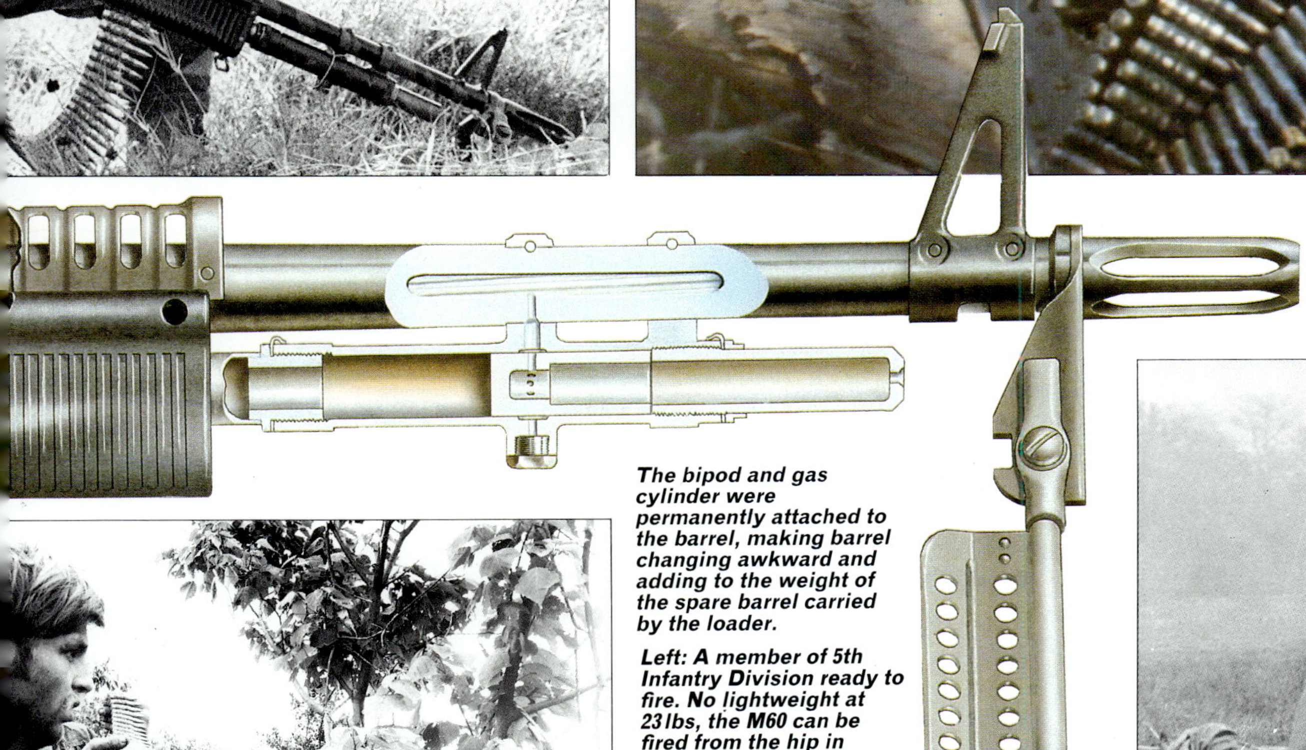

The bipod and gas cylinder were permanently attached to the barrel, making barrel changing awkward and adding to the weight of the spare barrel carried by the loader.

Left: A member of 5th Infantry Division ready to fire. No lightweight at 23 lbs, the M60 can be fired from the hip in emergencies, but without any great accuracy.

Right: The M60 armed a wide variety of vehicles, from trucks to helicopters. This M60-armed jeep of the 17th Cavalry is seen securing a landing zone during operation Junction City.

THUNDERCHIEF

Plagued with reliability problems, requiring a huge runway to take off when loaded and unmanoeuvrable when compared with other types, the Republic F-105 Thunderchief shouldered the brunt of operations against the North throughout the 1960s. In the end few aircraft were loved more by their pilots, mostly on the type's ability to soak up much punishment. It should not be forgotten that the F-105 racked up the impressive total of 28 MiG kills, and formed the basis for the highly successful 'Wild Weasel' anti-SAM programme.

"I could hear the strike force withdrawing. I knew those fighter bombers would be back, right over this area. I made up my mind to stay until I got that SAM site or it got me"

Above: Armed with 750-lb bombs, this Republic F-105D Thunderchief approaches the tanker on its way to a mission.

Above: F-105s taxi out at Takhli RTAFB at the start of another mission.

Left: ECM-equipped F-105Ds of the 34th TFS, 388th TFW drop their bombs from medium level during an attack on North Vietnam.

Below: Fully-armed F-105s could not reach their targets and back without the aid of inflight refuelling.

watched helplessly, the North Vietnamese overran the landing area, killing all the wounded GI's on it save three who escaped by playing dead. By the time the weather changed enough to let reinforcements come in, only nine of the original 27 air cavalrymen were alive. Among them was Sergeant Glaspie, who next day went into action again with a new squad. And Paul Revere ground on. (6)

At the end of Paul Revere II, the 1st Cavalry Division moved a couple of battalions to the very south of the II Corps area, to Binh Thuan Province, until late January 1968. This contingent carried out "economy-of-force" patrol operations which resulted in 849 Communist casualties. The rest of the division remained at its base at An Khe and participated in Operation Irving, a month-long effort in Binh Dinh Province with the ARVN and the South Koreans. Irving produced 681 NVA and VC dead during October. Following Irving, the 1st Cavalry Division initiated Operation Thaver II in the province's Kim Son and Luoi Ci Valleys. Lasting from the end of October 1966 until February 12th, 1967, the operation claimed 1,757 enemy lives. Also operating in Binh Dinh was the South Korean Capital "Tiger" Division, which conducted its own offensive (Operation Haeng Ho 6) between September 23rd and November 9th, killing a further 1,161 Communist troops.

Farther south, in III Corps, active operations got under way in mid-1966. The Viet Cong 9th Division ran foul of the US 1st Infantry Division and the ARVN 5th Division in Binh Long Province and lost 855 men. This operation, El Paso II, started in the beginning of June and lasted until mid-July. The 196th Light Infantry Brigade, rushed from training in the US, deployed in August and was thrown into the War Zone "C" area of Tay Ninh Province to commence Operation Attleboro on September 14th.

Within a month it had uncovered a large base complex (as well as the 9th VC Division and the 101st NVA Regiment) and additional units were committed to back it up, including the 1st Infantry Division, the 4th Infantry Division's 3rd Brigade, and the crack 173rd Airborne Brigade. By the end of the operation (the largest to date), on November 24th, the Communists had suffered 1,106 casualties.

In the Saigon area, Operation Fairfax was initiated at the end of November as a joint US-ARVN venture. Brigade-size participation by the US first included a battalion from each of the US infantry divisions in the area (1st, 4th and 25th), but was soon taken over by the 199th Light Infantry Brigade which had arrived in December as a security force for US installations around Saigon. At the conclusion of the operation in mid-December of 1967, the 199th handed over to the ARVN 5th Ranger Group after having inflicted some 1,043 casualties on the enemy.

Combat losses

American deaths, for all services, totaled 6,053 during 1966 (5,008 in combat and 1,045 non-hostile). Another 30,093 men had sustained wounds requiring hospitalization. In the same period the ARVN lost 19,000 dead and over 116,000 men deserted. Over the year the US Army lost 260 helicopters, 94 in combat and the other 166 to operational losses. All but 3 of the combat losses were from enemy ground fire. The rest were destroyed at bases. Marine air losses for the year included 45 helicopters (16 operational and 29 to ground fire) and 36 fixed-wing aircraft (12 operational, 23 to ground fire and 1 to SAMs).

Rolling Thunder starts

Rolling Thunder got under way in February of 1966, after a 37-day pause in the bombing schedule

Right: The flightline at Takhli bristles with Republic F-105Ds eager to get at the North. A date of late 1965 is indicated by the fact that only some of the aircraft have exchanged their peacetime colours for three-tone tactical camouflage.

Left: Groundcrew prepare an F-105F 'Wild Weasel' for a mission.

Below: During the early part of the war Douglas EB-66 ECM aircraft accompanied F-105s on blind bombing missions, the Thunderchiefs dropping their bombs on command from the Lead aircraft.

Above: Fuze extenders on the bombs caused them to explode above the ground, thereby causing maximum blast effect. The tailcode 'RE' denoted the 44th TFS, 355th TFW from Takhli.

Most potent version of the Thunderchief to reach Southeast Asia was the F-105G, tailored for 'Wild Weasel' operations. Able to launch Standard or Shrike (illustrated) anti-radiation missiles, the F-105G also carried ECM equipment in fairings scabbed on to each side of the fuselage. The unit was Detachment 1 of the 561st TFS based at Korat.

failed to encourage Hanoi to come to the bargaining table. Once more the emphasis was on transportation targets, with a number of rail bridges on the routes to China being struck. B-52s were used against the northern terminus of the Ho Chi Minh Trail in April, with a raid on the Mu Gia Pass leading out of North Vietnam.

For 37 days the skies over North Viet Nam had been free of U.S. fighter-bombers, while the U.S. vainly probed Hanoi for some sign of willingness to talk peace. When at last patience was exhausted, the code message flashed out from the Pentagon via Pearl Harbor to Saigon, and last week American jets roared aloft to end the bombing pause.

First off the mark were Navy planes from the U.S.S. *Ranger*, which dropped a bridge twelve miles southwest of Dong Hoi and blasted a ferry landing near Quang Khe. Only minutes later, on target – a highway-ferry complex at Thanh Hoa – were Air Force F-105s, and another Air Force wing was soon battering a cluster of barges with 20-mm cannon. The first day's bombing took a toll of three U.S. planes shot down by antiaircraft fire – one measure of the use to which Hanoi had put the pause.

Now, after the Communists' five weeks' grace, the flak flew thicker over virtually every target. Moreover, reconnaissance showed that Ho Chi Minh's men had hastily implanted ten new SAM sites, bringing to 60 the number of nests across the country able to cradle Ho's Russian rocket launchers. Even the North Vietnamese air force took advantage of the free skies to give its pilots some hasty refresher work in the MiG fighters that Hanoi has largely refrained from using so far. Hanoi also used the hiatus to pump perhaps 6,000 fresh troops down the Ho Chi Minh trail into South Viet Nam and put thousands of laborers to work round the clock feverishly repairing previous bomb damage to roads, bridges, ferries and supply dumps.

It was these limited targets that Washington began hammering again last week. No strikes were being permitted north of the narrow waist of North Viet Nam, thus sparing the enemy's industrial heartland around Hanoi and Haiphong. (7)

The bombing of North Vietnam prompted the Vietnamese to deploy a truly formidable air defence, one that was to cost the lives of many American pilots. Guns, such as these Soviet-supplied 57-mm S-60s were teamed with a strong surface-to-air missile component.

In July the priority shifted to POL (petroleum/lubricants) targets, and most of North Vietnam's fixed storage capacity was destroyed. The effort came too late, as much of the POL had been shifted to dispersed sites. In 148,000 Rolling Thunder sorties, US air arms delivered 128,000 tons of bombs in 1966, but with no noticeable effect on North Vietnamese resolve. The interdiction effort along the Laotian infiltration routes increased as well, rising to

100 sorties per day by July. By mid year the North Vietnamese had over 100 SAM sites and 70 operational fighters, including new MiG-21s. Toward the end of the year both figures would nearly double. USAF losses during 1966 totaled 374 fixed-wing aircraft, 78 to operational causes and 296 in combat. The great majority of combat losses (265) were to ground fire, with a further 18 to SAMs, 8 to enemy fighters, and 5 destroyed on the ground.

Naval operations

Throughout 1966, the Navy surface force on the gun line averaged 1 heavy cruiser, 4 destroyers and 3 fire support ships, with slight augmentations in April and May. The Sea Dragon gunfire program against the North Vietnam coast got into high gear in October, and by the end of November had destroyed 230 enemy vessels. As in 1965, Task Force 77 aver-

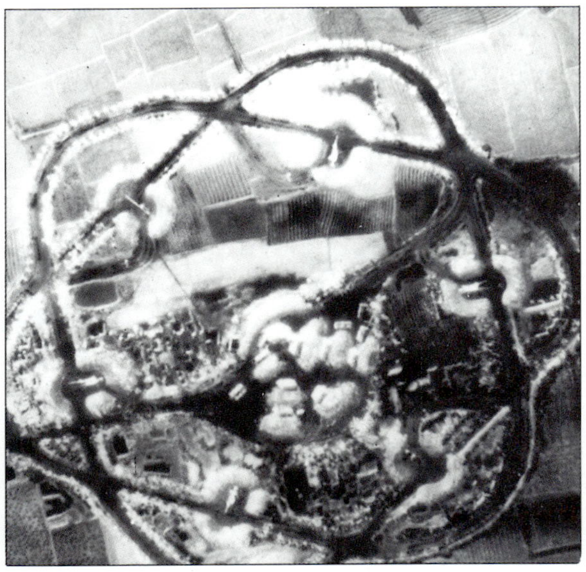

The distinctive shape of an SA-2 'Guideline' SAM site, as seen by a USAF RF-101 some 35 miles north-west of Hanoi in November 1966.

aged 3 large deck and 2 small deck carriers through 1966. Rolling Thunder operations continued, as did close air support (in South Vietnam). The first of the Navy's major aircraft carrier fires ocurred on October 26th on the Oriskany destroying four jets and two helicopters, and killing 43 men.

Amid gentle swells 50 miles off the coast of North Viet Nam, the aircraft carrier U.S.S. *Oriskany* swung north-ward into the wind. Four A-4E Skyhawk jet bombers soared gracefully off the flight deck. At 7:38 a.m. four more were being readied in a hangar bay far below, when a shouting sailor burst from a 15-ft-square locker near by. Behind him was an ominously hissing stack of 700 Mark-24 magnesium parachute flares. He barely had time to dog down the hatch on the locker and race for a phone when the flares began to explode. Fire bells clanged: klaxons sounded the call to general quarters. Loudspeakers shrilled: "This is no drill! This is no drill!"

Helpless Horror. Superbly trained fire crews dragged hoses toward the burning locker. Other crewmen fought desperately to roll four planes to the far end of the hangar deck: three of them were already laden with bombs: the fourth, a tanker, carried 900 gal. of JP-5 jet fuel. The fire fighters watched in helpless horror as the steel bulkheads of the flare locker started ballooning under the 7,000° heat inside. The steel hatch blasted open with a great gout of flame that engulfed the hangar and sent fireballs rocketing down every passageway, igniting two helicopters. Five sailors were burned alive.

The automatic sprinkler system opened up, spraying curtains of water into the lower-deck compartments. But the magnesium-fed fire continued to burn, turning sections of the flight deck above into a sizzling skillet. Choking clouds of dense, dirty-grey smoke poured through seven decks of the *Oriskany's* forward sections. Two more blasts sent flames belching along the flight deck, where red-shirted ordnance experts worked feverishly to jettison 500-lb., 1,000-lb. and 2,000-lb. bombs; (8)

The Navy lost 163 fixed-wing aircraft during the year. Operational losses claimed 39 of these and the

MEKONG WAR

From its source high in the Himalayas, the Mekong winds through more than 2,500 miles of South East Asia, before entering the sea via a huge delta. The Mekong Delta covers most of the southern portion of South Vietnam. The Viet Cong were present in the Delta in large numbers, and US Forces fought a long 'Brown Water' war for control of the region. Operation 'Market Time' started in August 1965 concentrating on coastal surveillance, with the inshore and riverine operation 'Game Warden' following in December.

A PCF inshore patrol craft, also known as 'Swift' boats, operated in coastal waters as well as in the Delta. They were often used to ferry Navy SEAL special warfare teams into action.

"This is the most densely populated area of all Vietnam. You can't walk five steps down here without stumbling on a gaggle of ducks, some kids and a little old lady selling soda pop. One old man near Dong Tam doesn't know where his village stands. The kids are helping Americans fill sandbags, the young men are off with Viet Cong guerrillas and the women are doing the laundry for the soldiers"

An ASPB (assault support patrol boat) is damaged during a patrol into the Mekong Delta in June 1968. A stopped boat provides little protection from VC fire, so while frantic attempts are made to repair the hull the crew return fire with a will.

On the Lon Tau river in the Mekong Delta, July 1967. A US Navy ATC (Armored Troop Carrier) lands US Army troops from the 9th Infantry Division at the start of Operation Concordia-Six.

Riverine operations called for good co-operation between helicopter and patrol boat.

Lack of base facilities ashore on the Delta was no problem for the US Navy. This is the auxiliary barracks ship USS** Benewah, **mother ship to a variety of riverine forces.

other 124 were in combat, with ground fire dow 105, SAMs getting 15, and MiGs bringing down 4.

THE US NAVY IN VIETNAM

By April 1966, all US Navy activities within Vietnam came under a Saigon headquarters known as Commander US Naval Forces Vietnam (COMNAVFORV). Naval air, gunfire support, and amphibious operations were directed from outside, with command moving from Pacific Command to Commander Pacific Fleet, to Commander 7th Fleet. COMNAVFORV's first and most successful mission was Operation Market Time, the interdiction of Communist supplies entering South Vietnam by sea. Market Time was carried out by the Coastal Surveillance Force (Task Force 115), which worked closely with the South Vietnamese National Maritime Police. From its headquarters at Cam Ranh Bay, Task Force 115 (TF-115) coordinated a network of five Coastal Surveillance Centers, which directed patrol operations in nine areas.

Patrol craft

To patrol one thousand miles of coastline TF-115 employed 81 armed PCFs (Patrol Craft, Fast or "Swift Boats"), 5 Coast Guard high-endurance cutters (WHECs), and 24 armed Coast Guard patrol boats (WPBs). Seven radar picket escort ships (DERs) served with TF-115 on a rotational basis from Cruiser-Destroyer Force Pacific, and minesweepers (MSOs and MSCs) were provided by Mine Force Pacific. Thirty-nine small patrol craft of the Inshore Undersea Warfare Group (Operation Stable Door, also under TF-115) protected merchant ships in port against the threat of swimmer attacks. Surveillance assistance was provided by five SP-2H Neptunes and several P-3A Orion multi-engine patrol aircraft. After a tentative start, TF-115 virtually closed down Communist seaborne resupply, formerly the easiest infiltration route available to Hanoi.

From the first moment it was spotted, the dingy, olive-drab trawler seemed suspicious. It flew no flag. It carried no markings except simply the number 459. And for three days it zigged and zagged on a curious path, first heading west toward the South Vietnamese coast, then veering out to sea. Finally, when it turned coastward, apparently making for the mouth of the Sa Ky River, south of the U.S. base at Chu Lai, U.S. coastal surveillance vessels closed in on the ship and asked it to identify itself. The answer was a burst of fire, and in response the U.S. ships sent a round of mortar fire into the trawler's pilot house, setting off a raging fire on the deck. Out of control, the ship ran aground, and next morning, with the first light, U.S. and South Vietnamese Navy men went aboard.

On the ship, the boarding party found only one dead body. The rest of the crew of the trawler had fled, leaving behind an enormous cargo of arms and supplies that had been destined for the Viet Cong. It was, reported a Navy spokesman last week, the biggest catch yet for Operation Market Time.

Begun in March 1965, Market Time, a combined Navy-Coast Guard-South Vietnamese operation under the over-all command of the Navy, has played an effective if relatively unsung role in containing the flow of enemy men and arms into South Vietnam. Any junk, sampan or even any unscheduled U.S. or Vietnamese ship traveling within 12 miles of the shore is subject to surveillance by Market Time's patrol planes or radar-equipped picket ships. If a ship seems suspicious, it is soon intercepted by a gunboat or one of the high-speed coastal patrol boats called "Swifts" that the Navy has had specially designed for use in Vietnam. In many cases, a quick examination from alongside a junk or sampan is enough to determine that it carries no contraband. But perhaps half the time, U.S. and Vietnamese naval officials are sent aboard to investigate. "We search a junk or a sampan an average of every minute and a half," says one Navy officer. "And that is 24 hours a day and 365 days a year." (9)

MONITORS IN ACTION

Search and destroy missions into the depths of the Mekong Delta were the only way of dealing with the omnipresent yet largely invisible Viet Cong guerrillas. It required expert troops and special equipment to be effective, and there was always the threat of attack from the all-concealing vegetation lining the banks. ATCs (Armored Troop Carriers) convoyed troops about the waterways, and the Monitors provided protection. Impressively armed with heavy machine-guns, 20-mm and 40-mm cannon, flamethrowers, 81-mm mortars and 40-mm grenade launchers, the Monitors were the best solution to the problem of VC ambushes.

The Fire-Support Monitors of the US Navy were the 'Battleships' of the brown-water war, and proved very successful.

"The only things which prevented a massacre were the 'battleships' of the riverine fleet. Called Monitors after the Civil War vessel, they are heavily armed and armored. They swung down the Rach Gia river, got behind the Viet Cong and let fly with 40-mm cannon and 81-mm mortars. The Monitors' firepower literally chopped down the mangroves and eventually put the enemy to flight. Alpha Company survivors made it out to the paddies and back to the boats, losing 48 dead and 143 wounded"

US Navy Patrol Air Cushion Vehicles return to base after attacking the Viet Cong in the Plain of Reeds.

Complementary to Market Time was Operation Game Warden, patrolling the waterways of the Mekong Delta and the Rung Sat Special Zone (Saigon's outlet to the sea). From March, 1966 Game Warden was conducted from the Bonh Thuy headquarters of Task Force 116, the River Patrol Force. TF-116 carried out day and night patrols to stop guerrilla use of the river system for troop and supply movement. It operated from 7 fixed and 3 mobile bases in the III and IV Corps areas. Mobile bases consisted of modified LSTs (Landing Ship Tank), which served as a docks for river patrol boats (PBRs). Every one of the Navy's 220 PBRs was capable of 20 knots, and was armed with three .50-cal. machineguns and a 40mm grenade launcher, which gave them welcome firepower to assist South Vietnamese Regional Forces and ARVN regulars in blocking Viet Cong escape routes. Usually 10 PBRs were assigned to each River Section (of which there were 20), and 2 to 5 River Sections constituted a River Division. Each of the five River Divisions had an area of responsibility in the Delta. In May, 1967 the Navy activated Helicopter Attack Squadron Light 3 (HAL-3), the "Seawolves", which supported TF-116 with 22 UH-1B armed helicopters. Navy SEAL (Sea-Air-Land) counterguerrilla teams also worked the rivers with TF-116. The other major mission of the River Patrol Force was keeping the Long Tau River channel clear of mines for the 45 miles through the Rung Sat up to the port of Saigon. For this purpose it had 6 mine sweeping boats (MSBs) from Mine Force Pacific, and 6 medium landing craft (LSMs) which were converted to the task. In response to Communist activity during Tet '68, a detachment (Task Force Clearwater) was sent north to provide security in several I Corps rivers. In all, TF-116 stopped the enemy using many *major* waterways in the Delta, but occasionally it shot up unwary civilians who broke the curfew travel restrictions as well.

The River War

The Mobile Riverine Force, of which the Navy component was River Assault Flotilla One (Task Force 117) was a joint Army-Navy operation. Riverine warfare aimed to take advantage of waterways to conduct offensive operations, especially during the June to November period when high water actually increased mobility in the Delta. Vessels built or converted for the Force consisted of 24 Monitors (ex-LCM 6), each mounting an 81mm direct-firing mortar, a 40mm gun, a 20mm gun, two .50 cal. machine-

The Monitors' heavy armament was well suited to destroying riverside bunkers impervious to normal small-arms fire. Most awesome of the weapons deployed were the flamethrowers.

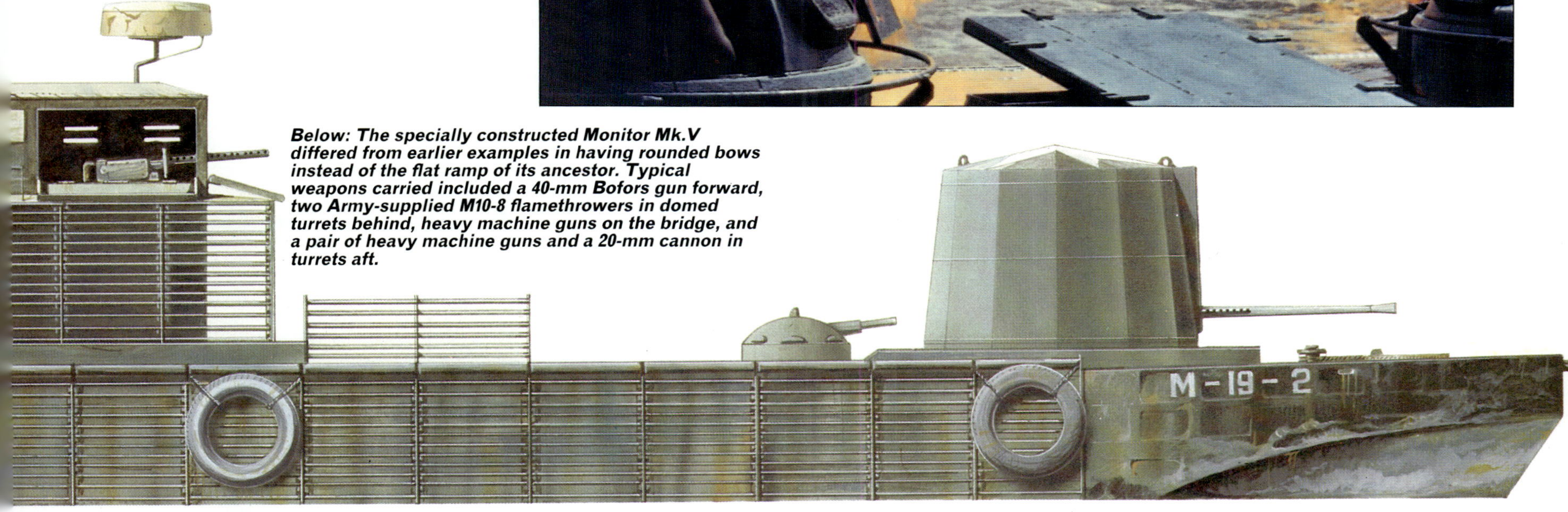

Below: The specially constructed Monitor Mk.V differed from earlier examples in having rounded bows instead of the flat ramp of its ancestor. Typical weapons carried included a 40-mm Bofors gun forward, two Army-supplied M10-8 flamethrowers in domed turrets behind, heavy machine guns on the bridge, and a pair of heavy machine guns and a 20-mm cannon in turrets aft.

guns, and two Mk.18 automatic grenade launchers; 48 Assault Support Patrol Boats (an escort similar in armament to a Monitor); 92 Armored Troop Carriers (40-man), each with a 20mm gun, two .50 cal. machineguns and two Mk.18s; and 7 Command Communications Boats (similar to the Monitor). About one-sixth of these were undergoing repairs at any one time, and the remainder were divided into two River Assault Squadrons (9th and 11th). Both of the River Assault Squadrons had two divisions, each of which operated 2 or 3 Monitors, 1 Command Communications Boat, 8 Assault Support Patrol Boats and 13 Armored Troop Carriers. A number of accommodation and maintenance vessels supported the Flotilla.

Not since the Mississippi flotilla was deployed to fight the Civil War battles of Vicksburg and Shiloh had the U.S. Army found use for an assault force designed especially for river warfare. But the war in Vietnam has seen the revival of many tactics and weapons of earlier days, and last week a U.S. river-borne assault force went on the attack in the Mekong Delta, its most important vehicle an unwieldy-looking craft that bears a striking resemblance to the ironclads of a century ago. The force was called "River Assault Flotilla One," and its overall mission was to root out the Viet Cong from the river and swampland south of Saigon. In the forefront were the "battleships" of the riverine fleet, the converted World War II landing ships the GI's call "Monitors" after the Civil War vessel. They are heavily armor-plated and heavily gunned and, luckily, the Monitors were able to swing down the Rach Gia River and get close in behind the Viet Cong position. Then they let fly with their 40-millimeter cannon and 81-millimeter mortars. The Monitors' firepower literally chop down the mangroves. (10)

The Army element of the MRF was the 2nd Brigade of the 9th Infantry Division. The brigade had three infantry battalions of 3 rifle companies each (it never converted to the 4-company organization like the rest of the Army in Vietnam) and a 105mm howitzer battalion. Since heavy weapons and wheeled vehicles were hardly appropriate to the conditions, personnel from these units filled in as riflemen. Routinely, one battalion and one battery operated ashore from Dong Tam, while the remainder of the brigade was afloat. The artillery fired from special platform barges. The MRF began operations in January, 1967 and continued until July, 1969. As a unique Army-Navy command, it proved itself adept at offensive operations and fully able to control any area within 30 miles of its base afloat.

Attack: Hour after hour, the men of the Fourth Battalion, 47th Infantry, Second Brigade, plodded through the sodden rice fields without so much as the sight of a Viet Cong. At midday, Alpha Company commander, Capt. Robert L. Reeves, 25, of Roswell, Ga., was leading his men across a wide stretch of water 10 inches deep and bordered on each side by the ominous mangroves. The men did not move in along the edge of the palms because that is where the Viet Cong usually plant their booby traps. Instead, they headed across the open field, then toward one of the banks of mangrove. When they were about a hundred yards from the trees, the Viet Cong opened up. Automatic weapon and recoilless rifle fire poured out of the palms from the front and right, pinning Alpha Company down in the rice field.

"During the initial contact," Reeves recalled later, "I had approximately 50 men wounded. Some of them died almost instantly." Added PFC Frederick Haag, 19, of Brooklyn: "We had nowhere to go. We just dove into the water." The Americans tried to keep down, but they had to keep their heads above water to breathe, and the Viet Cong snipers were picking them off with deadly precision. The river-based artillery and the jets that had been called in began to work over the

GUNS OF THE NAVY

Although the major US Navy effort in terms of ships and resources was the carrier war, it was the efforts of the men sweating in the gun turrets of smaller ships just off the coast that were most appreciated by the grunts on the ground. Naval gunfire was one of many battlefield luxuries available to US combat troops operating near the coast. Destroyers, cruisers and even on occasion the awesome power of a battleship were on call, able to lay down heavy and sustained fire in support of ground operations.

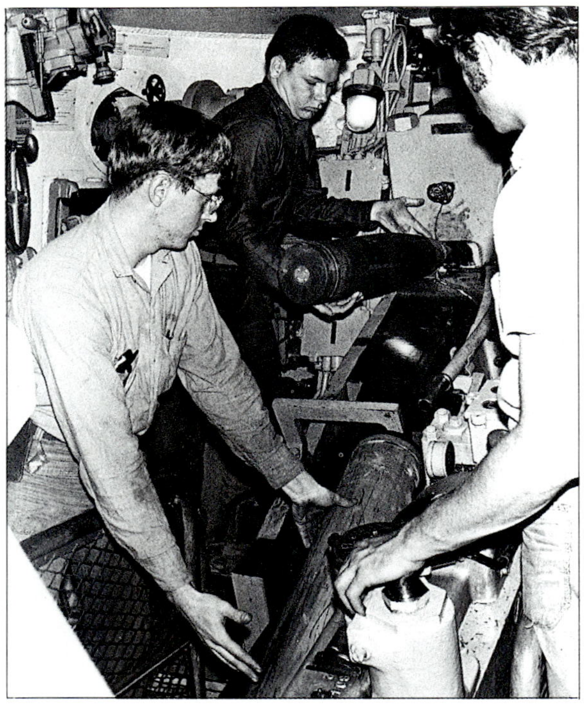

Above: Ammunition for the 6-inch guns of the guided missile light cruiser USS* Oklahoma City *are laid in a loading tray, prior to firing a mission in May 1972.

Above: Shells from the destroyer USS* Orleck's *5-inch guns (foreground) slam into the hills near Vung Tau in April 1966.

Above: The guided missile destroyer USS* Lynde McCormick *is fired on by North Vietnamese shore batteries in the Gulf of Tonkin, 1967.

Viet Cong positions; still the heavy enemy firing continued. To make matters worse, the tide came in and the men were soon neck-deep in water; and – in another instance of a mechanical failure that has been taking place with distressing frequency – many of their M-16 rifles had jammed. (11)

The Navy's other missions within Vietnam included providing advisors to the South Vietnamese Navy, base construction projects (under command of the 3rd Naval Construction Brigade, Da Nang), and the movement of supplies and personnel to Vietnam by sea. The last mission was undertaken by the Military Sea Transportation Service, which coordinated the mixed fleet of container ships, aircraft ferries, tankers, troop ships, roll-on/roll-off ships, and various refrigerated and dry cargo ships which were employed to sustain the war effort.

On May 20th, 1965 the first shore bombardment by a US destroyer was conducted in South Vietnam and, thereafter, ground units within range of the coast could count on fire support from the "gun line" – properly known as Task Unit 70.8.9. Beginning in October, 1966 shore bombardment extended to targets in North Vietnam under the title Operation Sea Dragon. Subject to the same target restrictions as Rolling Thunder, Sea Dragon destroyed enough North Vietnamese coastal shipping to be worth the investment of a cruiser and four destroyers.

A Navy destroyer shells North Vietnamese coastal defences.

Cruisers in action

Several cruiser classes participated in the gun line including heavy types like the Canberra (six eight-inch and ten five-inch guns, plus SAMs) and St. Paul (nine eight-inch and ten five-inch guns), and light cruisers such as the Providence (three six-inch and two five-inch guns, plus SAMs). Destroyers predominated, with modern types such as the C.F. Adams class (with SAMs) and the Forrest Sherman class, and older types like the Fletcher. The real work horses were the Summer and Gearing classes (usually known as "FRAMs" from their modernization programs). Purpose-built fire support ships (IFS and LFR) also were deployed, carrying a typical armament of one five-inch gun and eight 30-round five-inch rocket launchers. The premier naval gun platform was the USS New Jersey, with nine sixteen-inch guns and twenty five-inch guns, which served from October, 1968 to March, 1969. With the firepower of even a two-gun destroyer

"A marine told me that when New Jersey fired her guns the eastern sky lit up like sunrise and the shells sounded like an express train going overhead. Aboard, there were times when you could watch the 16-inch shells flash from the guns, arc lazily along their trajectories and coming down explode on the shore. Most of the time though, the targets were too far away to see"

***Above:** The massive, 30-mile-range 16-inch guns of the veteran battleship USS **New Jersey** provide awesome support for ground troops near the DMZ.*

***Right:** **New Jersey** fires one of the 3,615 16-inch rounds that pounded **NVA** positions between September 1968 and May 1969.*

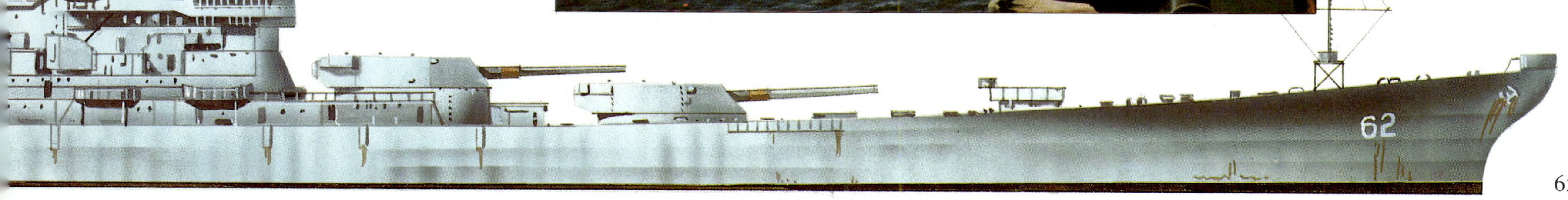

***Below:** In 1968 USS **New Jersey** was the world's only active battleship. She was used as a floating firebase until being decommissioned in August 1969. In the 1980s she returned to service, armed with missiles.*

being considered equal to that of a 105mm field battery, the might of the battleship can be seen in its proper perspective.

During America's combat participation in the war the Navy flew 52 percent of the sorties over North Vietnam, compared to 43 percent by the Air Force and five percent by the Marines. Naval aviation was under the command of the 7th Fleet's Attack Carrier Striking Force (Task Force 77), which executed raids on North Vietnam from a position known as "Yankee Station" (17 degrees 30 minutes north, 108 degrees 30 minutes east). Early in the war however, an alternate station ("Dixie" – 100 miles southeast of Cam Ranh) was used to provide air support in South Vietnam until the Air Force could take on that responsibility. Between May 20th 1965 and August 4th, 1966 the Navy kept one carrier assigned to Dixie Station. Throughout the 1965-73 period, four or five carriers would be deployed in support of operations in Southeast Asia, except during 1970-71 when the figure fell to three. Deployed carriers actually spent about 75 percent of their time at sea.

The Carriers

Attack Carriers (CVAs) fell loosely into two categories, the more modern "large deck" types and the smaller, older classes. The large deck types included the Kitty Hawk, Forrestal and Midway classes, as well as the nuclear-powered carrier Enterprise. The smaller types were surviving representatives of the Ticonderoga, Essex and Oriskany classes. Two anti-

The Air Officer aboard an attack carrier directs night air operations from the primary flight control station high on the carrier's island superstructure. The superior radar of the Phantom facilitated night operations.

submarine support carriers (CVSs) served in a limited attack role as well, the Intrepid (Essex class), and the Shangri La (Ticonderoga class). Aircraft carriers deployed with groups of escorting destroyers and replenishment ships. Each carrier operated an air wing with a mix of fighter and attack squadrons (nominally of 12 aircraft per squadron), and supporting detachments for reconnaissance, refueling, etc. Normally one fighter squadron was retained for combat air patrol (CAP) to protect the carrier, while other fighters were available to escort strikes. Early in the war, small deck types carried two F-8 fighter squadrons, two A-4 attack squadrons, and one A-1 attack squadron, while large deck carriers deployed two F-4 fighter squadrons and three (or even four) A-4 attack squadrons. Odd examples like the Intrepid carried an all-attack force, consisting of 32 A-4s and 24 A-1s for use over South Vietnam. The first A-6 all-weather attack planes joined TF-77 in June, 1965 and they were followed by A-7 improved-day-attack aircraft in December of 1967. The A-1, A-4, and F-8 squadrons were phased out, except for those based on the small deck carriers which could not operate A-6s or F-4s. During the latter half of the war the large deck carriers had a complement of two F-4 fighter squadrons, two A-7 attack squadrons and one A-6 attack squadron.

THE CARRIERS

Nowhere was the peculiar nature of the war more apparent than at sea. The most powerful navy in the world could deploy its carriers a few miles from the enemy coast with relative impunity. There was no submarine threat, and little more from the North Vietnamese Navy. The few aircraft attacks were dealt with peremptorily by the long range missiles of escorting cruisers and destroyers.

Above: USS** Hancock **in the South China Sea. The first strikes against the North were flown from this veteran ship in 1965.

Above: USS** Midway**, was commissioned in September 1945. She was rotated to duty with Task Force 77 throughout the war.

Below: Then the world's largest warship, and first nuclear-powered carrier, the** Enterprise **shipped up to 100 aircraft.

> Every 20 seconds one rocket-laden jet bomber after another is hurled off the carrier's 4.47 acre deck with a banshee howl from the tail pipes and a whoosh of steam from the catapult

Above: USS Kitty Hawk*, with a selection of her available aircraft on show. In April 1966 two of her A-6As knocked out one third of NVN's electricity supply in a night raid on Uongbi power station.*

Right: Approaching the Midway*'s angled flight deck for a landing. Some 19 carriers saw active service off Vietnam, operating from either Yankee or Dixie Station.*

Below: USS Forrestal*, best known for one of the grimmest tragedies of the war – an accidental fire that killed 134 men and destroyed 21 aircraft on 29 July 1967.*

At precisely 8 a.m., the carriers Kitty Hawk and Ranger, escorted by a convoy of combat-ready destroyers, turned into the brisk wind and catapulted their cream-colored planes into the smog-filled sky. On the drafty navigation bridge of the Kitty Hawk, Rear Adm. James R. Reedy pulled on a black Filipino cigar as plane after plane screeched off the steaming deck. "We anticipated the President's decision," said the mild-mannered Reedy. "All we had to do was pick up a folder marked 'Report of Intention,' containing all the elements for the mission, and we were ready for business."

Over the open sea, the Navy's A-4C Skyhawks, F-4B Phantoms, prop-driven A-III Skyraiders and A-6 Intruders rendezvoused with the Air Force's Thunderchiefs. Then, the combined armada wheeled in formation and headed for North Vietnam. Within a matter of minutes, the Navy pilots, hampered by poor visibility and a 400-foot ceiling, unleashed their 250-pound bombs, rockets and cannon fire on their assigned targets between the port cities of Vinh and Dong Hoi. Ground fire, they reported to their mother ships, was only "light to moderate." (12)

In April 1966 the Navy was assigned North Vietnam's coastal route packages (2, 3, 4 and 6B), while the Air Force picked up the inland packages (5 and 6A). North of the DMZ, Route Package 1 was an Air Force zone, under the direction of MACV. The Navy's all-water approach allowed for more secure

An A-4E of Attack Squadron 23 over South Vietnam unleashes a salvo of 3-inch rockets on Viet Cong positions.

access to the target areas than did the Air Force's long haul over land, but also made the recovery of downed pilots who did not make it to the sea a very difficult proposition. Subject to the same frustrating restrictions as the Air Force, the Navy conducted Rolling Thunder missions in the face of ever-increasing North Vietnamese air defenses. After the first Navy loss to SAMs, the "Iron Hand" SAM suppression program was started in August of 1965. By October the first SAM site had been destroyed by a Shrike radar-homing missile fired by an A-6. Another sophisticated munition, the Walleye TV-guided bomb, reached the fleet in March, 1967 but while it improved accuracy against point targets, the Walleye didn't have the punch necessary to destroy monsters such as the Thanh Hoa bridge.

Kill ratios

While only 16 of the 473 Navy and Marine planes shot down over North Vietnam were lost to enemy fighters, the 59 MiGs killed by USN/USMC pilots represented a legitimate achievement. As air bases were not approved bombing targets for most of the war, MiGs had to be destroyed the hard way – in aerial combat. In contrast to the Navy's efforts, the Air Force lost 60 of its aircraft to enemy fighters, while downing 137 MiGs. The best air-to-air kill ratio was achieved by the Navy F-8 Crusader, which shot down 18 MiGs while suffering 3 losses to them for a 6 to 1 record. Navy F-4 Phantoms were nearly as successful, with a 5.42 to 1 kill ratio, while the Air Force trailed with a 3.07 to 1 record for its Phantoms and a 1.37 to 1 ratio for the F-105 "Thud".

FIGHTING MiGs

Due to the nature of their respective missions, the US Navy enjoyed greater success over the MiGs during the early part of the war than the Air Force. Its two principal fighters, the F-4 and F-8, shared the spoils of a high kill-loss ratio, and there was good-natured rivalry between their pilots. As the Crusader was phased out, so the Phantom took on the mantle of 'MiG master'.

Commander Richard M. Bellinger, CO of VF-162, alights from his Vought F-8E Crusader. After having been downed by a MiG-17, Bellinger got his revenge by downing a MiG-21 with a Sidewinder on 9 October 1966.

Above: Closely watched by his wingman, a Crusader pilot ejects safely following a strike against the North.

Below: Vought's Crusader was a superlative dogfighter, accounting for at least 17 kills. This example is from VF-53.

Right: Maintenance crew relax under a South China Sea sky after a hard day's work. The F-4 Phantom bore the brunt of naval fighter operations.

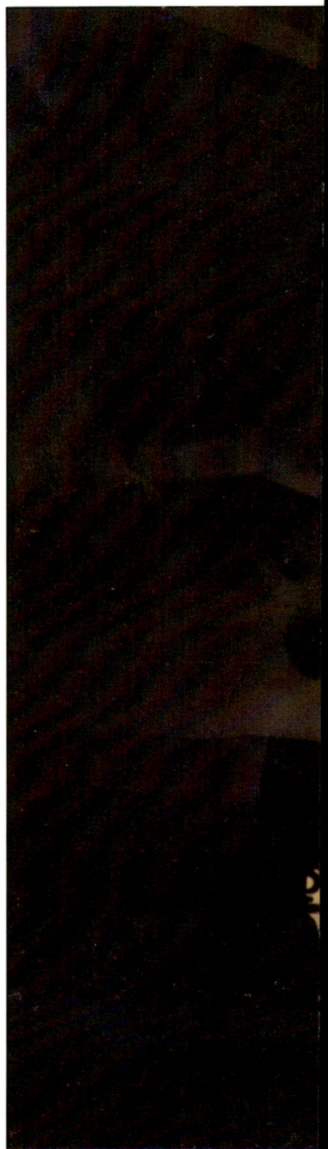

Below: Most of the Navy's Phantoms were employed on air-to-air duties, although they occasionally carried bombs. This aircraft is an F-4B, wearing the colours of VF-142. This squadron notched up seven cruises in the war zone, and collected five kills.

I paused for settling time, then fired two AIM-7s in a ripple. The first missile guided to a direct hit, with the second guiding to within 20 feet but failing to detonate. From the time I spotted the MiGs heading east, turned south, made my first pass, overshot, rolled back and got a kill the total elapsed time was about 45 seconds

Left: A VF-92 Phantom launches from **Constellation**. *In addition to the F-4 and F-8, the Douglas A-1 Skyraider and A-4 Skyhawk also claimed kills in Navy service.*

Right: A VF-211 'Fighting Checkmates' Crusader launches for another air-to-air mission. The squadron was the highest-scoring F-8 unit in the Navy with seven kills to its credit.

Below: Although possessing a healthy kill-loss ratio in air-to-air combat, US Navy aircraft were hit hard by groundfire. This Crusader was fireballed over Hanoi by North Vietnamese guns.

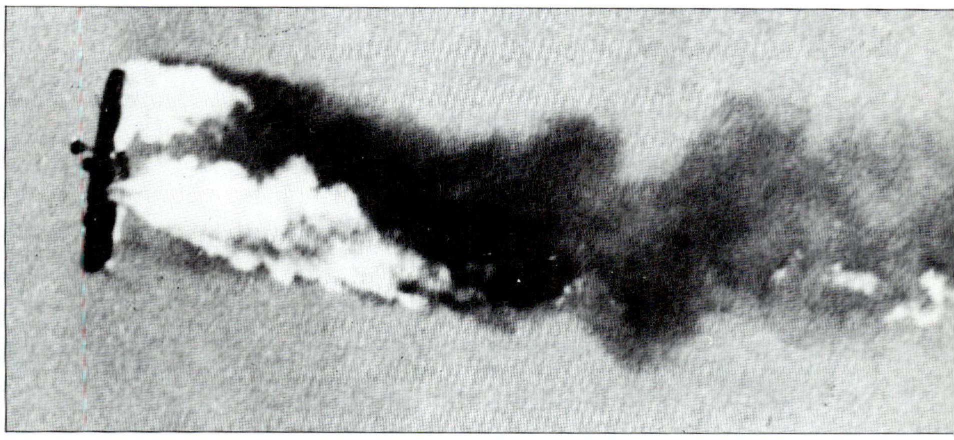

Above: VF-111 'Sundowners' were better known for their Phantoms, but operated the F-8 before them. This voracious Crusader is being checked for foreign object damage prior to flight. Its pilot, 'Tooter' Teague, shot down a MiG in 1972, flying an F-4B with VF-51.

CHAPTER FIVE

THE BIG BATTLES 1967

1st Division helicopters ferry troops into a landing zone near Phouc Vinh, at the end of Operation Junction City. This was the biggest US operation up to that time, with at least 22 battalions involved.

There were indications in 1967 of a tide of public disenchantment with the war in the United States. By the middle of the year, opinion polls showed that at least half of the country had no confidence in the administration's handling of the war, and an equal percentage held the opinion that the US was losing. Militant opposition to the war also hit a high point in October, when 50,000 demonstrators converged on Washington and surrounded the headquarters of the Department of Defense – the Pentagon. Regular Army units were deployed to protect the building. One brighter spot was a degree of stability in the Saigon government. National elections held in September, honestly or otherwise, gave Thieu and Ky four-year terms as President and Vice President/Premier respectively.

In January and February, 1967 the US 9th Infantry Division completed its concentration in Vietnam with the arrival of its 1st and 2nd (Riverine) Brigades. It joined up with the Navy's Task Force 117 and began operations in the Mekong Delta. In November, the 2nd and 3rd Brigades of the 101st Airborne Division joined the 1st Brigade, already in country. Non-divisional reinforcements during the year included the 41st Artillery Group (May), the 198th Light Infantry Brigade and the 108th Artillery Group (both in November), and the US Marine Regimental Landing Team 26 (April). Reinforcements boosted the total of US Army personnel in Vietnam to 319,000 by the year's end, and US Marine strength grew to 78,000. For the first time during the war the Marine Corps had to resort to the draft to replace losses, conscripting 19,000 men during the year. The ARVN brought its regular strength to a level of about 200,000 in 1967, and in addition, in October, Thailand sent its elite "Queen's Cobra" Regiment as the forerunner of a division-sized force. The NVA and VC hard core main forces numbered at least 250,000 within South Vietnam.

Secretary McNamara, still seeking technological solutions to strategic problems, ordered the construction of an anti-infiltration barrier along the DMZ. Comprised of fences, electronic sensors, and field fortifications, the barrier was derisively known as "McNamara's Wall" among the grunts on the northern border of South Vietnam. In February, the 3rd Marine Division inflicted 693 casualties on the NVA in the vicinity of the DMZ during Operation Prairie II, terminating on March 18th. During the operation's immediate followup (Prairie III), the Marines (then the Special Landing Force) lost 29 dead and 230 wounded – a high casualty rate for a single battalion in 12 days of combat. In a daring move to recover the initiative, the NVA infiltrated a regiment-sized force across the DMZ in early April and launched a raid against Quang Tri, killing 4 Marines and 125 ARVN while wounding another 27 Marines and 180 ARVN.

Quang Tri is a city in waiting – waiting for what many Vietnamese and Americans here expect to be a full-scale Communist assault within the next week or so. In the U.S. compound, where a hundred-odd American military men and a handful of civilians are quartered, GI's stand guard duty throughout the rain-drenched nights and try to fight off sleep. One night last week, in fact, the Americans became convinced that the Communists were finally making their move. Without warning, mortar shells began to thump into the city, smashing into the old French citadel and killing a number of civilians in nearby houses. The Americans poured automatic-weapons fire back, and South Vietnamese tanks rumbled through the streets to prearranged strong points. But half an hour later, the heavy Communist shelling ceased and no infantry assault followed. Said one U.S. officer, half relieved and half apprehensive: "I guess they were just registering their mortars for the big push."

The next day, it became clear that the Viet Cong had done somewhat more than that. During the night, in what seemed to be part of a concentrated campaign to isolate Quang Tri from the south, they had attacked four bridges in the northern provinces and destroyed two of them.

'Instant Recruiting': To many Americans, all this suggested just one thing: a big Communist offensive south of the DMZ in the near future. For one thing, the mortaring of Quang Tri marked the second time in two weeks that it had been hit hard by the Viet Cong. Two weeks ago, in one of the most daring raids of the war, at least 1,500 black-garbed Viet Cong, like a cluster of invading locusts, swarmed into Quang Tri in the dead of night. For about two hours they effectively controlled the city. Then, after freeing more than 250 Viet Cong prisoners, they disappeared back into the night. "That hurt," commented an American adviser. "It's instant recruiting of nearly a battalion." (1)

There was also a concerted effort to make life miserable for the Marine outposts along the DMZ (Con Thien, Cam Lo, Camp Carroll, Dong Ha and Gio Linh) by heavy shelling from North Vietnamese territory. In a subsequent move to secure the southern half of the DMZ (Operation Prairie IV), elements of the ARVN 1st Division and US Marine Regimental Landing Team 26, reinforced by the SLF, sustained heavy casualties, including 164 Marine dead and nearly a thousand wounded.

The division's 3rd Marine Regiment was sent to Khe Sanh, near the Laotian border in the extreme northwest corner of South Vietnam, where an air strip was being enlarged and completed. The Marines were not enthusiastic about the position, but General Westmoreland saw it as an excellent opportunity to extend the war of attrition against the NVA. In order to hold the base, the Marines had to clear the surrounding hills of NVA positions which overlooked the airfield. Between April 24th and May 5th, two battalions of the 3rd Marines suffered 160 dead and 746 wounded in some of the most bitter, close-in fighting of the campaign. Throughout the

FIREFIGHT

Pitched battles were relatively rare in Vietnam. With the kind of firepower America could bring to bear, formal combat was not a Viet Cong objective, and except for in special conditions neither was it very popular with regular North Vietnamese troops. So most action came about when small units were involved in ambushes and counter-ambushes. In such cases contact could lead to a vicious little firefight, sometimes lasting a few seconds but occasionally all day.

Above left: Marines rush to the aid of their buddies under heavy fire in February 1967, on an infamous stretch of road between Hue and Quang Tri City – the 'Street Without Joy'.

Left: The 7th Cavalry return fire near No Jay in I Corps, May 1968. Using a standard tactic, the enemy had been lying in wait for the patrol in a tree line 100 yards distant.

"Every way we turned, they'd fire on us. We decided it was a lost cause and we said we'd fight on till we were all dead"

Search and Destroy missions were designed to flush the Viet Cong from cover and cut them off from their support in the villages. Without that support, their cause would be lost, so enemy contact on such a mission usually meant a firefight. These Marines are on a I Corps sweep in February 1967, and are putting their Stoner rifles to use after coming under fire.

Left: Point man from a company-size patrol of the 196th Infantry Brigade near Hep Doc, January 1971, shows the direction of enemy fire. At this stage in the war, with US troop levels being reduced for political reasons and those in-country under pressure to avoid casualties, US tactics were often a matter of patrolling in the hope of provoking an enemy attack, rather than positive search-and-destroy missions.

Right: Hospital corpsmen of the 25th Infantry Division leave tank cover to aid comrades wounded by a mine in the Michelin Rubber Plantation, September 1970. With tanks in a convoy, the VC would wait to open fire with RPGs from distances of a few feet. If they had time before the ambush they would set up an array of booby traps off the trail, designed to catch unwary supporting infantry.

M79 BLOOP-GUN IN ACTION

Infantry squads in Vietnam often needed their own direct fire support to deal with things like Viet Cong bunkers. Many armies use rifle grenades, but the US Army could afford to equip members of the squad with a specialist grenade launcher. The M79 is a single-shot weapon firing spin-stabilized 40-mm grenades to a range of 300 metres or more. There was a wide variety of warheads, ranging from High Explosive and HE Air-Burst through smoke and illumination rounds in a bewildering variety of colours to buckshot and CS riot-control rounds.

Above: Weighing only 6.41lb, the stubby M79 was easy to hump through the boonies.

Right: A Leatherneck's M79 takes out a sniper during the battle for Hue in March 1968.

siege of Khe Sanh the following year, the hills remained in American hands.

The 3rd Marine Division picked up the pace again in mid-year with the initiation of Operation Buffalo, killing 1,281 enemy during the first two weeks of July, but the operation cost the Americans dear. The 9th Marines were hit by the 90th NVA Regiment near Con Thien and lost 96 dead and 211 wounded in one day. Reinforcements from the 3rd Marines had to be thrown in, and the 9th Marines never fully recovered from the engagement.

For weeks, some of the bitterest fighting of the war has raged around the U.S. Marine outpost of Con Thien, at the narrow top of South Vietnam. With North Vietnamese regulars infiltrating across the Demilitarized Zone and through the mountain passes on the Laotian border, the marines of late have been hard pressed to contain them. Seeking out the enemy, the marines last week walked into an ambush south of Con Thien and suffered their bloodiest loss yet in a single engagement in Vietnam. As they brought out their dead from the ambush, survivors related a grim and moving story of the action.

The area had been quiet for weeks, but in the midst of a routine sweep early one morning, two companies of marines of the First Battalion, Ninth Regiment, Third Division, were suddenly hit by intense mortar fire. Then, as the marines sought cover, the North Vietnamese, perhaps a thousand strong, came charging out of the jungle on all sides. Alpha Company managed to form itself into a tight defensive perimeter, but Bravo Company was caught strung out along a narrow dirt road and was quickly cut off under heavy fire. A captain who had recently taken over as commander of Bravo Company tried to rally his men. "He was all up and down that line, shooting his .45," Sgt. Richard Huff recalled later. "He told me to get the mortars firing. Then he ran back up front and that was the last I saw of him alive."

Trap: In the enemy onslaught, one platoon was wiped out almost immediately. The rest of Bravo Company, firing back furiously, tried to dig in. "All you could do," said Cpl. Mike Pitts later, "was to protect your buddy's back and hope he was doing the same for you." Added Cpl. Mike Hughes: "We were all wounded, and the men were just lying there, firing. I shouted, 'get up and move back,' and somebody said, 'We can't.' I said: 'You want to live, you got to move'."

The marines inched back along the road, trying to consolidate their position, but enemy fire whined in from all sides. Corporal Hughes saw what he thought was a marine in a helmet and flak-jacket, firing at his men with a sub-machine gun at 30 yards. "Stop firing, we're friendlies," he cried out. "But then," Hughes recounted, "I saw his face and he was a gook. I dropped back and my machine gunner, Garza, cut him down."

By now, U.S. planes and helicopters were strafing and bombing the enemy positions, but the North Vietnamese kept popping back up, blazing away at the trapped marines. Everyone was fighting back bitterly, and Corporal Hughes told of propping up his wounded men so they could fire. "One with a shattered arm," he said, "asked for help in loading a last round." No medics or bandages were left. Cpl. Margarito Garza was wounded three times before he died.

Rescue: By noon, the company had been badly mauled, and the only reason Huff, Hughes and some of the others finally made it out alive was the relief force sent into the area under First Lt. Gatlin Howell. At the head of a column of tanks and marine infantrymen, Howell – a former commander of a Bravo Company platoon – crashed through the bush and through a ring of North Vietnamese, his tank guns blazing. "When I heard those tanks, I cried," said Sergeant Huff. "All around, men of Bravo Company lay dead or wounded, but when they saw Mr. Howell," said another noncom, "they started to cheer."

Howell then pushed his force, along with the remnants of Bravo, back toward an abandoned marketplace in a destroyed village. Bodies of dead American marines lay everywhere, and there was evidence that the North Vietnamese had executed some of the

Above: Portable artillery at work. Fourth Infantry Div M79s bombard an enemy-occupied village in Quang Ngai in 1967.

Above: Reconnaissance by fire. Many soldiers could shoot the 'thump gun' accurately at up to 200 metres without aiming.

Below: A SEAL and an M79. The weapon's long range (350-metres), simplicity and killing power made it a favourite.

Above: Taking careful aim. The M79 could loose off up to seven rounds per minute.

Below: Besides the spin-armed HE round, the M79 fired a close-range buckshot charge.

"One enemy machine gun kept firing from the edge of the woods, until a soldier fired an M79 grenade that burst with terrible accuracy. Later, three VC bodies were found arranged head to foot like the spokes of a wheel – but the machine gun was gone"

wounded after overrunning the U.S. positions. The enemy fire was still pounding in, but Howell sent back his four tanks to pick up casualties. The tanks made it out, but on their return to the marketplace, two were knocked out, reportedly by the enemy's RPG-7, a new Soviet anti-tank gun. A bazooka-like weapon, its projectiles fly at almost 1,000 feet a second and can penetrate eleven inches of steel armor. "Those weapons can do a job on any tank we have," said one U.S. officer somberly.

Exit: With North Vietnamese mortar fire now zeroing in on his battered little force, Lieutenant Howell finally was compelled to pull out, leaving many Marine dead behind. And not until three days later, after the North Vietnamese had faded away, possibly across the Demilitarized Zone into North Vietnam, was another relief column able to get in and retrieve the bodies. The marines, wearing gas masks because of the smell of the decomposing bodies, carefully wrapped their dead comrades in rubber ponchos, piled them on the rear decks of their tanks and moved out.

It had been, all told, a bitter defeat. Lt. Gen. Robert E. Cushman, the Marine commander, tried to put the best possible face on the events south of Con Thien, claiming that 275 of the enemy had been killed in the battle. But that figure was impossible to confirm. On the U.S. side, Bravo Company had been destroyed as a fighting unit. The dead: 95. The wounded: over 200.

3rd Division Marines, part of Operation Chinook, wade through swampland near the infamous 'Street Without Joy' some 12 miles northwest of Hue in February 1967.

Late in the week, sporadic action continued to flare in the sector around Con Thien. Enemy heavy artillery, firing from across the Demilitarized Zone in North Vietnam, sent murderous barrages into U.S. positions, killing fourteen marines and wounding another 25. But the marines were also taking a heavy toll of the enemy. In one action south of Con Thien, Marine tankmen, aided by air strikes, killed sixteen North Vietnamese; and – in what appeared to be the biggest success of the week for U.S. arms – a company of marines caught 200 North Vietnamese troops moving through open territory northeast of Con Thien and pounded them with artillery and small-arms fire. When the battle was over, 150 of the Communist enemy lay dead, a defeat inflicted without the loss of a single American life. (2)

From mid-July until the end of October, the 3rd Marine Division extended its operations close to the DMZ with Kingfisher, producing 1,117 more NVA casualties, but losing 340 Marines dead and 3,086 wounded. From November, 1967 until the end of February, 1969 the continuing operations around Con Thien (dubbed Operation Kentucky) caused the NVA a further 3,921 dead.

Farther south, in the I Corps area, the US 1st

Marine Division inaugurated Operation Union on April 21st. By the end of the operation on May 17th, the 1st Marine Division had killed 865 NVA soldiers in Quang Nam and Quang Tin Provinces. The follow-up operation by the division's 5th Marines, Union II, caused another 701 enemy casualties to two regiments in the Tam Ky area of Quang Tin, while the Marines lost 73 dead and 139 wounded. The division's last major operation of the year (Swift) occupied the first two weeks of September and led to 517 more Communist dead. Once again the 5th Marines took the brunt of the enemy's fire and lost 114 men themselves.

Southern I Corps' Quang Ngai Province was the target of Operation Lien Ket 81, carried out by one of the ARVN's less enthusiastic divisions, the 2nd. Nevertheless, the one-week operation in February claimed 813 enemy casualties. The South Korean 2nd "Blue Dragon" Marine Brigade also operated in Quang Ngai, and in a two-month effort called Dragon Fire, killed 541 Communists.

In order to bolster US strength in southern I Corps, and free Marine units to reinforce their comrades on the DMZ, the 1st Cavalry Division shifted its 3rd Brigade north from II Corps in October.

Members of the 173rd Airborne Brigade leave a UH-1D during as assault near Pleiku in June 1967. It was part of operation Francis Marion.

In addition, the newly organized Americal Division undertook two large campaigns in I Corps, beginning late in 1967. The year-long Operation Wheeler/Wallowa started on November 11th and involved two brigades in Quang Nam and Quang Tin Provinces, and caused ten thousand enemy casualties. The division's remaining brigade carried out Operation Muscatine in Quang Ngai Province from December 19th, 1967 to June 10th, 1968 accounting for 1,129 NVA and VC killed in action.

In the provinces of Kontum and Pleiku in the II Corps area, border surveillance by the 4th Infantry Division and elements of the 25th continued under the name of Operation Sam Houston, producing 733 Communist casualties over a three-month period beginning in January. This was followed in April by the 4th's Operation Francis Marion, which lasted until mid-October and added another 1,203 NVA to the toll. The division remained in the Highlands until the end of January, 1969 continuing its operations under the banner of Operation MacArthur, and inflicting a further 5,731 casualties on the enemy.

The 173rd Airborne Brigade, which had moved up to II Corps after Operation Junction City (see below), began a murderous association with the town of Dak To in Kontum Province. In June, one company lost 80 dead and 34 wounded out of its 130-man complement during a large NVA ambush. The enemy body count was only 106.In further heavy fighting the next month, one battalion lost 75 casualties (including 26 dead) out of 400 troops in the bush on a single day. The fighting around Dak To reached a peak in November, when four NVA regiments of the "B3 Front" closed in on the 173rd and the 1st Brigade of the 4th Infantry Division

SEARCH AND DESTROY

Against a mobile, elusive enemy who had little regard for a conventional stand-up fight new tactics had to be evolved. Locating the enemy was hard enough, but to destroy him required good teamwork. Often, a force would be sent in to 'flush the game', sending the enemy straight into a blocking force placed across his escape route. The troops involved could be a company, or a brigade. It could involve helicopter assaults, or tanks, or just foot slogging. Whatever the force, the aim never changed: seek out the enemy, make contact and destroy him.

Above: Search and destroy missions could be gruelling, foot-slogging, small-unit actions depending on skill and stamina.

Below: APCs act as a blocking force for any fleeing enemy while ARVN infantry search for NVA troops at Phu Loc, 1968.

Below: Armour can do only so much: faced by dense jungle, the 11th Armored Cavalry dismount to stalk the enemy during Operation Cedar Falls in January 1967.

"Armor has proven highly successful in search and destroy operations. With their rapid reaction and firepower a mechanical battalion can control twice as much terrain as infantry battalions. Rapid penetration into VC areas secure LZs for airmobile units and provide added security for aircraft as well as personnel mechanized units back and forth through an area keeps the VC moving and creates targets for friendly ambushes, artillery and air"

Above: Constant patrols of the labyrinthine Mekong Delta did much to detect enemy movement in a traditional VC stronghold.

Below: Airmobility was the key to deploying large forces to pin down and destroy enemy troops wherever they were found.

(reinforced by the ARVN 42nd Regiment and two ARVN Airborne battalions). The Communist position broke when Hill 875 was taken on Thanksgiving Day, after a loss of 158 troopers of the 173rd. Total US losses for the November battle amounted to 285 dead, 18 missing and 985 wounded. Thirty of the 173rd's fatal casualties were caused by a friendly air strike and artillery fire ripping into the 2-503rd Infantry in the fight for Hill 875.

Still in Binh Dinh Province, the 1st Cavalry Division followed up its previous year's operations with a drive against the NVA 610th Division, called Operation Pershing. Lasting the greater part of a year (until January 19th, 1968), the operation claimed a total of 5,401 NVA and VC dead before the 1st Cavalry moved up to I Corps. Operation Bolling (September 19, 1967 to January 31, 1969) in coastal Phu Yen Province occupied units of the 173rd Airborne Brigade and, initially, elements of the 1st Cavalry. This long effort failed to produce many Communist casualties, just 715 being counted.

Korean divisions in action

Elsewhere in II Corps the South Koreans, charged with security of the coastal area, mounted two large operations. From March 7th until April 18th, both the Capital "Tiger" Division and the 9th "White Horse" Division engaged in Operation Oh Jac Kyo I, killing 831 enemy. Late in the year, the Capital Division mounted another operation, Maeng Ho 9, which concentrated in Binh Dinh Province and cost the Communists another 749 casualties.

In the critical III Corps area, the US mounted Operation Cedar Falls during the month of January. Aimed at the Communist stronghold north of Saigon known as the "Iron Triangle," the operation involved the 1st Infantry Division, most of the 25th, the 173rd Airborne Brigade, and the 11th Armored Cavalry Regiment. The score was 1,208 Viet Cong, 720 dead and 488 captured, a poor showing for the large forces involved. Although the Army plowed over the Iron Triangle and resettled its population of VC sympathizers elsewhere, it did not succeed in eliminating the Communist power base in the area.

It was early Sunday morning when Operation Cedar Falls began. Their loudspeakers blaring, U.S. helicopters flew over populated areas telling the people that next day they would be evacuated along with their belongings. "Anyone seen running away," crackled the speakers, "will be considered a Viet Cong." The others would be sent to government controlled areas to escape "the terror of the Viet Cong."

Operation Cedar Falls is directed at the Iron Triangle, a tangled patch of jungle northwest of Saigon that has been Viet Cong territory for over twenty years. Somewhere in the Iron Triangle's dense, heavily tunneled fastness is hidden the headquarters for all guerrilla activities in the area of the capital. Recently, a series of stinging raids against U.S. installations at Tan Son Nhut air base had been launched from the area. It was high time, U.S. commanders reasoned, to smash the triangle, and to do the job, Operation Cedar Falls – "an operation with a difference" – was put into motion last week.

Waffle Iron: With upward of 30,000 U.S. and Vietnamese troops committed, Cedar Falls qualified as the biggest single operation of the war. Before a foot soldier moved, no fewer than ten B-52 raids thundered across the triangle until, said one major, "the whole place looked as if it had been put in a waffle iron." Then elements of the U.S. First Division ("the Big Red One") moved in from the north. The 196th Light Infantry Brigade and 25th Division cordoned off the strip to the west, across the Saigon River. The Eleventh Armored Cavalry sent its tanks and armored personnel carriers racing round the roads that form the perimeter of the area, while the 173rd Airborne began a systematic combing of the triangle itself. And though, by the end of the week, no major contact had been made with the Viet Cong, the U.S. reported its forces had killed 286 of the enemy in a series of scattered actions.

From the start, however, the U.S. officers emphasized that the main purpose of Cedar Falls was not to kill huge numbers of Viet Cong but to deny them the use of the triangle as a base. And so, in addition to the combat troops, the operation provided the most impressive show yet by the U.S. Corps of Engineers.

ARTILLERY

For over 350 years, the guns of the artillery have been one of the dominant factors on the battle field. Artillery was the great killer in the First World War, and it had its place in the wide ranging battles of the Second World War. It was a key element in the US Army's operations in Vietnam, providing massive fire-support from hilltop fire bases wherever American troops operated. The artillery pieces in use ranged from the air-portable M102 105mm howitzer to the massive M107 and M110 self-propelled guns and howitzers. Even the smallest infantry patrols could usually call down fire on the enemy.

Above: A WWII vintage M101 105mm howitzer fires at enemy positions north of Loc Ninh, on the Cambodian border.

Above right: A 105-mm howitzer of 3d Bn, 319th Arty – the first US Army artillery battalion in Nam – in action in 1968.

Below: A 175-mm M107 SPG of 2d Bn, 32d Arty. The gun fires a 147-lb high-explosive shell to a range of over 20 miles.

“The battalion had more ammo than it could safely store, including 90 odd rounds of green smoke. On 17 March – St. Patrick's day – the Marines fired it all on known enemy positions”

Above: A 155-mm howitzer of 1st Bn, 30th Arty, in Binh Dinh.

Below: An M107 about to fire during Operation Junction City.

Below: The M110 8-inch self-propelled howitzer was developed in the late 1950s. The ordnance can throw a 200 pound shell over 18,000 yards. In anti-personnel action a system known as 'Killer Senior' was developed. A timer could be set to explode a high explosive shell 30 feet over the heads of the enemy at ranges between 200 and 1,000 yards.

Skytroopers from the Seventh Cavalry, part of the 1st Cavalry Division (Airmobile) advance towards a Viet Cong bunker near Bong Son.

Along the northern border of the triangle, where most of the people lived and worked in the rubber plantations, dozens of bulldozers plowed through the brush and sharp-edged "Roman plows" sheared off rubber trees, carving a 1,000-foot-wide swath through the jungle so that future Viet Cong movements might be easily spotted from the air. In other sections of the triangle, engineers cut through the fields with ditch diggers, hoping to slash into the fabled network of tunnels that runs beneath the area like a subway system. Still other engineers slid into the dank tunnels alive with bats and scorpions to search for the Viet Cong and to map them for the work of the demolition squads.

Barges and Carts: Along with demolition of the tunnels and clearance of some of the brush, the aim of Operation Cedar Falls is to remove more than 6,000 peasants from the area and resettle them in government-supervised refugee camps. And while the experience was an unpleasant one for some of the GI's, they did their best to make it as painless as possible for the uprooted. Before the evacuees were bundled on to barges and carts, they were permitted to collect their food and livestock and furniture to take along on the journey.

But it was made clear that there would be no going home. Even as the last of the evicted still poked around their wood and thatch huts assembling their belongings, U.S. troops began to burn and bulldoze their villages to the ground. And when all the peasants and their huts are gone, the Iron Triangle – once a sanctuary where the Viet Cong swam freely as fish in a sea – will be declared a "free-fire zone." Then, the whole area will be watched constantly by spotter planes and helicopters, and anyone caught in the triangle will be fair game. With the operation still in progress at the end of last week, one U.S. officer confidently predicted: "Charlie's monkey business in the Iron Triangle is going to be through for good." (3)

An even larger operation, Junction City, was launched on February 22nd. This pitted the 1st and 25th Infantry Divisions, elements of the 4th, the 173rd Airborne Brigade, the 196th Light Infantry Brigade, and the 11th Armored Cavalry against the Viet Cong base area in Tay Ninh Province known as War Zone "C". As with Cedar Falls, there was ARVN participation as well. Unique to Junction City was a parachute drop at the start of the operation by the 2nd Battalion 503rd Infantry (Airborne), of the 173rd Brigade. In March, both the 1st Infantry Division and the 173rd Airborne Brigade

HELICOPTER WORKHORSES

In many ways, Vietnam was the first 'Helicopter War'. Making air assaults into hot LZs was certainly the most dangerous of tasks, and heavy armament was carried to that end, but the vast majority of helicopter missions were very different. Delivering mail and new personnel, flying men on R and R to their departure points and returning with men full of the pleasures of Hong Kong, Tokyo or Australia, providing a taxi service for the brass or for television crews, replenishing ammunition and stores at isolated fire support bases . . .

Above: An Army CH-47 Chinook moves equipment from a temporary fire support base during November 1967.

Above: A Chinook brings home a Huey gunship shot down by enemy ground fire near Tan An City in 1967. The 115-mile range CH-47 could carry up to 44 troops or take a slung cargo of up to 10,366lb.

The ubiquitous 'Huey' served in a multitude of roles in Vietnam. It was primarily a transport, hauling men and supplies everywhere US Forces went.

Right: Smoke pops to mark the LZ for an Army UH-1D Huey. The color of the smoke was always confirmed by the chopper pilots by radio before the final approach to landing, to avoid enemy decoys.

became heavily engaged and sustained many losses. Junction City, which ended in mid-May, produced 2,728 VC casualties.

At 0900 hours on 22 February 1967, Brigadier General John R. Deane, Jr., stood in the door of a C-130 aircraft. When the green light flashed, General Deane jumped, leading the first U.S. parachute assault in the Republic of Vietnam, and the first such assault since the Korean conflict fifteen years earlier. This parachute jump of the 2d Battalion, 503d Infantry, signalled the beginning of Operation Junction City Alternate. The original plan, as conceived in November 1966, called for the 1st Brigade of the 101st Airborne Division to make the parachute assault; but, much to their chagrin, they were engaged in other operations and the honor was to go to the 173d.

Operation Junction City employed the 1st and 25th Infantry Divisions, the 11th Armored Cavalry Regiment, the 196th Light Infantry Brigade, elements of the 4th and 9th Infantry Divisions, and South Vietnamese units, as well as the 173d Airborne Brigade. Their target was enemy bases north of Tay Ninh City, in the area the French had named "War Zone C." The decision to make a paratroop assault was based on the urgency to place a large force on the ground as quickly as possible and still have enough helicopter assets to make a sizeable heliborne assault as an immediate follow-up.

The helicopter and the principle of airmobility meant that conventional airborne operations were comparatively rare over South Vietnam, though combat drops did occur.

The requirement for helicopter lift on D-day was substantial. The 1st Infantry Division had five infantry battalions to put in by air assault and the 173d had three infantry battalions. In addition to the requirement for the Huey slicks, there was a tremendous requirement for CH-47 lift for positioning artillery and resupply of ammunition. The 173d had computed that they would free 60 Hueys and six Chinooks for support of other forces by using the parachute assault technique. The paratroopers were assigned landing zones farthest to the north – areas that would have cost many extra minutes of flying time for lift helicopters. The practical aspects of making more helicopters available were perhaps colored by the emotional and psychological motives of this proud unit which was anxious to prove the value of the parachute badge; nevertheless, the jumpers contributed strongly to the overall attack.

The 173d was placed under the operational control of the 1st Infantry Division for this operation and developed an elaborate deception plan to avoid possible compromise of the drop zone. In the planning phase only the commanding general, his deputy, and two key staff officers were aware of the actual drop zone. The cover plan designated a larger alternate drop zone outside the planned area of operation. This permitted all the necessary staging preparations which must precede

Above: The Huey 'slick', or troop transport, had a 327-mile range and could take a maximum load of 14 GIs with equipment.

Below: A CH-54 Tarhe 'Sky Crane', capable of carrying a 20,760lb external load, takes a river patrol boat aloft.

> ***"1st Brigade flew heavy engineer equipment in small enough loads to be lifted by crane helos. The cranes had just enough JP-4 fuel to make the round trip, as they needed maximum lift to sling hoist heavy equipment across the ridgelines into A Luoi"***

an air drop and all necessary coordination with the Air Force. The actual drop plan for the airborne assault phase of the operation was not distributed to the units until 1900 hours on 21 February, the evening before D-day. After Lieutenant Colonel Robert H. Sigholtz, the Airborne Task Force Commander, briefed his troops on the operation, he sealed off his battalion area as a security measure. Thirteen C-130's were used for the personnel drop and eight C-130's for heavy drop of equipment. Jump altitude was 1,000 feet.

The battalion dropped on schedule and by 0920 hours on D-day all companies were in their locations around the drop zone. Out of the 780 combat troops who made the assault, only eleven sustained minor injuries. The heavy equipment drop commenced at 0925 hours and continued throughout the day. The 1st Battalion, 503d Infantry began landing by helicopter assault at 1035 hours and the entire battalion was in place shortly thereafter. No direct contact with an enemy force occurred during these early hours of D-day. Another infantry battalion, the 4th Battalion, 503d Infantry, conducted a heliborne assault into two other close landing zones at 1420 hours and phase one of JUNCTION CITY ALTERNATE was essentially complete. (4)

Members of Company B, 3rd Battalion, 60th Infantry, 3rd Infantry Division wade across a stream during a patrol in the Rung Sat Special Zone.

After Junction City the 25th Division moved directly south into Hau Nghia Province for Operation Kole Kole which ended on December 7th with 645 enemy casualties. This was immediately followed by two simultaneous operations, one being a return to War Zone "C" where the division killed a further 1,254 Communist troops during Operation Yellowstone, which lasted until the end of February, 1968. The remainder of the 25th Division stayed south to conduct Operation Saratoga, causing 3,862 NVA and VC casualties by March 11th, 1968.

Attack from Cambodia

Elsewhere in III Corps, the NVA 141st Regiment crossed the border from Cambodia into Binh Long Province and struck ARVN defenses in the vicinity of An Loc. The drive was repulsed, but only with the aid of tactical air strikes. Just to the south, the US 1st Infantry Division started Operation Shenandoah II in Binh Duong Province at the end of September, and ended up in northern Binh Long Province by November after inflicting 956 casualties – mainly on the 273rd VC Regiment, breaking its attack on Loc Ninh. In adjacent Bien Hoa Province, as part of the Saigon area security effort, the 199th Light Infantry

DELTA MUD

Vietnam is a land of contrasts. Much of the country is mountainous with a small coastal plain. To the south, however, the dominant feature is the mighty Mekong which rises high in the mountains of Tibet. Sweeping south-west for over 2,500 miles the river enters the sea through a massive delta. Some of the most fertile land in the world, the Mekong Delta provides much of Vietnam's food, and during the war its myriad waterways, paddies and villages proved a magnet to the Viet Cong.

US Navy SEALs leap from an assault river patrol boat to begin a raid on a VC base in the Rach Tho Rach Mo Cay canal complex, 50 miles south-west of Saigon.

Below: A reconnaissance patrol of the 9th Infantry Division moves through wet, waterlogged jungle 20 miles east of Saigon, early in 1967.

Brigade undertook Operation Uniontown. Between December 17th, 1967 and March 8th, 1968, the brigade eliminated 922 Viet Cong.

Delta operations

The 9th Infantry Division, operating as a riverine force in the Mekong Delta, was present in both the III and IV Corps areas. It began 1967 with Operation Palm Beach in January. Lasting until the end of May, Palm Beach concentrated in Dinh Tuong Province and accounted for 570 Viet Cong. A longer term operation, Enterprise, was initiated in conjunction with the ARVN and various South Vietnamese local forces in An Long Province. Enemy casualties amounted to 2,107 in the year-long effort which began in mid-February 1967.

Last month, for the first time in the Vietnamese war, a U.S. infantry battalion waded briefly into the labyrinthian mangrove swamps, coconut groves, and mud flats of the Mekong River Delta. They didn't stay for long; the whole operation was mainly an experiment to see how American troops would cope with the treacherous, watery terrain that has long been one of the Viet Cong's principal strongholds. Evidently the experiment was a success, for now Gen. William C. Westmoreland, acting against the advice of some of his own generals, has ordered the army to go back and build a delta stronghold of its own.

The site of the new U.S. base, selected by Westmoreland himself, is Dong Tam, 50 miles southwest of Saigon on the palmy shores of the half-mile-wide My Tho River. There, 90 acres of delta land are under an all-out assault by the army engineers. Gigantic bulldozers scrape the earth clean of the lush vegetation that festoons the placid little villages nearby. Ugly dredges sit anchored in the river, sucking away the Mekong's alluvial silt and draining rice fields where airstrips are soon to be imbedded. Deep-draft LST's and LCU's stream upriver from the sea to disgorge swarms of uniformed men, batteries of artillery and a cheery procession of bright red Coca Cola coolers. Onshore, a village of green tents has already taken root, complete with portable kitchens, showers and laundries for 2,500 men of the Ninth Infantry Division's Third Brigade. The Army intends to be around for some time.

Sabotage: There will be plenty of work to do once Dong Tam is fully operational. The Viet Cong, who call the rice-rich delta "the cradle of our guerrilla war," are estimated to have 82,000 men – roughly a third of their total force – in the area and the South Vietnamese, with a striking force of only three regular divisions, have barely been able to hold their own against them. The new U.S. force at Dong Tam, however, will be well positioned for quick strikes into the Viet Cong

Members of the US Army's riverine force disembark from a Navy ATC (Armored Troop Carrier) before a sweep along a river bank deep in the Delta region.

In the monsoon season, keeping yourself and your equipment free of mud is vital. When you have spent the day forcing your way through thick undergrowth it gets worse. All you want to do is collapse where you stand.

redoubts just south of the river and for exerting counterpressure to the north against the guerrilla threat to Highway 4. And though Viet Cong propaganda derides the base as "idiotic," the rebels have already given clear evidence that they are taking this latest U.S. gambit seriously: their frogmen managed to sink the huge hydraulic dredge Jamaica Bay, the fourth largest in the world, while it was on the job at Dong Tam.

But such sabotage is only a minor headache for U.S. strategists compared to the awesome problem of how to bring superior mobility and firepower to bear in the trackless morass of the delta. For one thing, this is the most densely populated area of all South Vietnam, and it is desperately difficult to carry out any major military action without risking serious losses in civilian life and property – a fact which helps to explain the Vietnamese Army's not infrequent reluctance to launch operations recommended by its U.S. advisers. As one American officer puts it, "You can't walk five steps down here

Members of one of the US Navy's elite SEAL teams fire on a Viet Cong bunker during Operation Crimson Tide in late 1967. While the body count was low, the operation some 67 miles south-west of Saigon destroyed a considerable quantity of VC materiel.

without stumbling on a gaggle of ducks, some kids and a little old lady selling soda pop." And the loyalties of the local populace are, at best, uncertain. Says a stoop-shouldered elder from a village near Dong Tam: "I just don't know where our village stands. The children are helping the Americans fill sandbags, the men have left with the guerrillas and our women do laundry for your soldiers."

Puzzle: Beyond that, there is the frustrating puzzle of how best to get around in the swampy delta countryside where roads are extremely scarce and where helicopters can never be quite certain of finding a solid landing-place. Critics of Westmoreland's delta foray conjure up nasty visions of U.S. forces becoming quite literally "bogged down" deep in unfriendly territory. American troops will have to become used to getting around in launches and "hovercraft" (vehicles traveling on a cushion of air), to crossing shaky bamboo bridges that demand the skill of a tightrope walker, to spotting signs of an ambush in the unfamiliar environment of mud and water palms.

U.S. commanders are confident that their men can do all this, but they have no illusions of quick or massive victories. "The nature of the terrain largely dictates the type of operations that we can effectively carry out," recognizes Lt. Gen. Jonathan Seaman, the tall, gaunt commander of U.S. Field Force One – which includes the Dong Tam garrison. "Large sweeps in a densely populated region where friends and foes are intermingled seem out of the question. We will have to take one small bite at a time." (5)

Overall, the US services lost 11,058 dead during the year – 9,378 killed in action and 1,680 in non-combat accidents and other circumstances. A further 99,742 men were wounded. ARVN losses included 11,135 dead, and allied casualties accounted for another 189. US and ARVN sources placed the number of NVA and VC killed at 90,400. Of the 551 Army helicopters lost during 1967, operational losses accounted for 335. The remaining 216 combat losses included 205 helicopters brought down by ground

AIR FORCE MiG KILLERS

Whenever Air Force aircraft went North, they were protected from MiGs by Phantoms, and these were called into action many times. During the hectic air-to-air fighting of 1972, three aces emerged (the fighter pilot Steve Ritchie and Weapon Systems Officers Charles de Bellevue and Jeffrey Feinstein) amid a mass of kills achieved by the Thailand-based fighters. After a poor start to the air-to-air war, the 1972 campaign underlined the importance of superior missiles and combat tactics.

Above: Captain Richard S. Ritchie was the US Air Force's only fighter pilot ace of the war in Southeast Asia, flying with the 555th TFS 'Triple Nickel'. He downed five MiG-21s between 10 May and 28 August 1972, flying a McDonnell F-4E Phantom.

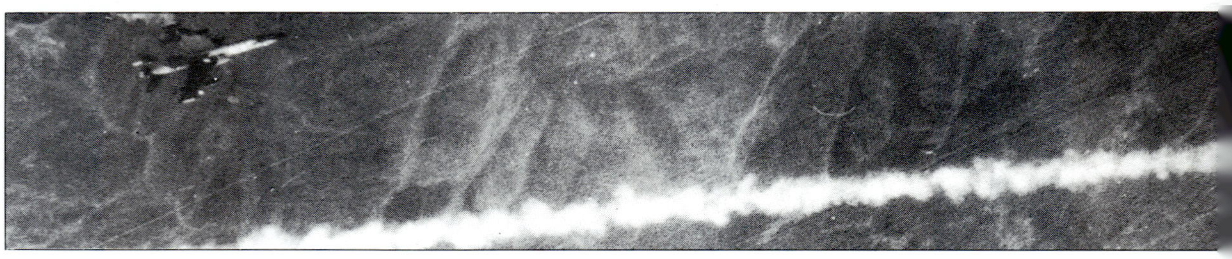

Above: Tactical aircraft attacking the North had guns, MiGs and SAMs to contend with. While MiGCAP fighters took care of the fighter threat, effective ECM tactics hoped to keep the SAMs under control. Near misses were commonplace, as evidenced by this SA-2 streaking past a lucky F-105D Thunderchief.

> **"I pulled the trigger, released, pulled again. The second Sparrow impacted the tailpipe producing a large orange ball of fire and a chute"**

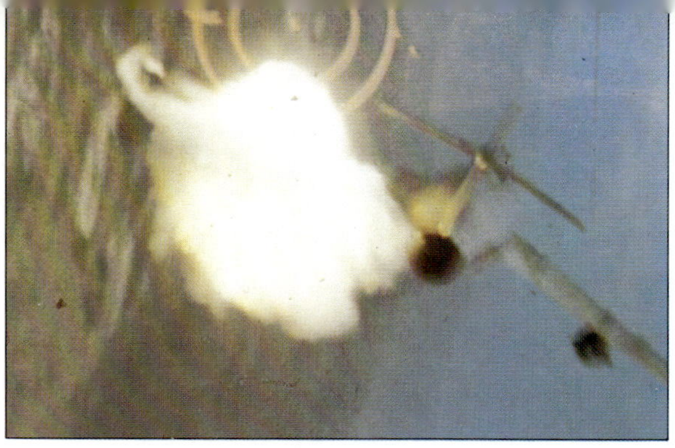

Left: It was not only the Phantom which scored kills against MiGs. This MiG-17 was shot down on 3 June 1967, hit by 20-mm shells fired from a Republic F-105. The Thunderchief is rarely credited as a MiG-killer, yet it accounted for 28, 11 more than the celebrated Crusader.

Above: This famous photograph depicts MiG-killing aircrew of the 555th TFS at Udorn RTAFB. From left to right are Lt. Col. Carl G. Baily (pilot, two MiG-21s), Captain Charles de Bellevue (Weapon Systems Officer, four MiG-21s and two MiG-19s), Captain Jeffrey S. Feinstein (13th TFS WSO, five MiG-21s) and Captain Richard S. Ritchie (pilot, five MiG-21s).

Above: Dogfighting in afterburner burned into the fighter's fuel reserves at an alarming rate, so many aircraft needed refuelling on the return journey after a hard fight. Going into battle with full tanks gave pilots the option to stay and fight where necessary.

Below: Lessons of earlier combat led to the reintroduction of an internal gun in the McDonnell Phantom. The F-4E mounted a 20-mm M61 Vulcan rotary cannon under the nose, but in practise only accounted for six kills.

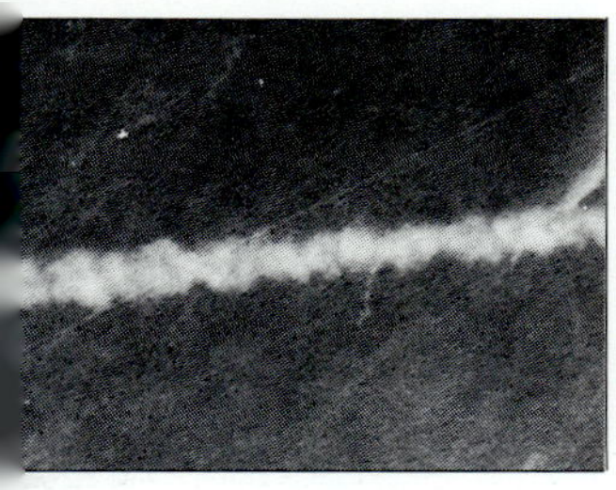

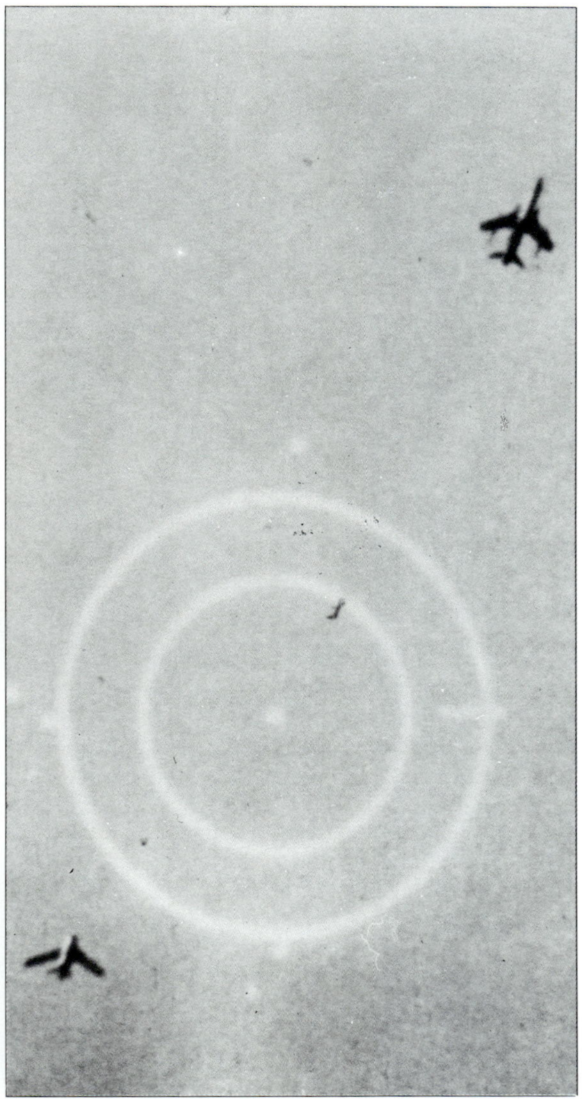

Left: The hunter hunted. Following a strike on the Paul Doumer bridge, this MiG-17 is attempting to gain a firing position on this F-105. The photograph was taken by another F-105, attempting to drive the MiG off his buddy's tail.

Right: Captain Jeffrey S. Feinstein was a WSO with the 13th TFS, 432nd TRW at Udorn, and took part in five MiG-21 kills between 16 April and 13 October 1972. His pilots were Major Edward D. Cherry, Captain Bruce G. Leonard Jr., Lt. Col. Carl G. Baily (two kills) and Lt. Col. Curtis D. Westphal.

During the hectic air-to-air action of 1972, the McDonnell F-4E Phantom claimed 23 of the 50 Air Force kills (others falling to F-4D [25] and B-52D [2]). This example sports three-tone tactical camouflage, internal M61 cannon, four AIM-7 Sparrow semi-active radar homing missiles and four AIM-9 Sidewinder infra-red homing missiles. It carries the markings of the 388th TFW, based at Korat RTFB with the 469th TFS.

fire and 11 destroyed at base camps. Marine helicopter losses amounted to 88, with 33 of those being operational, 50 to ground fire and 5 in base camps. Marine fixed-wing aviation lost 62 planes, with 23 being operational losses, 35 destroyed by ground fire, 2 to SAMs, and 2 by enemy attacks on bases.

Air force operations

For the US Air Force, 1967 started with a morale booster. Col. Robin Olds, commander of the 8th Tactical Fighter Wing out of Ubon, led his "Wolf Pack" to the largest one-day kill of MiG-21s during the war. Termed Operation Bolo, the plan rested on a tactical deception – substituting F-4C fighters for F-105 bombers in what appeared to be a routine Rolling Thunder strike formation. On January 2nd, assuming the "Thud" flight profile, the 8th TFW succeeded in drawing up 14 intercepting North Vietnamese MiG-21s. In a 12-minute fight the Wolf Pack

18 October 1967, and 20-mm cannon shells from a USAF F-105 pilot strike a North Vietnamese MiG-17 in a dogfight some 19 miles from Hanoi.

bagged four MiGs with Sparrow missiles and three more with Sidewinders, while losing none of their own. In May, North Vietnamese air bases were added to the Rolling Thunder target list for brief periods during the year, and the Air Force quickly destroyed 26 MiGs on the ground. Soon the North Vietnamese resorted to basing the majority of their MiGs in Red China.

Supporting Junction City

In South Vietnam the USAF flew 575 sorties on February 22nd in support of the opening of the Army's Operation Junction City – a one-day record up to that time. In March, the Royal Thai government granted permission for the USAF to run B-52s out of Thailand, shortening the response time for Arc Light strikes which formerly originated only from Guam. USAF losses during 1967 came to 411 fixed-wing aircraft. Combat accounted for 325 planes, and operational causes claimed the other 86. In combat, ground fire had brought down 252 planes, while SAMs shot down 28 and enemy fighters got 22. A further 23 were destroyed by enemy sappers while at their bases.

Naval bombardment

US Navy surface ships assigned to Sea Dragon extended their shore bombardment of North Vietnam all the way up to Than Hoa during February, 1967 concentrating their fire on transportation lines. Flying against Route Package 6B, the Navy was finally granted permission to bomb targets in the vicinity of Haiphong. Alfa Strikes (maximum effort raids) were conducted from the USS Kitty Hawk and the Ticonderoga on April 20th, but the targets were power generating facilities, and not the key docks. In fact, Washington even issued an apology to the Soviets when some stray bomb fragments hit the freighter Turkestan in the harbor! Further raids in the area were aimed at cutting the transportation lines from Haiphong to the interior. Only the rela-

THE COASTAL WAR

The Ho Chi Minh Trail was not the only source of supplies for the Viet Cong. From August 1965 Operation 'Market Time' was established. These coastal and inshore operations were designed to interrupt the flow of food, ammunition and re-inforcements reaching the Viet Cong by junk. They were the responsibility of US Navy Task Force 115, and used craft much more suited to the task than the 7th fleet's destroyers. Small, fast and heavily armed, the various US Navy craft operated with similar craft from the South Vietnamese Navy, with Navy helicopters and aircraft and with the Air Force.

October, 1968. The view from PCF-42 after shelling a VC supply dump along the coast from Cam Ranh Bay.

Below: A crewman of a PBR Mk II replies in kind with an M60 to VC fire while on Chieu Hoi operations on the Bassac River.

"Searching a fully loaded junk is difficult. There is no place to unload the cargo. Searches and personnel checks are handicapped by a language barrier. And many of the Vietnamese liaison people assigned to the Coast Guard cutters and Navy Swifts get seasick!"

Above: Early morning on the Mekong. Sun glints on helmets and a machine gun on LST USS St Clair County, May 1966.

Right: The Navy checks a fishing junk – a standard VC means of transporting arms, food and medical supplies to the South.

Above: Under fire from the shore, a Navy gunner answers back with a hefty burst from a shipboard .50 calibre Browning machine gun.

Left: An RVN Navy fast coastal patrol craft (FCF) makes a high speed run off the coast of An Thoi in January 1966.

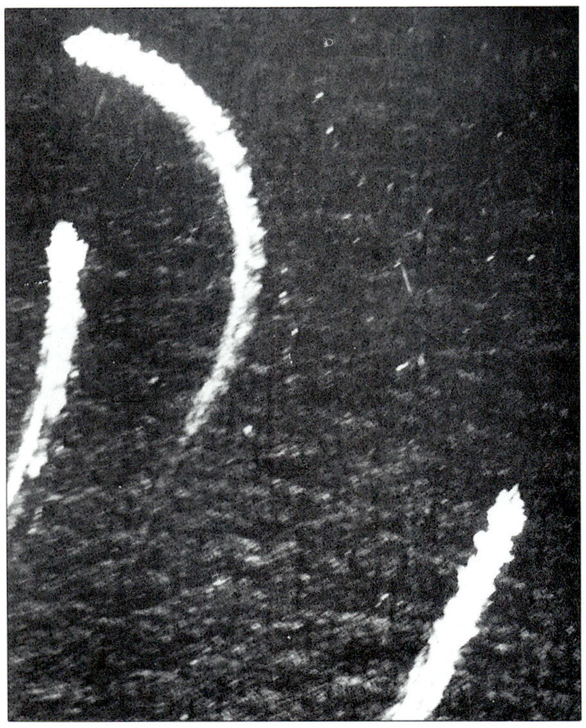

Right: Three North Vietnamese PT boats take evasive action after firing on a US Navy Phantom in the Gulf of Tonkin in July 1966. Two years previously an incident involving NVN torpedo boats in the Gulf brought US combat troops into Vietnam.

tively minor port of Cam Pha suffered from a direct raid on dock facilities, in September.

At the end of July, the USS Forrestal, just arrived at Yankee Station to begin air operations against North Vietnam, suffered a catastrophic fire when an electrical fault touched off a rocket which was mounted on a plane spotted on the flight deck. The resulting chain reaction of ordnance and aircraft explosions left 134 sailors dead and damaged 63 of the carrier's 80-odd aircraft, including 21 which were completely destroyed. The Forrestal was out of action, and never returned to Yankee Station during the war. In all, the Navy lost 186 fixed-wing aircraft during 1967. Operational losses totaled 52, and combat losses were 134, with 99 of those due to ground fire, 30 to SAMs, and 5 to enemy fighters.

Marine Corps at war

At the end of the Vietnam era, when President Nixon ended conscription, the call was that America needed a "modern volunteer army". A number of wags replied that the United States already had a modern volunteer army – the Marine Corps. For decades the Marines have occupied a special place in the popular imagination of the American people.

A US Navy UH-1E Huey helicopter patrols in company with the Vietnamese River Assault Group 22.

Renowned for their "fire brigade" role as an instantly ready force, the Marines built their reputation on interventions in the "banana republics" of the Western Hemisphere. The modern amphibious mission developed during the 1930s, and reached its peak during the Pacific campaign in World War II. Since then, only one large amphibious landing has taken place, at Inchon during the Korean War. Nevertheless, the Marine Corps remains the official repository of the amphibious mission in the US defense establishment.

Toughness

The Marines set themselves apart from the rest of the US services by the toughness of their training and discipline, their Spartan life style, and only partially by the uniqueness of their mission. The USMC's theory of organization and combat was also quite different than the Army's. Because of their expeditionary nature, the Marines were organized as Marine Air-Ground Task Forces of various sizes. In general, this meant that Marine ground and aviation units could be teamed up at any level from corps, (Marine Amphibious Force), down to battalion, (Marine Amphibious Unit), with the air units in

THE GREEN MACHINE

Up near the DMZ, it was a different war. Fighting was often against North Vietnamese regulars, and the people doing the fighting were special. They were the Marines. With a history dating back to before the signing of the Declaration of Independence, the Marines have the finest traditions of valour in the United States Armed Forces. In the early days in Vietnam, they remained a volunteer force, but by the end they were accepting draftees like everyone else. Nevertheless to be a Marine was something special, as battles from the taking of Hue to the Siege of Khe Sanh showed.

Above: A Marine Amtrack approaches the depot ship USS Cleveland during a 1968 training exercise with the 1st Amphibious Tractor Battalion.

"The Marines trapped the guerrillas. In three days they killed 291 VC and captured 65. 'If you're going to be a pro, be a ** pro, or get out of the *** ***** business' was the colonel's comment"**

direct support of the ground units. This practice ceased when the Khe Sanh crisis brought a single theater air manager into the picture.

Marine divisions were larger than their Army counterparts in every respect, right down to lowest level, where the Marines employed 13-man squads to the Army's 10-man squads. In practice the numbers of men at the "sharp end" were generally much lower in both cases, with many companies operating at half strength in both services. Tactically, the Army preferred to make contact with the enemy, stop, and call in artillery and air strikes to blast him out. The practice was expensive in ammunition instead of lives, but often failed to bring the NVA or VC to decisive engagement – they simply retreated. The Marines, while not eager to waste lives, were believers in the primary virtues of the infantryman, and thus more likely to force a decisive engagement through fire and maneuver. More than a few Marine units received the order "Fix bayonets!" prior to assaulting an enemy-occupied location. Although the Marines had a large helicopter contingent in

The Dock Landing Ship USS Monticello unloads landing craft off the Vietnamese coast just south of the DMZ. Operation Beacon Hill I involved a full-scale over the beach and helicopter assault by the Marine Corps.

Above: Early days in I Corps – an M60 gun team from 3d Bn, 4th Marines, fire on NVA troops on Hill Nui Cray Tre near the demilitarized zone, in September 1966.

Right: Esprit de corps – tattooed with the insignia of the Corps and gung-ho for action, a Marine personifies the USMC's fighting spirit. Early in the war, the Marines were able to maintain their tradition of taking only volunteers into their ranks.

Entering service in the mid-1950s, the LVTP-5 was a massive amphibian over 30 tons in weight and nearly 30 feet long. It could carry over eight tons of cargo or 25 Marines. The LVTH-6 depicted was the same but for a 105-mm howitzer turret.

Vietnam, their "birds" were mainly transport types like the large CH-46 as opposed to the Army's emphasis on "air assault", with the ubiquitous UH-1.

Using the same qualitative comparisons as presented in the US Army section, Marine units in Vietnam broke down roughly as follows: The 3rd Marine Division's 3rd and 4th Marines were excellent regiments, while its 9th Marines were good, but never recovered from early rough handling by the NVA. The 1st Marine Division's three regiments (1st, 5th and 7th Marines) were all good units. The independent regiments of the 5th Division which deployed to Vietnam were of declining quality, the 26th Marines being only "fair" as Marine units go, and the 27th Marines being poor (accounting for their speedy withdrawal). By the time the 26th and 27th went to Vietnam, there was a high proportion of drafted Marines in their ranks. Nevertheless, the primary Marine regiments in Vietnam (including the 26th) performed well when the chips were down.

Over the beach

The employment of the Marines during the war was something less than satisfactory. From the beginning there were divergent opinions on the role and location of the Marine effort. Logic would suggest that Marine expertise in amphibious operations and the Navy's supporting amphibious craft would be best used in the Delta area, where the primary means of transportation was by water. This was not to be. Rationalizing that the Navy/Marine capability for resupply "over the beach" would ease the logistical burden in South Vietnam's underdeveloped I Corps area, Westmoreland deployed the Marines in

During Operation Beacon Guide, part of a long series of operations in the De-militarized Zone these Marines 'liberated' a North Vietnamese flag from the body of an NVA soldier.

the northern provinces. This tied the Marines to sustained heavy combat along the DMZ, and wasted their intrinsic mobility. The commander of III Marine Amphibious Force, although a corps-level commander, could do nothing about this, because operations in Vietnam were under the control of MACV, and not through the Marine chain of command in the Pacific.

Counter-guerrilla expertise

Operationally, the Marines were prepared for counter-guerrilla warfare at the outset, one of their brigades having completed a major exercise along these lines just prior to the first landings at Da Nang in March, 1965. Marine theory centered around securing the population centers along the coast and spreading out like an "ink blot" to cover more villages and deny the enemy any support from the people. This worked quite well, and was enhanced by the Combined Action Program which teamed special volunteer Marine squads with Vietnamese Popular Forces platoons in village security schemes. General Westmoreland had other ideas, and ordered the Marines off into the sparsely populated interior to try to find the NVA while the Communist VC cadres reinfiltrated the populous areas.

MARINE AIR FIXED WING

Based at two large shore bases (Da Nang and Chu Lai), the Marine Corps fixed-wing assets were involved totally with supporting their 'grunts' on the ground. F-4s, F-8s, A-4s and A-6s regularly pounded communist forces in contact with Marine troopers, mostly in the area near the DMZ. Of course some Marine aircraft were deployed on board Navy carriers, where they took their place on Navy strikes. The only Marine MiG kill of the war was gained by a Phantom crew operating from a carrier.

Above: Da Nang was one of the busiest airfields in Southeast Asia, with Navy and Air Force detachments, numerous diverts from other airfields and several Marine units. Here the F-4B Phantoms of VMFA-115 and VMFA-323 are seen on their ramp.

Left: While Navy Crusaders 'mixed it' with MiGs, Marine aircraft were used exclusively to shift mud, armed with bombs and Zuni rockets.

Right: Workhorse of the Marine attack force was the Douglas A-4 Skyhawk. This pair from VMA-311 are seen at Chu Lai.

Above: VMF(AW)-232 F-8E Crusader seen on the runway at Da Nang, loaded with 'slick' bombs and Y-rack mounted rocket launchers.

Below: The adverse weather bombing accuracy and heavy weapon load earned the Grumman A-6 Intruder the name 'mini B-52'.

"The flight of Phantoms were operating against a 'suspected' enemy AA position. As Lt. Colonel Hagaman's F-4B, armed with Napalm and 250-lb Snakeyes, skimmed low over the treeline, the North Vietnamese cut loose and laced the belly of the plane with 50 caliber shells . . . The F-4B began to tumble end over end . . . the world outside was a spinning blur of blue and green . . . the Phantom flipped upright and the ejection cartridges blew the pilot from the flaming cockpit. Seconds later, the plane cartwheeled into the ground"

Above: Grumman A-6 Intruders occasionally used their sophisticated blind weapon delivery equipment to lead Douglas A-4 Skyhawks on medium level 'buddy-bombing' missions, the Skyhawks releasing their ordnance on command from the Intruder.

Below: For in-theatre transport and trans-Pacific refuelling support, the Marine Corps employed a fleet of Lockheed KC-130F Hercules. F-4J Phantoms are seen here deploying to the war zone: the unit had previously flown the F-8 Crusader.

Above: Tactical reconnaissance for the Marine Corps was handled by the McDonnell RF-4B Phantom, one of which is seen here being pulled from its hardened shelter. The parent unit, VMCJ-1, also operated EF-10B and EA-6A aircraft on jamming missions.

CHAPTER SIX

THE YEAR OF TET 1968

February 1968 saw the Marines fight their biggest battle since the Korean War. The struggle for the old Imperial capital of Hué was long and bitter, but in the end the Viet Cong were decisively defeated.

In January McNamara – constantly at odds with his military advisors and unable to see his way to a war-winning strategy – gave up the post of Secretary of Defense in favor of Clark Clifford. Clifford would quickly come to the realization that the administration had bungled the United States into a position where winning the war was no longer a viable option. President Johnson announced in March that he would not seek another term as President. This opened the field for Democratic contenders of all persuasions. One of Johnson's foremost critics, Senator Robert Kennedy, was assassinated in June, and the political violence in America was just starting. In the wake of major riots in various US cities, the Democratic Party Convention (held in August in Chicago) would shock the nation as events outside the convention hall exemplified anti-war extremism *and* police brutality. Republican challenger Richard Nixon won the presidential election in November on a "peace with honor" platform.

Prior to the Tet Offensive, the US Army deployed several additional units to Vietnam during January: the 11th Light Infantry Brigade, and the 16th and 164th Combat Aviation Groups. In response to Tet, several more formations were rushed from the States including the 3rd Brigade of the 82nd Airborne Division and the USMC's Regimental Landing Team 27 (both in February), and the 1st Brigade of the 5th Infantry Division (Mechanized) in August. By the end of the year, the United States had 359,800

AMERICAN PERSONALITIES

Vietnam was the first real media war. Saturation coverage on television and in the newspapers made stars of the main commanders. Of course, the presence of such a concentration of publicity machinery made the war an ideal place for an aspiring politician to be seen at least in the earlier parts of the war. Pentagon officials, senior officers, members of the administration, even news anchormen made their mark in visits to the war zone.

Above: General Lewis W. Walt, architect of the Marine build-up in Vietnam, 1965-67.

"Westy, as he is known to intimates, is not given to bluff talk, so his words carry some weight when he says that the USAF must continue to bomb the north as long as Hanoi keeps moving troops south."

Below: Richard Nixon with 3d Marine Division commander Frederick Karch at Chu Lai in 1965.

soldiers and 81,400 marines in South Vietnam. Further reinforcements were hard to come by, as many units in the US were on duty in the cities. The brigade of the 82nd Airborne lost most of its paratroopers to transfer soon after arrival, as they had been ineligible for deployment under prevailing Army Regulations. They were replaced by regular infantry drafts. Similarly, the Marines scraped the bottom of the barrel in dispatching Regimental Landing Team 27, and the unit was withdrawn from Vietnam by September. General Westmoreland had requested another 206,756 personnel, but the political climate in the United States simply would not allow it.

As of midnight on Sunday, June 23, the Viet Nam conflict became the longest war ever fought by Americans. It was 2,376 days since Dec. 22, 1961, when Viet Cong bullets killed the first American soldier. The U.S. death toll to date: 25,068. The previous longest U.S. conflict: the War of Independence, which lasted 2,375 days and, according to the Revolutionary Army's records, cost 4,435 American dead. (1)

In Vietnam, the Americal Division (also known as the 23rd Infantry Division), had organized its headquarters in September, 1967 and was formally assigned the 11th, 196th and 198th Light Infantry Brigades and its own aviation group (the 16th). The 101st Airborne Division converted from airborne to airmobile – a process not completed until July of 1969 – with the addition of its own aviation group. An *ad hoc* US unit known as Task Force South was formed in July in II Corps from a couple of spare infantry and artillery battalions, and it worked with the ARVN 23rd Division.

ARVN and Tet

The South Vietnamese organized a 3rd Brigade for their Airborne Division during the year, and strengthened their five Mobile Strike Force Commands (joint ARVN/US Special Forces reaction brigades). In I Corps, the ARVN raised two new infantry regiments (53rd and 54th). The Tet Offensive so rocked the South Vietnamese military that Saigon sent out an immediate call to mobilize 65,000 more men for the army. In June, President Thieu approved a general mobilization law to call another 200,000 conscripts to the colors. At mid-year, the Thais withdrew the Queen's Cobra Regiment and replaced it with the 1st Brigade of their Expeditionary "Black Panthers" Division.

Above: Vice-President Hubert Humphrey with Gen. William Westmoreland, at Chu Lai, 1967.

Below: Generals Westmoreland (left), Walt (centre) and Hochmuth (right) with ARVNs.

Above: Secretary of the Navy Paul R. Ignatius and V-Adm Elmo R. Zumwalt visit Cam Ranh Bay in 1968.

Below: Defense Secretary Robert S. Macnamara in Da Nang with Gen. Westmoreland, 1965.

August 1968. A Lance-Corporal in the Marine Corps teaches an ARVN gunner the ins and outs of the M60 general purpose machine gun.

The U.S had a Christmas gift for each of the men in South Viet Nam's 1st Regiment of the 1st Division, based just south of the Demilitarized Zone. It was the lightweight, fast-firing M-16 rifle, which packs far more punch than the older and heavier weapons that the ARVN (for Army of the Republic of Viet Nam) troopers had been carrying. The 1st Regiment soon had a chance to use them. During the Christmas truce, its scouts spotted a large North Vietnamese force moving into the Quang Tri coastal flats. As soon as the truce had ended, the ARVN moved to the attack, boxing the Communists into a four-sided trap with the help of a U.S. Marine blocking force. In a fierce day-long battle, the ARVN soldiers, using their new M-16s, killed at least 100 of the North Vietnamese *v.* only 15 ARVN dead, while allied air, artillery and helicopters killed another 100. A day later, another ARVN battalion flushed a Viet Cong unit in Quang Ngai province to the south and killed 40.

For the ARVN, such victories are quite a change. It was not so many months ago that General William Westmoreland felt obliged to pass the word down the U.S. chain of command: if you can't say something good about the ARVN, don't say anything at all. The resulting silence was almost as damaging to the ARVN as the heavy shellfire of criticism it replaced. Of late, however, the ARVN has been doing some pretty effective firing of its own on the battlefields. Its performance has enabled U.S. officers to talk about the ARVN again, this time in terms of results and performances from the DMZ to the Delta, including victories in 37 of the ARVN's last 45 major contacts with the Communists. (2)

Back in the United States, the Joint Chiefs once more pushed for mobilization of National Guard and Army Reserve forces, but had to make do with a call-up of just two brigades, the 29th Infantry (Hawaii) and the 69th Infantry (Kansas), which were brought to active duty in May. In the event, neither brigade deployed to Vietnam, but many of their soldiers were used as replacements. Several additional battalions were federalized, and a few of these were sent to Vietnam. One California National Guard unit, 1st Squadron 18th Cavalry, was selected for deployment and refused *en masse* to board the transport aircraft. After this virtual mutiny, MACV cancelled its request for the squadron's services.

The action which captured the imagination of the American public and the White House was the siege of Khe Sanh, lasting from late January until mid-

KHE SANH

In 1954, French forces were surrounded by the Viet Minh at a place called Dien Bien Phu, and their defeat pointed to the end of French colonial ambitions in Indo China. 14 years later in February 1968, a smaller force of US Marines found themselves similarly surrounded at a place called Khe Sanh. This time, the Vietnamese did not succeed. The difference between the two battles was the massive US use of air power, both to supply the 6,000 Marines at Khe Sanh, and to pulverise the attacking NVA from the air. The siege was eventually lifted after three months by a relieving force from the Cavalry.

Above: Keeping watch after four days of attacks on Khe Sanh by two NVA divisions. The battle was to last 77 days, with 6,000 allied troops facing up to 40,000 NVA regulars.

Below: Engineers dig an ammo bunker for 105mm howitzers of the 1st Cavalry Division, during their week-long fight to reach and relieve the defenders of Khe San in April 1968.

Above: Khe Sanh, 1968. An incoming North Vietnamese mortar round has burst directly on top of a fuel dump.

“Nobody seemed to have an exact count on the number of NVA out there. It was at least two crack divisions, maybe more”

April of 1968. The press was quick to compare the US position at Khe Sanh to the French position at Dien Bien Phu in 1954. This delighted General Giap, who had applied pressure to Khe Sanh to lure US troops away from populous areas for the forthcoming Tet Offensive. The propaganda was not lost on Lyndon Johnson, worried by the thought of a major US land defeat. Throughout the "siege", Johnson kept a terrain model of Khe Sanh in the White House briefing room and studied the situation every day.

The heavy fighting raged throughout the afternoon. Lieutenant Colonel Alderman, his operations officer, Major Matthew P. Caulfield, and representatives of the Fire Support Coordination Center (FSCC) flew from Khe Sanh to Hill 881S by helicopter so they could personally oversee the battle. During the action, Company I drew heavy support from the recoilless rifles, mortars, and 105mm howitzers on Hill 881S, as well as the batteries at Khe Sanh. In addition, Marine jets armed with 500-pound bombs streaked in and literally blew the top off the easternmost enemy hill, while

Marines from the 1st Battalion, 26th Regiment snipe at an enemy forward observer at Khe Sanh. The heavy M14 rifle was well suited to this task.

Left: *Supplies drop in by parachute for the besieged base. Some 65 per cent of the Marines' supplies arrived in this way, as enemy mortar and artillery attacks made the base airstrip a killing zone.*

Right: *A CH-46D laden with 3,000 pounds of ammunition heads for Hill 881, a westerly outpost of Khe San, where Company I, 3/26 Marines, withstood a constant barrage of rocket and shellfire.*

One of the major differences between the seige at Khe Sanh and the French disaster at Dien Bien Phu was the overwhelming fire support the Marines had on call. Even though cut off by the North Vietnamese, Khe Sanh was well within the range of guns such as the 175mm M107 at fire bases nearer to the coast. This M107 is from 'C' Battery, 2nd Battalion, 94th Artillery Regiment US Army and is firing in support of the Marines some 20 miles away.

other fighter/bombers completely smothered one NVA counterattack with napalm. A CH-46 helicopter from Marine Aircraft Group 36 was shot down while attempting to evacuate casualties but another Sea Knight swooped in and picked up the pilot and co-pilot. The crew chief had jumped from the blazing chopper while it was still airborne and broke his leg; he was rescued by Lieutenant Fromme's men. This, however, was the only highlight for the North Vietnamese because Company I had cracked the center of their defense and, under the savage air and artillery bombardment, the rest of the line was beginning to crumble.

Lieutenant Colonel Alderman realized that his men were gaining the advantage and requested reinforcements with which to exploit the situation. Colonel Lownds, however, denied the request and directed the 3/26 commander to pull Company I back to Hill 881S immediately. The order was passed on to Captain Dabney and it hit him like a thunderbolt. His men had been fighting hard all day and he hated to tell them to call it off at that point. Nonetheless, he rapidly disengaged, collected his casualties, and withdrew. The struggle had cost the enemy dearly: 103 North Vietnamese were killed while friendly losses were 7 killed, including two platoon commanders, and 35 wounded. As the weary Marines trudged back to Hill 881S, they were understandably disappointed at not being able to continue

Although Khe Sanh was never in the same danger as Dien Bien Phu 14 years before, it remained a perilous place to land an aircraft.

the attack. It wasn't until later that they learned why that had been halted just when victory was in sight.

Colonel Lownds' decision to break off the battle was not borne out of faintheartedness, but was based on a valuable piece of intelligence which came in the form of a NVA first lieutenant who was the commanding officer of the 14th Antiaircraft Company, 95C Regiment, 325C NVA Division; at 1400, he appeared off the eastern end of the runway with an AK-47 rifle in one hand and a white flag in the other. Under the covering guns of two Ontos, a fire team from the 2d Platoon, Company B, 1/26, took the young man in tow and, after Lieutenant Colonel Wilkinson had questioned him briefly, the lieutenant was hustled off to the regimental intelligence section for interrogation. The lieutenant had no compunction about talking and gave the Marines a detailed description of the forthcoming Communist offensive. (3)

In truth, the similarities between Dien Bien Phu and Khe Sanh were only superficial. A smaller American/ARVN force (26th Marines, 1/9th Marines [105mm], and 37th ARVN Ranger Bn) was surrounded by a larger Communist force (304, 320, 324B and 325C NVA Divisions), but all other factors were different. Unlike the French, the US controlled the high ground which dominated the area. The US position was also closer to friendly supply bases than Dien Bien Phu had been, making aerial resupply much easier. Lastly, US air power was overwhelming and probably decisive, as opposed to the comparatively ineffective French air support in 1954.

The initial relief of the combat base occurred at 1350 on 6 April when the lead company of the 3d ARVN Airborne Task Force was airlifted to Khe Sanh and linked up with the 37th Rangers. This move was primarily intended as a morale booster for the 37th. Two days later, after 2/7 Cav had completed the sweep along Route 9 and linked up with the 26th Marines, the official relief took place. At 0800 on 8 April, the 3d Brigade airlifted its CP to the base and became the new landlord. Relieved of its duties along the perimeter, Lieutenant Colonel McEwan's 1/26 saddled up and attacked to the west that day but made little contact.

Traditionally, the lifting of a siege has been the occasion for great emotional outbursts, bands, and stirring oration; in this regard, the relief of Khe Sanh was somewhat of a disappointment. General Tolson intended for the link-up to be "as businesslike as possible with a minimum of fanfare" so that he could get the Marines on the offensive again. A few newsmen at the base snapped pictures of Marines shaking hands with the Cavalrymen, but the men usually shrugged indifferently afterwards and went about their business. The defenders generally looked on the proceedings with sort of a "ho-hum" attitude; perhaps they felt that they had not been rescued from anything. In fact, they were right; the enemy threat had been squelched weeks before PEGASUS had gotten off the ground. "I've been at Khe Sanh for nine months," the regimental commander stated, "and if they keep me supplied, I could stay here another nine months." No doubt most men were glad they did not have to remain because the stand at Khe Sanh had not been "all peaches and cream," but, as far as the defenders being snatched out of the jaws of destruction – it just did not happen that way. (4)

Elsewhere in northern I Corps, the 3rd Marine Division's year-long routine "search and clear" missions were started in January under the title of Operation Lancaster II. These efforts netted a total of 1,801 enemy casualties by the end of November. A major campaign was also undertaken to clear the Cua Viet River, called Napoleon/Saline. With the help of Navy patrol boats, the operation eliminated 3,495 NVA and VC, and kept the line of communications open from the sea to Dong Ha. From April to mid-May the 101st Airborne Division, the ARVN 1st Division and the 3rd Brigade of the 82nd Airborne Division swept the coastal lowlands, killing 2,100 enemy in Operation Carentan II in the two northern provinces.

Relief of Khe Sanh

Prior to Tet, MACV ordered the 1st Cavalry Division to displace from Binh Dinh Province in II Corps to northern I Corps to aid the Marines. This involved a 200-mile move while the division was still engaged in Operation Pershing II. The strategic move was made in spite of operational and weather problems, under the banner of the Jeb Stuart series of operations. The 1st Cav had no sooner got its feet on the ground than the Tet Offensive got under way. The Communists lost 3,268 men. During the first two weeks in April the 1st Cavalry Division put its airmobile expertise to use in Operation Pegasus, the relief of Khe Sanh, along with an associated ARVN drive (Lam Son 207). The division broke through to the Marines (inflicting 1,044 casualties on the NVA) in an anticlimax to the seige. The 3rd Marine Division continued active operations in the vicinity of Khe Sanh after the relief. These sweeps netted another 3,311 NVA dead over nearly a year.

Some of the toughest fighting in I Corps develop-

BASE SECURITY

Bases in Vietnam came in all shapes and sizes, each with its own unique security environment. The Special Forces camp on the Cambodian border had to beware of large enemy formations. Guards at a major centre such as Long Binh had to watch out for sneak attacks by the Viet Cong, while at the same time being aware of possible infiltration amongst the hundreds of Vietnamese workers in camp. Security could involve armoured vehicles on the perimeter of a battalion headquarters, or lethal tripwire activated Claymore mines set up around an army helicopter base on the Kontum plateau. The enemy threat was everywhere.

Above: Two members of a quartermaster's company smash cans of fuel pilfered from the storage tanks at Qui Nhon, 1970.

Right: All along the watchtower: a military policeman shows the field of fire to an RVN Security Force member.

ed in the ancient city of Hué (the old imperial capital of Vietnam) during the Tet Offensive. On 31 January, the NVA 5th and 6th Regiments, reinforced by sappers, attacked the HQ of the ARVN 1st Division in the city. Initially, defenses were weak, consisting mainly of the understrength 3rd ARVN Regiment and some division troops. Both sides threw in reinforcements as the Communists gained the upper hand. The 8th and 9th NVA Regiments bolstered their comrades already in contact, and on the other side the South Vietnamese brought in an ARVN airborne brigade and a marine brigade.

Fight at Hue

A regimental-size task force of US Marines entered the fight, while the 3rd Brigade of the 1st Cavalry Division moved into position outside the city. Because of the cultural significance of the city of Hué there was a reluctance to use air strike, and most of the fighting was plain infantry work. The NVA and VC lost 5,113 men in Hué and another 3,000 in the vicinity, but the city was not secured until the 25th of February. During the Communist occupation over 5,000 civilians had been killed by the VC cadres and dumped into mass graves.

In the throne room of the palace at the heart of the old city of Hue, a Marine sergeant takes a break from the fighting.

Almost uniquely in Viet Nam last week, it was possible to follow clearly the progression of one battle: the block-by-block struggle of the allies to recapture the city of Hué from the North Vietnamese units that swept into it two weeks ago. The North Vietnamese had arrived to stay, and students from the University of Hué acted as their guides, in some cases donning the uniform of Viet Cong regulars. As the ancient capital of Viet Nam, Hué was a prime piece of captured real estate for propaganda purposes, and the NVA fought for every inch of it against ARVN troopers and a battalion-size force of U.S. Marines that moved in from the south.

At first, the Marines found the going not only tough but unfamiliar, since they had to retake the streets almost house by house. "The first two days, it was a matter of learning this sort of thing," said one Marine commander, Colonel Ernest Cheatham. "The Marines haven't fought a fight like this since Seoul, back in 1950." As more and more blocks fell to the Marines, they commandeered brightly colored Honda motorcycles, small buses and cars, to ferry themselves back and forth to the action.

Gradually, the battling turned the once beautiful city into a nightmare. Hué's streets were littered with dead. A black-shirted Communist soldier sprawled dead in the middle of a road, still holding a hand grenade. A woman knelt in death by a wall in the corner of

"The sentry watched until a hole was dug, then squeezed off a shot which detonated the mine that the VC sapper was about to plant"

Left: An M551 of the 4th Cav, 25th Infantry Div, patrols the perimeter of an LZ during a reconnaissance-in-force in August 1969.

Right: Claymore anti personnel mines were amongst the most effective weapons used in Vietnam, and were used in large numbers on defensive perimeters.

Above: Dogs struck terror into the VC – until they learned to put them off the scent by washing with American soap.

Right: Guarding against VC mortar and artillery attacks, men of the 82nd Airborne at Phu Bai work on a sandbag defence.

her garden. A child lay on the stairs, crushed by a fallen roof. Many of the bodies had turned black and begun to decompose, and rats gnawed at the exposed flesh.

Predawn Derring Do. Every so often the Marines came across pockets of American civilians, some of whom had been successfully hiding out for nine days. When they liberated the Thua Thien province headquarters, the Marines tore down the Viet Cong flag, one of the dozens the Communists had planted throughout the city, and raised the Stars and Stripes. Their commander had told them to run up the South Vietnamese flag, but two Marines had died and two others had been wounded in taking the building; they were not about to be denied the satisfaction of raising their own flag (though it later had to be lowered to conform with South Vietnamese law).

Meanwhile, the ARVN forces were making slower headway against the NVA defending the thick-walled battlements of the Citadel. They first tried to use armored personnel carriers to spearhead their attack, but the long straight streets of the old quarter enabled Communist gunners to knock them out from half a mile away. With only three of their original twelve APCs still operative, the ARVN troopers started the same house-to-house combat as the Marines on the other side of the fetid Perfume River.

In a predawn bit of derring-do, Communist frogmen swam down the Perfume and neatly dropped the center span of the last remaining bridge over the river, despite the fact that the allies held both bridgeheads. Boats thus became the main means of evacuation and supply, and each boat ran a gauntlet of NVA sniper fire. But at week's end the NVA pockets of resistance were slowly shrinking, and all of the city except a part of the Citadel had been seized by the allies. (5)

After the month-long battle for Hué, the 1st Marine Division launched Operation Houston, a six-month mop-up campaign in Quang Nam and Thua Thien Provinces, which accounted for another 702 Communist casualties. South of Da Nang the division eliminated 1,017 more enemy troops in the vicinity of Hoi An during Operation Allen Brook from May through August. In mid-April, the 1st Cavalry and 101st Airborne Divisions, along with the 196th Brigade and the ARVN 1st Division and Airborne Task Force "B", struck out into the A Shau Valley to prevent further NVA threats to Hué. This thrust, Operation Delaware (ARVN Lam Son 216), eliminated 869 Communist troops but failed to keep the NVA out of A Shau for long.

Marines of Company E, 2nd Battalion, 3rd Marines in action at Mutters Ridge during one of the phases of operation Lancaster II.

What has become known as the My Lai massacre took place in Quang Ngai Province in March. During operations in a hostile area, Lt. William Calley's platoon slaughtered at least 150 unarmed civilians. The US unit, poorly trained and badly led, was frustrated by its inability to find the enemy, and had suffered casualties from mines and booby traps. When let off the leash its performance was perhaps predictable, but inexcusable. Calley was singled out and the rest of the chain of command got off with mild censure. It is inconceivable that higher eche-

Left: A truck convoy carrying members of the 5th Marines to an operation near Tam Ky, May 1967. Troop movements by road presupposed a highly secure route.

Above: Noon on a road south of Da Nang. An inbound convoy escorted by LVT-5s passes a convoy heading out to support the Marine operation Oklahoma Hills.

"Of eleven vehicles, four ACAVs and one tank were destroyed. It showed what could happen on a routine mission. Indifference to unit integrity, lack of communications security, lack of planned fire-support, and wide gaps between each vehicle stacked the deck in the enemy's favour. In guarding a convoy, the escort failed to appreciate its own vulnerability"

Above: Convoy escorts sit atop their APCs before setting off. Convoys were favourite targets of the Viet Cong, and mines were always a problem.

Below: The M35 2½-ton 6x6 'Deuce and a half' operated all over Vietnam, and the chassis was used for a variety of tasks. It is still in service around the world.

Right: The 82d Airborne comes to Vietnam, February 1968. A truck convoy moves the newly arrived troops to a staging area before they are committed to the emergency response to the Tet Offensive.

lons were not aware of the events. At the least, there was some command oversight via the ubiquitous helicopters. But it is quite easy to envision the operations staff recommending that the area be "neutralized" and getting a nod of approval from the commanding general. By the time this filtered down to the platoon level, the translation was "waste 'em."

Mid-May saw three more operations commence in I Corps. The 1st Cavalry Division resumed the Jeb Stuart series in the area of Quang Tri and Thua Thien Provinces and eliminated 2,114 NVA by early November, when it was ordered to redeploy yet again – this time to III Corps. To their south, the 101st Airborne Division's Operation Nevada Eagle, lasting through February of 1969, claimed 3,299 Communist lives. At the same time the 1st Marine Division initiated Operation Mameluke Thrust in Quang Nam, accounting for 2,728 enemy dead by the end of October. In a followup operation (Henderson Hill) the next month, the division's 5th Marines killed 700 enemy at a cost of 35 Marine dead and 231 wounded. The 1st Marine Division ended the year with Taylor Common, a three-month operation in Quang Nam which started on 8 December and eliminated 1,299 NVA and VC.

The ARVN 1st Division had a busy year after Tet. In August its 54th Regiment, operating in Thua Thien Province, started Lam Son 245, while the 1st Regiment initiated Lam Son 261 the following month, and the 2nd Regiment embarked on Lam Son 271 in October. By the end of August 1969, when all three operations ended, the division had killed 1,963 NVA and VC. I Corps' ARVN 1st Ranger Group killed a further 695 Communist troops during Operation Le Loi I, a two-month effort beginning in December.

II Corps operations

In II Corps, the 1st Cavalry Division had begun the year with Operation Pershing II in Binh Dinh Province, when it was ordered to move north to I Corps. Still in the middle of this disruption, the division carried off the month-long operation and succeeded in eliminating 614 enemy soldiers before leaving II Corps. At the same time, the 173rd Airborne Brigade was in Binh Thuan (southern II Corps), engaged in Operation McLain. This pacification-support drive accounted for 1,042 Viet Cong. In March the brigade moved to Binh Dinh for Cochise Green, an operation which occupied it for the rest of the year, and accounted for some 929 enemy dead. The remainder of the year's large operations in II Corps were non-US efforts. In mid-February, the ROK Capital Division picked up where the 1st Cav had left off in Binh Dinh with Operation Maeng Ho 10, killing 664 NVA and VC in two weeks. In the southern part of the Corps Zone, the ARVN 23rd Division conducted another two-week effort in late August called Tien Bo, eliminating 1,091 enemy troops in Quang Duc Province adjacent to the Cambodian border.

The ARVN reaction to the Tet Offensive in III Corps took the form of a counteroffensive to mop up the Saigon area called Operation Tran Hung Dao. Using elite forces – two marine brigades, two airborne brigades and a ranger group – the ARVN cleaned out 953 Communist troops in two weeks of February. The followup operation (Tran Hung Dao II)lasting a further three weeks, killed 713 more Viet Cong. These were but preludes to Quyet Thang, a huge month-long effort around Saigon and adjacent provinces in March. Troops from the 5th and 25th ARVN Divisions (along with some South Vietnamese marines and paratroopers) were reinforced by the US 1st, 9th and 25th Infantry Divisions. The operation accounted for 2,658 VC. Following in April was the even larger Operation Toan Thang. Lasting nearly two months, this joint III Corps/II

INCOMING

The problem facing Americans in Vietnam was the difficulty in separating friend from foe. Who was to know if the base street sweeper went home in the evening, to put on black pyjamas and lead a raid by night on the base he worked in by day. Some facilities were hit more often than others, but there were few service establishments in Vietnam which had not been on the receiving end of some hostile fire. It might only have been a couple of rounds from a Kalashnikov, but it could equally have been a full scale attack with rockets, mortars and sappers. All you had to learn was where to dive for cover when the 'Incoming!' cry was heard.

Above: US Air Force B-57 bombers lie in ruins after a devastating VC mortar attack on Bien Hoa airfield during the night of October 31, 1964. Five B-57s were destroyed, eight were damaged, and four Americans died. This was the first VC raid on a US facility, and North Vietnam marked the occasion with a special-issue postage stamp.

Left: NVA soldiers set up a recoilless anti-tank gun in the jungle. By using portable equipment, making only brief contact and then vanishing into the bush, the communists maintained a harrassing campaign whose success was as much psychological as military.

Right: A Huey skims by a radar artillery and mortar detector set up at a forward command base near the Cambodian border. The device could spot an incoming round and compute the location of the attackers even before it landed.

Moved from II corps to I Corps, the 1st Cavalry division helped in the relief of Khe Sanh. These are troopers from D Company, 2nd Battalion 7th Cavalry.

Field Force drive involved the equivalent of nearly four US and four ARVN divisions, and netted 7,645 enemy casualties.

In the Delta of IV Corps, the US 9th Infantry Division cooperated with the ARVN in several major operations. Beginning in March and lasting through July, operations Truong Cong Dinh and Duong Cua Dan, concentrating in Dinh Tuong and Kien Tuong Provinces of northern IV Corps, eliminated some 1,251 Viet Cong and, for the first time in the region, regular NVA. From mid-July all the way through February 1969, the major ARVN commands in IV Corps (7th, 9th and 21st Divisions) engaged in Operation Quyet Chien, a blanket effort which claimed a total of 15,953 Viet Cong casualties. At the end of the year the US 9th Infantry Division embarked on Operation Speedy Express, lasting through May 1969.

US casualties

Overall, 1968 was the worst year for American casualties. The US services lost 14,589 killed in action and a further 1,919 dead from non-hostile accidents and other causes. The seriously wounded totaled 92,817. South Vietnamese military casualties more than doubled those of the US in killed and missing/presumed dead, 30,375 for the year. Another 70,696 ARVN were seriously wounded. Third-country allies lost 988 killed and missing plus 1,997 wounded. Communist casualties totaled a staggering 181,149 killed in action – about 45,000 during the Tet Offensive alone. While all of the statistics about NVA/VC losses are based on the highly suspect "body count", it should be remembered that after the end of the war, General Giap's accounting of actual Communist casualties came very close to what the US and South Vietnam had claimed. On the material side, US Army helicopter losses in 1968 totaled 889, with nearly half (414) due to operational causes. The 475 lost in combat amounted to 421 brought down by ground fire and 54 destroyed at their base camps. The Marines lost 103 helicopters and 74 fixed-wing aircraft during the year. Ground fire shot down 68 helicopters, and attacks on bases claimed 6 more, while the other losses were due to operational causes. USMC fixed-wing losses were to ground fire (50), SAMs (1), attacks on bases (8), and operational causes (15).

In one 24-hour period last week, 31 U.S. fighting men died in Viet Nam. Among them were 16 Marines helping to mop up a trapped enemy unit below Danang and

"I was lying in my bunk when the first round hit. I ran downstairs like hell and fell into the bunker. We were all hugging the ground, I was burrowing into the ground with my nose"

Even the largest bases might be hit. Here, photographers from the Audio-Visual Platoon, 69th Signal Battalion watch the base chapel at Tan Son Nhut burn down. It had been hit during a mortar and rocket attack, at the height of the 1968 Tet Offensive. At the time, Tan Son Nhut laid claim to being the busiest airport in the world.

Below: A C-130 burns on the airstrip at Dak To, the victim of an NVA mortar attack on 15 November 1967. A further mortar attack destroyed the base ammunition dump, in the prelude to a battle that was to involve four NVA regiments and last 22 days.

one infantryman in a patrol that was ambushed 40 miles north of Saigon. One of the 31, impossible to single out, became the 30,000th American to be killed in action in Viet Nam since the grisly log was begun on Jan. 1, 1961. Almost half of the total (14,400) died this year, many in the three major offensives launched by the Communists since the *Tet* holiday on Jan. 30.

Already the longest war ever fought by the U.S., Viet Nam now ranks as its fifth costliest (after World War II, with 291,557 battle deaths; the Civil War, with 220,938; World War I, with 53,402; and Korea, with 33,629). With the killed-in-action rate running at roughly 200 per week, Viet Nam should move past Korea into fourth place some time this spring – unless the negotiators in Paris make dramatic progress. The war has been far more expensive for native combatants. South Viet Nam has suffered 73,118 military dead in the past eight years. The Viet Cong and the North Vietnamese, according to an Allied estimate based on sometimes undependable body counts, have lost 422,979 dead since 1961. (6)

The shining moment for US air power was the battle for Khe Sanh. Not only did tactical fighters from the Air Force, Marines and Navy participate in the defense effort, but the big B-52 strategic bombers scored their greatest success so far in the ground support role. Able to establish a "presence" over the battle area the B-52s, aided by electronic guidance, stopped the NVA cold. From bases in Guam and

The awesome power of the B-52 was put to good use during the siege of Khe Sanh, devastating or destroying large formations of the NVA.

Thailand, the "Buffs" carpeted critical areas in conjunction with tactical air strikes and artillery to devastate attacking NVA formations.

In the early stages of the conflict, Arc Light strikes were not authorized within a prescribed distance of friendly lines. The same rule had applied during the heavy fighting at Con Thien the year before and the NVA had taken advantage of the buffer zone by moving troops and supplies in as close to the Marine base as possible to avoid the bomber raids. They tried the same thing at Khe Sanh. When American airborne observers noted enemy bunker complexes cropping up near the KSCB, the no-bomb line was moved in to about half of the original distance. At first the regimental commander was afraid that the resulting concussion would collapse his own bunkers and trenches; as it turned out, the enemy fortifications were the only ones which suffered. The first few B-52 raids inside the old line touched off scores of secondary explosions and undoubtedly snapped the North Vietnamese out of their sense of security. The closer strikes also served as a morale booster for the defenders who flocked from their bunkers to watch, what the Marines called, "Number One on the hit parade." (7)

The cessation of Rolling Thunder on 31 October brought the final shift of US air strategy during the Johnson administration – from targets in North Vietnam to interdiction in Laos. As aircraft stood down from Rolling Thunder, they were redeployed, tripling the sorties against the Ho Chih Minh Trail. The bombing halt was a bonus for Hanoi, which resumed moving troops and supplies in daylight throughout North Vietnam. Over the year, the US Air Force lost 380 fixed-wing aircraft, less than in 1967. Of these, 85 were operational losses

HUE

The country-wide uprising of the Viet Cong during the Tet (New Year) holidays of 1968 was nowhere more bitter than in the old imperial capital of Hue. The communists had managed to sieze the city, and immediately instituted a reign of terror, killing many thousands of people thought to be associated with the government. Before long, the US Marines were fighting their way through to the walls of the citadel, in the most vicious urban battle American troops had fought since the Korean War. From January 31 until March 2, two NVA regiments and two VC battalions fought 20 or more American and ARVN battalions.

Marines hoist 3.5' rockets to a launcher positioned on the roof of Hue University. Hue was the most ferocious Marine battle of the entire war.

Below: A lone Marine takes cover behind a tree to return fire into an enemy-held house. US troops, used to jungle warfare, had to learn urban combat techniques on the job.

Above: Marines bring a 106-mm recoilless rifle to bear on a house held by VC snipers. Bitter fighting in Hue cost one Marine unit one casualty for every yard of ground gained.

"Much of the city became a battle-strewn rubble, a No-Man's land where Marines crossing open ground became sniper targets. It was a strange, tense conflict, with Marines involved in their heaviest fighting for years. Casualties were high. VC casualties were higher"

Left: Refugees flood past a tank moving through southern Hue. Of a civilian population of 140,000, some 116,000 were made homeless by the month-long battle for the city.

Above: An M60 team fights towards the vast, virtually impregnable, NVA-held Citadel north of the Perfume River. 'We had to destroy the town to save it,' said a USMC officer.

Right: Against a backdrop of bullet-pocked walls, a Marine moves out under fire from a VC .50 calibre machine gun during the final stages of the battle to dislodge communist forces.

and 295 were combat losses. Ground fire caused 248 of the combat losses, enemy fighters caused 9, and SAMs 3. Attacks on air bases destroyed another 35.

Loss of the Pueblo

For the Navy, the worst incident of the war happened in January – and far removed from the Tonkin Gulf. The intelligence ship USS *Pueblo*, carrying out electronic surveillance in international waters off the Korean coast, was attacked by North Korean patrol boats and surrendered. The incident served as yet another diversion of US attention prior to the Tet Offensive, and also provided the Communists with a wealth of information about US electronic intelligence. Not only did the Navy fail to provide any covering support for the operation, but the captain

May, 1968. A US Navy Monitor of River Assault Flotilla One destroys possible ambush sites on both sides of a stream deep in the Mekong Delta

took no steps to scuttle – allowing his vessel to be first in the US Navy to surrender to an enemy in over a century.

In October the USS *New Jersey*, at the time the only battleship in commission, began operations off the coast of Vietnam. The ship was reactivated on the premise that it was more cost effective for bombardment of coastal areas than an equivalent aircraft squadron which would be vulnerable to air defense fire.

> From the moment *New Jersey* arrived on the gun line on 29 September 1968, there was no doubt in any man's mind that we were going to bash the hell out of some North Vietnamese.
>
> I can tell you, after talking to ground-pounders who saw the ship at work, that no sight of the entire war was as impressive as our battleship letting loose with its main battery of nine 16-inch guns. Each of those guns could fire a shell weighing 1,900 pounds over a distance of 32,500 yards, and there was nothing – *nothing* – which could withstand the penetrating force and the impact. The most heavily fortified North Vietnamese bunkers, even those with solid concrete roofs that were untouchable by Marine artillery, were blown away when our shells came howling down on top of them.
>
> One Marine told me that when *New Jersey* was firing her guns lit up the eastern sky like a sunrise and the shells sounded like an express train going overhead. On a 25 November 1968 firing mission , the big battlewagon was credited with destroying 117 North Vietnamese structures along the DMZ. Most of the time the targets – located by Skyhawk spotter planes – were too far away to see, but there were times when you could watch the 16-inch shells rising from the guns, arching over in their trajectory, and coming down to explode along the shoreline. (8)

In late February, limited naval air strikes were allowed within the Hanoi zone to hit dock facilities along the Red River. It was not quite the same as hitting Haiphong, and actually was too little and too late: at the end of March, President Johnson halted bombing of northern North Vietnam. By the end of October, all bombing of the north was stopped by the White House.

TACTICAL TRANSPORT

Shifting supplies from the major air bases to the troops in the field was another huge task facing the US Air Force, and it relied heavily on the excellent Lockheed C-130 Hercules to perform the task of in-theatre transport. Other transports were used to supply remote camps with only a mud airstrip, requiring short take-off and landing talents, combined with sturdy undercarriages. A large number of other aircraft were used, small jets hurrying about Southeast Asia on courier and staff transport duties.

Above: If any one fixed-wing aircraft could be called the workhorse of the Vietnam war, it would be the Lockheed C-130 Hercules, supplying airlift capability wherever it was required. It played an enormous part in the final evacuation from Saigon.

Below: Tactical airlift faced its most serious task during the resupply of the beleagured Marine camp at Khe Sanh. Evidence of the perils of operations into this camp are provided by this Fairchild C-123K, hit by mortars while taking off.

Below: Douglas C-47s played a part in transport operations, operated mostly by the VNAF. This example is seen being hit during a VC mortar attack on Tan Son Nhut in April 1966. Such attacks were a constant hazard of air operations in Vietnam.

"Air support of Khe Sanh was magnificent. Among the heroes were the C-123 and C-130 pilots who made short-field landings under heavy fire or, when the going got really tough, did low-altitude parachute extractions to get their cargoes out. It was a risky business. A Marine KC-130 carrying helicopter fuel was hit by NVA gunfire on 11 February. Trailing a red-orange plume of fuel-fire the Hercules touched down safely, only to explode in flames and swerve from the runway. Eight out of sixteen men aboard died"

Above: The de Havilland Canada C-7 Caribou possessed excellent short- and rough-field capability, vital to its role of supplying small outlying Special Forces camps with short, difficult airstrips.

Above: Fairchild C-123 Providers were widely used on Special Forces camp support, such as this turbojet-augmented C-123K taking off from Bu Dop camp after delivering vital supplies. A rugged aircraft was necessary for this sort of work.

Above: In addition to their tanking activities, the Lockheed KC-130F Hercules of the Marine Corps provided much in-theatre transport for the service.

Left: The Caribou was introduced to Vietnam by the Army, but transport assets were passed to the Air Force in April 1966. Conditions at Special Forces camp airstrips were abysmal, and it needed an extremely rugged aircraft to cope. The Caribou excelled.

Below: A large fleet of C-130 Hercules prepare for a mass launch in support of the Khe Sanh camp. Various means of air-dropping supplies were evolved and practised in Southeast Asia.

Staff transport, high-speed reconnaissance film transfer and the calibration of navigation aids were vital jobs of lesser glamour that required a fleet of small transports. This is a Lockheed C-140 JetStar of a calibration squadron, taking off from Cam Ranh Bay.

In all, the Navy lost 108 planes during the year – like the Air Force, less than the previous year. Operational causes destroyed 43 aircraft, while combat claimed 65, with 55 of those being downed by ground fire, 7 by SAMs, and 3 by enemy fighters.

THE TET OFFENSIVE

In 1967 it became apparent to the North Vietnamese leadership that its policy of matching US escalation was not succeeding. On the contrary, US attrition tactics – while operationally indecisive – were killing off NVA soldiers as rapidly as they could be sent south. Two positions emerged. General Nguyen Thanh advocated a step back to insurgency operations with an eye toward outlasting the Americans. General Giap, believing that a significant military victory could bring more benefits by reducing support at home for the US war effort, advocated a big push with all-out conventional and guerrilla participation. Politburo members decided in Giap's favor and the Tet Offensive plan was approved.

The Tet Offensive burst over Vietnam like a destructive tidal wave. This is Vinh Long after the first Viet Cong attacks on January 31.

Basically, the plan envisioned a simultaneous country-wide assault on most province capitals, autonomous cities, major military bases and, of course, Saigon, made possible by a series of border battles (including the siege of Khe Sanh) in the preceding months to lure major US units away from populated areas. Thus, NVA units would have an easier time infiltrating their targets, and would receive substantial aid from VC units which would be in place at the start. Surprise would be achieved by launching the attack during the Tet holiday when a truce was usually observed and when most ARVN units would be at low readiness because of the high number of soldiers on leave. Another feature of the plan was the anticipated "general rising" of the South Vietnamese population to welcome the Communists and participate in the overthrow of the Saigon regime. North Vietnam's revolutionary doctrine held the general rising as an article of faith, and there is evidence that the Hanoi leadership actually believed that it would occur.

Intelligence estimate

On the other side, prior to the Tet Offensive, the US "intelligence community's" top secret Special National Intelligence Estimate (SNIE) of 13 November 1967 stated that "The Communists apparently recognize that the chances of a complete military victory have disappeared, and they aim instead at a protracted war." The estimate could not have been more wrong. Ho considered that a massive blow would send the Americans reeling and lead to their withdrawal. Although many people – after the fact – claimed that they knew something was coming, the

GUNSHIPS

Few combat concepts introduced during the Vietnam war aroused such excitement and interest as the aerial gunships. Based initially on the venerable Douglas C-47, the concept involved an aircraft flying a left-hand orbit, its guns mounted in the port side of the fuselage firing on to a steady point at the centre of the orbit. The introduction of the Lockheed Hercules and ever more sophisticated weapons allowed the gunship to operate in the night interdiction mission, hunting trucks as they brought guns and ammunition to South Vietnam.

"Spooky 71 had been airborne for 4½ hours when word came of enemy action around Bien Hoa. As the Gooney Bird wheeled back towards home, the crew saw muzzle flashes from the perimeter of Long Binh below. The Viet Cong were busy, here also. The gunship orbited around the muzzle flashes. In two lightning quick attacks with mini-guns chattering, Spooky 71 slammed 3,000 rounds into the enemy's positions"

Below: A long time exposure records the orbiting of a Fairchild AC-119 over South Vietnam, with bursts of fire showing red. The destructive power of the gunships is difficult to imagine.

Left: A Fairchild AC-119 cruises over South Vietnam in daylight. All armament was carried on the port side.

Below: A Lockheed AC-130A featuring the 'Surprise Package' 40-mm cannon armament in the rear fuselage in addition to the two 7.62 mm machine guns and two 20-mm rotary cannon.

Above: An AC-130A lets fly with its 40-mm Bofors cannon. Aimed from a left-hand orbit, the cannon was particularly effective against vehicles moving along the Ho Chi Minh Trail.

Right: Under the 'Credible Chase' programme, the Fairchild AU-23 (illustrated) and Helio AU-24 were evaluated as mini-gunships, carrying a three-barrel gun in the cabin.

Below: Fairchild AC-119 'The Super Sow' shows the typical camouflage applied to gunships, with tactical upper surfaces and black below.

Below: One of a Douglas AC-47's SUU-11 7.62 mm six-barrel machine gun pods spews lead at a VC target. Cartridges were ejected into the cabin, and shovelled away by an airman.

Above: A close-up of an AC-130 reveals the open door for the night observation sight, the turret in the wheel fairing for the infra-red sensor, and the large radome for the 'Black Crow' sensor, which detected trucks.

Below: First and best-loved of the gunships was the Douglas AC-47, known as 'Puff the Magic Dragon' or 'Spooky'. Armament consisted of three SUU-11 machine gun pods aimed visually.

official position never hinted at an offensive of the magnitude of Tet.

Further complications arose from the compromises which went into the making of the SNIE. The document was a product of the inputs of MACV, CIA, DIA, etc., each of which had a different point of view. General Westmoreland, under political pressure to produce statistics which backed up his position that the US was winning the war, issued instructions to eliminate Viet Cong Militia from the order of battle estimates. This effectively lowered the enemy troop figures by up to 130,000 – using the rationale that these units were not offensive military forces. In reality, they would play a major part in tactics of the Tet Offensive by being the "in place" force. With the reluctant acceptance of the CIA, the SNIE allowed for 118,000 NVA and hard-core VC; 70,000 to 90,000 VC guerrillas; and 35,000 to 40,000 administrative support personnel, for a grand total (high estimate) of 248,000 enemy. The real total was somewhere closer to 463,000. Along with the elimination of the VC Militia, MACV had consistently underestimated NVA infiltration to the south. During 1967, MACV "top end" estimates of infiltration averaged 4,400 per month up through August, rising to between 5,000 and 8,000 per month thereafter. In fact, NVA infiltration was on the order of 25,000 per month for the five months prior to Tet. This alone would have been sufficient to produce an error of at least 85,000. Aside from the personnel numbers, there were significant unit discrepancies. The official estimate held 9 enemy division headquarters priot to Tet, with a total of 37 divisional and non-divisional regiments, or 202 divisional and non-divisional battalions. By the time the offensive jumped off Communist forces deployed 10 division headquarters in South Vietnam and a total of 52 regiments or 274 battalions.

Communist plans

From mid-1967 the Communist plan began to take shape, with the initiation of the border battles and a general reorganization of combat assault element. Regiments were task organized into regimental-size groups, including three infantry battalions, one sapper and one artillery battalion, and eight or nine special-mission companies. Massive casualties during 1967 forced the Communists to lower their standards in order to pump up units for the offensive. While the hard-core cadre leaders were tough and experienced, many of their new soldiers were youngsters who lacked training, experience and enthusiasm. To make matters worse, Viet Cong recruitment had fallen off from an average of 7,500 men per month in 1966 to 3,500 per month in 1967. Not only were 75% of the Communist regiments regular NVA, but 16,000 North Vietnamese soldiers were serving in regiments which were nominally Viet Cong.

ARVN strength

Prior to Tet, the ARVN consisted of 120 infantry, 20 ranger, 9 airborne, and 6 marine battalions. These each had an authorized strength of 650 to 700 men which allowed them to actually field about 400 to 450 men. Up to 50% of each battalion was granted leave for the Tet holiday, meaning that most ARVN battalions had about 200 men present for duty when the offensive struck. In a few units, commanders anticipated trouble and kept their men on duty. American units remained fully manned, but scaled back operations in observance of the traditional Tet cease-fire. In a fortunate turn of events, the general commanding II Field Force (Frederick Weyand) confided misgivings about the security of the capital to Westmoreland, who authorized the redeployment of a number of battalions from outlying areas to the Saigon vicinity. This factor weighed heavily in the promptness of the US response to the assault on Saigon.

The Tet holiday, the lunar new year for the "Year of the Monkey", began on the 30th of January, 1968. The Communist offensive kicked off at 0300 hours on the 31st, but things began to go wrong from the start. In an effort to preserve the security of the oper-

NAVY BOMBERS

The majority of aircraft within a carrier's air wing were attack types, and these were used to dramatic effect against targets in North Vietnam. Tactics ranged from highly organised mass raids (Alpha Strikes) to lone sorties against a single target. The aircraft used spanned a technology gap from the end of the war until the 1980s, beginning with the aged prop-driven Douglas Skyraider and culminating with the Grumman A-6 Intruder, still one of the few aircraft capable of true all-weather pinpoint bombing.

Above: The most potent attack platform used by the Navy was the Grumman A-6 Intruder. After problems with the nav-attack system had been overcome, the type proved excellent in the blind attack role, operating in foul weather with precision.

Above: Aircraft on* Kitty Hawk *and* Constellation *adopted experimental dark tactical camouflage schemes during 1966.

***Above: The first specialist tankers used by the Navy were hastily modified Douglas A-3B Skywarriors. This is an A-3B with fuselage drogue fairing of VAH-4 Det. 62 on* Independence.**

Left: As if battling with MiGs, SAMs and guns weren't enough, Navy pilots had to face the dangers of carrier landings. This Douglas A-4 pilot had a brake failure on landing, and had to eject as his aircraft fell over the side of USS Shangri-La.

Right: One can feel the deck shaking as bomb- and rocket-laden Douglas Skyraiders prepare to launch on an attack mission. Despite looking somewhat out of place next to the sleek jets on the carrier deck, the Skyraider was an excellent attack platform, with long endurance, heavy weapons load and the ability to absorb much more punishment than the sophisticated and delicate jets.

Above: Anti-radiation missions with Shrike missiles were handled by A-4s and Vought A-7 Corsair IIs (illustrated).

Right: A full salvo of unguided rockets is launched at VC positions. Navy Air Wings worked up against targets in the South before moving up North.

"In the last two months, my heart has pumped more adrenalin than it ever has before. You always get butterflies. This sort of thing never becomes routine"

For many years the prime heavy attack aircraft for the US Navy, the Douglas A-1 Skyraider continued its long career in Vietnam, where it served with distinction until replaced aboard the carriers by the Grumman A-6 Intruder. One of its great achievements was in downing two MiG-17s, one in June 1965 and the other in October 1966. After withdrawing from Navy use in 1969, the Skyraider continued its illustrious war career with USAF and VNAF units. This is an A-1H of VA-52, shown in the colours of the CAG (commander, Air Group).

ation, instructions from Hanoi regarding the starting date were sent out at the last minute and did not reach many commands on time. The resulting lack of coordination caused a few units to jump off a day early, and many to begin their attacks days later. Thus, the surprise and shock of a simultaneous blow was denied to the Communists.

The time was 0315, 31 January. The tower operator at Tan Son Nhut heliport, Mr. Richard O. Stark, had just received a call from an aircraft requesting to know if the field was secure. He replied in the affirmative. At 0325 the aircraft called again saying he had reports of enemy contacts in the area. Mr. Stark recalls, "I noticed sporadic tracer fire northwest of the helicopter tower, but I was not duly alarmed. Minutes later, when a C-47 departed from Tan Son Nhut and drew heavy ground fire, I realized that this was not nervous guards, but actual enemy contact." Tan Son Nhut Air Base was under attack!

This attack was one of many similar attacks which were launched against military installations and population centers throughout the Republic of Vietnam. These attacks marked an all-out Communist offensive that continued throughout the *Tet* holidays.

Within three minutes after the alert at Tan Son

Air Force security police move out to the perimeter of Tan Son Nhut in response to a Viet Cong attack on the air base during Tet.

Nhut, two "Razorback" fire teams consisting of four armed helicopters from the 120th Assault Helicopter Company were airborne and attacking the enemy. Major Ronald K. Kollhoff, commander of the 4th Gunship Platoon from this company, said, "The extent of the enemy buildup was surprising. When it first started we expected a small token diversionary force – a suicide squad – to divert attention from an expected mortar attack. But after a while it became evident that the VC wanted to actually take Tan Son Nhut very badly."

Major General Robert R. Williams, Commanding General, 1st Aviation Brigade, and his house guest, Colonel E. Pearce Fleming, Jr., were sleeping in the Long Binh BOQ when the alert sounded there. Within three minutes they were in a command Huey checking into the 12th Combat Aviation Group control net. There were ground attacks taking place in several areas of the Long Binh-Bien Hoa perimeter and a number of gunships were already airborne and were being directed to targets. Colonel Fleming reported, "I was impressed with the professionalism of all hands that I observed and heard during this period of the *Tet* offensive. The calmness and the voices of the men on the radio made you think they were merely calling for landing instructions at a peaceful U.S. airfield, and yet they were continuously in action for hours on end. When the sun finally came up on the morning of 31 January, I was surprised to find that the VC were continuing to stay and fight." (9)

The offensive employed a total of 323,000 Communist troops, with an initial assault wave of 70,000 men in 97 battalions: 35 against I Corps Zone, 28 in II Corps, 15 in III Corps, and 19 in IV Corps. The units which had infiltrated cities prior to the offensive caused initial problems but were not strong

TET OFFENSIVE

Saigon in the 1960s. You could still recognize the elegant French colonial city known as the 'Pearl of the Orient'. The shadowy world of Graham Greene might be found in the older bars, complete with dubious Europeans in linen suits making deals in hushed voices. Outside, the streets were alive, because Saigon was the great market place where anything could be bought and sold. Most of all, you were impressed, or terrified, by the traffic. Every hour was rush hour, traffic lights were just signals to start the race for the next junction. Yet you recognized a phenomenal nervous tension, because for most of the War Saigon was also a battlefield.

Above: 199th Light Infantry at Phu Tho racetrack, Cholon, a fiercely defended VC command post and field hospital.

Below: Vietnamese villagers picking through the burned-out wreckage of their homes after a Viet Cong rocket attack.

> **During late December 1967 and January 1968, Hanoi filtered troops and supplies into forward positions in the south. The initial assaults, employing about 84,000 Viet Cong and NVA troops, were mounted against 42 cities and provincial capitals, 64 district capitals, and 50 hamlets**

Below: ARVN troops return fire. At Tet 1968, ARVN responses were often heroic despite operating mostly at half strength.

Above: An M48 tank rumbles through Cholon. This Chinese suburb of Saigon was all but destroyed in the Tet battles.

enough to hold the way open for the units attacking from the outside. The "general uprising" simply did not happen and, in fact, the revelation of atrocities such as the massacres at Hué served to unite the South Vietnamese people in their opposition to the Communists.

Command and control problems plagued the NVA, which lost all communications with its Saigon front shortly after the attack started. Communist units in Saigon also failed to maintain liaison, resulting in disorder. For example, the two companies involved in the bitter fighting at the Phu Tho Race Track were there by mistake, having gotten lost on the way to their objective. The attack at Hué, initially successful, simply became prolonged agony for the NVA and VC. Their defense positions were weak, they lost direction during street fighting, their deployments were slow, as were their use of reserves, and they failed to concentrate their units because of the threat of air strikes. Elsewhere in the

Cholon, outside Saigon. Rubble litters the street after fierce house-to-house fighting between the ARVN and the Viet Cong.

country, the attacks followed a similar pattern. The assault forces generally failed to carry key positions within the cities they entered, often due to a lack of a heavy and responsive reserve to maintain the initiative. Communist troops attempted to force a continuous day/night battle and burned themselves out through fatigue. Many were demoralized when confronted with US or ARVN counterattacks.

Far from folding, as the Communists expected, the ARVN rose to the occaion and generally performed creditably during Tet. Some elements of the ARVN 45th Regiment were reported to have gone over to the enemy in the vicinity of Ban Me Thuot, and various VC sympathizers in Saigon headquarters units deserted as well. Most of the time, the available local leadership determined the performance of the ARVN. IV Corps turned in the most disappointing performance, which is not surprising. ARVN units in Chau Doc Province completely relaxed their defenses for the Tet Holiday.

At the lower levels, ARVN reactions varied from brave and stubborn resistance to calling in artillery on populated areas. After the initial assaults were repulsed the general tone of ARVN operations lacked aggressiveness, especially in IV Corps. Many units, already suffering from high leave and absence rates for Tet, took many casualties as well. The general morale of the ARVN was no better than fair to good except in a few elite units. Civilian support for the ARVN varied with the conduct of the troops. Many areas were very grateful for ARVN liberation or protection, while others blamed the ARVN for lack of security, looting, and destruction of property.

Communist disaster

Militarily, the Tet Offensive was a disaster for the Communists. With initial losses of 45,000 dead and large numbers of heavy weapons lost, rebuilding

TET-SAIGON

The violent outbursts which raced through South Vietnam in the Vietnamese New Year of 1968 did more to influence the end of the war than almost any other action. Militarily, it was a disaster for the Viet Cong, with many of their most committed cadres suffering crippling losses (more than 70% in some cases). In spite of an almost total American and South Vietnamese victory, the media zeroed in on incidents such as the raid on the US Embassy in Saigon, and presented Tet as a communist success. This provided fuel for the anti-war movement back home.

Above: The Viet Cong attack in Saigon, January 30 1968. The VC's Tet (Vietnamese New Year) Offensive was intended to trigger a mass anti-government uprising. It failed dismally.

Below: Member of ARVN 38 Ranger Bn pours fire at VC in a building near St Francis Church, Cholon, a Saigon suburb.

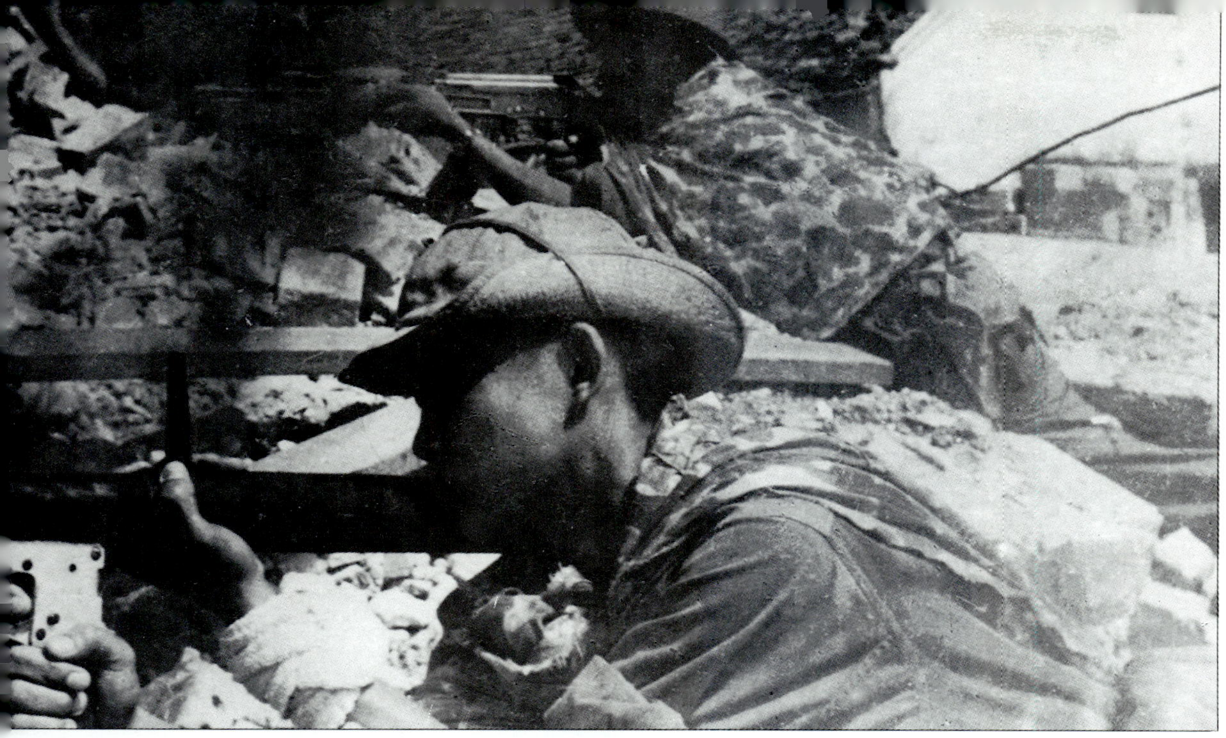

Below: Members of 38 Bn ARVN Airborne Division come under Viet Cong sniper fire in the village of Tan Son Nhut.

Above: ARVN Rangers in Cholon return Viet Cong fire from behind barriers set up days previously by the VC.

Above: A pushcart becomes a crude ambulance for the body of an RVN Marine killed in Saigon, May 1968. Surrounded by VC enclaves, the capital was under attack for months after Tet.

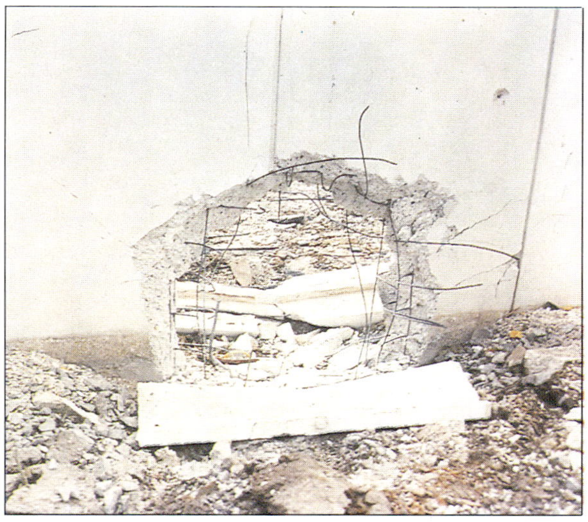

Above: Through this hole, 19 VC entered the grounds of the US Embassy in Saigon. The audacious attack helped fuel the popular impression that Tet was a communist victory.

Above: One of the VC shot dead in the US Embassy grounds, January 31 1968. Contrary to media reports at the time, none of the VC sappers succeeded in entering the embassy chancery.

“Into Saigon slipped more than 3,000 communist fighters armed with weapons ranging up to machine-gun and anti-tank rocket size. They tackled Tan Son Nhut airstrip and the adjoining MACV compound . . . getting close enough to put bullets through Westy’s windows. Other communist units raced through the city attacking US targets”

would take many months. Worse, the inplace Viet Cong political and military cadres were fully exposed due to the tactics of the offensive, and subsequently ruthlessly exterminated by the South Vietnamese. This VC infrastructure would be much harder to replace, making any return to "protracted war" a difficult proposition. In general, the Viet Cong bore the brunt of the casualties of Tet, and would never again be a major factor in the NVA conquest of South Vietnam. To a degree, this may have been shrewdly calculated by Hanoi in advance. Ho had always envisioned the reunification of Vietnam under under Northern leadership, and by eliminating the substance of the Viet Cong he could minimize any messy post-war accommodation with southern Communists.

Results of Tet

Although the South won Tet on the battlefield and proved that its army and people could take it, the ARVN lost about three percent of its strength in less than two weeks. Worse, Giap had been right about the American public's reaction to the offensive. A military loss had turned into a psychological victory for the Communists. The administration's pre-Tet assurances that the US was winning the war seemed to lose all credibility in the light of the furious offensive. Played to the hilt by the media, Tet *apeared* to be a tremendous setback for American arms.

The most daring attack of the week – and certainly one of the most embarrassing – occurred when 19 Viet Cong commandos of the C-10 Sapper Battalion made the U.S. embassy their target. When Ambassador Ellsworth Bunker opened the white reinforced-concrete complex last September, few American missions ever settled into more seemingly impregnable quarters. Looming behind a 10-ft.-high wall, the six-story symbol of U.S. power and prestige is encased in a massive concrete sunscreen that overlaps shatterproof Plexiglas windows. The $2.6 million building contains such an array of fortresslike features that Saigon wags soon dubbed it "Bunker's Bunker." Yet the Viet Cong attackers gained access to the embassy compound and rampaged through it for 6½ hours before all were killed and the embassy was once again secure.

At 3:03 a.m., supporting VC troops positioned around the embassy began lobbing mortar fire onto the grounds. The 19 commandos appeared, wearing civilian clothes (with identifying red armbands) and carrying automatic weapons, rockets and enough high explosives to demolish the building. Attacking simultaneously, some of the guerrillas blasted a hole in the concrete wall with an antitank gun and swarmed

SAIGON AT WAR

MACV made a political decision that the defence of the area around Saigon was to be left to the ARVN. As the celebrations of Tet Nguyen Dan (the Vietnamese lunar new year) approached the rumours of a major Viet Cong violation of the new year truce were discounted. As night fell on 31st January 1968, the sound of heavy weapons gradually emerged from the firework celebrations. The Tet offensive erupted all over the country, but in the Capital Command region there was fierce fighting at important bases such as Long Binh and Bien Hoa, with numerous regiment and battalion sized Viet Cong formations.

Above: Life goes on all around you: ignored by civilians, ARVN troops deploy against VC insurgents during Tet '68.

Below: Members of 9th Infantry mop up a shattered village just south of Saigon after the second battle of Tet.

"Saigon reminds me of Rabat and Casablanca . . . same architecture, odor, atmosphere. Could be called 'Scooter City'. Everyone has a pair of wheels and they ride in pairs . . . the girls ride sidesaddle in long slacks and split overskirts"

Below: Small sign of war: the US Combat Development and Test Center nestles in the midst of Saigon.

through it; others quickly scaled a rear fence. Though allied intelligence had predicted the attack, the embassy's defense consisted of only five U.S. military guards – just one more than normal. They fought back so fiercely that only their courage denied the enemy complete success. Sergeant Ronald W. Harper, 20, a Marine guard, managed to heave shut the embassy's massive teakwood front doors just seconds before the guerrillas battered at them with rockets and machine guns, thus denying the V.C. entry to the main building.

Unable to penetrate the main chancery, the V.C. commandos ran aimlessly through the compound, firing on everything they saw. Meanwhile, small groups of Marines and MPs began arriving outside the walls of the embattled embassy. The Viet Cong burst into the embassy's consular building and various other buildings in the compound, but the Americans on the scene threw such heavy fire at them that the guerrillas were kept too busy to set off their explosives.

Finally, just before 8 a.m., Pfc. Paul Healey, 20, led a counterattack through the front gate, personally killing five V.C. with grenades and his M-16 rifle. Minutes later, two paratroop platoons from the 101st Airborne Division at nearby Bien Hoa landed on the embassy's roof-helipad. Working their way down, they met no resistance. Though V.C. prisoners are usually turned over to the Saigon government, this time the troopers had orders to kill every V.C. in sight lest any had seen secret codes or plans in the embassy.

As the troopers advanced, a wounded guerrilla staggered into Mission Coordinator George Jacobson's white villa behind the embassy. When U.S. troops tried to flush him with tear gas, he started upstairs, spotted the 56-year-old retired Army colonel there, and fired three shots. The guerrilla missed, and Jacobson finished him off with a .45 that had quickly been tossed up to his second-floor window by troops below. That fearsome finale ended the 6½-hour battle. Five Americans lay dead, as did two Vietnamese chauffeurs for the embassy who were apparently caught in the crossfire. (10)

MPs from the 716th MP battalion peer across the pre-dawn street at the US Embassy, where a number of VC have penetrated the grounds.

In spite of the fact that South Vietnam and the US were in the best military position in years, and in good shape to exploit their battlefield success, Westmoreland's request for substantial troop reinforcements fell on deaf ears. The wave of the future would be US withdrawal – not US triumph. Hanoi's costly offensive had set in motion the events which would ensure its victory seven years later.

Above: Saigon was once known as the 'Pearl of the Orient', but by the 1960s it was afflicted by all the urban squalor imaginable. Exhaust fumes were everywhere, often generated by the hordes of small motorcycles which filled the streets. This is a typical intersection seen in 1968.

Left: A VC bomb rips apart a US military advisor's jeep parked in a Saigon street in 1964. Although such attacks were sporadic, no US personnel were safe from them – adding to the distrust among US troops towards the Vietnamese civilian population.

Right: M41 tanks support a column of ARVN troops in a search and clear operation in downtown Saigon during the Tet Offensive, 1968, seemingly unaware of the potential threat from the motorscooter – an ideal form of transport for a VC grenadier.

CHAPTER SEVEN

HIGH WATER MARK

1969

USS New Jersey unleashes the might of her 16-inch armament in support of Marines near the DMZ. The battleship served on the gun-line in 1968 and 1969.

In January, Richard Nixon succeeded Lyndon Johnson as President of the United States. Nixon appointed Melvin Laird to the post of Secretary of Defense, with a mandate to "Vietnamize" the war in preparation for scaled-down US participation.

US withdrawal, however, was linked to the state of the war and the state of the Paris peace negotiations – the first substantive session of which was held five days after Nixon entered the White House. US public opinion was still widely divided about the war, as polls indicated in March. At that time nearly one-third of those polled favored a more vigorous prosecution of the war, while slightly over a quarter favored withdrawal. The remainder split fairly evenly between supporting existing policy and "no opinion". Sensing likely public reaction to post-Vietnam American involvement in Asia, Nixon enunciated a new foreign policy doctrine in July which allowed for the US nuclear umbrella to protect Asian allies from external nuclear threats, but left conventional defense and internal security out of American hands.

In the aftermath of the Tet Offensive, the South Vietnamese were able to recover a good bit of territory from the Communists, and claimed that about three-quarters of the population were relatively secure from Viet Cong depredation. North Vietnam suffered the loss of Ho Chi Minh in September. The death of the charismatic Communist leader did not weaken northern resolve, however. His place was quickly filled by a committee representing the various power bases in North Vietnam, including General Giap (representing the military), Le Duan (Communist Party Secretary) Pham Van Dong (the

IN THE BOONIES

To the grunt, the easy life in the rear echelons was almost as much of a dream as life 'back in the world'. Day after day of patrolling through mud or dust, in scorching heat or driving rain left the soldier very different from the man in crisp green fatigues who had stepped off the plane Tan Son Nhut. He got his mail regularly, and there were a surprising number of places where some genius had set up a cooler well stocked with beer. Nevertheless, a year in the boonies would be enough to knock the civilization out of anybody.

"Helicopters, missiles, fancy radios, electronic gadgets . . . Listen here Marine, this war is like all the other wars before it. Its about humping. No, not that kind. It's about humping through paddy fields, or jungle, or low brush. Its about hacking your way through with knives, or slogging through knee-deep muck. Whatever, it's the same kind of war the Romans fought 2,000 years ago."

A Cavalry Sky Trooper marks off the few remaining days he has left in the Boonies (and in Vietnam) on his 'Short Time' helmet.

Above: The joys of C-rations. Grunts in Vietnam rarely went hungry, but you could grow weary of ham and lima beans.

In January 1969 Richard M. Nixon succeeded Lyndon Johnson with a mandate to scale down US participation in the war.

Premier), and Truong Chin (National Assembly Chairman). Their determination to pursue the war to a successful conclusion proved no less than that of Uncle Ho.

Sept. 4 – Neither joy nor sadness was evident in Tu Do Street today as dirty, barefoot boys hawked newspapers with headlines proclaiming Ho Chi Minh's death.

On the sidewalks limbless beggars, whispering black-market money changers and prostitutes conducted business as usual. Hundreds of motorbikes filled the streets with an endless buzz and fumes.

Students and taxi drivers shrugged indifferently when told that the most famous Vietnamese of their century was dead.

"The younger generation here doesn't care," said Tran Van Tuyen, a Saigon lawyer who served under Mr. Ho in the nineteen-forties.

"It is the younger generation in North Vietnam to be concerned about. They are more militant and extremist than the old leaders. Many of them have been trained in Communst China, and if they gain control they might fight the war to the end."

Above: Food and ammo fly in to the 1st Air Cav at Phuoc Bien, 1970. Unwanted American trash was recycled by the Vietnamese for various uses.

Above: Three Marines take an impromptu shower from their steel pots. Heat and humidity were exhausting in the boonies and a march lasting less than two hours 'back in the world' might take a day of backbreaking effort in Vietnam.

Above: A Pfc of the 1st Air Cav pauses to read a letter en route to an LZ. Mail was flown to patrols on a regular basis.

Above: Some walk, some ride, some wade. Even with an M-551 for transport, no journey in the bush was entirely simple.

At the old French opera house where the lower house of the National Assembly meets, many representatives acknowledged that President Ho's death was important but went no further. There were a few cynical comments.

A 'Truce' Is Proposed

Representative Ho Hu Tuong called for a truce while the Saigon Government sent a delegation to attend the funeral. "I would offer to head that delegation," he said.

"Let's have a toast to the death of Ho Chi Minh!" Another legislator shouted out at a cocktail party. His friends laughed.

President Nguyen Van Thieu, using the occasion for propaganda purposes, said that Mr. Ho's death would cause internal strife, instability and confusion in North Vietnam and would be "another blow to the already low morale of the Communist cadres and troops in North and South Vietnam alike."

In a communique, he added: "What is important for us is whether or not the Communist ruling clique in the North would still be the instrument of the Russians and the Red Chinese and continue their invasion of South Vietnam."

The most acid comment came from Vice President Nguyen Cao Ky, a Northerner, who said North Vietnam was now "like a snake without a head."

Ho Chi Minh led the Vietnamese Communist Party from before the Second World War until his death in September 1969.

Among older students of history there was a timid expression of both sadness and worry.

In a front-page editorial, The Vietnam Guardian, an English-language newspaper, said:

"With President Ho's death, a legendary, almost mythological figure disappears from the international political scene. Either one adores him or loathes him; no true Vietnamese can remain indifferent to his death for, to all of us, his life and actions have played an important role which was an integral part of our life."(1)

Half a million Americans

In April of 1969, US armed forces strength in Vietnam peaked at 543,400, of which some 360,500 were soldiers and 81,500 were marines. In June however, President Nixon announced the first troop withdrawals. July and August saw the 9th Infantry Division begin to phase down with the departure of its 1st Brigade and 2nd (Riverine) Brigade, and the Navy's turnover of Task Force 117 assets to the South Vietnamese. In I Corps, the 3rd Marine Division closed out its operations, withdrawing the 9th, 3rd and 4th Marines in August, September and November respectively, along with the helicopters of MAG 36. Other US withdrawals included 41st and 54th Artil-

THE UBIQUITOUS UH-1 'HUEY'

Despite the massive amount of tactical airpower brought to bear in Southeast Asia, it is best remembered as a helicopter war, and the abiding image is the unmistakeable outline of the Bell UH-1. Known universally as the Huey, this superb machine was used primarily for airmobile assaults. Many other roles were performed by the type, including gunship, river patrol, spraying, psychological warfare, cargo transport and liaison. It saw action with all four services.

Above: A heavily-armed UH-1 waits on a jungle clearing while a troop-carrying helicopter lands behind. Both are wearing the markings of the Royal Australian Air Force, which flew alongside the US Army on operations in South Vietnam.

Right: The Navy used the Huey as a gunship in the Mekong delta region on riverine patrol duties. Seen from behind the pilot, this Huey pops white phosphorus smoke markers into the jungle.

Left: Troops run from their Huey as another falls in behind. The LZ is obviously safe, as the pintle-mounted door guns are not manned.

Right: This UH-1B is typical of early Hueys, although bearing an unusual camouflage rather than the ubiquitous olive drab. It is seen in the markings of 'A' Company, 1st Aviation Battalion, 1st Infantry Division, and proudly wearing its 'Big One' insignia on the fin.

lery Groups in November, and the 3rd Brigade of the 82nd Airborne Division in December.

Morale problems

As the announced policy of US forces changed from combat to support for Vietnamization, a new feeling swept through the troops in Vietnam – no one wanted to be the last soldier killed there. Combat refusals, fraggings, and drug abuse started to increase, as did racial incidents. The continued lowering of standards did not help matters. The draft was decidedly rigged to provide exemptions for middle and upper class college students while sweeping in working class and minority youth. The inclusion of substandard category draftees and men who had the choice of going to the Army or to jail, insured a low order of ability in the field. Even the officer selection slipped, with the commissioning of more Officer Candidate School graduates from the ranks, in place of college graduates from the Reserve Officer Training Corps. As opposed to countries where the elite are expected to serve, the American upper crust was content to let someone else do the fighting. Unlike the First World War, there was never any danger of America losing its intelligentsia on the battlefields of Vietnam.

Wednesday, Aug. 27 – The company commander whose men refused to go into battle Sunday has been relieved of his job and is being transferred to a new post, his battalion commanders said today.

The commander of Company A, Lieut. Eugene Shurtz Jr., will be given a new assignment with the 196th Brigade of the Americal Division.

The battalion commander, Lieut. Col. Robert C. Bacon, said in a telephone interview from the battalion base camp south of Danang that he went out into the field Monday morning to relieve Lieut. Shurtz.

Company A at first refused to move again down the jungled rocky slopes of Nuilon Mountain into a labyrinth of North Vietnamese bunkers and trench lines after having made the same push and being driven back five consecutive days.

Lieutenant Shurtz reported to Colonel Bacon: "I am sorry sir, but my men refused to go – we cannot move out."

But after persuasion by Colonel Bacon, his executive officer, Maj. Richard Waite, and Sgt. Okey Blankenship, the company finally moved out.

A spokesman for the Americal Division and Colonel Bacon said that to their knowledge no charges were pending against anyone and no formal investigation was being conducted.

"The matter was not being further pursued," the spokesman said. "The men are still in the company and the company is still in the field." (2)

A sign of the decreasing US commitment which was visible at home came in September, when President Nixon cancelled draft call-ups for November and December of 32,000 and 18,000 men respectively. In an effort to apply some randomness to the inequitable draft system, the administration began the "draft lottery" at the end of the year – providing for call-up based on the luck of the draw according to birth dates for those unfortunate enough to be in a draftable category. In the mean time the government continued to search for alternatives to conscription.

ARVN increase

The Royal Thai Expeditionary Division was reinforced by its 2nd Brigade in January and its 3rd Brigade in July. In effect, the 3rd Brigade simply replaced the 1st Brigade, which rotated home to Thailand. The South Vietnamese began to consolidate some of their armored vehicle assets into corps-subordinated brigades, and increased their armed forces manpower by 150,000 during the year, to a total of over one million in all categories. Casualties from the Tet Offensive left the Communists short

"We ran head-on into about 350 men against our 30. Then those beautiful Hueys came in and circled the area. I threw up a pocket flare, we pulled back and he moved in. He was right on target, placing rockets right in the middle of Charlie. The next morning, if I had met that pilot, I'd have kissed him"

Above: The cabin of the UH-1D/H carried ten troops, with two flight crew. The crew chief and other maintenance personnel were carried to man the M60 7.62-mm door guns.

Right: When the Army moved, it moved everything, and in Vietnam that usually meant cramming men, materiel and pets into a Huey.

On heliborne assaults into the jungle, Hueys could often not set down in the difficult terrain. Hovering over the vegetation, troops had to leap the last few feet.

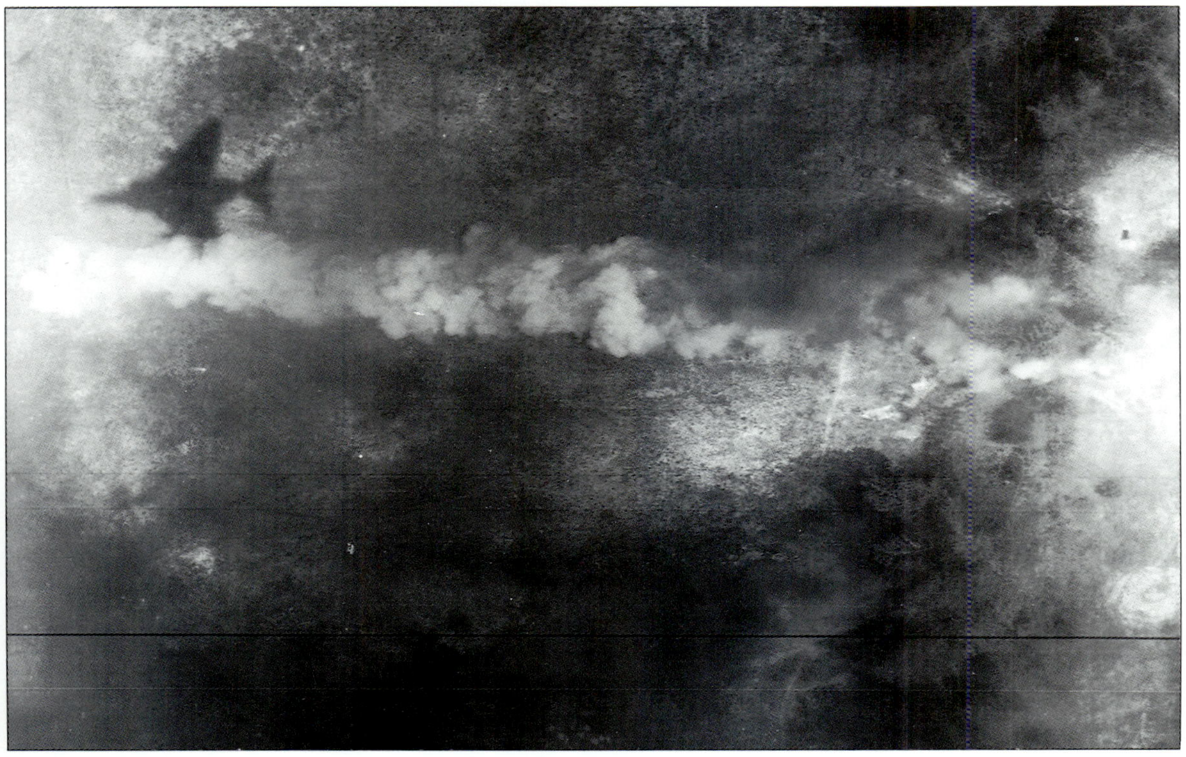

handed during the year, with about 240,000 men in the field in South Vietnam.

US operations in I Corps opened with a two month effort by the 9th Marines beginning in mid-January, called Operation Dewey Canyon. The Marines struck deep into the A Shau Valley and inflicted 1,335 casualties on the NVA. The 9th returned in May for another one-month crack at the A Shau, along with units of the 101st Airborne Division in Operation Apache Snow, netting 977 NVA casualties. This operation included the infamous battle of Hamburger Hill, (Hill 937, or Dong Ap Bia). The 101st's 3-187 Infantry (Airborne) was set down by helicopter into a North Vietnamese base area defended by the 29th NVA Regiment. Attempting to recon Hill 937, the 3-187th ran into fierce resistance and got hit by friendly helicopter gunships as well. Over 10 days and numerous enemy counterattacks, the battalion finally captured the hill against an opposition numbering perhaps 2,000 of the NVA's finest. Eventually most of the 101st's 3rd Brigade would be involved in the fight, cutting off the

Ground strafing to the south of the DMZ, an Air Force Phantom catches its own shadow ahead of the trail of destruction left by its 20-mm cannon.

enemy retreat route to Laos. As many as 1,500 NVA may have become casualties of some sort – the body count totaled 630. The 101st lost 56 dead and 420 wounded, most from the 3-187th. The scene of battle looked like something out of World War I, with stripped trees and muddy shell holes. The most unpalatable aspect of the action was that shortly after Hamburger Hill was taken it was abandoned and the troops redeployed elsewhere. Attrition had served its purpose.

Bad communications, misdirected artillery and confusion during the eight-day battle for Apbia Mountain in the Ashau Valley cost the American forces many of their early casualties, according to officers and men involved in the fighting.

Because of the heavy American losses on the exposed 3,074-foot mountain, it became known among the paratroops as Hamburger Hill. Controversy about the battle spread from Washington to military headquarters in Saigon after Senator Edward M. Kennedy of Massachusetts charged that the repeated assaults had been "senseless and irresponsible."

Military commanders maintained that the fight which began May 10 and lasted 10 days, had been necessary to inflict a toll on the enemy in the strategic Ashau Valley, which controls infiltration routes from Laos into South Vietnam.

The most frequent accidents involved rockets fired from heavily armed helicopters in support of ground troops. Officers say the rockets are fired at a rapid rate and sometimes bump each other in flight and so go off course.

The rockets went awry three times during the fight for the hill in the northern part of South Vietnam. On May 14 and 18, some of the rockets fell short of the enemy positions and struck the command area of the Third Battalion, 187th Infantry – a part of the 101st Airborne Division – which was commanded by Lieut. Col. Weldon F. Honeycutt. Colonel Honeycutt was slightly wounded both times.

One man was killed in the accident on May 14, and several were wounded.

The aerial rocket-fire also accidently struck members of an American unit assaulting the southern side of the hill on May 16.

On May 14, an artillery shell exploded amid the command group of one of the assaulting companies just as it reached the top of the hill for the first time. The shell wounded the company commander and his radio operator, and killed a sergeant. The accident blunted the United States drive and forced a retreat back down the hill. (3)

Troops from the 101st Airborne Division pass a truck mounted quad .50 cal machine gun. The 101st were heavily involved at Hamburger Hill.

Quang Nam Province saw the 7th and 26th Marines engaged in Operation Oklahoma Hills over a three month period beginning in March. The effort netted 596 enemy dead. Up in Quang Tri Province, the 3rd Marines initiated Idaho Canyon in late July, and eliminated another 565 NVA by the end of September. The 101st saw further action, in conjunction with the Americal Division, in Operation Lamar Plain in eastern Quang Tin Province. This three-month effort added another 524 enemy casualties between May and August. The 101st's last operation of the year was Randolph Glen on the end of the low-

DUST OFF

One of the most important tasks undertaken by the UH-1 was the evacuation of casualties from combat. The 57th Medical Detachment (Helicopter Ambulance) flew the first Hueys in Vietnam. In 1963, the unit adopted the call-sign 'Dust Off' and a legend was born. One of the 57th's early commanders was Major Charles L. Kelly, who before being killed in action set a standard for courage and coolness under fire that was to be an example to pilots for the rest of the war. It was not long before 'Dust Off' became a general term for all front-line medical evacuation helicopters.

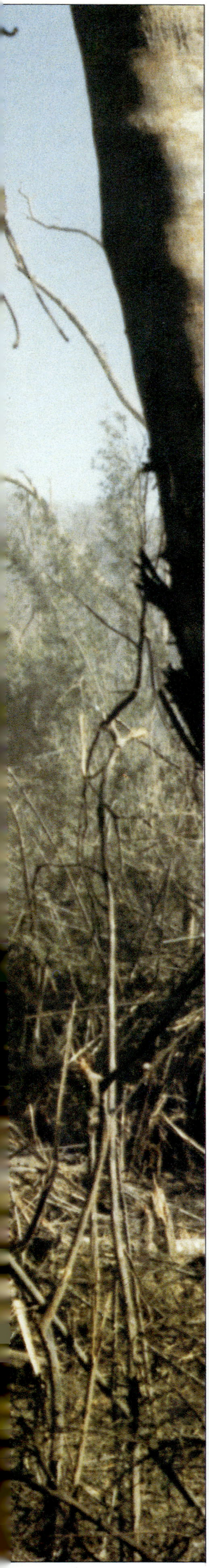

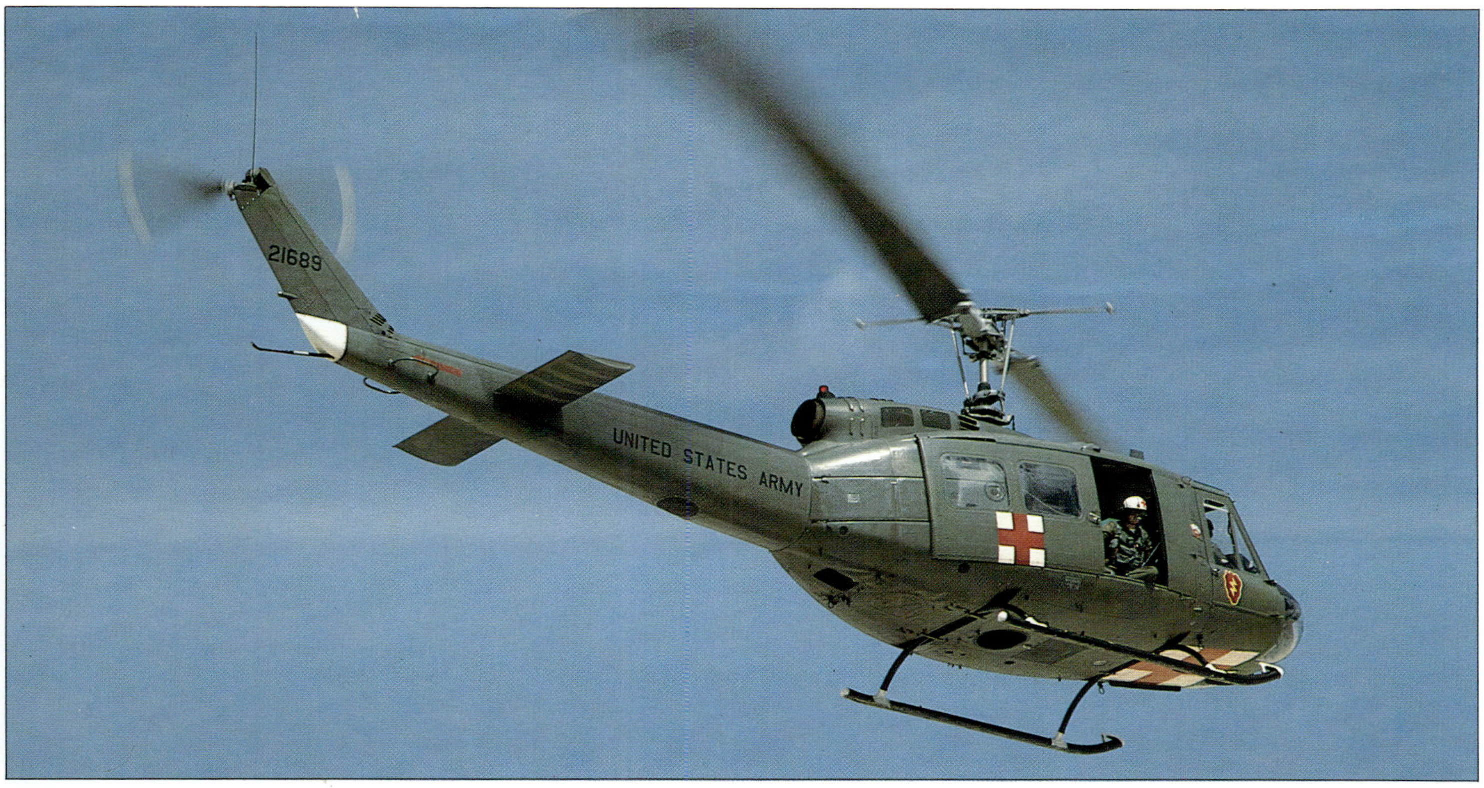

Left: *A small clearing near the* ***DMZ*** *in 1969. A* ***Dust Off*** *helicopter lands in the restricted space where casualties from the* ***101st Airborne Division*** *are waiting.*

Above: Dust Off *helicopters were marked with red crosses, although that did not stop the* ***Viet Cong*** *firing on them. Missions were dangerous, and losses were high.*

> ***The chopper leapt into the air. The wounded ARVN slipped off the ship, but Horvath kept hold and pulled him back in, falling to the floor and cutting his neck in the process***

Below: *Ambulance missions were perilous: the loss rate was almost twice as high as regular combat helicopter missions. Nevertheless the pilots kept on flying.*

Right: *The use of Air Ambulances in Vietnam contributed to the high percentage of combat wounded who reached hospital in time for their lives to be saved.*

lands of Thua Thien Province. The operation started in early December and lasted until the end of March, 1970, causing 670 NVA and VC fatalities.

The South Vietnamese had a busy year in I Corps, with the ARVN 2nd Division kicking off Operation Quyet Thang 22 in late February. This two-week push in Quang Ngai reported a body count of 777. The division's 4th Regiment kept up the pressure in late March with Quyet Thang 25, bagging another 592 NVA and VC. The regiment was active again from late August until the end of the year conducting Lien Ket 414, which eliminated 710 more Communist troops. The division's 5th Regiment undertook Lien Ket 531 at the same time, but moving north into Quang Tin Province. The operation reported an enemy body count of 542. To the north, in Quang Tri Province, the ARVN 1st Division's 2nd Regiment carried out Lam Son 277 from late April until late June, and claimed 541 Communist casualties. Elsewhere in I Corps, the ARVN 1st Ranger Group killed 688 NVA and VC in Quang Nam Province from the end of February to the end of June.

The American intent to disengage from the war meant that ARVNs like this sentry near Ban Me Thuot had to shoulder more responsibility.

The US 4th Infantry Division started operations in II Corps with Wayne Grey, an operation in Kontum Province during March and half of April, which eliminated 608 NVA. The division picked up again in late April with Putnam Tiger, extending operations south into Pleiku Province and netting another 563 Communist troops by the end of September. The 173rd Airborne Brigade's continuing operations in Binh Dinh Province, from mid-April 1969 until the end of 1970, went under the name of Washington Green. Primarily aimed at pacification in the An Lo Valley, the effort produced 1,957 enemy dead. South Vietnamese forces initiated several offensives in II Corps as well. The ARVN 22nd Division conducted Dan Thang 69 in Bin Dinh Province from late April until the end of the year, and reported 507 enemy dead. The division's 42nd Regiment and ARVN Rangers participated in Dan Quyen 38-A in Kontum Province from mid-May through early June, eliminating 945 NVA from the Dak To vicinity. The ARVN 23rd Division undertook two simultaneous two-month operations in southern II Corps' Quang Duc Province called Dan Tien 33-D and Dan Tien 40. Beginning in November, the push took out a total of 1,758 Communist troops.

ARMOR

Vietnam was not exactly ideal armor country. Jungles, mountains and swamps restrict a tank's mobility and allow enemy foot soldiers to get to close range, where manportable weapons such as rocket propelled grenades can do serious damage. Nevertheless, armored units made a significant contribution to the war, particularly when used for area and route security. It was not until US ground forces had withdrawn from the war that armor came into its own, when employed by the NVA in the 1972 invasion and ultimately in the 1975 conquest of South Vietnam.

***Above:** The most powerful armored vehicle used by the US Army in Vietnam was the M48 Main Battle Tank.*

***Above:** The major threat to tanks in Vietnam came from mines. The crew of this M48A3 tank waits for members of the 984th Land Clearing Company, 11th Cavalry to clear mines from the road ahead of its convoy in December 1969.*

***Below:** An M551 Sheridan from Troop A, 3rd Squadron, 4th Cavalry, 25th Infantry Division slogs through heavy mud while guarding the perimeter of landing zone 'Hampton'. The M551 had a complex 152mm gun/ missile system which caused many problems, but was gruesomely effective when firing canister shots against unprotected infantry.*

It was at Ben Het in March 1969 that American and North Vietnamese armor clashed for the first and only time.

Both Sergeant First Class Hugh H. Havermale and Staff Sergeant Jerry W. Jones of the 1st Bn., 69th Armor heard the sound of tracks and heavy engines through the noise of the artillery. With no free world tanks to the west, the probability of an enemy tank

> “Vietnam was strange. Contrary to tradition, armor was often used as a fixing force, while airmobile infantry made the encircling maneuvers. Armor by its nature had the protection and firepower to withstand mass ambush until supporting artillery, air and infantry assets could be brought to bear to destroy the enemy. Engagements with armored elements forcing or creating the fight and infantry reinforcing or encircling were typical of 1966 and 1967”

Above: Armed with a powerful 90-mm gun the M48 was a match for any vehicle it was likely to meet in Vietnam. This M48 from the 3rd Tank Battalion is seen operating near Dong Ma in 1967.

Left: The M551 Sheridan Armored Reconnaissance Vehicle was not a great success in Vietnam. It was prematurely deployed in 1969 when teething troubles and vulnerability to mines made it unpopular with its crews.

Right: The M42 Duster had no hostile aircraft to fire at in Vietnam. Used for perimeter defense and convoy escort the rapid firing 40mm guns proved very effective weapons.

Below: One of a long series of tanks starting from the M26 of World War II, the M48 entered service in the 1950s. On convoy duty, the inside of the turret grew very hot, and crews preferred to ride on top. Sandbags were added to provide some protection from small-arms fire.

attack sent everyone into action. High explosive antitank (HEAT) ammunition was loaded into tank guns and from battle stations all eyes strained into the darkness.

In his tank, Sergeant Havermale scanned the area with an infrared searchlight, but could not identify targets in the fog. Sergeant Jones, from his tank, could see the area from which the tanks sounds were coming but had no searchlight. Tension grew. Suddenly an antitank mine exploded 1,100 meters to the southwest, giving away the location of the enemy; the battle for Ben Het now began in earnest.

Although immobilized, the enemy PT76 tank that had hit the mine was still able to fight. Even before the echo of the explosion had died, the PT76 had fired a round that fell short of the defenders' position. The remainder of the enemy force opened fire, and seven other gun flashes could be seen. The U.S. forces returned the fire with HEAT ammunition from the tanks and fire from all other weapons as well. Specialist 4 Frank Hembree was the first American tank gunner to fire, and he remembers: "I only had his muzzle flashes to sight on, but I couldn't wait for a better target because his shells were landing real close to us." The muzzle flashes proved to be enough for Specialist Hembree; his second round turned the enemy tank into a fireball.

Captain Stovall called for illumination from the camp's mortar section and in the light of flares spotted another PT76. Unfortunately, the flares also gave the North Vietnamese tanks a clear view of the camp's defenses, and as Captain Stovall was climbing aboard Sergeant Havermale's tank, an enemy high explosive round hit the loader's hatch. The concussion blew Stovall and Havermale from the tank, and killed the driver and loader. Damage to the tank was slight.

Sergeant Jones took charge, dismounted, and ran to another tank which was not able to fire on the enemy main avenue of approach. Still under hostile fire, he directed the tank to a new firing position where the crew quickly sighted a PT76 beside the now burning

Mainstay of US tank units was the M48, which was a match for any NVA tank it was likely to meet.

hulk of the first enemy tank. The gunner, Specialist 4 Eddie Davis, took aim on one of the flashes and fired. "I wasn't sure of the target," Specialist Davis said, "But I was glad to see it explode a second later." Every weapon that could be brought to bear on the enemy was firing. Having exhausted their basic load of high explosive antitank ammunition, the tank crews were now firing high explosives with concrete-piercing fuzes. Gradually, the enemy fire slackened, and it became clear that an infantry assault was not imminent. In the lull, the crews scrambled to replenish their basic load from the ammunition stored in a ditch behind the tanks. Tank rounds were fired at suspected enemy locations but there was no return fire. The remainder of the night was quiet; the tension of battle subsided, and the wounded were evacuated.

Intelligence later revealed that the main object of the attack on Ben Het was to destroy the U.S. 175-mm guns. Whatever the enemy's intention, the camp was held by American tanks against North Vietnamese tanks. Not until March 1971, when South Vietnamese M41 tanks battled North Vietnamese tanks in Laos, would tanks clash again. (4)

REAR ECHELON LIFE

Millions of Americans served in Vietnam during the war, yet the nearest many of them came to combat was the stories in the news magazines from the PX. On the larger bases, living in air-conditioned splendour, young Americans led lives not much different to that they would have been leading stateside (except that entertainment facilities in Vietnam were probably better than those in some of the more remote duty stations 'back in the world'). Even so, there was always the chance of Viet Cong rocket attacks, or even full scale assaults like those of Tet 1968.

Above: Actress and singer Connie Stevens whoops it up with the help of GIs in a 1969 morale-raising concert.

Left: Air traffic controllers at Can Tho. Though disparaged as REMFS (rear-echelon mother fuckers) by front-line grunts, such troops always risked attack or sabotage from the VC.

Below: REMFs in a habitual state of relaxation in Saigon, 1967. In some postings it was possible to remain virtually untouched by the war.

Above: While grunts sweated in the steaming jungle, REMFs sweated only during personal time, in air-conditioned custom-built gyms.

Left: Even the most protected areas could be booby trapped. This explosives specialist is dealing with a bomb on a popular recreation beach near Cam Ranh Bay.

Below: Anita Bryant belts it out at the Bob Hope Christmas Show in 1968. Hope was one of relatively few Hollywood stars to publicly support the war.

"As well as entertaining servicemen with time-tested coffee, doughnuts, ice-cream, milk shakes, singers, dancers, musicians and pretty girls, the USO is now employing video-tape and closed circuit TV to bring the World Series to Vietnam"

MARKET TIME

While the majority of equipment entering South Vietnam to aid the Viet Cong travelled along the Ho Chi Minh Trail, a fair amount was infiltrated by sea using junks. 'Market Time' was the codename of maritime patrol aircraft operating against these vessels around the coast of South Vietnam, and also covered the general patrol and anti-submarine surveillance carried out to protect the US Navy assets in the South China Sea and Tonkin Gulf. Further inshore, smaller aircraft patrolled the waterways of the Mekong delta to trap any boast that had slipped through the 'Market Time' net.

Above: Patrolling the coastline of South Vietnam is the Martin SP-5M Marlin of VP-40.

Right: A Lockheed SP-2H Neptune checks out a Vietnamese junk during 'Market Time' operations.

Action in III Corps

III Corps saw a lot of activity initiated by the NVA and VC beginning in February with post-Tet Offensive rocket and mortar attacks directed against Saigon and many other locations. The effort, mounted by the 5th and 9th Viet Cong Divisions (manned mainly by NVA since Tet 68), aimed at the disruption of US logistical operations. It failed to provide more than a temporary interruption of US supplies. The Royal Thai Army's Expeditionary Division (1st & 2nd Brigades) base camp at Bear Cat was assaulted by a battalion-size VC raiding force in mid-June. The attack was repulsed with a loss of half of the VC force and minimal casualties to the Thais. Most US actions in III Corps yielded little in the way of Communist casualties.

Operation Rice Farmer

In IV Corps, the US 9th Infantry Division's operations took the name Operation Rice Farmer, lasting from January through the end of August. In conjunction with ARVN troops, the division cleared 1,860 VC out of parts of the Delta. The ARVN year-long operation in IV Corps was known as Quyet Thang, and involved all three of the deployed ARVN Divisions (7th, 9th and 21st). A grand total of 37,874 enemy casualties were claimed for the operation. In a subsidiary operation, Quyet Thang 21/38, the ARVN 21st Division's 32nd Regiment eliminated 721 Viet Cong from An Xuyen Province.

In 1969, US casualties went down to the level of 1967 from the peak reached during 1968. Losses amounted to 9,414 killed in action, 2,113 non-combat deaths and 70,216 seriously wounded. ARVN losses were 21,833 killed, 923 missing (presumed dead) and 65,276 wounded. Other allies of South Vietnam lost 867 dead and missing, and 2,218 wounded. Communist dead numbered 156,954 – less than the disastrous year of Tet, but more than they would lose in 1972 with the Spring Offensive. Over the year US Army helicopter losses continued to increase, with 949 destroyed. Again half (465) were from operational causes and the remaining 484 due to combat – 435 to ground fire and 49 at base camps. Marine helicopter losses declined, with 71 being brought down in 1969. Of these, 29 were operational losses and 42 were victims of ground fire. Marine fixed-wing losses also went down, with 13 operational losses and 34 losses to ground fire for a total of 47.

***Left:* VAH-21 operated a secret gunship version of the Lockheed Neptune on night interdiction missions over the Mekong Delta. Forward-looking infra-red and low light level television helped the crew detect VC targets, which were attacked with gun pods or light stores.**

***Below:* All three types of Neptune used in Southeast Asia are pictured here at Cam Ranh Bay. In the foreground are two AP-2H interdiction aircraft, alongside them is a regular patrol squadron SP-2H and in the rear row are Army-operated RP-2E aircraft, used for battlefield signals intelligence, pinpointing enemy radars.**

***Left:* VAL-4 'Ponies' OV-10 Broncos cruise over the Mekong Delta armed with rocket pods and cluster bombs for attacking VC positions spotted in the delta.**

***Right:* Marlins flew on coastal patrols until 1967, looking for junks infiltrating materiel into South Vietnam, before Lockheed P-3 Orions took over the role.**

"Maybe not as glamorous as flying a fighter from a carrier, but maritime surveillance has always been an important part of Naval aviation. About the first Navy aircraft into the fray were the elderly SP-2Hs of Fleet Air Wings Eight and Ten. Operating out of Cam Ranh Bay these watched for infiltrating communist trawlers and junks, bringing supplies to the Viet Cong"

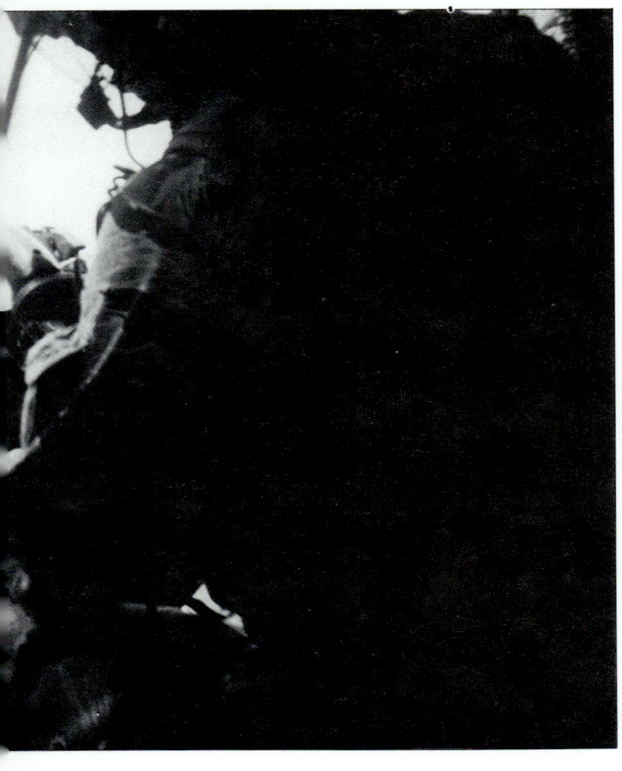

USAF rescue helicopters were kept busy aiding downed aircrew. Their UH-1s were armed with 7.62-mm mini-guns.

In March, President Nixon ordered USAF B-52s to commence a bombing program aimed at the disruption of NVA base areas in Cambodia. Called the Menu series of operations, the effort was carried out with the knowledge of Prince Sihanouk, then ruler of Cambodia, but kept secret from all but a handful of government and military leaders in the United States. The objective of the bombing campaign was to buy time for withdrawing US troops by destroying supplies needed by the NVA for offensive operations. The interdiction effort against the Ho Chi Minh Trail in Laos during 1969 increased by about 60% over 1968, as virtually all aircraft previously devoted to Rolling Thunder were directed at the Trail. The USAF's fixed-wing losses in 1969 totaled 269. Sixty-eight of these were due to operational causes and the remaining 201 were in combat (189 from ground fire and 12 from attacks on US bases).

By April 1969, all Ranch Hand planes had been converted to the jet-equipped UC-123K version. The extra power provided by the jets allowed Ranch Hand to fly some experimental spray runs at an airspeed of 180 knots, about 50 knots greater than the usual speed. This higher speed made the spray planes harder for gunners on the ground to hit, but it reduced the time available for the pilots to make flight path adjustments neccessitated by varying terrain and target shapes.

Ground fire was still a serious problem in early and mid-1969, as a mission on April 7 illustrated. On that date, a formation of seven Ranch Hand aircraft had planned to make three separate passes over their targets in the Delta. On the first pass, all but one were hit by .30- and .50-caliber machine gun fire. Two of the UC-123Ks lost an engine and proceeded at once to Bien Hoa. The five remaining aircraft received ground fire on the second pass, and the last plane in the formation lost effective aileron control as bullets penetrated its left wing and control surfaces. Like the crew of a UC-123 the previous December, the crew maintained limited directional control by using differential power settings on its left and right engines. After flying to the airstrip at Ben Tre for an emergency landing, the crew discovered a C-130 on the dirt runway which could not move clear in time for the damaged Ranch Hand plane to land. Unable to climb away from the field and return for another landing attempt, the crew chose to set the aircraft down in rice paddies 200 yards to the side of the runway. The crew escaped injury, but the UC-123K received extensive damage. In response to this incident, Seventh Air Force again restricted Ranch Hand's activities in IV Corps. (5)

Navy "Vietnamization" got under way early in 1969, when the River Patrol and Riverine forces began to turn over equipment to the South Vietnamese. Over 170 river craft of various types were given to the RVN Navy by the end of the year. Naval air losses declined over the year, with 61 fixed-wing "write-offs" – 45 operational crashes and only 16 combat losses, all to ground fire.

SPECIAL OPERATIONS

Special operations, in western parlance, were quite common to the Viet Cong and the North Vietnamese Army because of the very nature of the guerrilla-type war they waged. The Viet Cong specialized in urban and rural terrorism, assassinating an average of 4,500 South Vietnamese civilians a year and abducting an average of 7,000 more over the period 1966-72 alone. Planting bombs and conducting mortar attacks in or near US installations became a fairly regular occurrence during the war. Agents and VC sympathizers were present at all levels of military and government command in South Vietnam, making security a nightmare for US and ARVN forces.

The NVA and VC regular forces charged with special type operations were known as "sappers" – historically in western armies a type of combat engineer used for dangerous missions against enemy fortifications. Communist sapper units evolved an elite status through their reputation for skill, determination and high casualties in battle. Typical sapper missions involved infiltration of ARVN and US fire base defenses through stealth, raiding or preparatory to a major assault. Naval sappers would

In addition to their infiltration skills, Viet Cong sappers were masters of the booby trap. This sponge-bag bomb was found in a vehicle in Saigon.

make swimmer attacks on shipping with limpet mines or attack vessels from river banks with rockets. Due to the nature of their mission, most sapper elements operated in quite small units: squads, platoons and companies; but as they were elevated to an elite branch, sapper regiments (and even a division) were formed.

The Viet Cong Infrastructure (VCI) managed village intelligence networks which kept them informed of American and ARVN unit moves, strengths, and weapons positions. NVA radio reconnaissance units monitored US communications traffic for intelligence and deception purposes. US Army radio procedure was abysmal in Vietnam, with many units retaining the same call signs throughout their stay in country, broadcasting important information and locations in the "clear", and failing to authenticate "friendly" transmissions.

AIRBORNE SIGINT

One of the secret sides of the air war in Southeast Asia was the collection of electronic data. Performed by aircraft usually found patrolling the peripheries of the Soviet Union and China, this role of signals intelligence (Sigint) was vital to commanders plotting the military advances of the communist North. Eavesdropping on communications and analysing radars was the principal task for these spyplanes, a job they had performed since the early days of the Cold War.

Above: The most sophisticated Sigint type deployed to the war zone was the Boeing RC-135U 'Combat Sent', which arrived in the war zone in 1971. It could only spare a small amount of time in Southeast Asia due to its more important Soviet commitments, but in only a few hours could accomplish what had previously taken days of flying.

Below: The EP-3B Sigint version of the Lockheed P-3 Orion entered service with Fleet Reconnaissance Squadron One (VQ-1) in 1969, and began flying missions in the war zone from Japanese bases.

Above: Workhorse of the US Sigint effort was undoubtedly the Boeing RC-135M 'Combat Apple' which, during the middle part of the war, provided non-stop coverage of North Vietnam from its base at Kadena.

One of the best-loved and well-remembered Sigint types was the Douglas EA-3B Skywarrior. Serving with VQ-1, the EA-3B had the ability to operate from carrier decks, and was widely used from 'Yankee Station' during the war. Land-based operations usually took place from Da Nang, where this example is seen rolling out after landing. The venerable EA-3B is still in service after over thirty years in the Sigint role.

Above: Preceding the Boeing RC-135s in the theatre were various Sigint versions of the Boeing Stratojet. Above is an ERB-47H, of which only three were built, seen at Tan Son Nhut after a VC attack. Electronic surveillance Stratojets were used for general work, and for specific work with drones aimed at analysing the fuzing and guidance data for North Vietnamese SAMs, this latter under the program name 'United Effort'.

Above: Swooping on to the deck is another VQ-1 EA-3B Skywarrior, displaying to advantage the underfuselage canoe fairing and fin-top bullet fairing that distinguished the reconnaissance version. In addition to the three flight crew, four electronics operators sat facing rows of equipment in the fuselage cabin, illuminated by three side windows. Landing the EA-3B on a pitching deck was difficult, due to its narrow-track undercarriage.

"In those days, there wasn't much of interest in SE Asia. There'd be a handful of Chinese MiGs on Hainan, which we'd try to entice up. We'd punch out chaff, straying off course or broadcasting disparaging comments about Mao. No dice. We quickly learned to ignore the Vietnam area, because there was nothing happening, and likely nothing would happen. In fact the Gulf of Tonkin took on the new name Gulf of Tedium. We were hotshot Sigint operators, but we were sure lousy prophets"

During the late 1950s and 1960s, the EC-121K version of the Lockheed Constellation was the principal long-range electronic reconnaissance platform for the US Navy. Employed by VQ-1, these aircraft also flew the secondary task of weather reconnaissance, in particular hurricane warning. Often flying without unit markings, this example at Da Nang at least displays the name 'Miss Philippines', and its tailcode 'PR'. The latter gave rise to the famous callsign 'Peter Rabbit' for VQ-1's aircraft.

These lapses allowed the NVA to follow US units operations closely, and even employ imitative communications deception, for example, to call off US artillery fire at a critical moment.

Origins

The US Army's Special Forces originated in the early 1950s and made a home at Fort Bragg, North Carolina, site of the Special Warfare School. America has a rich history of special operations experience, dating back to the French and Indian Wars before the birth of the United States. The conglomeration of special units which existed in World War II disappeared, and interest in special forces only revived after Korea. Kept at a low strength, the Special Forces were generally only tolerated by the Army's higher command, whose members detested any units with pretentions to special or elite status. Army branch administrators discouraged officers who wanted to spend more than one tour in Special Forces on the basis that they would not be as valuable to their basic branch and thus be looked on unfavorably at promotion time. This mentality continued to exist up until the establishment of a separate Special Forces branch in 1987.

With the inauguration of John Kennedy as President, Special Forces became *chic* in government circles as the answer to Communist "wars of national liberation". Their original mission, organization of friendly guerrillas in enemy occupied countries, was subordinated to counterinsurgency and their numbers increased by several orders of magnitude. Deployed to South East Asia as part of what would become the 5th Special Forces Group, US "Green Berets" (a privilege granted by Kennedy) began to teach various tribes in remote Laos and Vietnam the fundamentals of reconnaissance and local defense. In November of 1963 the Special forces officially took over the CIA's border surveillance program in South Vietnam, with a mission of establishing outposts with "indigenous" tribal units to detect Communist infiltration from Laos and Cambodia.

Training

For this effort the Green Berets trained and worked out of fortified camps with "Civilian Irregular Defense Group" (CIDG) battalions of non-ethnic-Vietnamese. These CIDG troops were organized as camp strike forces (a total of about 42,000 area inhabitants) and mobile strike forces (around 10,000 men, recruited as reaction forces to serve anywhere in Vietnam). The border was so long and the Special Forces spread so thinly, that surveillance was never air-tight. Although Communist attacks on Special Forces camps started some of the largest main-force battles of the war, in retrospect the units used for border surveillance might have been put to better use in the pacification campaign in the populous areas of South Vietnam.

Beyond the Call

"If you lined up 100 officers and had to select the top five, he'd be one of them," a superior once said of U.S. Army Capt. Roger Donlon, 30, of Saugerties, N.Y. A West Point dropout who enlisted and won a commission and the green beret of the Special Forces, Donlon was in command of a mountain outpost in Vietnam last July 6 1964 when hordes of Viet Cong attacked by night. Shot in the stomach, he stuffed a handkerchief into the wound, cinched up his belt, and kept fighting. In fact, three more wounds didn't even slow him down. "He was a perfect target, silhouetted against the burning barracks, hopping on one leg, one arm useless, throwing grenades," a sergeant recalled. Last week, President Johnson presented Donlon with the first Congressional Medal of Honor of the Vietnamese war for "conspicuous gallantry, extraordinary heroism and intrepidity at the risk of his own life above and beyond the call of duty." (6)

Green Berets in Vietnam were subordinate to the 5th Special Forces Group, headquartered in Nha Trang.

USAF FAST MOVERS

The US Air Force employed most of its fast-movers during the Southeast Asia war on strikes against the North. Generally launched from Thailand, these missions relied heavily on the Thunderchief and Phantom, although during the early 1970s more advanced types such as the Corsair II and F-111 introduced better capability to the role. Other types were tried sporadically, proving less successful in coping with the hard environment encountered over the North.

Above: After the disastrous 'Combat Lancer' deployment, the General Dynamics F-111A returned to Southeast Asia in 1972 to participate in strikes against North Vietnam. These aircraft were detached to Udorn in Thailand from the Nellis-based 474th TFW.

Above: While some Phantoms took on MiGs, others were busy dropping bombs. This F-4E is returning to Udorn following a strike into Cambodia in 1973.

"I'll never forget my first night mission. I'd been up north before, of course, but never at night. Believe me, that AAA opened up like a circus underneath us, together with the searchlights they used to stalk us"

Left: An F-4E on the tanker over Thailand. This model had first appeared in the theatre in November 1968, and was widely used in the fighter role.

It exercised control over operations through a "C" Detachment at each Corps headquarters. Under the "C" Detachments, "B" Detachments controlled variable numbers of individual 12-man "A" Teams or special projects. In common with the rest of the Army, the Special Forces suffered from a lack of unit cohesion through the one-year tour system and rapid expansion to meet wartime manning levels. The 5th Group numbered 3,542 men at its highest strength (in September 1968), but by that time many replacements were not the high caliber to be expected in the Special Forces. When General Abrams replaced General Westmoreland as commander of MACV, he regarded the Green Berets and their CIDG wards as an expendable force to absorb casualties that would otherwise accrue to US units. Coupled with his appointment of a non-Special Forces officer as commander of the 5th Group, Abrams nearly single-handedly destroyed the morale of the Green Berets in Vietnam until he was overruled by Westmoreland, then Army Chief of Staff. As US forces started to withdraw from Vietnam, CIDG border operations were turned over to the ARVN Rangers, and US

Special Forces were often educators and social workers as much as warriors, visiting remote villages to provide red cross services.

Left: The Lockheed F-104C Starfighter did not impress in Vietnam, carring too little for in-country operations, and not having the range for operations over the North.

Below: October 1972 saw the first Vought A-7Ds deployed to Thailand by the Air Force, just in time for them to take a large part in 'Linebacker II'. They were the last tactical aircraft to leave Thailand, after involvement in the Koh Tang rescue in 1975. This example is from the 3rd TFS, 388th TFW at Korat.

Left: This is one of the Northrop F-5As evaluated by the US Air Force for South East Asia operations under the 'Skoshi Tiger' program. For nearly two years the F-5 was employed on mainly in-country operations, before it was considered as too lightly armed and too short on range for USAF use. It did form the basis of VNAF jet operations from 1967 onwards.

Below: Bearing the brunt of strike operations against the North during 'Rolling Thunder', the Republic F-105D Thunderchief had a poor reputation when first entering combat, but progressive improvements to its reliability made it a popular machine. Its take off run led to several appropriate nicknames such as 'Ultra Hog', 'Lead Sled' and 'Polish Glider' and performance at high altitude was sluggish. However, at low altitudes it was fast and surprisingly agile, and able to absorb much damage.

Special Forces worked much more closely with the local vietnamese than other American servicemen.

Special Forces were out of the surveillance business by the end of 1970.

Special reconnaissance

While the bulk of Green Beret activity in Vietnam was taken up with the CIDG border program, very effective work was performed by various special reconnaissance projects. The first of these was born in mid-1964, Project Delta, under the command of Detachment B-52. Delta was the dirty tricks element of Special Forces, carrying out missions such as recon of Communist sanctuaries, airstrike control in remote areas, bomb damage assessment, hunter-killer raids, rescue of prisoners and downed aircrew, mining, communications intelligence, special purpose raids, and a host of other activities as well as a training establishment for US Army Long Range Reconnaissance Patrol (LRRP) teams. Project Delta had at its disposal 16 recon teams in its Strike Recondo Platoon, and eight CIDG "Roadrunner" teams (disguised as NVA or VC). For camp security it included a company of native Nung tribesmen, and for a reaction force had control of the ARVN 81st Airborne Ranger Battalion.

On 11 September 1966, Projects Omega and Sigma were initiated under Detachments B-50 and B-56

THE STONER SYSTEM

Vietnam saw the rapid development of military technology. One of the less successful experiments was the Stoner system. This was a family of small arms with common and often inter-changeable parts. Light and handy to use, Stoners should have been ideal for the peculiar combat conditions in SE Asia, but after a limited trial they were dropped. A perfectly good weapon, in combat the Stoner was found to require too much care and attention.

Left: The M63A1 light machine gun on a tripod. Addition of a heavy barrel would give the Stoner sustained fire ability. Belt-fed, the ammunition is stored in a box attached to the left of the receiver.

Right: A US Navy SEAL waits in ambush, his Stoner at the ready. The Stoner family ranged from short carbines to medium machine guns and saw extensive trials with the Marines as well as with the SEALs.

Below: US Navy SEALs with a variety of weapons including Stoners, prepare to set out on a mission. The SEALs made good use of the Stoners, their extra weapons skills allowing them to maintain their weapons more effectively in the field.

respectively, to provide Special Forces reconnaissance support for I and II Field Forces. Conceived as scaled down versions of Project Delta, the two projects were organized similarly but with fewer recon and roadrunner teams, and airborne CIDG companies for reaction forces. In late 1967, both of these projects were resubordinated to MACV-SOG.

Intelligence projects

In April of 1968, Project Gamma was initiated at Nha Trang under the command of Detachment B-57. Gamma was the Special Forces intelligence effort aimed at Cambodia's NVA base areas, and initially employed nine two-man collection teams. The project grew to a total of 17 agent nets, handling nearly 100 agents and providing three-quarters of the intelligence information about NVA presence in Cambodia.

MACV had its own reconnaissance project which was not under the 5th Special Forces Group, but made use of Special Forces personnel. Called MACV-SOG (for "Studies and Observation Group"), the unit was formed in 1964 with a charter to operate anywhere in South East Asia and southern China. Operationally, MACV-SOG undertook the same type of missions as Project Delta, and developed a reputation as one of the best covert mission organizations ever fielded.

Once trained, Popular Civilian Forces were often very effective. These are setting off for a river ambush at night.

The most famous Special Forces mission of the war was the raid on the Son Tay Prison complex in North Vietnam on 21 November 1970. Planned and rehearsed for months, the raid aimed to rescue US prisoners of war. Using Air Force helicopters and 56 Green Beret volunteers from stateside Special Forces units, the plan was executed flawlessly – except that the US prisoners had been removed to another location some months previously. Through a failure of intelligence the raiders came up empty handed.

For two years no bombs had fallen in the Red River Valley in North Vietnam, and only occasionally had the sirens disrupted Hanoi's nights when unarmed U.S. reconnaissance flights triggered radar shields. Suddenly, in the early morning hours, radar screens all over North Vietnam blossomed in menacing blips. Across communications nets flashed word that waves of U.S. planes were bombing heavily south of the 19th

SPECIAL FORCES

The Green Berets were among the first Americans in action in Vietnam. Operating in small teams with larger numbers of native auxiliaries (often only marginally less hostile to the government in Saigon than to the Communists), they ran patrols from remote sites on the Cambodian border into the heart of the Ho Chi Minh trail. As advisors in the more settled parts of Vietnam, the Special Forces were assigned by MACV to provide anything from teaching and health advice to unarmed combat and demolitions instruction.

Above: A member of 5th SF Group on watch in 1969 near An Khe, with Colt Commando, bush hat and other unconventional gear.

Below: An airboat advisor with 5th SF Group mans a .30 MG during a canal patrol. Note the characteristic 'tiger stripe' camouflage suit.

Above: Members of the CIDG based at Ben Het give the location of a VC bunker complex to a 5th SF officer.

parallel: north of the DMZ, east of the Laotian border. That had happened before in the interim since the bombing halt – five times, in fact. But this was something far more.

Scores of fighter-bombers were weaving back and forth across North Vietnam north of the 19th parallel in what appeared to be bewildering bombing patterns. Flares were drifting down to illuminate the vulnerable ships and docks of Haiphong harbor. As North Vietnam's air-defense commanders opened up with cannon and missilery, MIGs scrambled into action all across the country, and South China also went into a state of advanced military readiness. To many North Vietnamese, it looked as if the U.S. were invading their country. It was 2 a.m. when allied monitors in South Vietnam heard the top-priority emergency transmission crackling from Hanoi: "There's a landing! There's a landing!"

Landing, yes: invasion, no – although the confusion and panic engendered by the illusion of invasion was precisely the aim of the U.S. planners. In one of the most daring and meticulously rehearsed operations of the long war, a fleet of U.S. helicopters was skimming into North Vietnam at treetop level, slipping through the narrow "windows" or gaps in Hanoi's radar system frantically preoccupied with the fighter-bombers high in the Vietnamese sky. Aboard the choppers were about 40 Green Beret and Ranger troops led by Army Colonel Arthur ("The Bull") Simons, 52, a near-legendary veteran of World War II, Laos and Vietnam. He is considered by many to be quite simply the finest derring-do combat commander in the U.S. Army. Like the 20 or so Air Force specialists manning the helicopters, all the raiders had been volunteers for a mission unknown, one with only a fifty-fifty chance of success: for many on board the choppers, it had been enough to know that The Bull was in charge.

Their target was a scant 20 nautical miles from the center of Hanoi: Son Tay, an American prisoner-of-war compound. As the tiny fleet scuttled into North Vietnam, National Security Adviser Henry Kissinger followed its progress at the Pentagon. The radio monitors in Washington were only two minutes behind the actual events. When the choppers passed their first checkpoint, they were seven minutes ahead of schedule. Kissinger made a quiet joke to a high-ranking officer about the plan's being off. Just wait, Kissinger was told. By the time the squadron passed the last checkpoint, it was only a minute ahead; the raiders came down on Son Tay, guns blazing, right on the dot. Incredibly, they had not been detected by the North Vietnamese until one minute before touchdown.

All but one of the helicopters were HH-53s, giant ships able to fly at almost 200 m.p.h. carrying 38 fully armed infantrymen and refueling in mid-air. The exception was a single HH-3 chopper, in which rode

The Montagnards were the Special Forces star pupils, being tough tribesmen with a long history of emnity towards ethnic Vietnamese.

Above: The Special Forces insignia, based on a motif from the US Great Seal. The motto means 'Freedom from oppression'.

> ***"The heart of the Special Forces operation in Vietnam remain its 'A' Teams . . . They operate with local mercenaries, who are not strictly soldiers, and are free to leave the camps when they want. Sometimes this could be in the middle of a Viet Cong attack"***

Above: Aerial view of the Than Tri SF camp in Kien Tuong, less than two miles from the border with Cambodia.

Left: An SF medical advisor with MACV HQ calls in on the horn after a visit to a village on the Song Co Chen River.

The Bull and his initial assault squad. The smaller craft came down inside the cramped camp yard; as its rotor tips whacked into trees, the pilot deliberately crash-landed it in the middle of the compound. Simons probably wanted to waste no time under fire while positioning for a landing. The other choppers landed outside the compound. There was a smattering of ground fire as the troops came in. The soldiers expected to meet as many as 100 guards, but there were only an estimated half a dozen. Colonel Simons found himself yards from one North Vietnamese, who, he reported wryly, seemed very surprised to see him.

Unhappily, the Americans were surprised as well. There were no American prisoners to be found. For some 50 minutes, the soldiers dashed from building to building, breaking locks and searching the abandoned cells. Though U.S. fighter-bombers rocketed and strafed nearby antiaircraft batteries and troop areas to prevent a North Vietnamese reaction force from reaching Son Tay, some North Vietnamese reinforcements did arrive. One American was slightly wounded by an AK-47 automatic-rifle burst. Another broke his foot in the crash landing of the HH-3 helicopter; which was blown up before the Americans left. There were no

Montagnards were tough hill tribesfolk, who lived in primitive fashion in the highlands of South East Asia.

other casualties; there was only an awful sense of dismay. All the courage, the long training, the perfectly executed mission, had come to naught. Said First Lieut. George Petrie, one of the raiders: "When we realized that there was no one in the compound, I had the most horrible feeling of my life." (7)

Outside of Vietnam, US Special Forces in Thailand (eventually designated 46th Special Forces Company) trained the first Royal Thai Army elements which went to Vietnam (the Queen's Cobra Regiment). In 1971 it undertook training of Thai mercenary troops to be deployed to Laos under the codename of Project Unity. After the overthrow of Prince Sihanouk in Cambodia, Special Forces were invited to train some 85 Cambodian light infantry battalions. Additionally, Cambodian Special Forces received Green Beret training from April, 1972 through February of 1973. Operating throughout South East Asia in unmarked fixed-wing aircraft and UH-1 helicopters, the CIA's 'Air America' covert transport force flew missions in support of irregular units in Laos. Air America played right through the period of the war, from start to finish, and eventually disbanded at the insistence of Congress.

An LLDB sergeant corrects a CIDG recruit's ground fighting position during an unarmed combat course.

Vietnamese Special Forces

The South Vietnamese Luc Luong Duc Biet (LLDB), patterned loosely after the US Special Forces, originated in the late 1950s and quickly assumed the position of an anti-coup force for President Diem. Staffed mainly with political cronies, the LLDB proved corrupt and inept in the face of the Viet Cong, and much more enthusiastic in the role of intimidating Diem's domestic opposition. Even after the demise of Diem, the LLDB never regained the stature of a trusted fighting unit. Eventually, the LLDB was dropped and a new force raised, called the Special Mission Service. The SMS was to be the Vietnamese equivalent of MACV-SOG and began operations in January of 1972, after a year of intensive training. The most successful South Vietnamese special operations program was Phuong Hoang (Project Phoenix), which flourished between 1968 and 1971 with CIA and Special Forces assistance. Aimed at rooting out the Viet Cong Infrastructure, Phoenix was carried out by Vietnamese Provincial Reconnaissance Units. Based on intensified intelligence efforts, files were opened on suspects who were subsequently turned to the government side, jailed, or shot. Although given a bad press, Phoenix proved more effective than most other efforts even though it was sometimes used to settle private scores. Post war Communist statements have revealed that they considered it the number one threat to their covert organization in South Vietnam.

SEALs

Rising slowly from the murky waters of the Mekong, the black clad figure slipped silently towards his target. In the dark, he struck, placed his explosive charges and slipped away. The SEALs had struck again.

Arising out of the Underwater Demolition Teams of World War Two, SEAL (Sea Air Land) Teams are the US Navy's special warfare fighters. Equally at home underwater, or under a parachute, the SEALs were amongst the most effective US fighting men in South East Asia.

Above: Without relaxing their guard, a SEAL team takes a brief rest after discovering a Viet Cong 'punji bed' – a concealed pit of sharpened stakes that were designed to stab the feet of the unwary and were sometimes poisoned with human excrement.

Left: A SEAL demolition team leader and hospital corpsman on an exercise near the Chowan River, North Carolina, in readiness for upcoming combat in Vietnam in mid-1969. SEALs were widely regarded as the best-trained counter-terrorist troops serving in SE Asia.

Below: SEALs in the Mekong Delta during Crimson Tide, 1967. The day-long operation netted five Viet Cong dead, with 153 enemy structures and fortifications, 120 sampans and 75 bunkers destroyed.

*Above: Sailors from **UDT** (**Underwater Demolition Team**) 13 about to set out on a riverine mission near **Da Nang** in early 1971.*

*Above: Two **SEALs** pause for water during **Operation Crimson Tide**, 1967. These troops were highly trained in survival techniques.*

***Above: A SEAL** prepares to take out a Viet Cong bunker – one of hundreds that protected the **VC** from conventional attack.*

***Above:** Training in the Virgin Islands. Besides counter-insurgency, **SEALs** specialized in intelligence missions.*

***Below: SEALs** enter **Rung Sat** swamp, January 1967. This notorious **VC** stronghold was a natural target for **SEAL** skills.*

***Below:** Checking out an enemy bunker along the Rach Thom/Rack Mo Ray canal, 1968. Every **SEAL** was his own 'tunnel rat'.*

" SEALs would use their razor-sharp combat skills to avoid or take out guards, infiltrate the objective and carry out the mission – intelligence gathering, kidnap, sabotage, rescue or assassination. They'd do it silently if possible, but if they got into a firefight their weapons would be put to venomous use "

CHAPTER EIGHT

PULLING BACK 1970

US Navy SEALs aboard a riverine assault craft set a suspected Viet Cong hut ablaze in a 1970 Delta operation. By this time, the 'Brown Water War' was being handed over to the South Vietnamese as part of the process of Vietnamization.

American public support for the war continued to decline. A February poll indicated that the percentage who favored immediate US withdrawal from Vietnam had risen from 21% to 35% since November 1969. Fifty-five percent of those responding still rejected an immediate withdrawal, but by the end of September 1970, the figures had nearly reversed. On the diplomatic front, the stalled official talks in Paris prompted President Nixon to dispatch his chief advisor, Henry Kissinger, to meet with North Vietnamese Politburo member Le Duc Tho for secret negotiations on several occasions over the next few years.

US withdrawals picked up in 1970, with the 26th Marines departing in March, and the 7th Marines pulling out in August. The departure of III Marine Amphibious Force Headquarters in March left the US Army's XXIV Corps Headquarters in charge of American units in the I Corps area. The 1st Infantry Division left Vietnam in April and moved to Fort Riley, Kansas, replacing the 24th Infantry Division (which disbanded) there and in West Germany, where it stationed its 3rd Brigade. The 4th Infantry Division's 3rd Brigade returned to the States in April, followed by the remainder of the division in December. Moving to Fort Carson, Colorado, the 4th replaced the 5th Infantry Division (Mechanized), which disbanded like the 24th. The 3rd Brigade of 9th Infantry Division, which had lingered on as an independent unit, was out of the country by the end of September, when its parent division disbanded. The 199th Light Infantry Brigade was also gone by October. The 25th Infantry Division, minus its 2nd Brigade, returned to Hawaii before the end of the year. By mid-1970, US strength in Vietnam totaled 298,600 soldiers and 39,900 marines.

Communist forces in the south began the year with 8 division headquarters and a total of 57 divisional and non-divisional regiments, or 271 divisional and non-divisional combat maneuver battalions and 58 combat support battalions. Manpower included 133,000 main force soldiers, 52,000 guerrillas, and 58,000 administrative and support troops for a total of 243,000 in the field. The Viet Cong Infrastucture (VCI) and political cadres added perhaps 84,000 more. In a period of rebuilding, the Communist forces kept activities at a low key. Weapons supplied from the USSR and China continued to pour into the north and upgrade the NVA's firepower after the Tet Offensive of 1968. Available heavy weapons included 122mm and 107mm rockets; 120mm, 82mm and 60mm mortars; 107mm, 82mm and 75mm recoilless rifles; RPG-2 and B-40 anti-tank weapons; and 14.5 and 12.7mm heavy machine guns. Small arms consisted of the ubiquitous 7.62mm AK-47 assault rifle and the RPD light machine gun.

> In a few weeks, according to the American estimate, the number of North Vietnamese and Viet Cong dead by actual body count since Jan. 1, 1961, will pass 600,000 men and women. There have long been honest doubts about the accuracy of the body counts, and despite all the genuine efforts of the U.S. military to verify tolls and improve the accounting techniques, the doubts are not likely to vanish. The odd thing is that the North Vietnamese and Viet Cong may have suffered even more heavily than the Allied tallies indicate. American figures do not include the thousands of dead enemy troops borne off the fields by their comrades, or the thousands more wounded who have later died of their wounds.
>
> Counting their battle dead, their captured, victims of fatal disease and the 140,400 who have deserted to the Saigon cause, the North Vietnamese and Viet Cong forces have probably been drained of about 1,640,400

Vietnamization meant that more of the burden of defending their homes lay with peasants, such as this Delta farmer.

> men during the war. Applying such a loss to the U.S. population base (there are 21 million people in North Vietnam, plus over 100,000 Viet Cong, *v.* 200 million in the U.S.), that would be the equivalent of about 15,500,000 Americans lost. And this does not even count the Vietnamese who have died in the U.S. bombings of the North. Proportionately, the North Vietnamese have taken among the heaviest casualties in the history of warfare. (1)

With Vietnamization, such as it was, in full swing, the US Army's primary mission became an orderly evacuation of major combat units at the least cost in lives. Major combat operations were to be turned over to the ARVN. In I Corps, the 101st Airborne Division mounted Operation Texas Star from April to the beginning of September. Dedicating one brigade to pacification support, the remainder of the division conducted sweeps through the western portion of South Vietnam's two northern provinces, Quang Tri and Thua Thien. A total of 1,782 enemy casualties were counted for the five month effort.

PACIFIC AIR BRIDGE

The huge military involvement in Southeast Asia required an equally large logistics effort to supply the forces in-country. At the heart of the effort were the US Air Force's transport wings, ferrying men and materiel across the Pacific in a non-stop shuttle. Such was the huge need for airlift capability that civil contractors were called in to join the effort, principally on trooping flights. Airlift crews worked tirelessly supplying the war effort, until the final evacuation from South Vietnam in 1975, where Air Force crews, and their civil counterparts, toiled bravely to complete a successful withdrawal.

Substantial contracts were awarded to civil airlines during the war to ferry personnel. This Pan Am Boeing 707 is at Da Nang in 1966.

Below: Douglas C-9A Nightingale flying hospitals were instrumental in evacuating wounded troops to the Philippines in the last years of the war.

Above: Introduced on the airlift effort during August 1971, the Lockheed C-5A Galaxy greatly increased the ability to transport large equipment by air. One was tragically lost carrying war orphans in April 1975.

Below: The Lockheed StarLifter was the workhorse of the trans-Pacific air bridge, using its speed and internal volume to ferry vital equipment into the war zone in enormous quantities.

"Gentlemen, welcome to in-country processing. The snack bar and ice-cream shop are off limits until you have completed your processing . . . Gentlemen, there will be absolutely no talking while you are processing. Gentlemen, I want you to prepare to process"

Below: Used sparingly on the airlift was the Boeing C-135B Stratolifter, one of which is seen here unloading at Tan Son Nhut.

Above: Despite taking several days to complete a round trip to and from the war zone, the lumbering Douglas C-124 Globemaster was much valued on account of its gaping clamshell doors and capacious fuselage. This 'Globie' runs up at the start of another intrepid journey back to the States from Thailand.

Left: Another elderly type on the transport effort was the Douglas C-133 Cargomaster, valued too for its good internal capacity. This aircraft is seen at Bangkok alongside a C-124 Globemaster and a Royal Australian Air Force Sabre, the latter used for base air defence duties.

Above: Although its small internal capacity rendered it obsolete as a cargo transport, the Douglas C-118A Liftmaster was employed as the primary aeromedical evacuation aircraft for most of the war. It served in this role until 1972, when the Douglas C-9 took over.

Tan Son Nhut outside Saigon was one of the world's busiest airports during the war, and this holding point photograph graphically illustrates the differing types using the base. Two F-100 tactical fighters, a C-1 carrier onboard delivery aircraft, C-47 special operations aircraft, Lockheed C-141 StarLifter transport and Continental Airlines Boeing 707 trooper wait their turn for take-off.

The operation was marred by a forced withdrawal from Fire Support Base Ripcord (40km west of Hué) when the position became untenable in the face of a large NVA buildup. The last US offensive, Jefferson Glenn, was the 101st's combined operation with the ARVN 1st Division in Thua Thien Province, lasting from September 1970 until October 1971 and producing 2,026 enemy casualties.

In Cambodia, Prince Sihanouk was ousted by General Lon Nol in March. Lon immediately moved to reorganize and strengthen the weak, 32,000-man Cambodian Army (*Forces Armées Nationales Khmeres*, or FANK) with US Special Forces assistance, and closed the port of Sihanoukville which had been a covert source of supply for Communist forces in the III and IV Corps areas. This provided an interesting situation in which Cambodia, now anti-Communist instead of "neutral", was perceived in danger not only from the fledgling domestic Khmer Rouge Communists, but from the angry NVA as well. It was not fully appreciated in Washington that

Cambodian mercenary troops make a combat assault from a US Army Huey. Such soldiers had long been supported by the CIA.

BODYCOUNT

One of the most religiously sought after statistics in Vietnam was the Body Count. The statistical wizards at the Pentagon had decided the best way to measure success was to count the number of dead enemy bodies left after an action. As a result, troops would be more interested in killing the enemy rather than capturing him. This often meant that the first hint of contact with the enemy would bring down a profligate hail of fire to that position. Of course, one Vietnamese looked just like another, and who was to tell if that Vietnamese was a Viet Cong or just a villager in the wrong place?

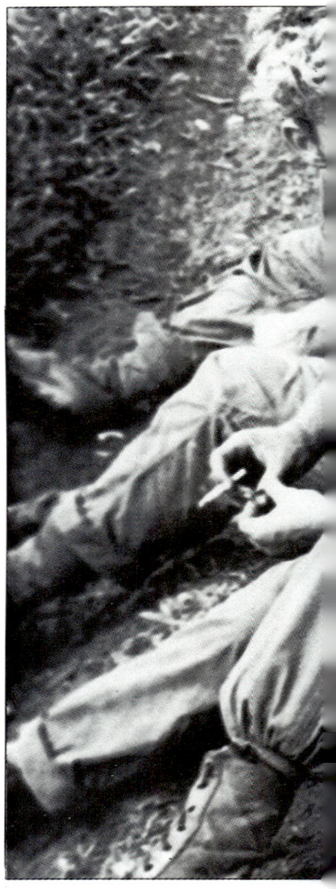

Above: 1st Bn, 7th Marines return fire on Charlie Ridge, 17 miles south-west of Da Nang, in February 1970, using an assortment of weapons: M14 and M16 rifles, M79 grenade launchers and M60 machine guns.

Left: Under fire from the NVA near Da Nang, troops of 1st Bn, 26th Marines take cover, February 1970. With Viet Cong forces demoralized after the failure of their 1968 Tet offensive and the success of the CIA Phoenix program, two thirds of the 125,000-strong communist forces in the south were now NVA regulars.

Right: Body counts are one measure of success. For hard information in a firefight you need prisoners. An 11th Cav training team and a Kit Carson Scout demonstrate the right way of getting one.

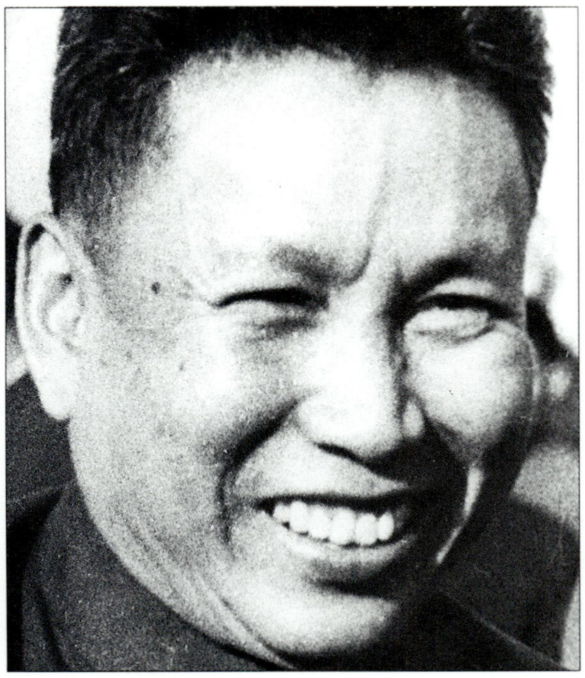

One of the great monsters of history, the Khmer Rouge leader Pol Pot was responsible for the deaths of millions of Cambodians.

in spite of outward appearances, the Khmer Rouge and the NVA were antagonistic and as liable to clash with each other as with the FANK. Nevertheless, there was sufficient justification for the Nixon White House to authorize a limited "incursion" into border areas of Cambodia, along with ARVN troops, for the purpose of disrupting Communist base areas. The objectives of the operation would be to take pressure off US units during the withdrawal by destroying NVA supplies, and to nip any Communist attempt to topple Lon Nol before he established himself. An added bonus would be the capture of COSVN – the Central Office for South Vietnam – the Cambodia-based North Vietnamese headquarters for Viet Cong activity. In fact the NVA did move quickly to overrun vast areas of eastern Cambodia to protect the Ho Chi Minh Trail, and the ARVN had responded with a number of minor cross-border attacks.

Into Cambodia

Allowing for weather and favorable terrain, the attack into Cambodia was scheduled for 1 May 1970. South Vietnamese units taking part in the offensive included the ARVN 9th, 21st, and Airborne Divisions; one regiment each from the 22nd, 23rd and 25th Divisions; five Ranger groups and one Marine brigade of three battalions each; and about half of the ARVN's armored assets, organized in 9 armored cavalry squadrons (company-size units). US participation was planned for several of the dozen ARVN thrust lines across the border. ARVN units were programmed to advance up to 60 km into Cambodia, while US units were restricted to a 30 km advance and a time limit for withdrawal by the end of June. Operation Toan Thang 43 was aimed at the supply area around Snoul (called "The City"), north of III Corps. Forces along this axis included the ARVN Airborne Division's 3rd Brigade (supported by armor), and the US 1st Cavalry Division's 3rd Brigade (reinforced by armored and mechanized battalions), as well as the 11th Armored Cavalry Regiment. Huge caches of supplies were uncovered, but the NVA refused combat and left only delaying detachments in contact. The remainder of the 1st Cav moved by helicopter farther into Cambodia where, at Bu Dop (called "Rock Island East"), large stores were also destroyed. Between the 20th and 30th of June the 1st Cavalry Division withdrew without having discovered the illusive COSVN.

"I'd like to see the look on Fulbright's face right now," said a rotund American lieutenant colonel as he stuck a

Above: Soldiers of the 1st Cavalry look over material found in an enemy bunker near Mi Mot, Cambodia, in May 1970. Some 20,000 US and ARVN troops took part in the controversial incursion into Vietnam's neutral neighbor, in an attempt to destroy communist supply lines to the south.

Above right: Dead VC killed at Illa Illo Island in the Cua Dia estuary. In a war with no conventional front lines, the 'body count' became the only measure of military success – leading to inflated claims from commanders, a widening credibility gap and loss of public support for the war.

Right: A company commander of 3d Marine Division gives orders to redeploy after contact with the VC. Two enemy dead lie in the foreground.

plug of chewing tobacco into his right jowl. "This is really something, ain't it?"

It was really something, everyone seemed to agree. If by no other means, you could tell a lot of allied troops were in this part of Cambodia – South Vietnamese infantrymen and their American advisers – simply because of all the U.S. beer cans lying around.

In a stubbled rice field just outside of this village, four miles inside the Parrot's Beak area of Cambodia, the brand was Carling Black Label, and after two warm cans, the South Vietnamese commander of a squadron of armored cavalry troops flopped on a mat in the shade of one of his armored personnel carriers and promptly fell asleep. "War is hell, even in Cambodia," said an American sergeant – one of two advisers with the squadron.

About four miles north of Chipou, as South Vietnamese planes dropped their loads of bombs and napalm on a nearby house where a sniper had taken refuge, a small, dirty pig walked boldly across a dusty rice field, past two armored personnel carriers loaded with South Vietnamese troops and up to within 20 feet of a United States helicopter parked on the ground, next to some captured Vietcong medical supplies. He stopped and lifted his nose.

The Americans, two pilots and two door gunners, spotted him and charged. The pig darted away and the chase was on. Three South Vietnamese soldiers jumped off their vehicles and tore after the pig. After a three-minute chase, one of the door gunners, in a flying leap, jumped on the pig, tied a piece of twine around its neck and led it back toward the helicopter. The pig squealed and strained at the twine.

"Chalk up – one P.O.W. pig," said the door gunner. They planned to take it back to South Vietnam, but their passenger – an American colonel – objected. So the pig was freed, and it ambled away in the direction of the house, now burning, where the sniper was. (2)

The next operation, Toan Thang 44, jumped off on May 6th, and featured elements of the US 25th Infantry Division. Again, some supplies were found and destroyed, but once again the NVA chose to withdraw rather than stand. The troops moved back to III Corps on May 14th. Starting from II Corps, Operation Binh Tay I included the US 4th Infantry Division and the ARVN 40th Regiment. Advancing into Cambodia, the force encountered stiff resistance south of the tri-border area and made only perfunctory attempts at further movement. The 4th Division simply went through the motions and avoided casualties. By the 30th June there were no more US units left in Cambodia. The ARVN stayed on longer, but lacked the aggressiveness necessary for a successful pursuit. In general, the incursion was a qualified success. On the plus side, the NVA logistic effort was set back by 6 to 9 months. Enough small arms were captured to equip 54 Communist battalions, and enough heavy weapons to equip 27. A 9 to 12 month supply of ammunition for Communist forces in III Corps (2,500 tons) was destroyed along with a 4 to 6 months supply of rice (7,023 tons). The

Vietnamese volunteers patrol the Cambodian border while a large part of the ARVN is engaged in operations across the rontier.

HO CHI MINH TRAIL

The Ho Chi Minh Trail stretched from North Vietnam along the Annamese mountains, through Laos and Cambodia to terminate in the Mekong Delta. It was a network of interlocking roads and trails through which supplies and reinforcements for the Viet Cong passed. In spite of years of bombing and the 1970 US and ARVN incursion into Cambodia, the Trail was continually improved. The journey to the Delta which in 1959 could take three months, had by 1975 been cut to less than a weeks travel. In the final offensive, the NVA was able to use the trail, by now almost a highway, to concentrate its forces to great effect.

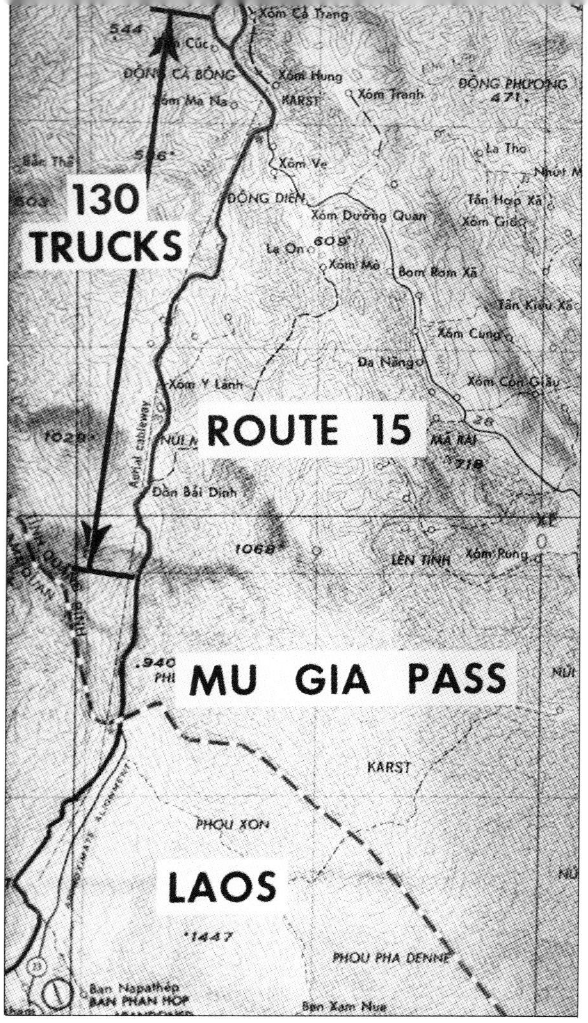

Above: The 1st Battery of the Song Gianh Anti-Aircraft Brigade in the NVA 4th Military Zone encircling Saigon. The Ho Chi Minh Trail stretched into this area – a long-standing communist stronghold – from the 'Parrot's Beak' in Cambodia.

Left: From the air, the De-Militarized Zone along the Song Ben Hai river and 17th parallel separating North and South Vietnam is a pockmarked morass from B-52 and tactical air strikes. Despite its name, the zone was invested by five NVA divisions, who launched heavy artillery, rocket and ground attacks from here against US and ARVN positions in the South.

Left and above: Aerial recon photo taken in March 1967 of part of a 130-strong convoy of trucks on Route 15, which wound through North Vietnam to the Mu Gia Pass on the border with Laos. Men would be trucked down this highway to Mu Gia, then continue on foot down the Ho Chi Minh Trail through Laos to infiltrate South Vietnam. Most SVN provinces could be reached within six weeks, but to reach the Mekong Delta could take three months.

Above: A North Vietnamese anti-aircraft unit operating in Thanh Hoa. In June 1967 the battery claimed an astonishing tally of 2,000 US planes (USAF combat losses from 1962 to 1973 totaled only 2,257 planes). Thanh Hoa province contained numerous supply depots and the key highway, Route 1A, to the Ho Chi Minh trail, and was constantly shelled and bombed by the US Navy and Air Force. In March 1967 alone, 19 separate air attacks were mounted.

Left: A convoy destroyed on the Ho Chi Minh Trail near An Loc in 1972 by aircraft from the carrier USS Constellation. At this stage in the war the 'trail' had been upgraded to a full-fledged all-weather highway system complete with jungle filling stations.

" I came close to the trail, but never reached it. No Laotian guide would take me, because all patrols sent into the area get wiped out "

Above: Men of 3d Marine Division's 3d Reconnaissance Bn with captured 12.7mm NVA anti-aircraft guns in 1969. Such equipment was brought down the Ho Chi Minh trail in pieces, often strapped onto bicycles or carts – and, sometimes, on elephants.

CAMBODIA

The North Vietnamese and the Viet Cong established secure base areas in Cambodia, from which to raid the South. In 1970, Cambodia fell into chaos following the overthrow of Prince Sihanouk and to forestall any communist attacks President Nixon authorized a cross-border 'incursion'. In 13 major operations over the two months from April 29 1970, Corps sized American and Vietnamese units killed at least 10,000 enemy, and captured or destroyed enormous quantities of weapons and ammunition.

***Left:** May 1970, and US Troops prepare for the incursion into Cambodia. Their jumping off point is the former Marine base at Khe Sanh.*

***Above:** ARVN M-41 tanks roll into Cambodia in an attempt to cut off the supplies reaching the Viet Cong from the Ho Chi Minh Trail.*

body count of NVA and VC totaled 11,349, and the prisoner bag totaled 2,328 more. On the minus side, COSVN was not found and destroyed, US units were not allowed the latitude necessary to force the NVA to fight a decisive engagement, and the whole operation got adverse media attention in the United States. Communist countries, the American press and anti-war elements denounced the move as an "invasion" and widening of the war in spite of the fact that it was undertaken for defensive purposes, had limited objectives, and terminated precisely according to Nixon's promised schedule. The worst fallout came in early May when rioting students at Kent State University in Ohio were fired on by nervous National Guardsmen who were not trained to handle civil disturbances.

FIRE SUPPORT BASE EUNICE, South Vietnam, June 28 – Twenty-one-year-old S. Sgt. Stanley Zeager of Rocky River, Ohio – one of the more than 30,000 soldiers sent to Cambodia – is back in Vietnam and glad of it.

"Now, oh yes, definitely!" he said today.

But he felt exhausted, and so did his platoon, after setting up a fire support base, Eunice, about three miles inside South Vietnam. They were flown here yesterday.

"The officers like to use us as their little toy, but we get the job done," said Sergeant Zeager, whose glasses are smeared with reddish dust and who looks thinner than the 150 pounds he say he weighs.

The sergeant and his outfit left Cambodia two days before the June 30 deadline announced by President Nixon.

The leader of an infantry platoon in Company B, Second Battalion, Eighth Cavalry, First Air Cavalry Division (Airmobile), Sergeant Zeager says he did not really want to go in the Army. He enlisted with a "back-of-the-mind hope" that he could "kill time in the States" at a noncommissioned officer's school.

"I could have went to college but I knew the Army was looking for me," he said. "I knew I'd be in for two years and I'd give it all I got."

Like most men in his platoon – their faces look flattened by fatigue – he believes that the use of American forces to clean out the Communist sanctuaries in Cambodia was a good idea.

"I think it was one of the best moves in the Vietnam war 'cause it put a hurt on the North Vietnamese and the VC which could help our withdrawal here, and Stanley Zeager is in favor of that," he said.

Pfc. Rex West, the 20-year-old medic for the platoon, looked at the filth under his fingernails and sighed.

"We were so tired yesterday we hardly knew we

Firebases were moved to the Cambodian border, serving as jumping off points for the invasion as well as providing the usual artillery support.

Above: The 11th Armored Cavalry return from Cambodia. Allied forces captured or destroyed enough supplies and equipment to maintain as many as fifty Viet Cong Main Force battalions for a year.

Below: Air mobility and large scale employment of armor meant that most military objectives were achieved. At home, however, massive antiwar protests and the Kent State tragedy were what hit the headlines.

were here, back in Nam," he said. "There are too many gooks in Cambodia. I just didn't feel right there; it gave me kind of a spooky feeling. Especially since we found all that stuff in the caches, they'll be coming back to find out what's left and they'll be coming in mad." (3)

US casualties during the year dropped to half of the 1969 total. The services lost 4,221 killed in action and 1,844 in non-combat circumstances. US wounded totaled 30,643. ARVN casualties exceeded 1969 levels with 23,346 dead, 71,582 wounded, and 950 missing. South Vietnam's other allies lost 715 killed and missing, and suffered 1,830 seriously wounded. Communist casualties dropped by a third from 1969 to 1970, with a body count of 103,638 for the latter year. The Army's helicopter losses declined for the first time in 1970, with 359 operational and 441 combat losses for a total of 800. Thirty of the combat losses were from attacks on US base camps and the remaining losses were from enemy ground fire. US Marine helicopters suffered 41 losses (17 operational

The process of Vietnamization accelerated through the year, with the VNAF receiving many surplus USAF planes.

and 24 due to ground fire) while Marine fixed-wing losses totaled 22 aircraft (5 operational and 17 due to ground fire).

In May, US B-52 operations in Cambodia (Menu) were expanded and renamed Freedom Deal. This offensive included support for Lon Nol's Cambodian Army in its new role against the Communists. The missions did not end until mid-August 1973, by which time the effort had involved a total of 16,527 B-52 sorties. A brief break in the North Vietnamese bombing halt was authorized in connection with the Son Tay POW rescue attempt on November 21st. Over 200 sorties were flown against various military targets throughout the country, ostensibly in reaction to the North Vietnamese shooting down of unarmed US reconnaissance planes. During 1970 the USAF lost a total of 160 fixed-wing aircraft. Forty-one of these were from operational causes, 117 from enemy ground fire, and 2 from attacks against US bases.

A US Navy 'Swift' boat ferries Vietnamese Marines around a barrier in a joint operation on the Ca Mau peninsula.

The last combined US/South Vietnamese river operation took place in conjunction with the Cambodian incursion. In early May a South Vietnamese Navy patrol force of 110 river craft started up the Mekong in the direction of Phnom Penh to destroy Communist base areas and supplies along the river. A force of 30 US Navy boats joined the push, but were limited by the 30 km restriction on movement into Cambodia. By September, the effort had been reinforced by an additional 90 South Vietnamese river craft and 1,500 Marines to comb the NVA base areas between the Mekong and Bassac Rivers. At the end of December, the South Vietnamese received the last 125 of 650 US Navy river patrol vessels that were turned over in connection with Vietnamization, and the USN's "brown water navy" in Vietnam officially went out of business. To further reinforce the closure of Sihanoukville as a Communist supply terminal, the South Vietnamese instituted a blockade of Cambodia with coastal patrol craft beginning in May. This stopped North Vietnamese supplies being lightered ashore or brought into small harbors. As the need for carrier air support declined, US Navy fixed-wing air losses in 1970 dropped to 44 planes – 30 lost to operational causes and 14 to enemy ground fire.

THE VILLAGE WAR

Pacification, in the context of the war in Vietnam, refers to the attempts which were made to provide security to the inhabitants of rural areas in connection with civil development projects such as construction, education, farming, medicine, and local government. As such, the enemy was generally not main force NVA, but the so-called Viet Cong Infrastructure (or "VCI"), which was present to various degrees throughout South Vietnam. The VCI presence in Saigon-controlled areas might be very low key and consist mainly of secret agents, saboteurs,

FIRE BASE

Although Vietnam was a war of lightning operations, helicopter assaults and small-unit patrols, artillery still played a major part. There was no defined front line, and troops could be in action almost anywhere. To provide fire support in such situations, the Fire Support Base was evolved. Situated on commanding hilltops the FSB could usually bring down fire on a huge area, and would do so on request of units in the field. Guns in use ranged from air-portable howitzers to self-propelled 8-inch weapons. Long range guns were able to support the Marines at Khe Sanh, from FSBs as much as 20 miles away.

The AN/MPQ Mortar locating radar was used to locate enemy shells, backtrack their trajectories and direct counter-battery fire.

Above: Two members of the 82nd Artillery clean the tube of a 105mm howitzer. The gun had a full crew of eight men.

Above: The crew of gun No 2, Battery C, 14th Arty wait for a fire mission to be called in at FSB Fat City, June 1970. An innovation in Vietnam was to allow patrol commanders in the boonies to call on artillery support at need although the danger of inexperienced observers calling in short rounds was always present.

Above: The commander (far right) of Battery C, 1/321 Artillery, counts down to a salvo from his howitzers.

Below: Flame belches and the breech block blurs as a 105mm howitzer sends out a round.

Above: The heart of Fire Support Base Jackson. Operating in support of units of the 25th Infantry Division, FSB Jackson had a variety of towed and self-propelled artillery pieces to call on ranging from pack guns to 8-inch howitzers.

Above: Marines ram a shell into a 155mm howitzer as they fire missions in support of Khe Sanh.

Below: A jovial welcome. FSBs were sited in commanding positions, but not for the view.

"Westy said that they'd done a great job under tough conditions. He took his hat off to them. Then he took off in his helo. You could see the gunners cursing as the gritty yellow dirt blew across the firebase"

and VC recruiters and sympathizers. In areas of marginal or contested control, the VCI could expand to a "shadow government" complete with local terrorist organizations, propagandists, support elements for Communist field troops, and bully boys to extort "taxes" of rice and "labor volunteers" from the local villages. In areas of little government presence or in hard-core Viet Cong areas, the VCI virtually ran things – at least at night – and included a local covert militia, part-time guerrillas, elaborate hidden storage facilities for the supplies of Communist forces, and elements to enforce the conscription of young Vietnamese into the Viet Cong.

Political control

Essentially, in a war for the political control of the population, pacification is of paramount importance. The war in Vietnam was conducted on several levels by the Communists, which tended to blur the ever-present insurgency aspects at times. At first though, insurgency was the major threat and Diem's efforts to counter it were lamentable. Like most things in Diem's regime, the very concept of pacification was corrupted along with its execution. Using the inapplicable model of the British experience in Malaya, Diem pushed a program of *strategic hamlets* and *agrovilles*, designed to provide security by concentrating peasants in fortified locations where they could be managed. The idea ran counter to Vietnamese culture in which the farmer is inseparable from his land. The strategic hamlets ended up failing to provide the security advertised, and turned out to be VC recruiting grounds for dissatisfied farmers. Other aspects of ,Diem's pacification effort were equally unsuccessful. Local security forces were a joke, with little training and few weapons. The National Police were more involved with the suppression of domestic opposition than the elimination of the VCI. The ARVN was geared to withstand a conventional invasion, like that in Korea, and proved poor at dealing with civil affairs.

A Vietnamese Skyraider diving on a small hamlet demonstrates one way of controlling the Viet Cong in the villages.

America's role

Although pacification was always the responsibility of the Saigon government, and carried out mostly by the South Vietnamese themselves, America began to take a more active role during the Kennedy administration due to the heightened awareness of Communist insurgency strategy. Unfortunately there was no attempt at central direction in the American effort. Each interest group of the government (CIA, USAID, State, Agriculture, USIA, the Embassy, etc.) had a different approach and a comparatively low budget for pacification assistance. By 1965, the US perceived that the Communist insurgency was just close to winning and North Vietnam perceived that the insurgency was just close to losing. The resulting race to introduce

IGLOO WHITE

Detection of traffic moving along the Ho Chi Minh Trail was hard. One of the more sophisticated methods in use was the 'Muscle Shoals'/'Igloo White' programme, which used air-dropped sensors to relay information back via an airborne relay to an Infiltration Center. These sensors detected truck movements, and proved fairly successful in helping to direct strike aircraft to targets. They were also of great value in breaking the siege on Khe Sanh, plotting the communist moves around the camp.

Air dropped seismic sensors fall away from a Lockheed OP-2E Neptune during a seeding mission over the Trail.

Above: A pair of Beech QU-22B 'Pave Eagle' relay platforms display the strange geared propeller installation.

Above: The Beech YQU-22A was used in Southeast Asia to evaluate the unmanned radio relay concept.

Above right: Radio relays direct from the sensors to the ground station were handled in the early days by Lockheed EC-121R aircraft of the 553rd Reconnaissance Wing based at Nakhon Phanom.

Right: Also at Nakhon Phanom were the Lockheed OP-2E Neptunes of the Navy's VO-67 squadron. Used for dropping sensors, these aircraft were often armed (note the Minigun pods) to suppress ground fire during sensor seeding runs.

After the QU-22B was introduced as the first radio relay in the link from sensor to ground station, the vulnerable EC-121R could move back away from danger and relay data from the QU-22 to ground.

Below: As ground defenses increased in capability, so fast-mover sensor delivery had to be adopted. The F-4D Phantom was often used, exemplified here by an aircraft carrying six sensors, a Sparrow missile, ECM pod and bombs.

Above: The trusty Douglas A-1 Skyraider played its part in 'Igloo White' operations, dropping sensors such as these 'Spikebuoys' over the Trail.

"Developed by the Defense Communication Planning group, the air-planted Igloo White sensors had to be dropped accurately to monitor the trail which meant flying low and slow. This became more and more dangerous as the North Vietnamese deployed an ever increasing number of anti-aircraft guns along the trail"

regular troops is recounted in earlier chapters, but suffice it to say that US military perceptions settled on the "big unit war" and lost interest in pacification.

A Talk With the Berets
The 11 Green Berets of the advisory team are not men who talk easily with strangers and they dislike civilians. They suspect questions, even innocent ones, which make them even more suspicious. They do not seem at ease with the 14 members of the South Vietnamese Special Forces. The Green Berets seem bored – and able to stand anything but boredom.

When they talk of the montagnards – uncorrupted by the cities, physically superior to most South Vietnamese, less sophisticated in their outlook – the Americans are fiercely possessive. They remind a visitor of the manner in which the British military once talked of the Gurkhas of Nepal.

Because the Green Berets enjoy their own toughness, they appreciate some of the more primitive aspects of the montagnards' habits. They even exaggerate them, and they hope the montagnards will never change.

A young lieutenant has a dog that he never lets off a leash except when it is in his lap. "Well," he said, "if I let it loose the Yards would eat it for sure. Wouldn't want that to happen." (4)

While Westmoreland concentrated on finding and destroying the NVA in the back country, the vast majority of Communist actions (taking in everything from assassinations to shellings to major attacks) were conducted at levels lower than the battalion. This was part of the North's strategy to maintain pressure on several "fronts" simultaneously. While the chance of successful insurgency faded with the commitment of US troops, the guerrilla effort did succeed in occupying the attention of considerable security forces, and distorted most American perceptions about the war. Most of all, it provided a climate which encouraged US withdrawal some years later.

By 1966, inefficiency and half-hearted attempts to coordinate pacfication efforts inspired President Johnson to appoint Robert Komer as his special assistant for pacification, with direct access to the White House. In May 1967, on Komer's recommendation, Johnson placed the responsibility for US pacification assistance under MACV, which had the

Vietnamese villagers are questioned about enemy activity by an interpreter attached to the 1st Cavalry Division.

PBR PATROL

Operations on the shallow and treacherous waters of the Mekong Delta and in the marshes of Rung Sat called for specialized craft. The PBR (Patrol Boat River) was made from glass-reinforced plastic. The PBR drew less than one foot of water, and was propelled by a pump-jet. Normal propellers would have had a hard time of it in the weed-choked swamps and canals. Some 500 were built, most serving with Navy Task Force 116 as part of the River Patrol Force codenamed 'Game Warden'. Heavily armed for such small craft, the PBRs saw a considerable amount of action.

Left: A river patrol boat chugs in reverse in the sunset. The mobile riverine force – the 'brown water navy' in Vietnam – was a unique combination of forces from the Army's 9th Infantry Division and the Navy's Task Force 117 and SEAL teams.

President Thieu attempted to cut off Viet Cong support at the grass roots by means of agrarian reform.

resources and the clout to get things done. Westmoreland was assigned General Creighton Abrams as a deputy with a charter to enhance the ARVN, and "Blowtorch Bob" Komer himself as a deputy for CORDS (Civil Operations & Revolutionary Development Support). The pacification effort, for the first time, came under a unified civil-military chain of command which reported to Westmorland through Komer, and featured a single manager for pacification support at every level of the South Vietnamese government.

Pacification with teeth

Komer worked with the Vietnamese to develop a national pacification plan with teeth. The part-time local security units (Regional Forces at the district and province level, and Popular Forces at the local level) were given better weapons, and their US advisors were subordinated to the CORDS chain of command. US Army Mobile Advisory Teams made the rounds of RF/PF units to conduct needed training. The South Vietnamese National Police (called "white mice" by GIs because of the color of their hats and accoutrements) were integrated into the fight against the VCI along with intelligence forces

Below: Mainstay of the riverine forces in Vietnam, the river patrol boat or PBR MK II. The 32ft-long boat was armed with twin .50 calibre machine guns forward and a single .30 calibre gun aft. A radar set housed in a mast-mounted dome monitored enemy activity on the shore. Top speed was 20 knots.

"We stop and search anywhere the grass is bent, or it looks like a boat's been beached, or at the mouth of a canal. Coconut palms usually mean an abandoned village, and they're likely spots as well"

Left: A Navy crewman at the aft gun of a PBR patrolling the Go Cong river in 1967.

Right: A Huey gunship and a PBR at speed. Riverine operations were broad in scope. The Navy's river patrol force, Task Force 116, was supported by a helicopter attack squadron, while the combined Army-Navy force included a supporting artillery battalion equipped with 105mm howitzers. Typical riverine operations would involve heliborne assault troops, artillery and tactical air support from 'fast movers' as well as shipborne troops and firepower.

Above: The Mobile Riverine Force was indeed mobile – it could move 150 miles in 24 hours and be in combat within 30 minutes of anchoring.

Below: PBR thrashing through the water. Mark I ships had a fiberglass hull; Mark IIs were faster, aluminum-hulled boats. Both had a crew of four.

PADDYFIELD SOLDIER

Vietnam is a tropical country, and its main crop is rice. During the wet season, most of the flat areas of the country are either a sea of glutinous mud, or are completely under water. Of course, the paddy fields are ringed and criss-crossed by dykes making travel relatively easy but they are also the easiest sites for booby traps, and patrols had to be extremely wary about where they placed their tropical boots. Patrols could use the dykes for cover, but it was difficult to cross several hundred exposed yards of waist deep mud just to close with the foe.

Above: A Marine of H Co, 2/5 Marines, leaps across a break in a rice paddy dyke while on a search-and-destroy mission during Operation Colorado in August 1966.

Left: A rifleman from HQ Bn, 1st Marine Div, during a sweep of paddy fields near Da Nang, in search of Viet Cong. The soft hat allows better hearing than a helmet.

Right: Near Quang Tri in I Corps, Marines ford a jungle stream during Operation Medina in October 1967. Water in all its forms hampered quiet, swift movement of US ground troops throughout Vietnam.

and the sinister Provincial Reconnaissance Units. These elements carried out the controversial Phoenix program (Phung Hoang). Between 1968 and 1971, Phoenix identified some 65,000 members of the VCI. Of those, 20,000 were killed, 28,000 jailed, and 17,000 turned towards the Saigon government. Although not simply an assassination program, as has been alleged, it was capable of mistakes and abuses. Its highest praise, perhaps, came from the North Vietnamese, who admitted its effectiveness after the war.

Pacification and Tet

Pacification reform had not yet gotten up to speed when the Communists launched the 1968 Tet Offensive. In an effort to attain maximum Viet Cong penetration of the offensive's targets, the VCI was employed for active missions. In the resulting carnage, many of its members were exposed. Tet left a power vacuum in rural South Vietnam as the VCI disappeared, and pacification forces had to cope with refugee resettlement and the reestablishment of the government in numerous areas. Komer convinced the Saigon government to adopt the Accelerated Pacification Campaign late in the year, which filled the gap left by the depleted VCI.

Too often the villagers who were caught in the middle of the struggle received nothing but tragedy and death.

Left: Members of a US Navy Underwater Demolition Team crouch down on the lookout while a further team member prepares to blow up a Viet Cong bunker hidden in the paddy field nearby.

Above: Members of G Co, 2/7 Marines emerge from the jungle during Operation Harvest Moon in December 1965. Spreading out across the rice paddy makes them a harder target for any VC in the treeline.

"The middle of the year, when the Monsoon floods the Mekong Delta, water is everywhere. The canals are the roads of the region and they run long and straight from the swollen rivers. All war plans involve boats. The communists cart their troops and supplies by night in flotillas of long, narrow, shallow draft sampans. The same boats carry Charlie away when he retreats"

The village war was often best fought by combined US and CIDG operations such as here near Van Thien in 1970.

Between 1969 and 1971, CORDS enjoyed considerable success in boosting the efforts of the South Vietnamese Revolutionary Development cadres. Additionally, President Thieu's genuine land reforms over the period 1970-73 went a long way toward relieving age-old rural grievances. By all standards, including the highly suspect *Hamlet Evaluation System* statistics, pacification was a success. This was due, in part, to the rationalization of the US and South Vietnamese pacification support structure and its funding, and also in part to the North Vietnamese themselves. It has always been suspected that part of Hanoi's hidden agenda for the Tet Offensive was the crippling of the Viet Cong. Certainly their long term goals did not include a meaningful VC role in post-war leadership – a fact which has been confirmed by subsequent events. Even the Communist return to low key guerrilla tactics after Tet did not seem to inspire a drive by Hanoi to resurrect a strong VCI, which undoubtedly would have facilitated the Communist strategy. It is quite likely that North Vietnamese leaders had already decided that the conquest of South Vietnam would be by main force, and they simply wished to bide their time while awaiting the inevitable US withdrawal. As the US disengagement course became clear, Hanoi could afford to default in the village war – a massive conventional invasion would render pacification inconsequential.

Are the U.S. and its allies still trying to "win the hearts and minds of the people" in South Vietnam? Not any more, at least in those terms. According to a new directive entitled "Let's Say It Right," the allied effort is intended to "develop community spirit." Prepared by the U.S. Command in Vietnam for military press officers, the directive bans or substantially alters 22 terms that once were used frequently in briefings for correspondents in Saigon. Instead of "search and destroy," U.S. briefings officers should now say "search and clear." U.S. troop withdrawals are to be described as "U.S. redeployment" or "replacement by ARVN" (Army of the Republic of South Vietnam). A Viet Cong tax collector should be called a V.C. extortionist. V.C. defectors are to be called ralliers.

The term "body count" is banned. Hamburger Hill is to be mentioned only by its metric name: Hill 937. Press officers also are sternly enjoined from referring to "the 5 o'clock follies," the name given by newsmen to

Above: An advisor identified as 'Mr. Cash' and a Special Forces sergeant conduct an orientation for Vietnamese Rangers in 1970.

Below: The CIA had its own airline, Air America which operated all over SE Asia. This turbo powered Beech 18 is seen at Tan Son Nhut.

CIA AT WAR

The CIA played a major but secret part in the war in South East Asia. Their operations covered a wide range of legal and less than legal activities, including gathering intelligence, conducting clandestine operations against the Viet Cong, providing logistic support for the temporary USAF rescue helicopter landing zones deep in Laos, or inspiring and leading some of the many ethnic minorities in Vietnam into battle. The CIA controlled Air America, which at least part of the time operated as a genuine charter airline. The CIA stayed in Vietnam to the bitter end.

the frequently fanciful official recitation of the day's events. From now on, the briefings will simply be called briefings. (5)

The US Marine Corps entered the war with its own strategic thinking about counterinsurgency warfare. The "ink blot" system provided for a constantly spreading pacified area under the protection of Marine units. As MACV had operational theater control, Army methods were forced on the Marines, and the ink blot dried up. An outgrowth of the original thinking resulted in the Combined Action program, started in 1965. Specially selected Màrine combat veterans were put together in volunteer squads, which were given instruction in Vietnamese culture, and teamed up with Popular Forces platoons. The Marines trained the Popular Forces, aided the villagers, and – most important of all – lived with them. Most ARVN and US units moved on and the Viet Cong moved back in to punish villagers who cooperated with the government. The CAP Marines stayed, and could call on their neighboring units for assistance. The concept worked well enough for the Marines to organize four Combined Action battalions by 1968. Westmoreland responded that he didn't have the resources to waste on such a program, so the Army continued its search and destroy tactics – leaving unprotected the people it was there to defend.

Night of Death

The Communist attack opened suddenly with a fiery burst of 60- and 81-mm mortar fire that jolted the residents of Thanh My and two nearby hamlets out of their sleep at 1:30 a.m. one night last week. Many of the shells were white-phosphorous ones that set fire to the flimsy huts.

The Communists, apparently a mixed force of North Vietnamese sappers and Viet Cong guerrillas, skillfully pinned down one platoon of U.S. Marines and one of the Popular Forces that were on night ambush duty near by. A Regional Forces platoon was trapped inside its compound near the village's only military target, a bridge across the Ba Ren River. After pounding the three hamlets with some 200 mortar rounds, enemy troops slipped into Thanh My. By then, many of the residents, trying to escape the mortar explosions, had taken refuge in bunkers. They soon became graves.

The Communist troops moved through Thanh My hurling various sorts of explosives – grenades, satchel charges and homemade devices called "Chicom grenades," which are fashioned from Coca-Cola cans filled with plastique or TNT, rocks and nails. Explosives

A Vietnamese fires his M60 at suspected enemy positions. By the end of 1970, ARVNs were taking over US combat tasks.

Left: Laos, September 1972. A CIA helicopter heads for the town of Long Chen, headquarters of the Clandestine Army of General Vang Pao. The CIA were providing support and advice against the nearby NVA, who were shelling the town.

Above: An Air America Huey lands on a Navy ship during the final evacuation of Saigon.

Below: The Caribou was one of several types used by the CIA to support clandestine operations.

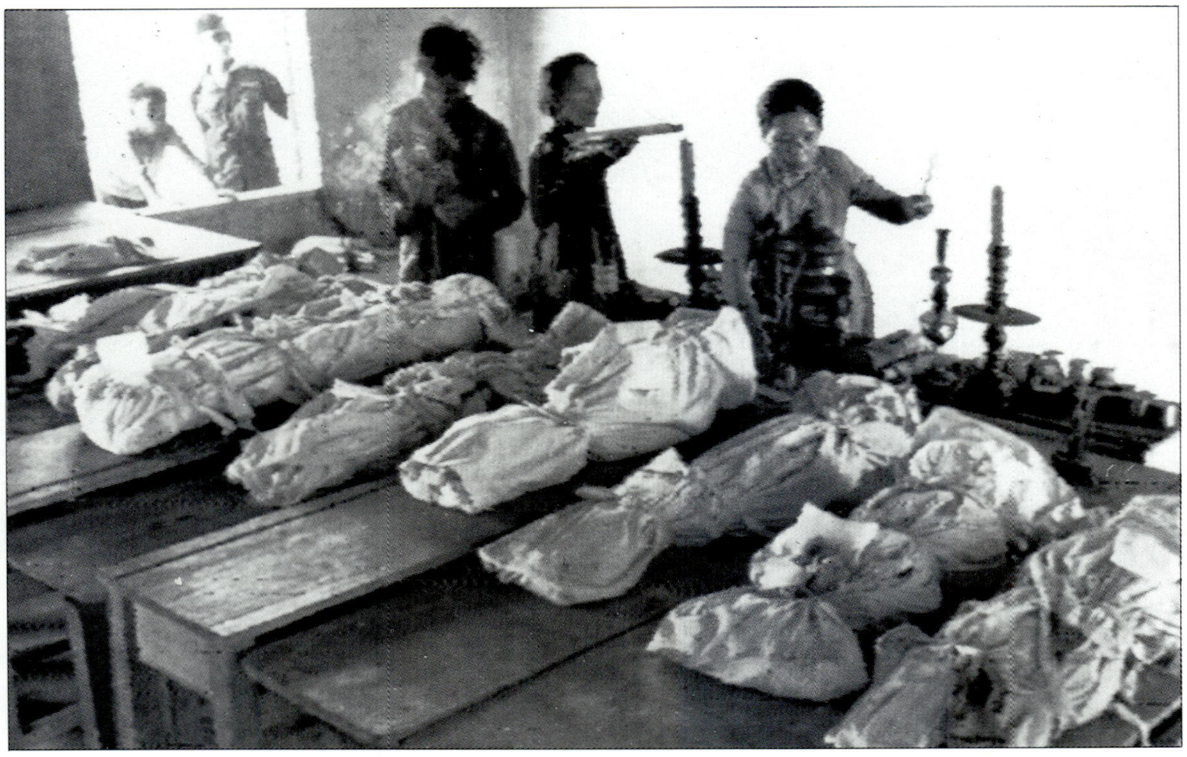

dumped into one large bunker killed 24 persons. "When the V.C. came, they shot every house," says Hoan Than Tick, 56, a resident who escaped. "When people ran, they shot them too. Then they threw grenades into the bunkers."

All the hamlets were heavily damaged, and Thanh My was virtually destroyed. At least 114 inhabitants died in the raid in the worst Communist massacre since the deathly days of the 1968 *Tet* attacks. The survivors wandered dazedly through the smoldering ruins of their homes. One old dwarf carried two severed hands wrapped in paper – all that he could find of his twelve-year-old son, who was in one of bunkers. Even as the people of Thanh My mourned their dead, the women of a village controlled by the Viet Cong only a few miles away showed up to carry off the 16 Communists killed during the attack. Neither group of mourners disturbed the other.

Thanh My, located 18 miles south of Danang, had been considered one of the safer points in I Corps' Quang Nam province. The Communists apparently had no objective in mind other than to break that reputation by killing as many of Thanh My's men, women and children as they could in one night of terror. (6)

The remains of mass murder at Hue should have given warning to the villages of the true nature of the Viet Cong.

CHAPTER NINE

HANDING OVER THE WAR 1971

A Marine Staff Sergeant from the 1st Marine Division on a Patrol in support of the large ARVN operation into Laos, Lam Son 719. US troops were confined to the Vietnamese side of the border.

As the year began, Congress sought to head off any further operations like the Cambodian Incursion by prohibiting the movement of US ground forces into either Cambodia or Laos. Public opinion was restless, and the publication of *The Pentagon Papers* in mid-June did nothing to make it less so. The *Papers*, a classified history of the US decision-making process in the war, got into the hands of the *New York Times* by way of Daniel Ellsberg, who felt that the government's classification of the report was intended to avoid embarrassment rather than protect defense secrets. In general, *The Pentagon Papers* confirmed that the Johnson administration really didn't know what it was doing.

Johnson's decision to fight the war with young draftees produced another spinoff in July 1971 when the US voting age was lowered from 21 to 18 by the ratification of the 26th Amendment to the Constitution. Again, the public felt that it was wrong that young men were being asked to die for their country without the benefit of representation in government.

His mother spotted him first, and as the slender young marine entered the crowded terminal at Oakland International Airport, she rushed forward and threw her arms around him. Then it was his father's turn, and the two shook hands vigorously. Finally, his 8-year-old brother stepped forward, and the marine reached out and tousled his hair. Minutes later, the family was driving home to Castro Valley, south of Oakland

Throughout the country last week, the familiar scene was played out as families greeted long-absent sons and daughters who were coming home for the holidays. But for this marine, the homecoming was special. Like thousands of other GI's, the 19-year-old was home this Christmas on "Operation Reunion" – a two-week furlough for servicemen who are midway through their tour of duty in South Vietnam.

The program has been a resounding success ever since it was started a month ago. Although the GI's must pay the fare out of their own pockets, the 80-odd flights offered by two charter airlines have sold out. The young lance corporal stationed with the First Marine Division at Da Nang had his parents draw $350 from his savings account. "It took my new car away," he said. "I was going to buy one when I got back from Nam." But it was worth it. "I wanted to see this girl," he said, "-plus I wanted to get home." (1)

President Nixon, feeling secure in his "peace with

TRAINING

Arriving in Vietnam, fresh out of training, the conscript was thrown into action in a completely alien environment. It was clear that many Stateside lessons would have to be relearned. For a while the only classroom available was the real thing, where the pass mark was survival. It took some little time, but training programmes were established in-country. Some enterprising units had their Kit Carson Scouts give a graphic display of VC ability by demonstrating the extraordinary infiltration skills of the VC sapper battalions.

A survival exercise is completed at Nha Trang. Such in-country training was essential in Vietnam's hostile terrain and climate.

Below: Members of the 7th Cavalry climb a rope ladder to a waiting Chinook – to practise rapelling out the other side.

honor" policy, was ready to apply whatever pressure he could to reach some sort of face-saving agreement with North Vietnam. Along with military means, this included diplomatic efforts to isolate Hanoi. In July he announced a forthcoming trip to Beijing for the purpose of reopening a dialogue with the People's Republic of China.

Returning home

The 1st Cavalry Division began to return home in March and April, with the 3rd Brigade remaining on in Vietnam until mid-1972 in an independent capacity. Returning to Fort Hood, Texas, the "Cav" replaced the 1st Armored Division which, in turn, transferred its flag to Germany. America's first and most successful airmobile division would change its configuration to a short-lived TRICAP (triple capability – airmobile, armor, attack helicopter) experimental structure and then revert to being a straight armored division. The 11th Armored Cavalry Regiment also departed in March for Germany (another flag transfer in 1972), leaving one squadron behind for another year in Vietnam. The 1st Marine Division's 5th Marines were out by April and its 1st Marines were gone by the following month. The 2nd Brigade of the 25th Infantry Division were back in Hawaii by April, completing the division's rotation. The 101st Airborne Division's 3rd Brigade moved to Fort Campbell, Kentucky in December, while the rest of the division prepared to follow. Other units returned from Vietnam to face disbandment, including: 52nd Artillery Group (June), 173rd Airborne Brigade (August), 1st Brigade of the 5th Infantry Division [Mechanized] (August), 108th Artillery Group (November), and the Americal Division (less the 196th Brigade) in November. At mid-year, US Army strength in Vietnam numbered 190,500 and the Marine presence was all but gone, with only 500 personnel in country.

April 12th:

The war had long been "winding down" in Quang Tin province, and no one at the 23rd (Americal) Division's Fire Support Base Mary Ann had seen the enemy for quite some time. "Man, we thought for us the war was over," muttered one grunt, while another at the soon-to-be-abandoned base recalled: "We weren't expecting anything, and we especially weren't expecting what we got." Certainly no one at the woefully undermanned fire base last week expected the savagely successful enemy attack that left 33 Americans killed and 76 wounded, the largest single American combat loss in a year. (2)

The heavily armed UH-1 'God of Hell Fire' takes off from the old combat base at Khe Sanh during operation Dewey Canyon.

Left: An M60 Machine Gun is put through its paces along with a line of other weapons at an impromptu 25th Infantry Division range session. The tight range organization normal in peacetime weapons training is notable by its absence. Note the size of the M60 gunner; carrying and firing the 'Pig' was a physically demanding job.

"Now the legs have been playing hide and seek with Charlie. You've got to find him before you can kill him. So they've come to us, the Special Forces Recondo School, for help"

Below: Rappelling out of a Huey to join the rest of the squad below.

The most important operation of 1971 was Lam Son 719, billed as the first big test of Vietnamization. It was an ambitious plan for other reasons as well, being the largest airmobile operation of the war, and the first airmobile operation to be attempted against a serious air defense environment. The object of the offensive was to disrupt the Ho Chi Minh Trail opposite northern I Corps to delay anticipated Communist offensive activity. The targets were NVA Base Area 604, at Tchepone, and Base Area 611, paralleling the border in a southerly direction. The NVA had anticipated such an offensive by as much as five months, and had reinforced the area with Front 70B, including the 304th, 308th, and 320th NVA Divisions and some 20 air defense battalions with guns ranging up to 100mm.

90 Days

Lam Son 719 was to be conducted over a 90-day period in four phases. The first of these was a US operation, Dewey Canyon II, which was to secure Highway 9 to the Laotian border to provide a jump-off point for the main attack by ARVN I Corps. The 1st Brigade of the US 5th Infantry Division (Mech) would perform this operation, along with supporting units from US XXIV Corps. For political reasons, US ground troops and advisors were not permitted to accompany the ARVN into Laos – only helicopter and fixed-wing air assets could participate. The assault (Phase II), was planned with an axis of Highway 9 for 40km toward Tchepone. It would be carried out by a ground and airmobile force consisting of the ARVN 1st Armored Brigade, 1st Ranger Group, 1st Division, Airborne Division, Marine Division, and the 5th Regiment of the 2nd Division. When Tchepone was taken, and supporting firebases secured to guard the flanks of the drive, Phase III would begin. This phase encompassed the destruction of NVA supplies uncovered in the vicinity. The fourth phase was to be the withdrawal prior to the heavy monsoon rains.

On January 30th, Dewey Canyon II was launched with the seizure of the old Khe Sanh base as an assembly area for the ARVN. The Phase II main effort kicked off on February 8th, with the ARVN armor moving down Highway 9. The flank operations involved airmobile assaults to seize dominating terrain on either side of the axis of advance. This was where the US helicopter force came into play. Rotary wing assets were task organized under the command of the US 101st Airborne Division (Airmobile), and consisted of 659 helicopters: 64 scouts (OH-6A and OH-58), 177 gunships (AH-1G and UH-1C), and 418 transports (UH-1H, CH-47, CH-53 and CH-54). Airmobile assaults to the north of the road were undertaken by the ARVN Airborne and Ranger units, while those to the south involved the ARVN 1st Division. B-52 strikes and suppressive fire from helicopter gunships were used to "prep" the landing zones.

To the modern American cavalryman of the air, the plunge into Laos has been something like an old-time charge on horseback: admirably heroic, stunningly effective – and terribly costly. For four weeks now, American helicopter pilots have flown through some of the heaviest flak in the history of the Indochinese war. One day alone last week, the Army admitted to losing ten aircraft to the unexpectedly heavy North Vietnamese ground fire, and there were reports from the field that the actual losses had been much worse. As a result, the customary bravado of the American chopper pilot was beginning to wear a bit thin. "Two weeks ago," said one gunship skipper, "I couldn't have told you how much time I had left to serve in Vietnam. Now I know that I've got 66 days to go, and I'm counting every one." Another flier added anxiously: "The roles are reversed over there. In Vietnam, you have to hunt

HOT LZS

The new helicopter tactics gave US forces unprecedented mobility, allowing large units to swoop upon the enemy with little or no warning. It was not long before the Viet Cong and the North Vietnamese army learned of the limitations of the technique, however. In the jungles and mountain forests of Vietnam the guerrillas soon learned that by waiting at potential Landing Zones, they could catch the Americans at their most vulnerable.

Above: Helicopter door gunners lay down suppressive fire as they leave a landing zone (LZ) near Bien Hoa. The troops they have just landed move warily across the rice paddy towards the treeline, from where retreating VC snipers and a mortar team have the LZ under fire.

Above left: Inserted into the Mekong Delta, some 40 miles south-east of Saigon, a GI hangs on to his helmet in the wash from the slick's rotors. Note the size of his pack: while airmobility meant that troops could be moved to trouble spots at great speed, they had to be prepared to survive in the bush for days at a time without resupply.

Left: A pathfinder advises incoming helicopter pilots of ground conditions during an assault by ARVN Rangers in the Central Highlands, 1970. The pathfinders' task was to test a potential LZ for hostile activity and clear the ground of obstacles, such as brush, trees or booby traps, before the main body of heliborne troops was inserted.

for the enemy. But in Laos, man, they hunt for you."

Despite the risks, it was inevitable that U.S. helicopters should be deeply involved in the Laotian campaign, for more than any other artifact of war, the chopper has become the indelible symbol of the Indochina conflict. Helicopter pilots were among the first Americans killed in the war a decade ago, and, under President Nixon's Vietnamization program, they will probably be among the last to leave. In the years between, the chopper's mobility and firepower have added a radically new dimension to warfare, and the daring young American pilots have scooped up their Silver Stars, Distinguished Flying Crosses and Air Medals by the bushel – along with Purple Hearts. In the opinion of many military experts, the helicopter has been the difference between a humiliating U.S. defeat in Vietnam and whatever chance remains of attaining some more satisfactory outcome. (3)

The ARVN 1st Division was able to conduct Phase III operations almost immediately in the vicinity of Base Area 611. North of Highway 9, the ARVN Rangers and Airborne met considerably more opposition, including a counterattack by NVA tanks. In the center, the ARVN armored advance was stalled by the end of February when it ran head-on into NVA armor. The ground advance on Tchepone was thus halted in favor of an airmobile assault by the ARVN 1st Division. On March 6th, two of the division's battalions were lifted into Tchepone by 120 helicopters in the biggest air assault of the war. B-52 strikes had stunned the defenders and killed hundreds. Again the ARVN destroyed tons of supplies and weapons – though not in the quantities that had been found in Cambodia in 1970.

Increased pressure

The Communists increased the pressure by throwing in even more forces including the 324th NVA Division, the 202nd Armored Regiment and several other tank and heavy artillery units. The Phase IV withdrawal was conducted under the most severe conditions. ARVN armor found it as hard to retreat as to advance, and very few of the troops of the Highway 9 axis made it back to South Vietnam. The fire support bases on the flanks came under constant attack, making extraction difficult and, in a few cases, impossible. By the end of March, all of the ARVN's viable units had withdrawn.

The outcome of the operation was something of a tactical draw. The ARVN leadership credited Lam Son 719 with delaying the next NVA offensive for nearly a year. On the other hand, the ARVN had been run out of Laos in 45 days, and had suffered a psychological shock at the hands of the NVA. Casualties for both sides were high – perhaps as much as 50% of both forces involved. ARVN dead and missing totaled 1,392 according to official statements, but may have been as high as 4,575. Between 4,236 and 5,200 ARVN troops were wounded. US air crews suffered 155 dead and missing plus 215 wounded. Communist casualties were estimated at nearly 14,000 dead alone, with 167 captured and 6,657 weapons recovered. The US lost 90 helicopters (with another 453 damaged), while the ARVN lost 96 pieces of artillery and 71 tanks. The NVA lost between 100 and 120 tanks. The ARVN performed fairly well in the face of overwhelming opposition, and did not deserve the bad press reports which followed the operation. It should be remembered however, that without US air support Lam Son 719 could have been a genuine disaster.

Not long after the South Vietnamese Army plunged across the border into Laos, a Vietnamese major sat down for a private chat with a reporter in an outpost near Khe Sanh. "Aren't you afraid that the North Vietnamese might be luring your forces into a Dienbien-

Troopers from the 173rd Army Airborne Brigade race from their helicopters for cover in a 1965 operation outside Saigon.

Left: Men and machine under fire. Choppers made large and tempting targets, and crews ran constant risks when inserting and extracting GIs. Yet a staggering total of 7,547,000 assault sorties were flown by US helicopter pilots during the course of the war.

> ***"I thought we'd fly a lot better without our cargo of ARVNs. Suddenly, green tracers whipped in front of us, I heard someone say "Shit, we're hit""***

phu-style trap in Laos?" asked the journalist. A smile of satisfaction crossed the officer's face. "Nonsense," he replied. "Did the French have helicopter gunships?" And he swept his hand low over a table in a swift, darting gesture to imitate the flight of a helicopter. "Did the French have jet fighter-bombers?" His hand swooped downward. "And the French, I can assure you, did not have B-52s," he declared – and his fist thundered on to the table.

That kind of confidence seemed justified enough in the early days of the Laotian invasion – and, to a degree, even during the tough battles between U.S. helicopters and Communist anti-aircraft guns that followed. But last week brought another sharp reminder that the North Vietnamese do not always knuckle under to explosive American air power, and that the outcome of the war in Indochina still depends largely on foot soldiers slugging it out on the ground. Throughout the bomb-blasted moonscape of the central Laotian panhandle troops of the South Vietnamese Army (ARVN) and Communist forces waged some of the bloodiest ground battles of the war. And when the fighting died down, the ARVN troops seemed to be scurrying back toward their own border. As the Pentagon described it, the South Vietnamese were engaged in "mobile maneuvering." But in the eyes of many observers, it seemed more like a plain old-fashioned retreat. (4)

US troops watch helicopters depart from a fire-support base near Chu Lai. By this time, ARVNs did most of the ground fighting.

In mid-April the ARVN launched Lam Son 720, a push into the A Shau Valley with elements of the Marine Division and US helicopter and air support. The heaviest fighting of the operation took place in the last half of May during determined NVA counterattacks. The drive was a threat to NVA Base Area 607. By mid-June Lam Son 720 involved two marine brigades as well as several ARVN regiments. A follow-up operation, Lam Son 810 took place in September to try to pre-empt further Communist supply stockpiling along the Laotian border. Another ARVN divisional drive took place in November in the Central Highlands, the target again being Communist base areas. Another Communist base, the U Minh Forest in South Vietnam's southern IV Corps, was attacked during September, with the ARVN eliminating 400 VC at the cost of 113 ARVN dead and another 183 wounded.

Communist raids

At the end of April, Communist units staged dramatic raids on the major base complexes in South Vietnam. Their most noteworthy successes included detonating Da Nang's aviation fuel storage tanks and blowing up the Qui Nhon ammunition depot. Sappers continued their work in May, igniting six aviation fuel tanks at Cam Ranh Bay. During the late-August South Vietnamese elections, the Communist terror campaign stepped up to discourage voter participation and, for dramatic effect, paid another visit to Cam Ranh to blow up the ammunition dump.

In Cambodia, Lon Nol's government was in trouble. With the Communists occupying the main road between the port of Kampong Som, as Sihanoukville was now called, and Phnom Penh, vital supplies for the capital had to be flown in or shipped up the Mekong from South Vietnam. After two months, the road was finally cleared by FANK and ARVN troops on January 22nd, but at the end of March the Communists again seized enough of the road to block traffic for a further month.

South Vietnam continued its border campaign in February with a division-size drive in Cambodia's Kompong Cham Province in cooperation with the FANK and with US air support. In mid-May the ARVN launched a regimental-size attack into the Cambodian Parrot's Beak area, again using US helicopter and air support. During September, the ARVN struck north from Tay Ninh to clear Highway 22 into Cambodia and relieve the pressure on beseiged ARVN fire bases in the area. By November the ARVN were able to take the offensive against the VC 7th and 9th Divisions at Chup, northeast of Phnom Penh, with a combined ARVN/FANK force of 27,500 men. They succeeded in capturing the town with US air support in December, and destroyed some supplies. Communist forces closing in on Phnom Penh from the north, via Highway 6, routed opposing FANK units, and pressed to within 16 miles of the capital in early December.

CIA in Laos

The US Central Intelligence Agency's involvement in the war in Laos came to light in August when the administration revealed that various non-Communist troops were organized and paid by the CIA. The US believed that regular units of the *Forces Armees Royales* (FAR or Royal Laotian Army) were ineffective, just as the North Vietnamese regarded the *Neo Lao Hak Xat* (NLHX or Pathet Lao) as unsatisfactory. Thus, the seven FAR Groupements Mobiles (GMs or Mobile Groups of about brigade size) operating in Laotian Military Regions III and IV (opposite North Vietnam) were supplemented by seven GMs of Laotian Irregular Forces and additional units backed by the CIA (including the Air America transport service). The effort in Laos was further enhanced in October, when US Special Forces began Project Unity, training special Thai mercenary light infantry battalions for service in the 014 Division in the Laotian panhandle. The Communists generally matched these moves in quantity and quality, first by integrating NVA cadre with selected Pathet Lao units, and finally by the commitment of regular NVA combat units. Beginning in 1970, the NVA 968 Group pursued a vigorous security campaign for the Ho Chi Minh Trail. It included the 9th, 19th and 29th NVA Regiments, reinforced by armor and artillery and the independent 39th Regiment. Both sides had to contend with their allied Laotian neutralist elements, which proved to be unreliable politically and militarily. The FAR had to put up with GMs 801 and 802 of the *Forces Armees Neutralistes* (FAN), while the Pathet Lao suffered similar units of Dissident Neutralists on its side.

US fatalities in 1971 reached their lowest level since 1965, dramatically emphasizing the reduction in operations. American killed in action totaled 1,381, while non-hostile causes claimed another 968 lives. US servicemen seriously wounded amounted to 8,936. South Vietnamese casualties registered only a slight decline from the previous year, and

WILD WEASEL

Surface-to-air missiles shot down only a small number of US aircraft due to an active campaign to provide adequate countermeasures. While electronic warfare types jammed the radars, 'Wild Weasel' aircraft carried out anti-radiation attacks, using missiles which homed on the enemy radars controlling the SAMs. Under the program name 'Iron Hand', these aircraft were feared greatly by North Vietnamese SAM crews, and their reputation was well-founded, for they destroyed numerous sites.

Entering service in the 'Wild Weasel' role during the last months of the war was the McDonnell F-4C Phantom. This example, complete with Shrike anti-radar missiles, is seen refuelling from a Boeing KC-135 during 'Linebacker II'.

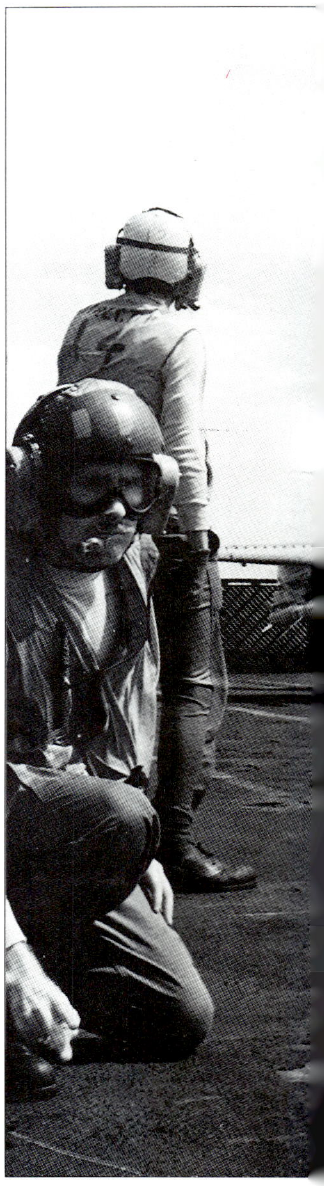

Above: Navy 'Iron Hand' anti-radiation missions launched from the smaller carriers were handled by the Douglas A-4 Skyhawk, suitably modified with a radar homing and warning system and provision for Shrike missiles.

"The rattlesnake tone in Leo's headset buzzed in time with the flickering strobes on Harry's scope. Already the enemy missile crews were warming up the SAM radars and searching for American aircraft"

Left: Republic F-105s hit the tanker en route to their targets 'up North'. 'Wild Weasel'-configured F-105s flew ahead of the strike packages to soften up the SAM defences.

amounted to 22,738 dead, 2325 missing (presumed dead) and 60,939 wounded. Third country allies lost 528 dead and missing plus 1,148 wounded. Communist casualties also dropped slightly, with a body count of 98,094 for the year. US Army helicopter losses dropped to 491. For the first time operational losses (155) were substantially lower than combat losses (336). Nineteen of the combat losses were from attacks against US camps, 316 were due to ground fire, and the remaining loss was from a MiG intercept. The Marines lost only 6 helicopters (2 operational and 4 to ground fire) and a single fixed-wing plane (to ground fire).

Preventive reaction

In January, the concept of *protective reaction* strikes (i.e., the bombing of air defense sites which shot at recon aircraft) was expanded to include a multitude of other targets in southern North Vietnam. NVA SAM sites which fired across the border to engage US aircraft in Laos got particular attention. By April, air strikes were being carried out as far as 250 kilometers north of the DMZ. Between

Although US combat troops were withdrawing, aviation and artillery were heavily involved supporting ARVN operations.

Below: In the later years of the war the Vought A-7 Corsair II was the Navy's prime 'Iron Hand' weapon. It was widely used during the 'Linebacker' raids on anti-radiation missions. This VA-146 aircraft carries bombs and Shrikes.

Above: A Republic F-105F 'Wild Weasel' departs on a mission. The F-model featured a second seat for the electronic warfare officer.

Left: The F-105G model introduced internal ECM and Standard anti-radiation missile capability.

Right: F-105s line up at their Thai base, awaiting orders for a strike North. Without the 'Weasels' these missions would have been almost suicidal.

late September and the end of December, air strikes against North Vietnam increased in size and intensity, with daily efforts often including 250 or more aircraft. Nevertheless, Air Force fixed-wing losses dropped to 83 during 1971 – half that of 1970. Sixteen losses were operational and the other 67 were in combat, with 61 due to ground fire, 4 to SAMs, and one each to MiGs and enemy attacks on US bases.

The US Navy averaged one small-deck and two large-deck carriers on Yankee Station during 1971, only slightly less than during 1970. Naval air losses, however, were half the 1970 total, and amounted to only 21 fixed-wing planes. Sixteen of these were operational losses, 4 were to ground fire, and SAMs got the remaining plane.

NORTH VIETNAMESE LOGISTICS

Had the war been only an insurgency, logistics would not have presented the North Vietnamese with many problems. With locally confiscated food, an insurgency could have lingered on indefinitely with just periodic shipments of small arms and ammunition. An insurgency however, would not have satisfied Hanoi's goal of *reunification under North Vietnam* and, in any case, could never have been decisive in South Vietnam – especially after Tet '68 and the pacification efforts which followed. To accommodate North Vietnamese military and political objectives, a large and complex logistical system was developed which eventually supported a 20-division army equipped with modern assault rifles, plentiful tanks and heavy artillery. Several critical elements contributed to the success of this system: outside supply of modern equipment and ammunition; a diversified transport and distribution network from North to South Vietnam; and secure base areas near the combat theater, where supplies could be stockpiled and units refitted.

North Vietnam did not have the industrial capacity to produce heavy or high technology weapons such as tanks, aircraft, or surface-to-air missiles (SAMs). These, and most other military supplies were provided by the Chinese and the Soviets. Initially, most small arms and personal equipment were supplied by the Chinese Communists and, indeed, Chinese material assistance was largely responsible for the NVA as it existed in 1965. At that time however, the Soviet Union, in competition with China for influence with Ho Chi Minh, began to provide advanced weaponry to Hanoi. In early May of 1965, 25 new all-weather fighters and eight Il-28 jet bombers (capable of striking US facilities in South Vietnam) were delivered by the Soviets. In July the

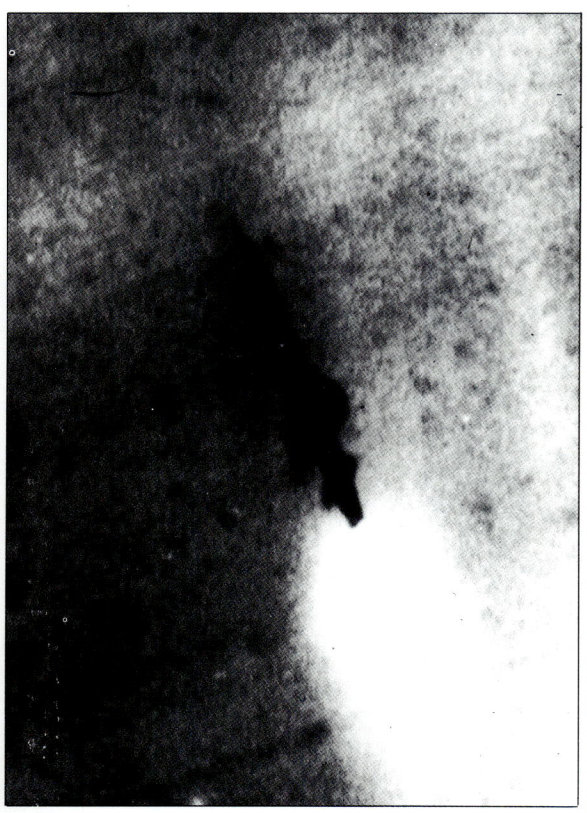

North Vietnam is one of the poorest countries in the world, and relied upon aid from China and the USSR for high tech weapons such as this SA-2.

HELO GUNSHIPS

The agility and flexibility of the helicopter led it naturally to be developed as a weapon-carrying platform, and to this end early helos in Vietnam were hastily fitted with forward-firing guns. So useful did they prove that dedicated versions of the Huey appeared, armed to the teeth with guns and rockets. Successes with these led to the hastily produced Bell AH-1G, designed from the outset as a gunship, and proving immensely valuable in areas of stiff opposition from the ground.

Above: The AH-1G Huey derivative gunship proved a major success in Southeast Asia. This aircraft is seen refuelling from the hover during the 1970 Cambodia campaign.

Resplendent in shark's mouth markings, this Bell AH-1G is typical of the many that served in Vietnam. It is armed with a 40-mm grenade launcher and 7.62-mm six-barrel machine gun in the nose turret, and pods for 52 rockets. Often extra Minigun pods were carried on the inboard pylons. The first type to adopt the classic gunship configuration, the AH-1 Cobra carried the gunner in the forward cockpit, affording him a commanding view of the tactical situation.

Above: *Helicopter gunship experience was first gained with various versions of the Bell* ***UH-1*** *Huey, armed with varied guns and rocket pods. While proving quite effective, the 'Hog' Hueys had difficulty keeping up with the 'slicks' carrying troops.*

Above: *Three shark-mouthed* ***AH-1Gs*** *cruise purposefully towards their operational area.* ***D****uring combat operations they would fly considerably lower, and they had to use their speed, agility and firepower to overcome heavy groundfire.* ***D****uring the war 173 were downed by hostile action.*

"A lot of people thought that a semi-skilled skeet shooter, or even a sling-shot artist could knock a helicopter out of the sky at close range, and that an attack on real AA defenses would be suicidal. It's an understandable attitude in duck hunters, whose targets don't shoot back. In reality, of course, armed helos can and do hit back, hard and accurate"

first SAM-associated missile equipment arrived. The NVA steadily improved in capabilities, and by the Tet Offensive of 1968 was employing PT-76 light tanks and 122mm rocket launchers in South Vietnam. The 1972 Spring Offensive featured heavier T-54 tanks and 130mm field guns which outranged most ARVN artillery. At the time of the 1975 offensive, the NVA fielded over 600 tanks and a number of armored personnel carriers.

Weapons and supplies entered North Vietnam by two major routes. The first and most important was through the port of Haiphong, which handled 70% of North Vietnam's total imports and perhaps 85% of its military imports. Virtually all Soviet and East Bloc aid entered through Haiphong, as the Chinese were inclined to delay or deny use of their railways for overland transport from the USSR. The northeast and northwest rail lines from Hanoi to China handled the remaining 30% of North Vietnam's imports. These three entry points were the most critical nodes of the North Vietnamese logistical system. Their closure would have virtually ground the NVA to a halt. US military leaders had suggested

F-105s hit Hanoi's main railroad car repair works, aiming to cripple North Vietnam's logistics.

RANGER PATROL

Rangers have a long and honourable history in the United States armed forces. Ranger qualified soldiers were of exceptional skill, capable of operating effectively deep behind enemy lines. During the Second World War the famed Merrill's Marauders carried out many such operations and were later to become the nucleus of the 75th Infantry, formed in 1954. In the early years in Vietnam, Ranger tasks were carried out by Long Range Patrol Companies attached to major units. In January 1969, all such companies were reassigned to the 75th Infantry (Ranger), making it one of the elite formations in the United States Armed Forces.

Right: A Ranger from Company 'C', 75th Infantry takes cover on a mission in Tuyen Duc province. Before 1969 the company was a 20th Infantry LRP unit.

Below: 9 December 1970, North East of Xuan Loc and along the Dong Nai river. Members of Co. 'H', 75th Rangers are on a recon patrol.

the mining of Haiphong and other North Vietnamese ports, and the destruction of rail lines and bridges leading to China, from early in the war. This would have been the most efficient way to stop Hanoi's war machine. Instead, the Johnson administration settled for the haphazard Rolling Thunder air campaign, which placed these vulnerable nodes in virtual sanctuaries, and succeeded in destroying perhaps 30% of the imported war material at best. By the time Nixon ordered the Linebacker air offensives and the mining of Haiphong, there was no question of continuing the war to a successful conclusion. Even at that late date however, the awesome impact of a concentrated bombing campaign was felt in North Vietnam.

Moving south

Moving equipment and supplies south involved a two-stage process. In North Vietnam itself, road and rail lines carried materials to pick-up points for shipment over strategic passes on the Laotian border. From there, trucks and porters carried supplies down the Ho Chi Minh Trail through Laos and Cambodia. The "Trail" was actually a network of trails and roads which were steadily improved over

Wreckage of a North Vietnamese convoy litters a road in the South after Navy bombers strike.

the course of the war to become two-lane paved roads and a fuel pipeline. In the early days, a trip from North Vietnam to the Mekong Delta could take as much as six months, but when the Trail's upgrading was complete a truck could cover the distance in as little as a week.

January 1966:

The U.S. has long suspected that a branch of the Communist "under-ground railroad" – the Ho Chi Minh trail – cut through Cambodia. But proof was hard to obtain: so wild and enemy-infested is the Viet Nam side of the Cambodian border that no allied troops had ventured to the border since the French left in 1954.

That was remedied last week in a massive assault called Operation Matador. Swooping down on to the Vietnamese side of the Ton Le San River, which forms the border with Cambodia, went four sizable units of the 1st Air Cavalry Division. Planes and rocket-firing helicopters first softened the riverbank landing zones with shells and napalm, and "the First Team" rode in on their choppers. In some places the brush was too thick and high for a proper landing, so the troops leaped 15 ft. to the snake-infested ground, producing several sprained ankles, one broken leg – and two very bullet-riddled 12-ft. pythons. In other spots, the troop-

"The helicopter danced seemingly aimlessly over the countryside, landing for seconds here and there. But it's not aimless. Inside, a squad of Rangers prepare to set out on a long-range patrol. Somewhere along the line the squad gets off, ready for action"

Above: Operation Bushmaster, August 1971. Rangers leave the LZ.

Below: Operation Bushmaster was a long-range Search and destroy mission.

Below: Company 'L' in camouflage before Operation Bushmaster.

Above: Point man, Company 'C', near Da Lat, 4th March 1970.

EYES OF THE NAVY

Like the US Air Force, the US Navy operated two main types on tactical reconnaissance duties, in this case the North American RA-5 Vigilante and the Vought RF-8 Crusader. On missions over heavily-defended targets, both types often required a fighter escort by F-4 or F-8. Other more specialised photo-reconnaissance needs were filled by the Douglas RA-3 Skywarrior. Both the Vigilante and the Skywarrior had started their careers as bombers, while the RF-8 was an adaption of the Crusader fighter and provided the Fleet with a fast reconnaissance capability long after the standard F-8s were retired from Navy service.

Rockwell's RA-5C Vigilante provided high speed reconnaissance from the larger carriers. SLAR and infra-red reconnaissance sensors were carried.

Below: Most tactical reconnaissance for the Navy was furnished by the Vought RF-8 Crusader, usually escorted by fighter versions of the F-8.

Below: Experiments were undertaken on Kitty Hawk with tactical camouflage, and even this RVAH-11 Vigilante could not escape the paintshop. The experiment was short-lived, the RA-5 returning shortly to its grey and white scheme.

One of the most bizarre colour schemes of the war was this three-tone camouflage applied to several Douglas RA-3Bs of VAP-61 and VAP-62, to render them less vulnerable to detection during low level reconnaissance missions. Cameras were the only sensors, although these often used infra-red film to detect heat sources such as truck engines.

ers shinned down 60-ft. aluminum ladders swaying from Chinook copters overhead, and one special reconnaissance team slid down a rope in seven seconds from a chopper hovering a full 150 ft. above the jungle carpet.

The 1st Air Cav's mission was to determine if the Communists were indeed using Cambodia as both funnel and sanctuary for troops infiltrating from the north. If so, the First Team hoped to provoke an attack, giving the U.S. a chance to act on last month's warning that pursuit across the Cambodian border would henceforth follow a continuing attack from the other side.

Doubt about the enemy's use of Cambodia was quickly dispelled. Beside one clearly defined crossing point on the riverbank stood a camp with 400 lean-to structures, 200 foxholes and a small hospital – fit for a regiment and freshly evacuated. Tethered on the opposite Cambodian bank of the shallow river, only 55 ft. wide at that point, were ill-concealed sampans loaded with ammunition boxes. At one point, a G.I. patrol even caught sight of twelve uniformed North Vietnamese soldiers hastily paddling across the river into Cambodia. 1st Air Cav Lieut. Colonel Kenneth Mertel took his helicopter down the middle of the narrow stream, hoping to draw fire, which presumably would have justified a U.S. response. None came. But now that the U.S. had penetrated right to the threshold of what had long been the enemy's privileged domain, chances were it would come soon enough. (5)

Left: The trail was not the only resupply route to the Viet Cong. Every small sampan along the coast could ferry supplies from Cambodia.

Above: A USAF Super Sabre destroys a Viet Cong headquarters and storage area about 60 miles from Ban Me Thuot in South Vietnam.

Before the Trail became an all-weather transportation route, supplies were generally moved south during the winter monsoon when the Laotian trails were dry and easy to negotiate. At that time, before trucks became the principal means of hauling supplies, most shipments were carried by porters, bicycles or carts. Depending on the slope of the terrain, a man could carry 30 to 55 pounds of rice or 22 to 44 pounds of other supplies for 15 to 25 kilometers in daylight or 12 to 20 kilometers at night. Unburdened infantry could manage up to 50 kilometers a day on footpaths.

Needless to say, interdiction of trucks and porters throughout a wide-spread network of jungle trails proved a much tougher proposition than hitting bridges and rail lines in North Vietnam. The Trail was highly organized, with different routes for supplies and personnel, way stations for porters and troops, anti-aircraft defenses, and 150,000 construction and maintenance personnel. The US Com-

"Offensive operations included armed recon sorties by small flights. Recon flights would be accompanied by TARCAP fighter protection. Some recon operations were carried out from the large Naval Air Base at Da Nang"

Above: For night operations the RA-3Bs adopted a gloss all-black scheme, but this could not prevent heavy loss. Although most missions launched from land bases such as Da Nang, RA-3Bs occasionally deployed aboard carriers.

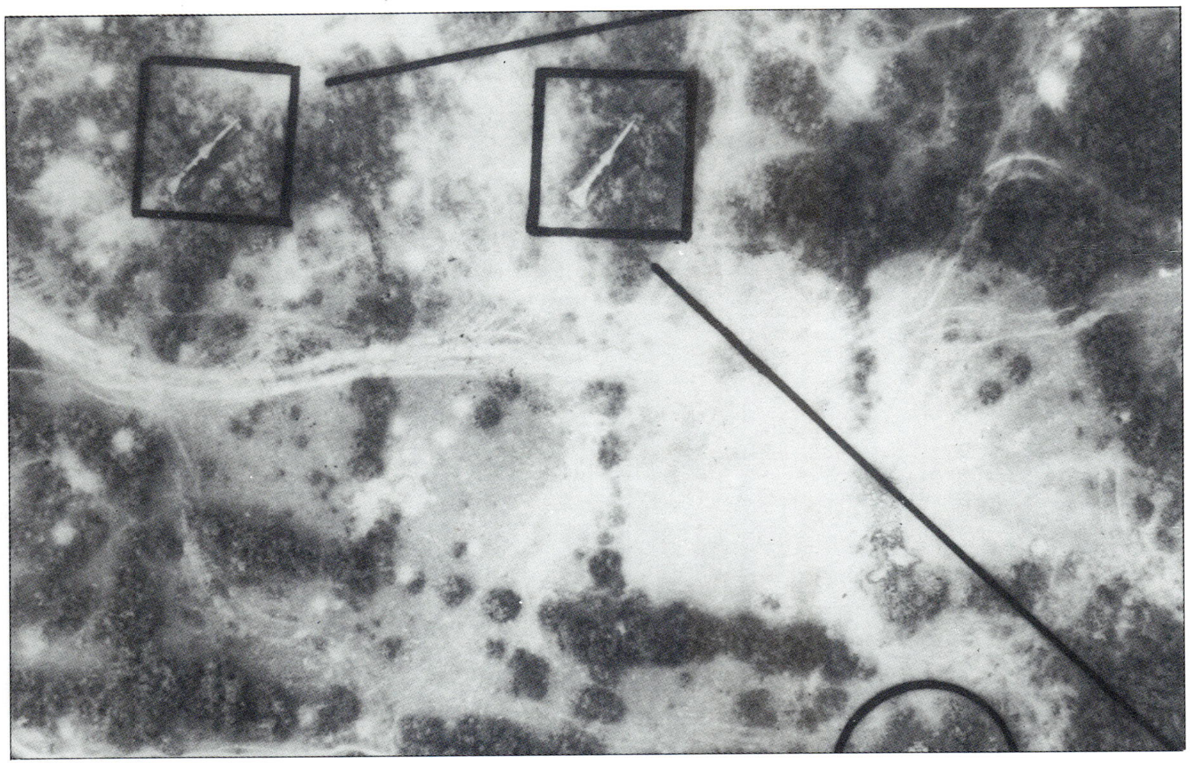

mando Hunt and other interdiction operations destroyed maybe 10% of the supplies and 5% of the infiltrating personnel on the Trail between 1965 and 1968.

1972:
DANANG, South Vietnam, March 19 – "The bad guys have gone 20th century," the young Air Force pilot said. He was still shaken by a barrage aimed at his small observation plane by antiaircraft gunners on the Ho Chi Minh Trail in Laos.
First Lieut. Robert Schur of Bricktown, N.J., had brought his twin-engine OV-10 Bronco back unscathed to Danang, the largest remaining American air base in Vietnam, concerned about the heavy fire. His concern is shared by senior United States commanders in Vietnam.
The officers say that the North Vietnamese are defending their infiltration and supply routes in southern Laos with more determination and imagination than ever before, and counterattacking more effectively, with more up-to-date weapons, the American aircraft that range over them every day.

A reconnaissance photo shows a SAM site in the southern panhandle of North Vietnam that was later destroyed by USAF fighter bombers.

TUNNEL RATS

The Viet Cong burrowed deep in their undermining of South Vietnamese society. Literally. Originally boltholes for escape, or bunkers from which to fight, the tunnel systems of South Vietnam became fortresses, with extensive though primitive facilities. Hospitals, food stores, weapon stores, rest areas, all could be found in a maze of workings. In areas like the Iron Triangle, the workings would be so extensive that they would be literally under the US Army's feet! In spite of the best American efforts, the Viet Cong tunnels were never completely eradicated and remained a source of trouble to the end of the war.

A Marine rousts Vietnamese civilians out of a Viet Cong cave system about 15 miles south of Quang Ngai.

Armed with a .45 Colt and a flashlight, a tunnel rat reaches for a hand out of a Viet Cong tunnel. The length of a rifle was a handicap in the confined spaces underground.

Until late 1970, the American bombers that drop hundreds of tons of bombs on the North Vietnamese truck traffic, supply dumps and antiaircraft sites on the twisting dirt roads of the trail went largely unchallenged, except in the critical mountain passes at the entrance to the trail.

But then the enemy began to fire surface-to-air missiles across the border at the bombers over Laos. With the advent of this year's dry season, the firings became more frequent and significant numbers of missile launchers and heavy-caliber automatic antiaircraft guns were moved farther south along the trail and deeper inside Laos than before.

The change in the air war over Laos, where the majority of all American missions are flown daily, was put this way by First Lieut. Ray Noftsinger of Roanoke, Va., a forward air controller: "The air defenses out there are so heavy now that there are certain areas we just don't fly in. We just don't have unchallenged air superiority any more in some parts of Laos." (6)

An alternative supply route utilized junks to infiltrate along South Vietnam's 1,000 mile coastline. At first this was a low-risk, high-payoff method of bringing material south. In March of 1965 the Coastal Surveillance Force (Task Force 115) was established to combat this infiltration. Using US and South Vietnamese Navy vessels and aircraft, as well as US Coast Guard cutters, waterborne infiltration became hazardous and costly, and generally declined to a small fraction of the supply effort.

US Navy divers had to watch for Viet Cong sappers in ports such as Da Nang. Any coastal craft could carry supplies or VC swimmers.

Much more important was the use of the "neutral" Cambodian port of Sihanoukville for direct shipment of supplies to the vicinity of III and IV Corps. By May of 1966, the Sihanoukville operation was in full swing, with Communist agents picking up weapons and supply shipments from the docks and trucking them to NVA and VC base areas on the border with South Vietnam. Nothing could be done to halt this activity because of the fiction of Cambodian neutrality. It finally came to an end in March of 1970 when Lon Nol overthrew Prince Sihanouk and cut off the port from Communist use. This was a major setback, and it took two years for the NVA to build up the Ho Chi Minh Trail to the point where it could replace the supply flow into the southern half of South Vietnam.

Recent attacks by the Vietcong on shipping in the Saigon River have emphasized the importance of what the Navy calls inshore, coastal, shallow water, or "riverine" warfare.

"Troops of the US Army's 1st Infantry Division have been trying to sweep Vietcong guerrillas from their tunnel systems with 1000° blasts of air. The technique involves using Mighty Mite blowers that normally force tear gas down tunnels. The air is heated by a battery powered generator"

Sgt. Rodriguez, a member of Troop E, 17th Cavalry, 173rd Airborne Brigade, investigates a Viet Cong tunnel during 1970 operations in Valley 506.

Contact with the enemy in the tunnels meant firefights at point-blank range. Occasionally, however, prisoners were taken underground. Here there is even enough room to use an M16.

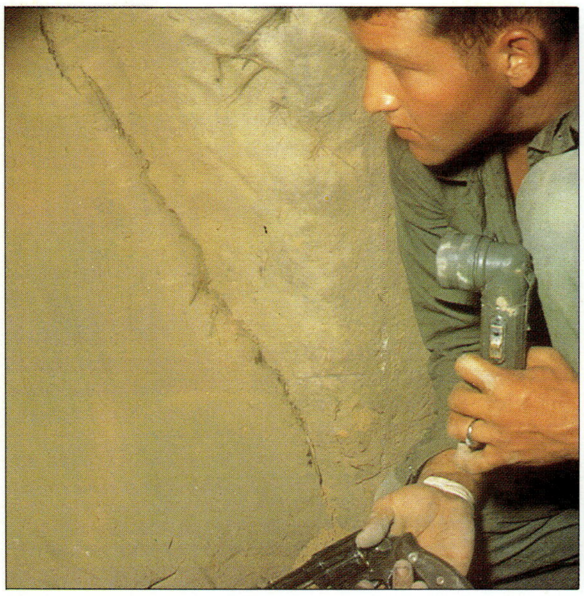

A featureless wall might hide a hidden doorway, or as here, a stash of Viet Cong supplies.

It took a special kind of courage to hunt the Viet Cong in his element underground.

More powerful lights might be used to light tunnels where power cables could be run from the surface.

Rear Adm. Norvell G. Ward, chief of the Naval Advisory Group of the United States Military Assistance Command in Vietnam and also commander of the Navy's Coastal Surveillance Force, points out that much of the war in Vietnam is conducted in an "aqueous environment."

Most of the inhabited regions are along the coast. River systems penetrate into the interior. The Vietcong try to use the seas and waterways for supply and reinforcement, and in the Mekong Delta area waterways are the principal routes of communication.

The dimensions of the problem of controlling coastal and shallow water in Vietnam are illustrated by statistics:

The coastline of South Vietnam is about 1,500 miles long and about 9,000 junks pass through coastal waters each week.

There are about 8,000 miles of navigable rivers and canals during the rainy season in South Vietnam principally in the delta and about 2,000 in the dry season, with a mean depth of about six feet of water. Along these rivers and canals cruise hundreds of junks and thousands of sampans.

The control of this traffic to prevent its use by the enemy and the use of these waterways to move troops and supplies is the objective of both the United States and the South Vietnamese. (7)

On arrival in South Vietnam (or border areas of Laos or Cambodia), supplies and replacements would move into Communist base areas. These complexes were underground fortresses – immune to most bombing and artillery. The tunnel networks were developed over decades and included barracks, hospitals, supply rooms, training areas, headquarters, and fighting bunkers. The most famous of these base areas in the "Iron Triangle", War Zone "C" and War Zone "D", were never eradicated

A GI checks the uncovered entrance to a bunker near Cu Chi. Huge VC tunnel complexes were never completely eradicated.

completely during the war. Aside from the large base areas, local tunnel networks performed the same functions on a much smaller scale in Communist dominated regions. Any village could have a tunnel system, and it was the unenviable job of soldiers known as "tunnel rats" to explore and clear these.

The functioning of the Communist supply ststem required a lot of planning, organization, and hard work. By its nature, it lacked flexibility – there was no chance of rapidly changing a main effort tens or hundreds of kilometers away on short notice. Ironically, one of the major reasons for its success was that the Americans allowed it to succeed by fighting it at the diversified end instead of at the top.

HIGH FLIERS

Two of the United States' most controversial reconnaissance aircraft saw widespread use in Southeast Asia. U-2s were committed to the war effort throughout the conflict, providing both photographic and electronic intelligence. With its long endurance and slow speed, it was a master at communications intelligence, operating from Vietnam and Thailand. On the island of Okinawa lurked the SR-71 'Blackbird', its operations shrouded in secrecy and denials. In addition to other commitments in Asia, it regularly patrolled the war zone, providing high resolution photographs and useful Sigint from its altitude of above 80,000 ft.

Above: Trailing smoke from its J75 engine, a Lockheed U-2R launches on a mission around the periphery of North Vietnam. This was the most important version used in the Southeast Asia theatre, blessed with phenomenal endurance and large sensor payload.

Right: Ground crew work on a U-2C. This version performed the strategic reconnaissance task during the early years of the war, gaining an all-black colour scheme.

Below: A U-2R lounges in front of its hangar at U-Tapao RTAF base in Thailand. The structure in the foreground is the aircraft access steps and 'howdah' sunshade.

Left: Dwarfed by a visiting C-5 Galaxy, a U-2R taxis for a mission from U-Tapao. The paddle-shaped aerials under the wing were used for the gathering of communications intelligence (Comint) during long endurance missions.

Below: A Lockheed SR-71A taxis in post-mission past a line of Boeing RC-135s. Both types operated under a cloak of secrecy from Kadena AB on Okinawa, particularly the SR-71s, whose very existence on Okinawa was denied by Washington.

Kadena SR-71 operations were aimed at China, Korea and the Soviet Union in addition to war-related activities, and often encompassed more than one target nation in a single sortie. This aircraft approaches a tanker high over the South China Sea.

Below: When violent storms hit Okinawa, most units moved out of Kadena until they subsided. Not so the Lockheed SR-71s, which weathered the storm.

"Operation Dragon Lady saw high-flying U-2s on recon missions over North Vietnam from December 1963 and continued well after the official US withdrawal from the region. The U-2 was joined by the superfast SR-71, which overflew China and North Vietnam. Even now, little about these missions has been declassified."

Below: Comint-equipped Lockheed U-2R 'Dragon Lady' drifts across the landing threshold at U-Tapao following a mission.

Below: 'Habu' mission marks adorn SR-71A 64-17974, denoting sorties from Okinawa, where the Habu pit viper was a well-known local snake.

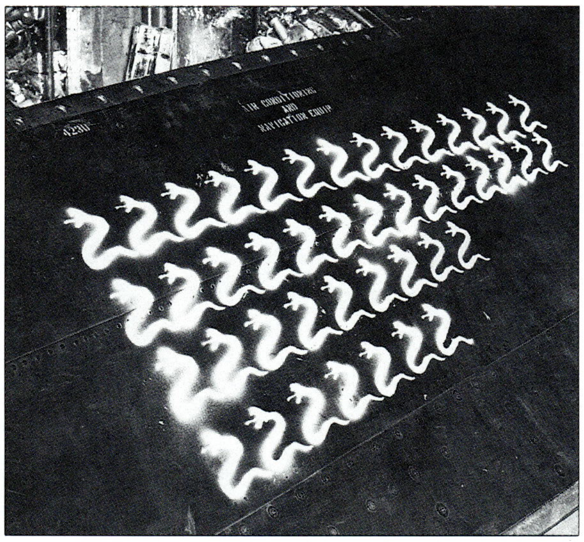

CHAPTER TEN

THE SPRING OFFENSIVE 1972

Catapult crewmen prepare to launch an F-4J Phantom from the deck of USS Constellation during operations to blunt the North Vietnamese Spring Offensive in 1972.

In February 1972, opinion polls in the United States gave President Nixon's war effort a positive rating. His trip to China, later that month, enhanced his stature further, and made the North Vietnamese apprehensive over the apparent accommodation with the Beijing leadership. Chinese military aid to Hanoi continued, but the People's Republic backed off diplomatically. Nixon's re-election in November appeared to be a mandate for "peace with honour", and he lost no time reassuring President Thieu that if the North Vietnamese violated the forthcoming peace agreement the full weight of US power would be brought to bear on them.

In January, the remainder of the "Screaming Eagles" 101st Airborne Division transferred to Fort Campbell, Kentucky. Removed from "jump" status, the division retained the historical airborne title and remained on in the Army force structure as an "air assault" division – a continuation of the airmobile concept. The 1st Cav's 3rd Brigade, which had remained as an independent unit in Vietnam was gone by June. The sprawling logistical complex at Long Binh was turned over to the ARVN in November. US non-divisional unit withdrawals included 23rd Artillery Group in January, the 2nd Squadron, 11th Armored Cavalry in April, and the 196th Light Infantry Brigade in June. True to form, elements of the 196th refused orders for routine patrols during the Spring Offensive – a dismal ending to this sad unit's existence.

Between April and July the US 9th Marine Amphibious Brigade stood by with four to six battalions to re-enter Vietnam by air and amphibious lift, and actually did provide security for several installations during the NVA Spring Offensive. This boosted Marine mid-year strength in Vietnam to 1,400. Army strength at the same time numbered 31,800, but the last ground combat battalion (3-21 Infantry) was gone by August. As if to highlight the American withdrawal still further, Nixon ordered that no more US draftees would be sent to Vietnam except on a voluntary basis.

The South Korean 2nd "Blue Dragon" Marine Brigade withdrew in February, and the Royal Thai Army Volunteer Force did likewise the next month. Remaining Korean units, scheduled to withdraw later, participated in combat operations until November 8th. For the South Vietnamese, the crisis of the NVA Spring Offensive prompted President Thieu to recall 45,000 conscripts, end deferments for college students and lower the draft age to 17.

Communist initiative

Prior to the Spring Offensive, the Communists took the initiative in I Corps in mid-March by launching a series of simultaneous attacks against ARVN Regional Forces and Popular Forces (RF/PF) outposts in Quang Ngai Province. At the same time, farther north in Thua Thien Province the ARVN 1st Division improved Hue's security by fighting west toward the A Shau, claiming over 900 enemy lives. South Vietnamese leaders were convinced that any major offensive would come from the west, and not across the DMZ.

In early January, II Corps launched a regimental attack into Cambodia to try to disrupt NVA supplies. This was followed up by an operation in the Central Highlands in early March with the same objective. As the South Vietnamese anticipated some sort of Communist effort timed to coincide with Tet, the ARVN bolstered III Corps defenses by withdrawing 10,000 troops from Cambodia in early January, and interposing them between Saigon and the northwest approaches. During February, IV Corps units made several thrusts into Cambodia, and this effort reached divisional proportions by the middle of March.

American air power in Southeast Asia is about half the size it was at the height of United States' involvement in 1968 and 1969. The cutback has been most visible in Vietnam, where it is easily observed. Most of the 450-plane bomber fleet is not here but on carriers and on bases in Thailand.

In mid-February, as fears of a North Vietnamese offensive grew, the air fleet was temporarily increased, with deployment of about 20 extra B-52s to Guam and the assignment of three rather than two carriers in the Tonkin Gulf off the coast of Vietnam. (1)

In Cambodia, the FANK began a multi-brigade operation in mid-February to try to drive the NVA from the ancient Angkor Wat temple site in the north west. Although outnumbered three to one, the NVA held and the FANK eventually retired back down Highway 6 toward Phnom Penh. In March the Communists continued their artillery and rocket attacks on the capital city, and got infantry units to within six miles of its southeast perimeter. In conjunction with the Spring Offensive, NVA troops secured the border areas of Cambodia during April, thus protecting the Ho Chi Minh Trail from potential FANK interruption.

US losses

With the US ground combat mission being wound down to nothing, American casualties in 1972 dropped to 300 killed in action, 251 non-combat deaths, and 1,221 wounded. The NVA Spring Offensive (detailed below) sent South Vietnamese casualties soaring to the highest level in any one year since the beginning of the war, with 39,587 killed in action, 13,200 missing (presumed dead), and 109,960 wounded. Allies of South Vietnam lost 455 dead and missing, and 739 wounded. The number of Communist dead rose to 131,949 over the year, but this was significantly lower than in 1968 or 1969, highlighting the reduction in allied firepower due to the American withdrawal. US Army helicopter losses in 1972 totalled 169, forty-four from operational causes, 4 from attacks on base camps, 115 from ground fire, and 6 were from the newly deployed SA-7 hand-held SAMs. Losses to Marine aviation increased due to efforts to stem the NVA Spring Offensive. Four Marine helicopters were lost during 1972, two from operational causes, one to ground fire and one to SA-7 SAMs. USMC fixed-wing losses amounted to 17, with 3 operational losses, 13 losses to ground fire and one plane shot down by MiGs.

US "protective reaction" strikes against NVA air defenses began early and strong in 1972, as did strikes against the Ho Chi Minh Trail. Most remaining US air units shifted their operational bases from South Vietnam to Thailand as Army security forces were withdrawn. The stepped up air activity in response to the NVA Spring Offensive and the Linebacker operations led to an increase in USAF fixed-wing losses during the year. Thirty of the total of 189 losses were due to operational causes, and the remaining 159 were from combat. 84 of the combat losses were caused by ground fire, SAMs accounted for 51, enemy fighters 19, and attacks on US bases 5. The North Vietnamese Air Force took a beating as well, and in August the USAF acknowledged its first "ace" fighter pilot of the war, Capt. Richard

LONG RANGE PATROL

The US forces were not really ready for the problems of fighting an insurgency war in the tropics. Regular reconnaissance methods were not too effective, so a special kind of unit was developed. Able to move in the jungle as easily as did the Viet Cong, living off their own resources, the long-range patrollers (LRPs, or Lurps) took the war to the enemy wherever he might be found. The Navy's SEALs did much the same job in the Delta, while up in I corps the Force Recon units gave the Marines a similar capability. Eventually, all the US Army recon units were gathered under the aegis of the 75th Infantry (Ranger).

Left: ***Recon patrolling varied considerably depending upon the terrain and the force involved. Marine recon units were largely employed scouting ahead of larger Marine formations.***

Right: ***In the Delta, patrols might involve long operations in the Viet Cong heartland. Here SEALs pause at a possible Viet Cong booby trap.***

Left: ***One of the functions of long-range patrollers would be to check out possible landing zones in advance of major operations.***

Below: ***Scout snipers operated in pairs, sometimes setting up in a commanding position, other times stalking a valuable target such as a NVA commander known to be in the region.***

Ritchie, who downed his fifth MiG near Hanoi. American pilots destroyed 47 MiGs in air-to-air combat between April and September.

The Pacific carrier forces experienced racial problems with a race riot aboard USS **Kitty Hawk** and mutiny on the **Constellation**. Some shore installations were also troubled, and a number of ships reported incidents of machinery sabotage. Naval aviation losses in 1972 increased four-fold over the previous year, totalling 91 – a level not reached since 1968. Twenty-four losses were operational, and the remaining 67 were due to combat. Forty-three aircraft were destroyed by ground fire, 22 were downed by SAMs, and 2 were shot down by enemy fighters.

The NVA spring offensive

North Vietnam's Spring Offensive (called the "Nguyen Hue Offensive" by the NVA and the "Easter Offensive" in the West) was the first that was primarily a conventional attack staged by the NVA in divisional strength. The 1968 Tet Offensive had seen widespread attacks by regimental and independent battalion groups and a large Viet Cong representation, in the hope of a psychological victory and perhaps the downfall of the Saigon government. The Spring Offensive, on the other hand, was mostly an NVA show. About 10 of the 14 available Communist divisions participated in the initial attacks, along with many of the 26 independent infantry and sapper regiments, and strong regimental groups of armor and heavy artillery (equipped with 600 tanks, and new 130mm field guns).

By 1972, an American serviceman had become almost a rare sight on the street of Saigon.

At Cam Ranh Bay, US Air Force pilots were abruptly wakened at 3:00 a.m. by a gaunt-faced sergeant who'd just heard the latest Intelligence. "It's hit the fan!" the sergeant shouted. "The bastards are coming down the pike with everything they've got!" Every GI in the country remembered where he was, that cool misty morning when the NVA punched. Because of the drawdown of US troops under the Vietnamization program, most of those on the front line of the assault were South Vietnamese. Specialist Six William Ferrand, advising an ARVN battalion on 2 April, watched enemy troops gaining momentum in the forested and rugged highlands north of Pleiku. Ferrand helped to position fire teams and called in mortars. Soon, the NVA were so close and so densely packed that it was like a shooting gallery. Ferrand shouldered an M16, popped off single shots, and saw one of them blow a man's head off. He and his comrades prudently began to withdraw. (2)

Above: The only National Guard infantry unit to see action in Vietnam were the long range patrollers of Company D, 151st Infantry, Indiana National Guard.

Below: Long range patrols travelled light. Their main function was to obtain intelligence, not to engage in firefights so numbers were small.

"All hell broke loose. We'd walked into the middle of a VC bunker complex. Within seconds we were under fire from six occupied bunkers, dug in a L-shape. We were only 7 meters from the nearest bunker"

As usual, Hanoi hoped for the collapse of the South Vietnamese government in the wake of a battlefield defeat. With the US forces gone, this seemed an attainable goal. Less spectacular would be the seizure of one or two northern provinces and perhaps the city of Hue, to improve the North Vietnamese position at any cease-fire negotiations. In any event the offensive could severely test, if not set back, the "Vietnamization" of Saigon forces.

Northern plan

The North Vietnamese plan appears to have tried to accomplish too much with the resources at hand. In trying to spread the ARVN's reserves, they were unable to achieve a decisive concentration themselves. The first, largest, and most successful wing of the attack was directed against I Corps across the DMZ – an option US and ARVN intelligence officers generally dismissed. The second phase of the offensive came out of Cambodia into the heart of III Corps, on an axis of Loc Ninh – An Loc, toward Saigon. The third major thrust was from Laos into the Central Highlands of II Corps for the traditional attempt to split the country in half – the strategy most expected by Saigon intelligence.

The Offensive in I Corps

Through most of South Vietnam, ARVN units were engaged in pacification support or raids on Communist supply bases. In I Corps, where the main attack would fall, some of the best – and worst – South Vietnamese troops were deployed. ARVN's two largest divisions, the 1st and 2nd, with four battalions per regiment, defended the center and southern provinces respectively. The 1st was Saigon's best regular division but the 2nd was only average. Guarding the DMZ, the recently formed 3rd Division was composed of two new regiments, the 56th and 57th, and the veteran 2nd Regiment (formerly of the 1st Division). The 3rd Division proved the weak link in the defense. Independent units were also attached to the Corps, including the 51st Regiment, the 1st Ranger Group, the 1st Armored Brigade (of sorts), and the crack 147th and 258th Marine Brigades attached to the 3rd Division sector. On the day the Communist attack commenced, General Vu Van Giai (3rd Division Commander), in spite of warnings, had his 2nd and 56th Regiments engaged in an administrative road march to exchange tactical areas of responsibility. As a result, neither regiment was in a defensive position or in tactical formation when the assault struck. This incompetence was so blatant that senior US Marine advisor, Col. Gerry Turley, suspected treachery on the part of the general.

The offensive in I Corps got under way on 30 March with a massive artillery and rocket barrage across the DMZ. Five NVA regiments spearheaded the push from the DMZ, while three more drove in from the west. Fire Support Bases were abandoned in haste as the green 3rd ARVN Division crumbled. By April 2nd the defense line had been pushed back from the DMZ to the Cua Viet River and, to the southwest, NVA units had advanced to within eight miles of Quang Tri City. The ARVN 56th Regiment, holding the northwest corner of the Quang Tri defenses, became combat ineffective by April 5th through desertion. That same day, the NVA 324B Division opened its attack against the western approaches to Hue, just to the south in Thua Thien Province.

DONGHA, South Vietnam, April 8 – Pigs sniffing around the corpses of North Vietnamese soldiers were the only things moving today in this battered town in the middle of the North Vietnamese offensive below the demilitarized zone.

Overhead, rockets sped southward and shells north. At the edge of the town was a South Vietnamese marine

CANINE WARRIORS

Mankind has used animals in warfare as far back as history records. In South Vietnam, war dogs were used in a variety of ways. The Military Police used dogs in their usual roles as sentries and guards, particularly around major bases such as Da Nang and Cam Ranh Bay. They were also used to guard Long Binh Jail, the military detention facility. Combat dogs were different. An animal's finely tuned senses could be used in a number of ways. Scout Dog platoons used their dogs to accompany patrols, giving warning of ambushes or traps ahead. Combat Tracker platoons were called upon to track down the enemy to his lair.

A Combat Tracker team from the 4th Infantry Detachment (War Dog Provisional) await a helicopter to the combat area.

Below: A well padded member of the 981st Military Police Company takes part in the training of a Sentry Dog at Cam Ranh Bay.

battalion whose job was to stop any northerners trying to cross a branch of the Cua Viet River.

Dongha, until four days ago a prosperous town of 18,000, is considered to be "holding out". But no humans move inside it. Any who do are killed by the marines here on the south bank of the river.

Three dead North Vietnamese soldiers lie beside the wreckage of the river's main bridge, which an American adviser blew up yesterday after enemy tanks approached the town and threatened to cross the river.

The North Vietnamese were killed by the marines at dawn as they tried to cross the river. Their topee style helmets lay beside them. (3)

The NVA attack on Quang Tri from the west received a bloody check at the hands of the South Vietnamese Marines at Fire Support Base Pedro on April 9th, losing an entire tank battalion and about 1,000 men. This success was short lived as NVA forces redoubled their efforts and steadily pressed the attack. By the end of April the defenders of Quang Tri were reduced to a pocket 5 miles in diameter around the city.

Similarly, an ARVN battalion holding FSB Bastogne kept the NVA attack on Hue at arm's length for some time, even though surrounded. FSB Bastogne finally fell on April 28th as the ARVN 1st and 3rd Regiments withdrew in the direction of Hue. Refugees from the city fled south along Highway 1.

In 1972 North Vietnam made its first attempt to conquer the South by conventional military action.

With the 3rd ARVN Division fleeing in panic, Quang Tri City fell to the NVA on the 1st May. The only effective defense left in northern I Corps was the line held by the 147th and 369th Marine Brigades, which had been redeployed to guard the northern approaches to Hue. By mid-month, South Vietnamese counterattacks began to take shape. With US helicopter support, the South Vietnamese Marines staged a raid into the Quang Tri area and killed about 300 NVA troops on the 13th. West of Hue, the ARVN 1st Division rallied, and in a week-long counterattack reoccupied FSB Bastogne on May 15th. After this setback, the NVA committed the 325C Division in early June to try to regain the initiative against Hue. By the end of July, it succeeded in forcing ARVN withdrawal from FSB Bastogne, but declined to occupy the position itself.

At the end of June, the ARVN I Corps counteroffensive was launched from Thua Thien Province northward toward Quang Tri. Spearheaded by ARVN airborne and marine brigades, and backed up by US naval gunfire support and B-52 strikes, the

Left: A scout dog and handler work out with an Infantry squad at the US Army Vietnam Training Detachment based at Bien Hoa. Most dog teams in Vietnam were assigned to Scout Dog Platoons or to Combat Tracker Platoons.

Right: Dog handlers of Co.D, 16th Armor, 173rd Airborne Brigade pause behind an M113 personnel carrier in August 1965. They are about to take part in a sweep through a village in Xuan Loc province, searching for Viet Cong.

Below: A dog handler 'hits the dirt' while on exercise, having been warned of a potential ambush by his dog's keen senses. USARV maintained a dog training detachment near Bien Hoa.

"There was Adolf, teeth bared, standing on a VC officer. He didn't want to move, and Kevin put a harness on him to pull him off. We didn't get many prisoners so this was a treat for us. Aside from a few teeth marks, the VC was alright – just scared shitless – and Adolf got a special award for bravery"

10,000 strong force moved forward cautiously. By July 7th the advance stalled two miles south of Quang Tri City. After a week of further pounding by B-52s and ships of the 7th fleet, the NVA withdrew into the city and ARVN advanced elements got to within one kilometer of the Citadel at the center. The elite 2nd Airborne Brigade led the house-to-house fighting through the city and suffered so many casualties that it was withdrawn and replaced by marines. By the end of the month the operation against the Citadel had taken on the characteristics of a siege. The position finally fell to the ARVN on September 15th. The beginning of December brought the monsoon, which stopped further ARVN advances in Quang Tri Province.

In late August the NVA had extended operations south in Quang Nam Province, seizing a district capital and routing ARVN troops from FSB Ross. Within two weeks they also overran most of Quang Tin Province against light opposition and pressed an attack into Quang Ngai Province.

A wounded ARVN soldier clings to a helicopter taking off from a landing zone during the bloody three-month siege of An Loc.

The Offensive in III Corps

On April 5th the NVA offensive against III Corps started with a drive south into Binh Long Province from Cambodia by the VC 5th, 7th, and 9th Divisions (actually mixed VC/NVA composition). While the 5th advanced south from Snoul to Loc Ninh, the 9th applied pressure directly on An Loc from the west, and the 7th maneuvered south and cut Highway 13 – the main Saigon-An Loc road. By 7th April the ARVN 5th Division was cut off in An Loc and the Communists were in possession of Loc Ninh. Between April 7th and 11th the garrison was reinforced by two ranger and two ARVN infantry battalions, moved in by helicopter. On April 9th, the ARVN began shifting units north from IV Corps to relieve An Loc, and over the next few days B-52s were committed to aid the city's defenders. In spite of these measures a Communist spearhead of four tank companies and a reinforced regiment penetrated An Loc's perimeter on April 13th. By the next day, the ARVN 1st Airborne Brigade had reached a position adjacent to An Loc by helicopter and effectively increased its perimeter.

Day after day, Air Force Captain Thomas Hammons, 32, chatted with the U.S. adviser sweating out North Vietnamese attacks on the besieged rubber town of An Loc. But Hammons learned neither his name, rank nor serious feelings about the situation: their conversations were carried on over a radio link between the ground and Hammons' tiny O-2A observation plane and confined to business. Hammons' job as forward air controller was to hover over the city, receive ground requests and direct the air armada of F-4s, A-7s, A-37s, F-8s and Cobra and C-130 gunships dispatched to help the beleaguered garrison.

"I'd like to napalm south of town, napalm and CBUs (cluster bomb units) in town and hard bombs seven klics northwest of town," the adviser on the ground

BOOBY TRAPS

The Viet Cong could not come out and face the Americans in pitched battles (the few occasions they did cost them heavily) so they had to think of other ways to strike back. The booby trap is as old as warfare, and the Vietnamese made extensive use of such devices. Booby traps are effective, costing almost nothing to produce. You can take several people out of action by injuring one soldier, as two or three others will have to be detailed to take the victim back for medical attention.

Above: A 155mm artillery warhead acquired by the Viet Cong, rigged with a pressure-sensitive trigger, and buried on a trail. Even if set off by a man walking point, the effect of this simple device on a patrol would have been devastating. Such explosive traps could also be remotely controlled.

Right: A simple, foot-sized trip hole cut into the ground. Known as the foot-fall trap, it was easily camouflaged under the jungle vegetation and could break an ankle – disabling a soldier without expense of ammunition or even the need to tie up scarce communist manpower in an ambush.

Left: The so-called Venus fly-trap. More elaborate than many 'passive' Viet Cong booby traps in its construction, it worked by causing the victim to stumble into the hole. This might break a limb; in any case, it was almost impossible for the victim to extract himself without further injury.

Below: The classic punji trap, a shallow pit filled with sharpened bamboo stakes on which the unwary could impale themselves. The stakes were sometimes poisoned with human excrement. Booby traps accounted for fully 11 per cent of American deaths in Vietnam, and 17 per cent of wounds.

"They're our biggest problem. Hardly a day goes by that a mine or booby trap doesn't hit some of our people. Only last month Dr. Bernard Fall, the noted historian and author, touched off a mine that killed him along with a Marine sergeant. They account for 50% of 1st Marine Division casualties"

would order in a typical conversation. Or occasionally, after a bombing run, "Babe, that was too close for us. Keep your stuff at least 600 meters to the east, O.K.?" During one attack on NVA positions around An Loc, a Cobra pilot complained when F-4 Phantoms running short of fuel were assigned his target. The man on the ground blew up. "We ain't playing no goddam game, boy. If you can't take it, you get your ass back to base until you cool off. You hear me, babe?" Hammons gauges a day over An Loc hopeful or hairy by the voice of his unseen colleague. "When he's calm, he stutters a little bit. When things are hot, he shoots those words out without a pause." (4)

Relieving forces, including the 21st ARVN Division from IV Corps, pressed north on Highway 13 during early May, only to be repulsed by VC 7th Division troops. Bolstered by battalions from the ARVN 9th Division, the 21st continued the attack and got to within two miles of An Loc by May 19th. On June 9th part of the relief force broke through to the city but the Communists resealed the gap and continued the siege. By the third week of June, the ARVN 9th and 21st Divisions from IV Corps were thoroughly exhausted by the An Loc relief effort and were replaced by III Corps' 18th and 25th Divisions. The Communists broke off the siege on July 11th and retired to Cambodia.

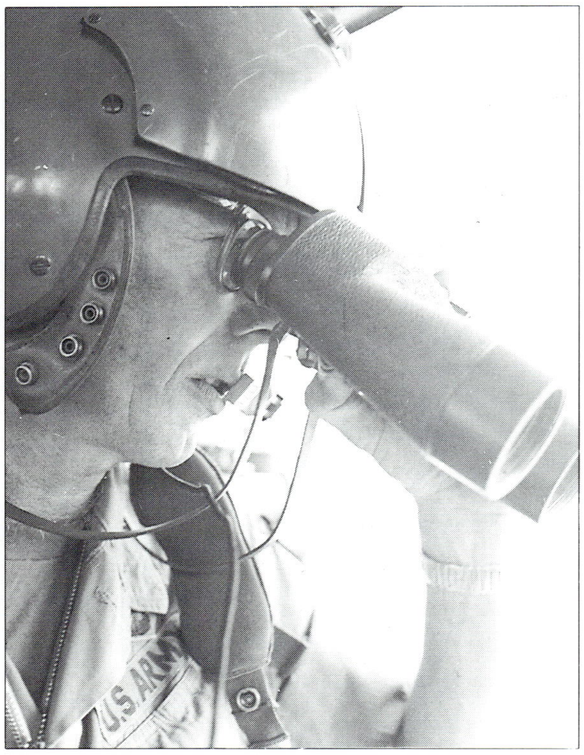

A US advisor to the ARVN 23rd Infantry Division conducts a reconnaissance in May 1972. By this stage in the war, US combat troops had been cut right back, and it was in the air that the Stars and Stripes most often went into battle.

In early August, Viet Cong efforts shifted to the Saigon approaches, where they cut three of the main roads to the city (Highways 1, 4 and 13). This diverted ARVN troops to keep the roadways clear. At mid-month sappers infiltrated the logistical complex at Long Binh and blew up major stores of ammunition. In early September they raided VNAF air bases at Bien Hoa and Tan Son Nhut, damaging 50 ARVN helicopters.

The Offensive in II Corps

In the Central Highlands the offensive began on April 8th with the NVA B3 Front's 2nd Division moving on Dak To from the north, while the 320th Division advanced from the west, immediately cutting Highway 14, the main Kontum-Pleiku route. B-52 strikes on April 11th assisted the ARVN 22nd Division in repulsing the attack on Kontum. Also within the II Corps area, the NVA 3rd Binh Dinh Division captured Hoai An along the important coastal Highway 1 on April 9th. The next day, the division seized the strategic Mang Yang Pass, cutting Highway 19 between Pleiku and the coastal city of Qui Nhon. (For clarity, this division will be referred to as the 3rd Binh Dinh Division to dis-

DOOR GUNNERS

Helicopters had to do their fighting at slow speed and close to the ground, and were natural prey for any communist carrying a gun. Although many were lost to groundfire, the number was reduced by employing suppressive fire by the helicopter itself. The best method of providing this was by the door gunner, firing a machine gun from the cabin at any movement on the ground he considered hostile. The nature of this operation led to a group of fearless men who spent their war leaning out of helos in tight turns feet above the tree-tops, all the time keeping their machine guns trained on the enemy.

Below: Door gunners were a much respected and fearless group. This 'Razorback' gunner fires back at VC ground forces as the helicopter flies past the target. The gunner will continue firing in a steep turn until the helicopter's forward-firing fixed weapons are brought to bear again.

Right: Heavily-armed Bell Hueys patrolled the Delta with Navy squadron HAL-2 'Seawolves'. This door gunner readies for action as his Huey helps a burning PBR after a Viet Cong attack.

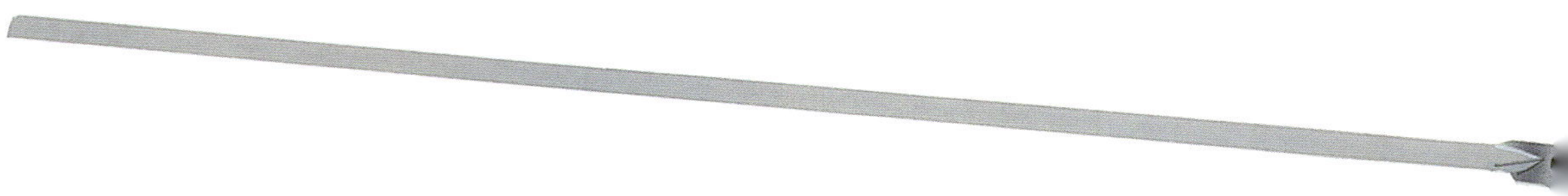

"As we made the last firing pass, I saw muzzle flashes and tracers all around us. I heard the pilots heavy breathing in my earphones. I looked at the North Vietnamese – almost close enough to see the whites of their eyes, as they said at Bunker Hill"

Left: With the helicopter in a turn, the door gunner could concentrate fire on to a small area, like a low-tech version of the fixed-wing gunships. The gun in this case is a 0.30-in Browning machine gun, and the helicopter one of HAL-2's Bell UH-1s, patrolling the Mekong delta.

Above: Two Navy gunships cruise over the waterways of southern Vietnam en route to their operational area. The door gunner has a M60 7.62-mm machine gun for trainable fire, while the pilot controls the forward firing armament of four fixed guns of the same calibre.

Door gunners were vital when suppressing enemy fire around landing zones, but before long more firepower was needed. Versions of the ubiquitous Huey were converted to provide greater firepower firing directly ahead.

tinguish it from the 3rd Phuoc Long Division which was formed late in 1974). By the end of the month, the South Korean Capital Division had retaken the pass and opened Highway 19.

Moving from the west through the "Rocket Ridge" area, the NVA 320th Division hit the ARVN 22nd Division positions at Tan Canh, and moved on Dak To from the south on April 23rd. The remnants of the ARVN 22nd Division fell back on Kontum where, by the end of the month, they were surrounded. In late May, Communist spearheads penetrated Kontum but were ejected by the first week in June. On July 19th, II Corps initiated a major counteroffensive against the NVA's 3rd Binh Dinh Division at Hoai An.

The Offensive in IV Corps

By the latter part of April, ARVN units in IV Corps had been sufficiently thinned out by the An Loc relief operation that the Viet Cong could open a new, and unexpected, fourth front in the Delta. VC regiments quickly established control in Chuong Thien Province in the heart of IV Corps. Taking advantage of the situation, the NVA 1st Division moved into the Delta from Cambodia in late May to consolidate the Chuong Thien position.

At the end of July, there was a real possibility that Highway 4 (the main route south from Saigon) would be severed by the VC. This prompted a regimental-size spoiling attack by ARVN Rangers into Cambodia's Parrot's Beak area to disrupt VC preparations. Nevertheless, the end of October saw a build-up of Communist strength in the Delta as new units from Cambodia moved across the border to consolidate gains before any negotiated settlement.

Allied Air Operations – Linebacker & Linebacker II

By the time the Spring Offensive kicked off, Allied air power in Southeast Asia had dropped dramatically from the peak years of 1968-69. USAF jet assets in the theater (Vietnam, Thailand, Guam) totalled 83 B-52s, 203 F-4s, 16 F-105s, 23 A-37s, and 10 B-57s. Prop planes included 15 A-1s, and a gunship force of 15 AC-119s and 13 AC-130s. The South Vietnamese had about 150 prop attack aircraft (mostly A-1s) and a F-5 jet squadron. By the 23rd May, the USAF brought 10 fighter squadrons, and electronic warfare squadron and a couple of C-130 squadrons to Thailand, and tripled the size of the B-52 force. These reinforcements included 180 F-4s (many being improved "E" models), 12 F-105Gs, 8 EB-66s, 32 C-130s, and 124 B-52s.

By the end of the war the USAF were using the Vought A-7 Corsair, known affectionately as the SLUF (Short Little Ugly F**)***

At the beginning of April, the B-52 force was put on standby for a massive operation to stem the NVA offensive. On the 6th the first break in the weather allowed fighter-bomber operations to re-commence, initially aimed at NVA units engaged below the DMZ. The forward deployment of Communist SA-2 missiles gave US aircraft their first taste of high intensity air defense within South Vietnam. By April

TACTICAL RECON

Few tasks are more important in war than reconnaissance, and varied schemes were adopted to monitor communist activity throughout Vietnam. In its most orthodox incarnation, reconnaissance for the Air Force was carried out by tac recon types such as the RF-101 Voodoo and RF-4 Phantom, both specialist variants of fighters. Their use was largely aimed at conventional military installations in the North, such as POL facilities, marshalling yards and airfields. Operating at low and medium level, they constantly ran a gauntlet of guns and SAMs. Despite the risk, they proved their worth in the bombing of 1972.

Below: The McDonnell RF-4C Phantom went to war wearing 'peacetime' grey and white and 'FJ' buzzcodes. Aircraft were soon repainted.

Above: A McDonnell RF-101C Voodoo transits at altitude. Despite lacking agility, it had a top speed of over 1,240 mph.

“The RF-101C Voodoo was the first combat aircraft operated in South East Asia by a USAF squadron. Even when no-one was shooting at you, the Voodoo was more difficult to fly than any other fighter in squadron service . . . but the ‘Long Bird’ undertook the fastest combat missions of the war. Other aircraft could reach greater speeds in a dash, but did not sortie at those speeds. Voodoo pilots had to slow down on those rare occasions when F-4C Phantoms escorted them”

Above: The RF-101C was the only version of the Voodoo to see service in Southeast Asia. It was instrumental in providing most of the USAF's tactical intelligence in the early years.

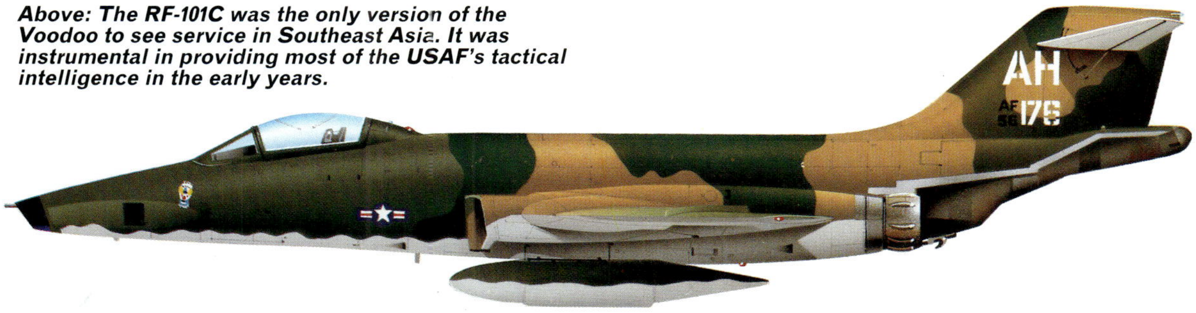

Below: Photographed by his wingman, this RF-101C photographs the North Vietnamese airfield of Kep, an important MiG base close to Hanoi. Target ingress and egress were made at low level, with a ‘pop-up’ to around 15,000 ft for the vital photo run.

Below: In 1968 the RF-101Cs of the 20th Tactical Reconnaissance Squadron were replaced by the RF-4Cs of the 14th TRS. This aircraft is undergoing a cartridge engine start at the Royal Thai Air Force base at Udorn.

Above: Wearing the markings of the 45th TRS, this RF-101C is typical of the type which served the USAF so well in the tac recon role. Sensors were entirely optical, with oblique cameras facing through side windows, and another camera facing forward.

Above: The commander of the Udorn-based 20th TRS enjoys a well earned glass of champagne after completing his 100th combat mission in the RF-101C. This was no mean feat for this dangerous undertaking.

Left: Streaking across the jungle, an RF-101C displays the small wing area and T-tail associated with the Voodoo. Known as the ‘long bird’, its speed was legendary.

Right: Third of the tac recon types operating for the Air Force was the Martin RB-57E ‘Patricia Lynn’. Serving in-theatre from 1963 to 1971, the RB-57Es compiled an impressive combat record, using their Reconofax VI infra-red sensors to spot VC targets hidden beneath the jungle canopy.

6th, airpower started to take its toll and slow the NVA advance on Quang Tri. In one instance two cells of 3 B-52s destroyed an entire NVA tank battalion on a road march in I Corps. In all, some 285 NVA tanks were destroyed by allied aircraft in I Corps alone during the four and a half months following the Communist assault.

B-52 operations

B-52 operations against North Vietnam began on April 9th, with strikes as far north as Vinh. Operations expanded over the next week to include most major target complexes from Thanh Hoa south. By the 16th, the areas immediately surrounding Hanoi and Haiphong were added to the B-52 target list. Nixon's concept of an expanded air offensive (Linebacker) incorporated isolation of North Vietnam from outside supply, destruction of stockpiles of material in the north, and interdiction of NVA supplies going south. By mid-May, missions in the southern route packages succeeded in knocking out the pumping facilities for the Ho Chi Minh Trail pipeline which supported tank and truck operations in the south. In line with the port mining operations in May, raids intensified against the rail lines to China and reduced these supply routes to a small fraction of their former capacity.

Hit by a SAM over North Vietnam, the pilot reported rapid loss of fuel, two engines completely out, and the adjoining two with only partial power. All fuel gauges were spinning, making it impossible to accurately determine the amount of fuel on board. The SAM had exploded close enough to the aircraft to blow off part of the tip tank and put some 400 holes throughout the airframe. It also knocked out some of the flight instruments and the cockpit lights. The pilot was instructed to try to make an emergency landing at Da Nang, since it was the closest available airfield that could handle B-52s.

When the aircraft arrived over Da Nang it was nighttime. The field was under instrument flight conditions (IFR) – that is, not visible from altitude – and was undergoing a rocket and mortar attack. At each end of the runway there were mine fields, and Viet Cong snipers with automatic weapons that previously had done their share of damage to U.S. planes.

Northern air defenses included numbers of Soviet supplied MiG 21 fighters. Some, but not all, of the pilots were very good.

The approaching and landing speeds of the BUFF vary considerably with the fuel on the aircraft at the time. Because of the spinning gauges and the massive fuel leaks, the crew could only estimate the fuel load. They properly estimated on the high side to keep from stalling out and and, as a result, when Capt Alward flared for landing he was "hot" and landed long. Then, when Capt Bob Davis, his copilot, pulled the handle to put out the large drag parachute to decelerate the aircraft, nothing happened. A SAM fragment had severed the drag chute actuator cable.

Faced with the upcoming mine field, the pilot elected to make a go-around. Handling a BUFF with two engines out on one side is considered a very serious emergency. One with two engines out and other battle damage, at night, in weather, with part of the flight instruments out and fuel spraying out of body tanks is

HANOI'S RING OF STEEL

During the later years of the war, the area around Hanoi became the most heavily-defended region the world has ever seen, ringed with a mass of anti-aircraft artillery emplacements and SAM sites. MiG fighters flew regularly against the US aircraft. While the MiGs and SAMs took their toll, they were effectively negated by fighter escorts and effective countermeasures. The guns, however, were more difficult to silence, and accounted for 88.6% of combat losses to US fixed-wing aircraft.

Above: Makeshift bamboo flak jackets provide these Vietnamese gunners with a measure of protection while operating their 57-mm cannon during a US bombing attack.

Above: Vietnamese MiG-21 pilot. All cockpit stencilling is in Cyrillic.

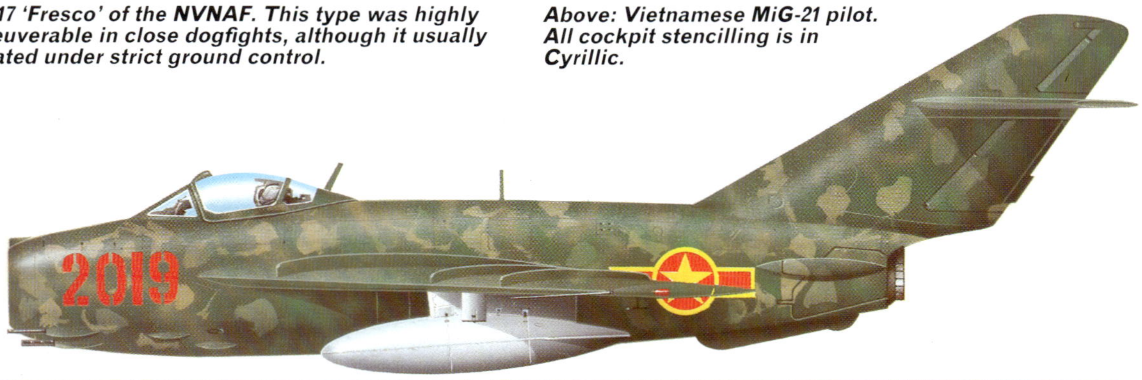

MiG-17 'Fresco' of the NVNAF. This type was highly maneuverable in close dogfights, although it usually operated under strict ground control.

Above: North Vietnamese pilots scramble to their MiG-21PF fighters, armed with two AA-2 'Atoll' air-to-air missiles.

Below: Quad 14.5mm machine guns blast away at US aircraft during the 'Linebacker II' raids, when Hanoi was protected by the 'ring of steel'.

Above: The 'star and bar' type national insignia may have caused some confusion for US servicemen, but the distinctive shape of the MiG-21 was difficult to confuse with anything else.

Above: SA-3 'Goa' missiles on their launchers. The impact of SAMs was not as great as might have been expected, their effect being largely negated by superior ECM and 'Weasel' tactics.

Below: Aircraft left behind by the retreating South Vietnamese armies were impressed into service by the communists. The most potent type was the Northrop F-5.

Left: MiG-17 'Frescos' are seen in their revetments at Kep, photographed by a recon drone.

Right: Photographed near Hanoi, this is a North Vietnamese MiG-21, armed with AA-2 missiles.

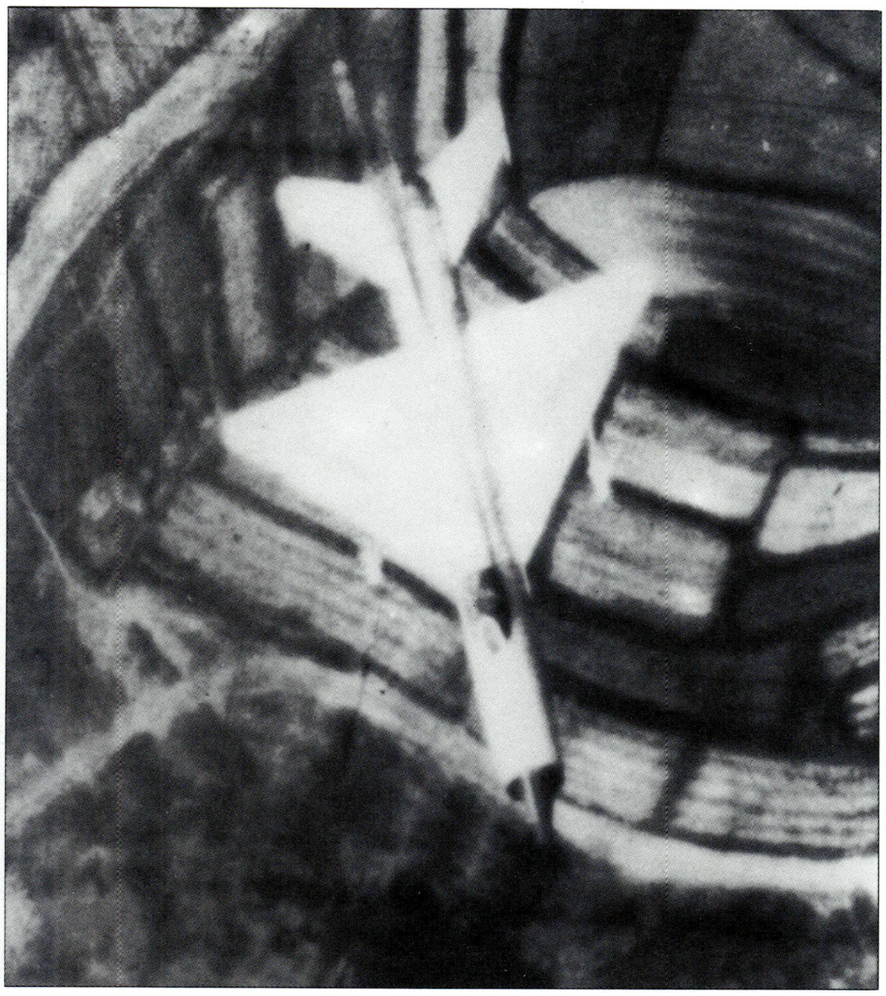

considered difficult even for a highly qualified instructor pilot to handle.

Captain Alward wasn't concerned with the impossibility of the situation. Using every bit of the long runway, he pulled his damaged aircraft into the air just prior to the wheels going on to the overrun and the minefield.

On the next approach, he was able to make a successful landing. Although severely damaged, the aircraft was eventually flown back to U-Tapao and repairs were completed. (5)

Aircraft taking part in the renewed air offensive against North Vietnam were equipped with new weapons which had not been available during Rolling Thunder. Laser Guided Bombs and Electro-Optical Guided Bombs of 2,000 to 3,000 pounds armed the strike planes of the 8th Tactical Fighter Wing (which had replaced its F-105s with F-4s). These bombs had the accuracy and the punch to destroy point targets which formerly required the attention of many aircraft carrying "iron bombs". In a three-month period the 8th TFW dropped the elusive Thanh Hoa and Paul Doumer bridges and 104 others throughout North Vietnam.

Airbase targets

North Vietnamese air bases were back on the target list, with Phuc Yen and several other fields being virtually knocked out in September along with 14 MiGs, destroyed or damaged on the ground. Finally, on October 24th, Nixon acknowledged Hanoi's apparently genuine desire to negotiate in good faith by halting all bombing north of the 20th Parallel. Linebacker and the port mining had reduced North Vietnam's supplies to 20% of the levels they had enjoyed at the start. By December, however, Nixon

The Ai Mo warehouse complex near Hanoi was flattened by bombs from B-52s early in the Linebacker II series of raids.

had had enough of further North Vietnamese intransigence and ordered a renewed bombing effort with the the stops pulled out – Linebacker II.

Linebacker II

Linebacker II was conceived as a strategic blow to the very heart of North Vietnam – Hanoi and Haiphong. B-52s would be the primary arm, complemented by strike support aircraft. F-111 fighter-bombers, with all-weather capability and terrain-avoidance radar, would go in ahead of the B-52s to take out airfields and SAM launchers. Beginning on the 18th December, the twelve-day effort included only one day of good visual bombing weather for the fighters.

Everyone was still hopeful that a truce would be reached in time for us to "get home in time for Christmas." All but a few bombing missions had been cancelled for December 17th. A meeting for all commanders was scheduled for 1400 on the 16th in the Eighth Air Force Commander's conference room.

AERIAL TANKERS

A large force of US Air Force tankers was built up in Southeast Asia, to support either tactical strike aircraft or B-52 bombing raids. With a full load of bombs and a great distance to travel, refuelling was usually necessary to reach North Vietnam and back, while the fighters had the added disadvantage of being involved in air-to-air combats which decreed the use of fuel-sapping afterburner. Tankers also flew from carriers and Marine bases, and crews from all three services exhibited a professionalism second to none in always being in the right place at the right time.

Above: Bomb- and Sparrow-armed F-4C Phantom refuels from a Boeing KC-135A.

Right: Tactical fighters required refuelling over northern Thailand to reach Northern targets.

Above: The Boeing KC-135A was the premier tanker employed in the theatre, tasked with refuelling most USAF aircraft types.

Below: Early fighters such as this North American F-100 required the KC-135A to attach a drogue to its boom. Navy aircraft required the same system.

Above: Fighters often topped off their tanks after the main refuelling so that all of the formation left the tanker with full tanks.

Below: Navy tanker operations largely relied on the Douglas KA-3B Skywarrior. Other attack aircraft were used in the refuelling role, carrying 'buddy' pods.

Above: During the first days of the war PACAF's fleet of Boeing KB-50Js was used on tanker missions, but these veterans were quickly retired due to corrosion problems.

Above: Carrying a useful fuel load from carrier decks was the KA-3B Skywarrior. This example is from Det. 4 VAQ-130, refuelling Vought A-7Es from VA-113.

Above: A welcome sight for any fighter pilot, a Boeing KC-135A in a racetrack orbit with boom lowered.

Below: Rescue helicopters such as this Sikorsky HH-53 refuelled from the Lockheed HC-130 tanker/command post.

What was in the air? Were they getting the airplanes ready for us to fly home? As I left the squadron on my way to the meeting I saw several crewmembers talking together.

One of them said, "Colonel, are we going home? Let's hope you have good news for us when you come back."

As we gathered for the meeting, speculation was running about fifty-fifty that we would be going home. Others of us had a premonition and were saying nothing. The General came in and the meeting got underway. The briefing officer opened the curtain over the briefing board, and there it was – we were not going home. Not yet, anyway. We were going North. Our targets were to be Hanoi and Haiphong, North Vietnam. At last the B-52 bomber force would be used in the role it had been designed for. The goal for this new operation was to attempt to destroy the war-making capability of the enemy.

The method of attack we were to use would be night, high altitude, radar bombing of all military targets in the area of the two major cities in North Vietnam. We would launch a raid each night beginning on the 18th of December and continue with a raid each night. Each raid would consist of three waves of varying strength, each hitting their targets at four- to five-hour intervals.

It would not be easy. We knew we would suffer losses. The Hanoi/Haiphong target complex was among the most heavily defended areas in the world. The combined number of surface-to-air missiles, fighter aircraft, and antiaircraft guns that surrounded the target area exceeded anything ever experienced.

As soon as the meeting was over, I went back to the squadron area to begin preparations for the missions. As I approached the area, the crewmember who had wished for good news when I left was still there. He said, "We're not going home, are we? We're going North instead. I can tell from the look on your face." (6)

The B-52s and F-111s operated regardless of the weather. In all, 15 B-52s were lost from a total of 729 sorties in 11 combat days. By the end of the period, bombing tactics had been refined to the point where 113 B-52s were all over the target area within the space of 15 minutes and suffered no losses. Indeed, so effective was the strategic interdiction effort that North Vietnam had expended the last of its SAMs and had no reloads left! In the wake of the most concentrated bombing campaign in history, the military targets in the Hanoi/Haiphong areas were utterly destroyed, with less than 1,600 civilian casualties. The offensive brought the North Vietnamese back to the peace talks – ready to make a deal.

An all-nuclear Battle Group consisting of the carrier USS Enterprise, the cruiser Long Beach and the frigates (light cruisers) Bainbridge and Truxton seen in the Gulf of Tonkin in 1972.

US Naval Operations

At the outbreak of the 1972 invasion the USN had two carriers on station, the USS Coral Sea and USS Hancock. From the US Naval Base at Subic Bay in the Philippines, the carrier Kitty Hawk was dispatched to the Tonkin Gulf (arriving on 3 April), and Constellation was recalled from Hong Kong (arriving on 8 April). Sailing orders were given to the

LINEBACKER

'Linebacker II' finally saw US air power let loose in the sort of role for which it was intended. Striking military targets within the Hanoi/Haiphong region between 18th and 29th December 1972, the heavy bombing was carried out by Boeing B-52s from U-Tapao in Thailand and Andersen AFB, Guam. A supporting cast of Navy and Air Force fighters, 'Iron Hand' aircraft and ECM jamming platforms softened-up targets and hit others. 15 of the bombers were lost, but the North's leaders hurried to the negotiating table for the first time during the war.

Above: A Boeing B-52D chases the sun as it sets out on a 'Linebacker II' mission from Andersen AB on Guam. North Vietnam lay 4,000 miles ahead.

Below: Boeing B-52Gs (foreground) and B-52Ds (background) litter every available parking space at Andersen during 'Linebacker II'.

Above: Many tactical aircraft took part in 'Linebacker II', including Vought A-7Ds. These aircraft are parked on a disruptive patterned apron at Korat.

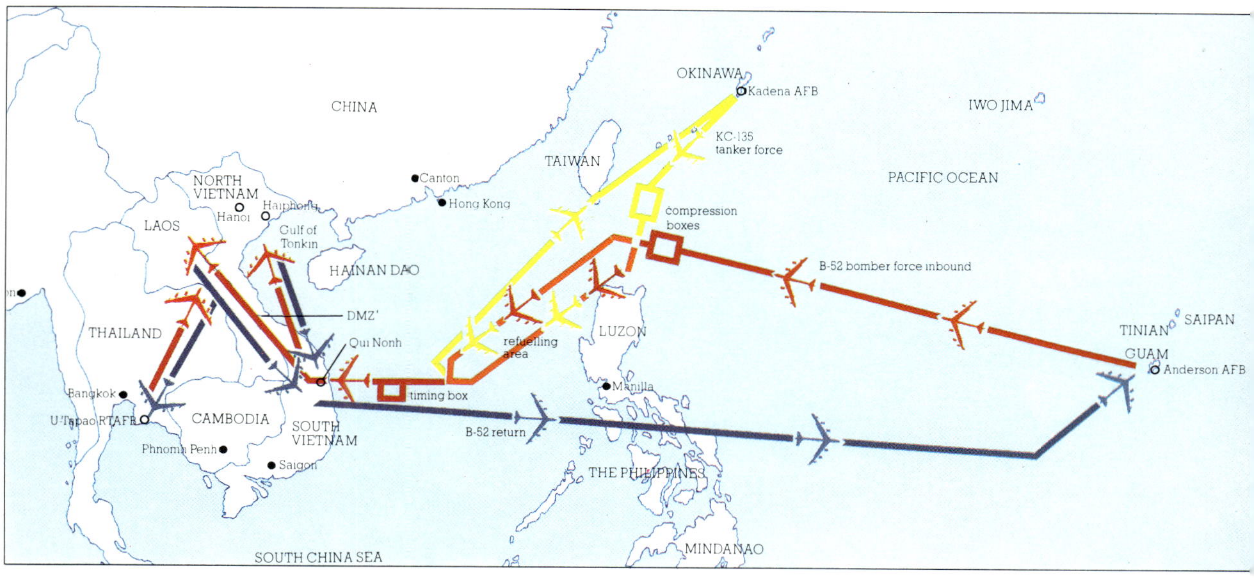

Above: This map shows the journey of the bombers from Andersen and U-Tapao, with their refuelling areas north-west of the Philippines.

Left: Among the smaller aircraft supporting the B-52s were McDonnell F-4 Phantoms armed with laser-guided bombs for precision attacks.

Left: Navy aircraft were used on anti-radiation missions as well as bombing targets of their own. This is a Grumman A-6 Intruder, a type heavily committed to 'Linebacker II'.

Inflight refuelling was vital to the B-52s heading for North Vietnam, as many had 8,000 mile missions to complete.

Above: By this time SAC's tanker effort depended on the Boeing KC-135A. Operating from Kadena, the tankers supported the bomber streams, while others flying from Thai bases refuelled tactical aircraft.

With the 'Big Belly' weapons bay modification and wing pylons, the Boeing B-52D could carry up to 84 bombs of 500-lb or 750-lb size. They were used to great effect during 'Linebacker II', even gaining two MiG-kills with the tail guns.

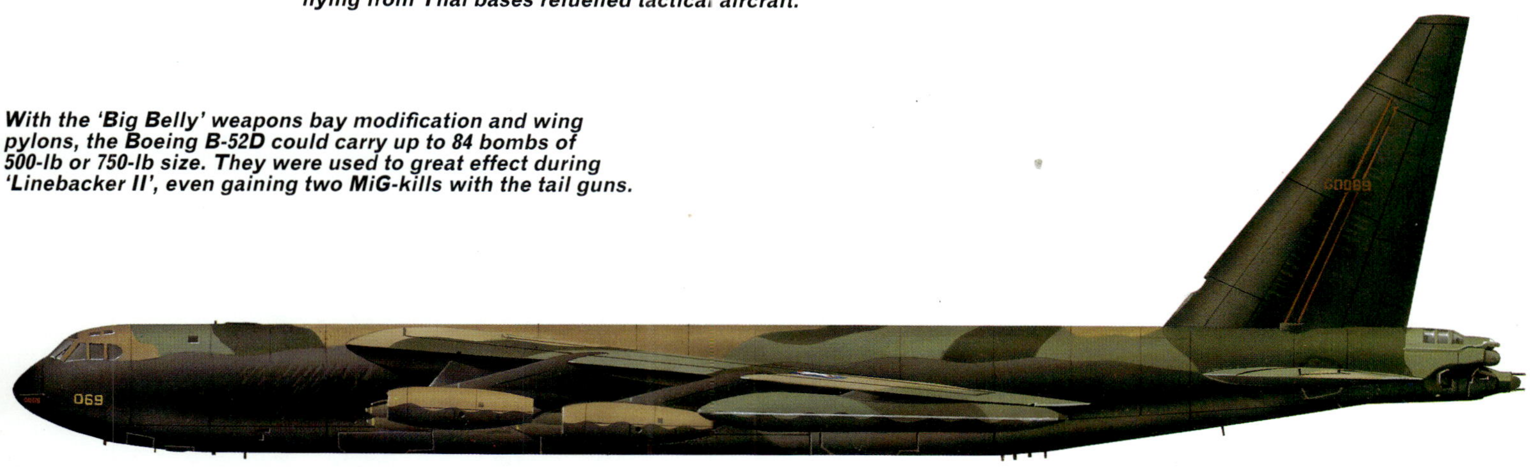

The upgraded B-52G version featured a smaller bomb load, shorter fin and redesigned gun turret with the gunner moved inside the cockpit. All were based at Andersen. During 'Linebacker II', 15 B-52s were lost to enemy action.

stateside carriers **Midway** (Eastern Pacific) and **Saratoga** (Atlantic) on the 8th. Of the six carriers eventually in the theater, at least four were on line at all times with about 70% of their aircraft combat-ready daily.

Marine aircraft reinforced the defenses with MAG 15's three F-4 squadrons arriving at the beginning of April to join a Marine A-6 squadron from the Coral Sea. Two A-4 squadrons arrived in mid-May, followed by another A-6 squadron and a further two F-4 squadrons.

Naval strikes

By mid-April, Task Force 77 had been given clearance to hit supply and fuel storage facilities in the vicinity of Hanoi and Haiphong. During these operations a **Shrike** anti-radiation missile (used for SAM suppression) was accidentally released by a

The light cruiser USS Oklahoma City unleashes a salvo of 6-inch shells in support of operations in I Corps. Other ships conducted bombardments of the North Vietnamese coast.

Navy fighter, and homed in on the electronic emissions of the guided missile frigate **USS Worden**. The missile put the ship out of action, causing severe damage to its antennae and inflicting a number of casualties in the combat information center.

Shore bombardment

USN surface forces conducting shore bombardment off the North Vietnamese coast had doubled by the end of April, and were effectively engaged by NVA 130mm gun batteries for the first time that month. The North Vietnamese also tried a number of torpedo boat sorties which were promptly sunk, and a few MiGs which were likewise shot down. On August 27th, a shore bombardment group including the 8-inch gun heavy cruiser **Newport News** hit Haiphong docks in a night raid and also destroyed a couple of North Vietnamese torpedo boats. In October, the **Newport News** was to suffer a major accidental explosion in its No.2 main turret, necessitating the removal of the center gun and leaving the turret inoperable for the rest of the ship's service life.

By the beginning May, there were six carriers on line at Yankee Station. They cheerfully received the news on the 8th that President Nixon had authorized the mining of Haiphong, Cam Pha, Vinh, Quang Khe, Dong Hoi, Thanh Hoa, Hon Gai, and the Red River Delta. This was accomplished, with the minimum of trouble, by May 15th. The United States, too late in the war, was finally getting serious about hitting the North Vietnamese supply line where it hurt. The mining operation effectively cut the main overseas supply route into North Vietnam. The only way that cargo could reach Haiphong was for a ship to stop outside the mined area and off-load into small boats – a process requiring up to a month for even a 5,000-ton freighter. In the days following the mining effort, naval air operations in the Hanoi and Haiphong areas grew in intensity. North Vietnamese MiG opposition provided Lt Randy Cunningham of the Constellation a record three kills in one day and an overall score of five, to make him the first US "ace" of the war.

COMBAT RESCUE

Few airmen in Southeast Asia commanded as much respect as the rescue crews. Much effort was ecpended by the military in bringing back downed airmen alive from the hostile jungles or sea, and the discipline of combat rescue was evolved rapidly into a highly tactical art, involving the use of sophisticated techniques and equipment. Nevertheless, it was the crews to whom the credit is due, their dedication and skill leading to some amazing rescues in the face of heav opposition. Such was the dedication that on a few occasions, more lives and aircraft were lost in the rescue than in the original incident.

Above: A Sikorsky CH-3E moves in to retrieve a downed pilot. Later another helicopter may be called in to retrieve the remains of the Northrop F-5.

Above: Members of the Sikorsky H-3 family were amphibious, although waterborne operations were seldom practised.

Above: First deployed in June 1964, the Kaman HH-43 Huskie was the first rescue helicopter deployed to the war zone. This example hovers over a crash site.

Above: Replacing the Huskie as the primary combat rescue platform, the Sikorsky CH-3 and HH-3 were known as the 'Jolly Green Giants'. This CH-3E hovers in the treetops during a rescue.

Right: Seven Douglas A-1 Skyraiders set out on a rescue attempt. In addition to close support and suppressive fire, the Skyraiders were often used to lay smoke screens during the helicopter's approach.

Above: More heavily-armed and armoured, the Sikorsky HH-53 'Super Jolly' introduced greater flexibility and endurance to the combat rescue role. This example is seen being marshalled across a temporary pierced-steel planking apron at Nakhon Phanom.

Above: One of the most dangerous parts of the 'Sandy' mission was trolling for fire – deliberately flying to draw enemy fire and so pinpoint the guns.

CHAPTER ELEVEN

BEFORE THE STORM

1973-1974

The North Vietnamese invasion of 1972 saw the south faced with new and more sophisticated weapons, such as these Soviet supplied D-74 122-mm field guns. They could outrange most ARVN artillery with ease.

During the so-called "Christmas bombing" of **Operation Linebacker II**, one US Air Force wag, ready to begin a bomb run on Hanoi, announced over the radio, "The Prince of Peace comes in from the East." So it appeared when the bombing prompted Le Duc Tho to resume negotiations with Henry Kissinger in Paris. By January 9th a rough agreement had been hammered out. North Vietnam's willingness to negotiate led Nixon to call off bombing north of the 20th Parallel and shift US air efforts back to South Vietnam on December 30th, 1972.

President Nixon addresses the nation, Jan 23 1973.

Good evening. I have asked for this radio and television time tonight for the purpose of announcing that we today have concluded an agreement to end the war and bring peace with honor in Vietnam and Southeast Asia.

The following statement is being issued at this moment in Washington and Hanoi:

"At 12:30 Paris time today, Jan. 23, 1973, the agreement on ending the war and restoring peace in Vietnam was initialed by Dr. Henry Kissinger on behalf of the United States and Special Adviser Le Duc Tho on behalf of the Democratic Republic of Vietnam.

"The agreement will be formally signed by the parties participating in the Paris Conference on Vietnam on Jan. 27, 1973, at the International Conference Center in Paris. The cease-fire will take effect at 2400 Greenwich mean time, Jan. 27, 1973. The United States and the Democratic Republic of Vietnam express the hope that this agreement will insure stable peace in Vietnam and contribute to the preservation of lasting peace in Indochina and Southeast Asia." (1)

The cease-fire document was signed on January 27th, 1973, and took effect the next day. The various major provisions included:

1. **A cease-fire.** It never really happened. Both sides refused to give up the chance of temporary gains.
2. **The withdrawal of US forces.** Between the end of January and mid-March, US Army strength in Vietnam dropped from 12,400 to 4,081. By the end of the month, all but the staff of the Defense Attache's Office and a few advisors had left. The agreement also called for the removal of mines that the US Navy had laid at the entrance to North Vietnamese ports. Sweeping was undertaken by Task Force 78, and was completed by July.
3. **The return of US Prisoners of War.** 591 POWs were acknowledged by Hanoi. The first were released on February 12th, and the operation was completed by March 29th. Some 2,483 US personnel were still listed as "missing in action" twelve years later, and a handful of these have subsequently been recovered from aircraft crash sites. To this day, rumors persist of POWs still in captivity in Southeast Asia.
4. **No NVA withdrawal from South Vietnam.** Saigon had insisted that the NVA withdraw, but was forced to compromise and accept the ludicrous provision which allowed the NVA to occupy 25% of South Vietnam and control 15% of its people.
5. **Removal of foreign forces from Cambodia and Laos.** The NVA never gave up its base areas in these two countries.
6. **Eventual reunification of Vietnam by political processes.** There was never any realistic chance for reunification while both sides held diametrically opposed ideological views.
7. **Temporary recognition of the DMZ as the North/South boundary.** As the entire area of the DMZ was in NVA hands, this was a moot point.
8. **Formation of an International Commission for Control and Supervision.** The ICCS was formed to monitor the cease-fire, and was composed of members from Canada, Indonesia, Hungary and Poland. It proved singularly ineffective in this role, and was routinely denied access to key areas by the NVA. Using their diplomatic status and protection, members of the Hungarian delegation regularly conducted espionage against the ARVN.
9. **No resignation of the Thieu government in South Vietnam.** Hanoi had insisted that Thieu be replaced, but finally accepted his continued presence in light of other concessions they received in the cease-fire agreement.
10. **North Vietnamese recognition of South Vietnam.** The right of self-determination of the South Vietnamese people was never seriously acknowledged by Hanoi, which continued to stick to its plan of reunification under its own terms.
11. **No further troop movements through the DMZ.** This provision was ridiculous and unenforceable. In

fact, the NVA built up its lines of communication through this area in anticipation of the final offensive.

12. **Renunciation of the use of force to unify Vietnam.** Wishful thinking, which failed to take into account Hanoi's long-standing commitment to annex South Vietnam at all costs, accomplished in 1975.

Saigon, South Vietnam, Jan. 24 – The last American soldiers in South Vietnam received the news today that the war was finally ending for them with emotions that ranged from elation and relief to disappointment, anger and resentment.

For some who had grown fond of the special life-style here, there was a sense of loss. And there were some young men who had lived with the war more than half their lives, who had been crushed when their hopes for peace were shattered late last year and simply refused to believe when they heard President Nixon announce the agreement to stop shooting at 8 A.M. Sunday, Saigon time.

"I just ain't going to believe it till Sunday and I see we don't go out anymore," said Specialist 4 John Victor Bilton, a 19-year-old radio operator from Miami, as he returned to the Bien Hoa air base this afternoon from an operation with a platoon of South Vietnamese rangers. (2)

Although the cease-fire agreement was ultimately a sham, it allowed Nixon to withdraw from the war claiming that "peace with honor" had been achieved. The major architects of the document, Kissinger and Le Duc Tho, were later chosen to receive the Nobel Peace Prize for their efforts and Le Duc Tho prophetically refused to accept the honor. It was clear that the North Vietnamese would only avoid major renewed fighting as long as Nixon's threat to intervene with airpower was valid. Nixon's assurances became increasingly less relevant as his administration slowly submerged beneath the Watergate scandal, which ultimately forced his resignation in August of 1974. Thieu and the South Vietnamese felt betrayed by the United States, which had presented the agreement as a **fait accompli**. While Thieu's outlook is understandable, one can't forget the years of blood and treasure that the Americans had poured into South Vietnam in order to keep alive a regime which ultimately failed.

US withdrawals during March were mainly made up of logistical and support elements, as well as remaining helicopter units (11th, 12th, 17th and 164th Aviation Groups) which turned over many items of equipment to the ARVN. At the same time, the South Koreans finally pulled out their Capital and 9th Divisions. American casualties in 1973 amounted to 237 killed in action, 34 non-combat deaths and 66 seriously wounded. South Vietnamese dead during 1973 totalled 13,788, about one-third of the 1972 toll. Communist dead for the year amounted to 45,057 – again about one-third of the previous year. Before the March withdrawal, the US Army lost 6 more helicopters in South Vietnam. Two of these were operational losses and the other 4 were to ground fire. In all, from 1962 to 1973, Army helicopter losses totalled 4,321 – nearly half of which were non-combat accidents. The Marines had a single operational helicopter loss in 1973, and this brought the total of Marine helicopters destroyed during the war to 424, of which 154 were from non-combat causes. The Marines had also lost a total of 276 fixed-wing aircraft since 1964, of which all but 82 occurred in combat.

USAF losses

Final USAF fixed-wing losses during 1973 amounted to 18 planes, operational accidents causing 7, ground fire bringing down 8, and SAMs being responsible for the remaining 3. Air Force losses since 1962 totalled 2,174 fixed-wing planes, 495 of them being operational. The Navy lost an additional

PSYOPS

A concerted psychological warfare campaign was waged in Vietnam, involving USAF, US Army and VNAF aircraft. Leaflets inviting the VC to defect were dropped by the million. 'Gabby' loudspeaker-equipped psy-ops ships taunted the VC into firing, allowing gunships to destroy positions thus revealed.

Above: Douglas C-47 parked at Nha Trang AB, South Vietnam. It is equipped with loudspeaker for psy-war operations.

Left: A Bell UH-1P cruises at altitude over South Vietnam. These helicopters were employed for many psy-war operations, serving with the 20th Special Operations Squadron 'Hornets' mostly in the III Corps region. The UH-1F version was also employed by this unit, and some of their aircraft were armed with a door-mounted 7.62-mm Minigun.

Above: The Vietnamese air force was also active in psy-ops, using various types of small lightplane such as the Cessna U-17 and de Havilland Canada U-6 Beaver (illustrated). Leaflet dropping and boradcasting were the main functions, the loudspeaker being mounted in the port fuselage.

Bell UH-1P of the 20th Special Operations Squadron. Helicopters were ideal for leaflet dropping and other psy-ops over small hamlets, where accuracy of dropping was required. While UH-1s were the principal type employed for this task, it had been performed earlier by Sikorsky H-34s, and the VNAF continued to use this elderly helicopter.

12 planes in 1973, 8 in operational accidents and 4 from enemy ground fire. This boosted the total of USN fixed-wing planes destroyed since 1964 to 830. Of these, 299 were operational and 531 were combat losses.

Project Enhance

After the NVA Spring Offensive of 1972, the US dumped a considerable amount of equipment on the South Vietnamese armed services, partly as replacement for lost items and partly as a last minute upgrade prior to American withdrawal. **Project Enhance** provided the ARVN with: 36 x 175mm SP guns (enough for 3 battalions); over 100 M-48 tanks (enough for 2 battalions); sufficient quad-.50 cal. and twin-40mm air defense weapons for 2 battalions; and 100 TOW anti-tank missile launchers (enough to provide a section for each maneuver regiment, brigade or group). Air Force systems also came under **Enhance**, and a follow-up program, **Enhance Plus**. Together, both programs provided the following aircraft: 23 CH-47 medium helicopters (2 sqdns); 286 UH-1 utility helicopters (increasing establishments and adding 3 sqdns); 90 A-37 light bombers (5 sqdns); 118 F-5 fighters (5 sqdns); 22 AC-119K gunships (1 sqdn); 28 A-1 attack planes; 4 C-7 transports (1 sqdn); 32 C-130 transports; 12 RC-47 photo-recce planes; 23 EC-47 electronic recce planes; 35 0-2 spotters; and 24 T-37 trainers.

The fiscal 1973 aid package granted South Vietnam 2.8 billion dollars in hardware and operations funding, but the Congress imposed a 1974 ceiling of 1.126 billion dollars. The FY-75 allowance slashed this figure by more than half again, to 500 million dollars in effective military aid. These figures translated directly into operational shortfalls in the field. In 1974, only slightly more than half of ARVN's vehicles had fuel to move – and that at a reduced level of employment. Lack of spare parts grounded 20% of South Vietnam's aircraft that year, as well as 35% of its tanks and 50% of its armored personnel carriers. At the same time, Soviet and Chinese aid to North Vietnam during 1973 was 150% of the 1972 level, and 110% of the 1971 level – the previous high point.

CLARK AIR BASE, the Philippines, Feb. 13 – There was general sympathy here today for one former prisoner of war who, after calling his wife in the United States, was said to have walked down a hospital corridor saying, "My God, she did it, she did it, she did it."

A fellow prisoner asked him sympathetically, "What did she do?"

The reply: "She bought a motorcycle." (3)

Operations – 1973

Both Laos and Cambodia felt the effects of redirected Communist efforts. In February of 1973, the Royal Laotian government of Prince Souvanna Phouma made an accommodation with the Pathet Lao Communists and agreed to a cease-fire. To the south, the NVA pushed the FANK 32nd Brigade away from the Cambodia/Vietnam border in May, and gained control of the entire frontier. Soon after, the NVA and the Khmer Rouge had a falling out over the requisition of rice in Cambodia, and serious skirmishes between the two sides began. The Khmer Rouge, proteges of the Chinese, never got along with the Hanoi Communists, and the situation continued to deteriorate.

Nixon honored Lon Nol's request to continue B-52 strikes against NVA and Khmer Rouge units operating in Cambodia. At this time the NVA had 9 regiments in Cambodia which were used in cross-border attacks against South Vietnam, and a further 4 which fought against Lon Nol's FANK. Nixon secured Congressional approval to maintain the B-52 efforts only until August 15th, 1973. Congress went further, in passing the War Powers Act (over Nixon's veto), which required Presidential notifica-

Above: A light utility type employed on psychological warfare operations was the Helio U-10 Courier.

Right: Wearing a non-standard camouflage, this Cessna 0-2B of the 9th SOS flew from Nha Trang on leaflet-dropping and broadcasting missions.

Below: A 5th SOS C-47 'Bullshit Bomber' flying from Nha Trang drops its load of leaflets over the jungle.

ELECTRONIC WAR

The Vietnam war saw the first major use of airborne electronic warfare systems. As the SAM threat grew and grew, so electronic countermeasures were introduced to negate it. ECM jamming platforms became a vital part of strike operations north of the border, while tactical aircraft themselves began carrying pods and fairings with equipment designed to protect them. Aircraft from the Air Force, Navy and Marine Corps were involved in this discipline, a task that has remained of utmost importance to this day.

The Douglas EF-10B Skynight was a highly effective ECM/Elint platform. Operated by VMCJ-1, USMC, the type's services were often requested by Air Force and Navy units. It served until 1969.

Douglas EB-66 Destroyer ECM operations began in May 1965, and lasted on until 1974.

tion and ultimate Congressional approval of any commitment of US troops to combat.

In January of 1973, the NVA launched a vigorous campaign on all fronts to secure last minute gains before the "cease-fire" officially went into effect. They lost about 5,000 men in the effort, but made no substantial headway. At that time, the Communists had about 123,000 NVA regulars and 25,000 main force VC in the field, making up 424 battalions, 94 regimental headquarters and 16 division headquarters. Three of the divisions (304, 308 and 312) had been seriously depleted in the 1972 Offensive, and were withdrawn to North Vietnam to refit. The ARVN had about 192,000 regulars in 264 battalions, 48 regiment and brigade headquarters and 13 division headquarters. In addition there were 497,000 South Vietnamese Regional Forces distributed in more or less static defense throughout the country.

SAIGON, South Vietnam, March 28 – The 60-day first phase of the Vietnam cease-fire came to an end today with fighting continuing, peace-keeping machinery in a state of disarray and the prospects for real peace in South Vietnam apparently remote.

The end of this phase is being marked by a momentous turning point in Vietnam's history: the complete withdrawal of American troops after more than eight years of intense involvement.

In the view of many Western and Vietnamese officials, this turning point does not mean that peace has come. "The cease-fire isn't working," said one highly placed Western diplomat in summing up the critical two months since the Paris peace accord was signed. "It hasn't been implemented as it should have been."

"There certainly has been no cease-fire," said a high-ranking American official who only a few weeks ago predicted that the fighting would soon end. "The best we have is a significantly reduced level of fighting – but we have had these lulls before."

"The thing is," still another well-informed Western official commented, "there's a war on." (4)

The cease-fire allowed the North Vietnamese to expand and improve their logistical system. Units began to move in daylight along the Ho Chi Minh Trail without fear of bombing, and there was a marked increase in truck traffic. In the northernmost province, Quang Tri, South Vietnamese aircraft had a difficult time operating in the face of 13 NVA air defence gun regiments and an SA-2 SAM regiment. In general though, there was little action in I Corps during 1973. The 1st and Airborne Divisions had a demoralizing time trying to hold on to isolated outposts in the face of increasing Communist strength, but the 2nd Division had somewhat more success mopping up VC remnants in the coastal lowlands. On the other hand the Viet Cong began a particularly brutal campaign of terrorism in the spring, aimed at the refugee resettlement villages in the northern provinces. All things considered, it was Saigon's unanimous opinion that US air power would be required for the ARVN to hold any of Quang Tri and Thua Thien in the face of a determined NVA attack.

What cease-fire?

The first renewed Communist offensive after the "cease-fire" came in March and April, 1973 in Kien Phong Province (IV Corps). The NVA had massed three regiments (174, 207 and 272) in Cambodia and struck south against the ARVN 15th Regiment (9th Division) which held Hong Ngu, near where the Mekong River crosses the Cambodian border into Vietnam. Determined resistance on the part of the ARVN, and B-52 strikes from Nixon's Cambodian effort succeeded in repulsing the attackers, leaving 422 Communists and 94 ARVN soldiers dead. Suc-

Grumman EA-6As began replacing EF-10Bs with VMCJ-1 from November 1966 onwards on the jamming mission. They also found time to perform Elint sorties.

For the early part of the war ECM support for Navy strikes was flown by the Douglas EA-1F Skyraider, EKA-3B Skywarriors took over the role for the latter part of the conflict.

"Army electronic warfare quite naturally was directed to help the troops on the ground. Battlefield ComInt and location of enemy radios were the prime missions"

Above: Distinguished by its wingtip pods, this is an EB-66C ESM/ECM platform, seen taking off from Takhli RTAFB in 1966.

Left: Seen approaching the tanker is an EB-66B, which was used solely for ECM duties. The EB-66s were the last Air Force tactical aircraft in the theatre to require probe and drogue refuelling.

Below: The 'RH' tailcode on this Douglas EB-66B denotes the 42nd Tactical Electronic Warfare Squadron, 355th Tactical Fighter Wing which operated all the EB-66s during the later years of the war from Korat RTAFB. Note the plethora of aerials, which grew steadily as ECM advances were made.

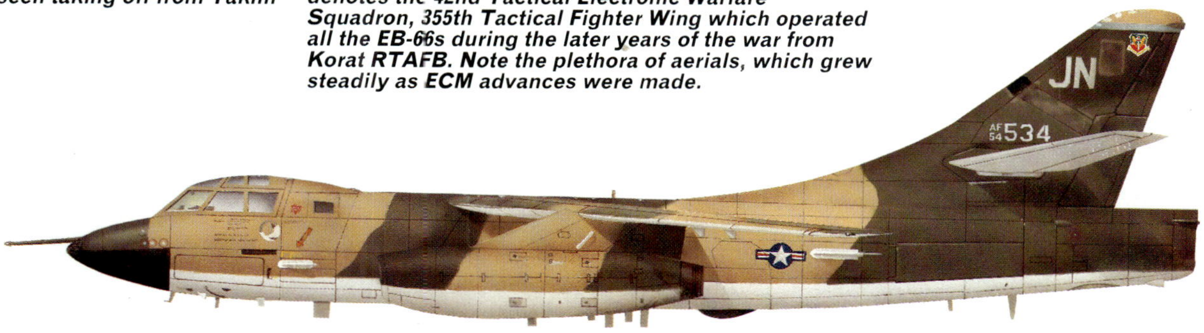

cess prompted the ARVN to take the offensive against the NVA 1st Division, holed up in "Seven Mountains" Base Area 400 in neighboring Chau Doc Province. The ARVN blockaded rice traffic to the area and, in July, launched an attack with the 4th Armored Brigade and the 7th Ranger Group. The blockade was so effective that by September the NVA 1st Division ceased to exist, and its 44th Sapper and 52nd Regiments were amalgamated with its 101D Regiment which retired to Cambodia.

In the Central Highlands, the NVA launched a summer offensive against ARVN's II Corps in 1973. The NVA's 3rd Binh Dinh, 10th, and 320th Divisions (a total of 8 divisional regiments plus 4 separate units) exerted pressure on the outposts guarding the approaches to Kontum and Pleiku. The ARVN defended with the 22nd and 23rd Divisions (a total of 7 regiments) plus the 2nd Ranger Group and reinforcements from the 7th Ranger Group. The Communists achieved local successes by concentrating against the thinly spread ARVN, but failed to carry any important objectives. Similarly, a fall counteroffensive by ARVN's II Corps, which hoped to destroy the NVA 320th Division, met with little success. In November the NVA gathered a division-size task force (with sappers, tanks and artillery

1972 saw the NVA bringing significant anti-air weapons into the south for the first time, with more following in 1973 and 1974.

attached) called "Unit 95" in Quang Duc Province – the southernmost in II Corps. Unit 95 gained initial success against the ranger border camps and RF/PF militia which they encountered. The ARVN 53rd Regiment was rushed to the area and absorbed the initial attack while the ARVN 23rd Division's 44th and 45th Regiments and the 21st Ranger Group prepared to reinforce. With operations continuing into January, 1974 the ARVN 23rd Division succeeded in throwing back the NVA, thanks in part to the rapid reinforcement made possible by air transport.

In III Corps, the NVA and VC were mainly limited to guerrilla and sapper operations during 1973 – the exception being the mauling the ARVN 5th Division received at the hands of the NVA 7th Division, engaged in isolating Phuoc Binh, the capital of Phuoc Long Province. In general, the NVA was busy establishing a strategic reserve in North Vietnam for serious offensive operations that were to follow. At Thanh Hoa they organized the NVA 1st Corps, consisting of the 320B, 308th and 312th Divisions – the last two refitting after substantial losses in the 1972 offensive. Also concentrating in North Vietnam for movement south were the 316th, 341st and 308B Divisions. The 316th had been in Laos, the 341st had been in static defense north of

DRONES

The large-scale use of air-launched reconnaissance drones was seen only during the Vietnam war. At the time a secret operation, it is only in recent years that the full extent of their major contribution to the war effort has been publicised. Many versions existed, able to perform most reconnaissance disciplines including electronic, photographic and real-time TV intelligence-gathering. Flying at altitudes from a few feet to 75,000 ft, the drones regularly penetrated hostile airspace to bring back data of inestimable value without placing a pilot in great danger.

Above:* Tom Cat *was an AQM-34H drone, a low-altitude photo-reconnaissance version. It notched up a remarkable 68 combat launches.

***Above left:* Ground crew programme an *AQM-34M* low-altitude drone with its guidance data.**

***Right:* Lockheed's *DC-130E* was the definitive drone-carrier.**

> ***"Peaking during Linebacker II, when 91 drones were launched in a 30 day period, recon RPV activites brought a wealth of information"***

the DMZ, and the 308B had been the Hanoi garrison. Similarly, the North Vietnamese organized the NVA 2nd Corps south of the DMZ. It consisted of the 324B and 325th Divisions, as well as the 304th Division when it had completed its refit in the north. While these units were gathering, the 968th Division (which had formerly guarded the Ho Chi Minh Trail in Laos) moved across into South Vietnam. Air defense in the south was strengthened reaching a total at the end of the year of two anti-aircraft divisions and 26 separate AA regiments. By the end of 1973, NVA artillery and armor holdings in South Vietnam were four times greater than in 1972. Virtually the entire strength of the NVA was massing for employment in the south. The only major units to be left in North Vietnam were four training divisions (304B, 330, 338 and 350), and of these the 338th was converted to a line division for use in the final offensive.

Operations – 1974

Early in January, elements of the NVA 5th Division and the Z-15 and Z-18 Regiments occupied the southern portion of Kien Tuong Province in IV Corps, threatening to cut off the province capital and the route to Saigon. The ARVN massed its 14th Regiment (9th Division) with the 10th and 12th Regiments (both 7th Division), for an attack on the NVA. By April the ARVN had decimated not only the Z-15 and Z-18 Regiments, but the VC Dong Thap 1 Regiment which had come to reinforce them. With a loss of only 100 dead, the ARVN had killed 1,100 Communist troops and forced the NVA 5th Division back into Cambodia.

A combined III and IV Corps effort that started at the end of April kept the NVA 5th Division off balance. Moving west into the "Angel's Wing" of Cambodia from III Corps' Tay Ninh and Hau Ngia, four armor/Ranger task forces, plus the ARVN 49th Regiment and 7th Ranger Group, swept the NVA assembly areas and forced the retreat of the E-6 and 174th NVA Regiments. From the east, out of Kien Tuong, IV Corps' ARVN 7th Division launched two task forces into the "Elephant's Foot" area and put heavy pressure on the NVA 275th Regiment. The operation was successful in stopping NVA thrusts into the III/IV Corps junction, but it was to be the war's last big offensive for the ARVN.

During the spring and summer of 1974, the Communists changed the emphasis of their operations in III Corps, nibbling away at the outposts which guarded various approaches to Saigon. In April they overran a Regional Forces post at Chi Linh and forced the abandonment of a Ranger battalion base at Tong Le Chon. North of Saigon, the NVA 9th Division overran a Regional Forces base and the town of An Dien on the edge of the Iron Triangle in May. In early June, an ARVN counterattack by elements of the 18th Division, 7th Ranger Group, and an armored task force, succeeded in recapturing An Dien from the north. The RF base was not recaptured until four months later, after persistent and costly attempts by III Corps. The other NVA division operating in the area, the 7th, moved on Phu Giao (south of Phuoc Vinh) in May in an effort to seize the bridge over the Song Be and cut local route 1A. The bridge was held by Regional Forces who stood firm until elements of the ARVN 5th Division and an armored task force repulsed the NVA.

At mid-year, the NVA 301st Corps Headquarters was established to command the NVA 7th and 9th Divisions, and independent regiments operating north and west of Saigon. During August, some of these NVA elements tried to overrun outposts guarding the Bien Hoa complex, but were unsuc-

Left: DC-130s and a collection of high-altitude drones wait outside in the South Vietnamese sun, protected against VC attacks by steel revetments. At the time an unsung achievement, only recently has the full extent of the drone's contribution to the war effort been publicized.

Right: Originally intended for launch from the back of a Lockheed A-11, the D-21 drone was a Mach 4 aircraft powered by a Marquardt ramjet for high-altitude, high-speed penetration of extremely hostile airspace. Tests were conducted from B-52H carriers, and many rumours persist that they were used operationally in the Southeast Asia theatre. Little has been released about the drones, but this picture exists of the aircraft slung under a B-52 of the 4200th SRW.

Above: A drone descends during mid-air recovery slung under its main parachute.

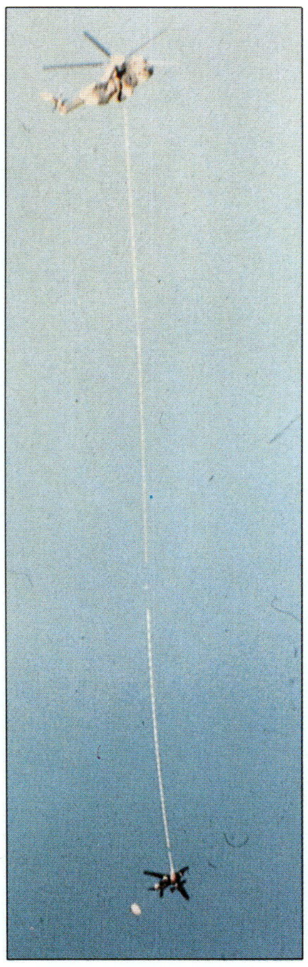

Right: A successful mid-air catch, and the helicopter now has to reel in the drone. The small drogue chute keeps the drone steady in transit.

Above: The recovery helicopter prepares to set down the drone at its base.

Left: Throughout the war the recovery helicopter used was the Sikorsky CH-3E, operating from Da Nang or Nakhon Phanom. This drone is a high-altitude AQM-34R, with long range tanks.

cessful. To the east of Saigon, near the strategic junction of Xuan Loc, the NVA 33rd and 274th Regiments initiated a summer campaign to cut Highway 1 and occupy several key villages. The ARVN 18th Division was reinforced by elements of the 5th Division and the 7th Ranger Group and cleared the NVA over the next few months. Also during August, the NVA 6th Regiment attacked three RF outposts near Tay Ninh City but was eventually forced to retreat into Cambodia because of losses inflicted by the Regional Forces and the ARVN 46th Regiment.

More losses

During May, the NVA 324B Division's 29th Regiment (with tank and anti-aircraft support) invested an ARVN Ranger camp called Dak Pek, in northwest Kontum Province. This was another case of the ARVN attempting to hold insupportable outposts deep in the interior – in this case II Corps. The 88th Ranger battalion was pounded into submission and forced to surrender. At the end of the month a Regional Forces post was overrun, this time Tieu Atar northwest of Ban Me Thuot. In July, the NVA 10th Division's 66th Regiment hit another northern position, Mang Buk, in Kontum Province. Defended by just a couple of RF companies, the base was overwhelmed by mid-August. As Mang Buk fell, the NVA 320th Division moved to attack the ARVN 82nd Ranger Battalion camp at Plei Me. Unlike other outposts, Plei Me was in range of supporting ARVN 105mm and 175mm artillery, the base itself was well fortified and the 82nd Ranger Battalion had an additional company attached. The NVA 320th Division's attack involved five of its own battalions plus the 26th Independent Regiment, and support from artillery and heavy mortars. The assaults all failed, with heavy NVA casualties, and they broke off and withdrew in early September. Between Mang Buk and Kontum lay Chuong Nghia, another Regional Forces post in a remote location. In October the NVA 28th Regiment had little problem overrunning that position, which was outside the range of any ARVN supporting artillery. Financial and fuel restrictions had left II Corps unable to reinforce its outlying units by airlift or helicopter.

In the I Corps area, the NVA 2nd Division (formed out of the remnants of the disbanded 711th Division) launched a series of probes beginning in May in Quang Tin Province. This threat to Highway 1 was met by the ARVN 2nd Division and Rangers from I Corps, who stiffened the Regional Forces and stood fast. Just to the north, in Quang Nam Province, the ARVN 3rd Division and some Rangers drove elements of the NVA 2nd Division from Tien Phuoc in July. As the NVA suffered these reverses, they organized a new headquarters, NVA 3rd Corps, to take over operations in Quang Nam. It thrust the NVA 2nd Division, reinforced with the 36th Independent Regiment, into action against the ARVN 78th Ranger Battalion at Da Trach in July. The situation deteriorated rapidly for the South Vietnamese, and the ARVN 3rd Division required reinforcing regiments from other I Corps divisions, as well as the 12th Ranger Group, to hold the line. A little to the north, at Thuong Duc, elements of the 14th Ranger Group came under attack from the NVA 29th Regiment in late July. The post was overrun on August 7th, before reinforcements from Saigon (1st Airborne Brigade) could reach the area. Continued NVA pressure exhausted the ARVN 3rd Division by the fall, and to the south, in Quang Ngai Province, the ARVN 2nd Division was spread thin by calls for reinforcements to other areas. Along with the 11th Ranger Group, it fought a losing battle against the gradual pressure of the NVA 52nd Brigade, which began picking off RF and PF positions in August. By the end of the year, the ARVN 2nd Division's battalions were averaging only 300 men apiece.

ARVN counterattacks

Over the summer, the new NVA 2nd Corps deployed units in Thua Thien Province to threaten Hue from the south. At the end of August the Corps' 324B Division launched a four-regiment attack (6, 271, 803, 812) against the ARVN 3rd Regiment (1st Division). By the end of September, in spite of heavy ARVN reinforcements (51st & 54th Regiments), the NVA controlled the high ground on the southern approach, dominating the air base at Phu Bai. The heavy fighting had rendered the NVA 803rd and 812th Regiments ineffective, along with the ARVN 3rd Regiment. ARVN counterattacks regained a slim foothold on some of the heights by December, and kept the NVA from exploiting its position.

As 1974 drew to a close, the South Vietnamese felt the strain of depleted fuel, spare parts and ammunition. Pressed everywhere, the ARVN was just about holding its own. Worse, the strategic reserves had all been committed. The stage was set for the final offensive.

THE ARVN

When the US and North Vietnam began serious escalation of the war in 1965, the Army of the Republic of Vietnam ("ARVN") had nine infantry divisions: 1st and 2nd in I Corps; 22nd and 23rd in II Corps; 5th and 25th in III Corps; and 7th, 9th and 21st in IV Corps. In 1966, the 10th Division was formed in III Corps from three formerly independent regiments, and next year was redesignated as the 18th Division because its commanding general thought that "10" was an unlucky number. The last infantry division to be formed was the 3rd, in I Corps, in October of 1971. It was formed by raising two new regiments and transferring the 2nd Regiment from the 1st Division, which in turn picked up the independent 51st Regiment.

QUANGNGAI, South Vietnam, April 22 1966 – Five battalions of United States marines and South Vietnamese soldiers swept toward the South China Sea today in the cleanup phase of an operation in which 322 Vietcong regulars have been killed.

The drive was the first joint operation in recent months in which Vietnamese troops reported having killed more enemy soldiers than the American participants did.

In the Allied sweep, the South Vietnamese said that by 9 P.M. they had killed 201 Vietcong soldiers and captured 90 and 8 heavy weapons including mortars and recoilless rifles. The marines' haul of weapons was 29 small arms and 9 heavy weapons.

"This is a good healthy sign," said Maj. E. N. Snyder of Oceanside, Calif., operations officer of the Seventh Marine Regiment. "Our role here is to help the Vietnamese win the war. In this operation, we appeared to be assuming the proper role: Instead of us fighting their war, they did it and we supported them." (5)

Each of these divisions had three infantry regiments (except the 1st Division which normally operated four) of three battalions each, except for the 1st and 2nd which had four battalions per regiment. A division had two battalions of 18 105mm howitzers until 1969-70 when the number was increased to three. At first there was no heavy artillery assigned to divisions. The Army had independent 155mm towed-howitzer battalions, and these grew in number from 6 to 12 by 1969. The next year, each division was given one of these battalions. Each division was normally assigned an "Armored Vehicle Battalion" (called "armored cavalry squadrons" by the US) with one M-41 tank company and two M-113 APC companies. In practice, these divisional units often

POWs

Oriental minds can rarely understand the Western regard for the sanctity of human life, and in war eastern peoples are rarely solicitous of a prisoner's welfare. Americans were being captured in Vietnam from the beginning of the war, when A-4 pilot Eb Alvarez was shot down over the North. US prisoners were often badly treated, even tortured. Prospects of escape were bleak. Even if you did get out of the prison or the camp, a six foot tall caucasian or negro would stand out a mile in an Asian country most of whose people were six inches or more shorter than you, making evasion impossible.

Right: An American PoW talks to others, held behind bars, in a Hanoi detention camp in 1973. Prison conditions were appalling for captured GIs, and torture was commonplace.

Below: Captured US airmen, dubbed 'air pirates' by North Vietnam, are paraded for public humiliation in Hanoi.

operated with corps-level armored brigades.

Organization

Line infantry divisions had tactical areas of responsibility which tied them territorially to a defined portion of real estate. In addition, personnel normally served in the same corps area in which their families resided, making it very difficult in practice to use an ARVN division anywhere except in its home Corps. With the division commander responsible for a large area, the operating organization of a division was anything except "lean and mean". For example, the 21st Division, in the Delta in 1966, looked like this:

21st DIVISION
Division Mobile Reserve
33rd Regiment
42nd Special Mobile Corps Bn (i.e. "ranger") (attached)
44th Special Mobile Corps Bn (attached)
1 x Company of 2nd Armored Vehicle Bn
21st Reconnaissance Co

"A" Brigade
32nd Regiment
An Xuyen Sector Garrison
21 x Regional Forces Companies
1,693 x Popular Forces personnel

"B" Brigade
31st Regiment
Chong Thien Sector Garrison
9 x Regional Forces Companies
2,865 x Popular Forces personnel

Phong Dinh Sector Command
2nd Bn, 23rd Regiment
14 x Regional Forces Companies
3,169 x Popular Forces personnel

Bac Lieu Sector Command
8 x Regional Forces Companies
1,812 x Popular Forces personnel

Ba Xuyen Sector Command
11 x Regional Forces Companies
5,424 x Popular Forces personnel

Division Artillery
211th FA Bn (105 towed)
212th FA Bn (105 towed)

ARVN quality

The quality of ARVN infantry divisions varied considerably, and often was a direct reflection of the leadership rather than the fighting material. A general evaluation of ARVN divisions follows, using the same qualitative descriptions as used for the US Army earlier in the text (i.e., **excellent, good, fair, poor, and bad**). In I Corps, the 1st Division could be rated **good** in absolute terms. It was the best of the ARVN regular infantry divisions, and could be counted on as steady through most of the war – with the exception of the abortive coup in I Corps between April and June, 1966. By the end of 1973 however, the strain of constant combat and weakening leadership began to tell and the division's performance declined. Even changes in command were not enough to turn the 1st Division around thereafter. I Corps' 2nd Division should be rated **poor** by comparison – about average for an ARVN division. Throughout its history the 2nd Division generally showed little enthusiasm, as amply demonstrated by its high desertion rate. The unfortunate 3rd Division can only be rated as **bad**. The one pre-1971 unit of the division, 2nd Regiment, had been built up to a strength of five battalions before **Lam Son 719**, but

Above: An unwilling GI surrenders in Trung Bo, 1970.

Below: The 'Hanoi Hilton' in 1973, emptied of its US guests.

Above: B52 pilot Maj. R. E. Johnson, captured in NVN, 1972.

Below: Two PoWs and mail from home. Did they get to read it?

"The guards would hoard food meant for prisoners, but you could sometimes rectify the situation by complaining to prison camp officials. A lot depended on the camp commanders. In seven years I ran into dogs and real jewels. Some people I would invite into my home today for a drink. Others I'd invite behind a woodshed and only one of us would come out again"

was so badly mauled in that operation that it virtually had to rebuild from scratch like the division's two new regiments. With little time to train as an effective unit, and with an incompetent or even treasonable commander, the division took the brunt of the 1972 Spring Offensive – defending an area previously held by elite and heavily armed US Marines. It is no wonder that the 3rd Division cracked. That it could subsequently reorganize and perform in a creditable manner was quite an achievement.

II Corps' 22nd Division delivered very mixed performance. In general, its 40th Regiment was **fair**, the 41st Regiment **bad**, and the 47th Regiment **poor**. The 23rd Division can be rated **poor** overall (42nd, 45th 53rd Regiments), with its 44th Regiment being rated **bad**. For an ARVN division, this was fairly respectable.

Bad

In III Corps, the 5th Division must be accorded a rating of **bad**. Originally stationed near Saigon as an anti-coup force, it had very low fighting ability. MACV considered the division "marginal" and "barely effective", and had asked for its disbandment in 1966. The 18th Division's overall rating was **bad**. Throughout most of the war it was the worst ARVN division – nearly combat ineffective – though during the final defense of Saigon, the 18th Division was heavily reinforced by paratroopers and armor, and fought creditably in the battle of Xuan Loc. The 25th Division's performance was questionable through much of the war. It was generally marginal in effectiveness, but improved with better leadership. Its rating can be considered **poor**.

CHONTHANH, South Vietnam, April 8 1972 – The survival of South Vietnam's surrounded Fifth Division and control of the northwestern approaches to Saigon appeared to be in the balance tonight as the opposing forces positioned themselves for a major battle.

The probable site of the potentially decisive clash seemed likely to be at or near this small district capital 40 miles north of Saigon.

To the south, Vietnamese airborne units supported by tanks and artillery were moving cautiously toward the town up a road that has been called "Bloody Route 13" because of the constant ambushes mounted along it in earlier years of the war. Commanders today were taking no chances of stumbling into an ambush or surprise flank attack.

A few hundred yards north of a small police checkpoint here, enemy troops could be seen darting across the paved highway, and it was assumed they were moving rapidly south through scrub jungles near the road.

Farther to the north, in a pocket around Anloc, the capital of Binhlong Province, the Fifth Division awaited new onslaughts by the encircling North Vietnamese.

The division fell back to Anloc yesterday after abandoning the district capital of Locninh 15 miles to the north at the end of Route 13 near the Cambodian border.

Just how grave the situation is indicated by the decision to evacuate United States advisers from critical areas not only in Binhlong Province but in neighboring Tayninh Province as well. (6)

The 21st Division of IV Corps had been one of ARVN's better divisions, and it performed well in the Cambodian operation. Thereafter, its discipline and effectiveness declined until it was the worst in IV Corps. By 1974, it was only marginally combat effective. A rating of **fair** sums up the 21st overall. The Corps' 7th Division could be considered poor. Through most of the war it was barely effective, but it did well during the 1972 Spring Offensive and enjoyed a brief period of superiority over the NVA and VC in 1973 – due mainly to the inspired leadership of its commander, Maj.-Gen. Nguyen Khoa Nam (later the IV Corps commander). The 9th Division's rating could be **bad**. It was generally one of the worst ARVN divisions.

Airborne

The Airborne Division (properly Division Airborne), was the best ARVN division, and should be

ENDSWEEP

The Democratic People's Republic of Vietnam relied on powerful friends for help just as much as did its foe in the south. Military equipment and economic aid was provided by China and the USSR, some coming across the mountainous border with China but by far the major part being shipped by sea into the port of Haiphong. When President Nixon allowed the B-52s free to bomb the North to the conference table, he also authorized the mining of the waters around Haiphong. The strategy successfully encouraged the North to a peace agreement, but left the problem of the mines in Northern waters. It was agreed that the US would clear Haiphong, and operation End Sweep got under way in March 1973. The Seventh Fleet Mine Countermeasures Force, known as Task Force 78, began by deploying 10 ocean minesweepers and a number of airborne minesweepers. Navy instructors trained North Vietnamese personnel in minesweeping techniques. Haiphong was re-opened on July 26, 1973.

***Above:** The 'Aggressive' class ocean minesweeper USS Inflict sails the waters off the North Vietnamese port of Haiphong. Dating from the 1950s, these wooden hulled minesweepers made up the bulk of US Navy MCM capability right into the 1980s.*

***Above:** A Marine CH-53 towing a magnetic sweep clears mines from Hon Gai, to the north of Haiphong. The area was mined because it was on the coastal route from China to North Vietnam.*

***Right:** CH-53s of the US Navy's airborne MCM squadron HM-12 tow sleds meant to detonate acoustic mines. The 'Endsweep' operations around Haiphong were the first major test of such techniques.*

rated excellent. Its units undertook some combat parachute assaults (usually battalion or smaller in size), but it normally operated as infantry using airmobile or air-transported movement. In 1965 it had a total of six battalions in two brigades, and the next year was augmented by another two battalions. The division added a 105mm artillery battalion in 1968, another in 1969, and a third in 1970. Over the same period, it completed its expansion to a full three-brigade division. In late 1974, the 4th Airborne Brigade was formed to try to establish some sort of reserve, as the rest of the division was heavily engaged in I Corps. Throughout its history, the division was considered elite, and was assigned to the General Reserve directly under the Joint General Staff. As such it was used in a "fire brigade" capacity to reinforce any part of the country. The division was sent to I Corps during the 1972 Spring Offensive, and by the end of 1973 it had lost 3,200 killed and missing plus 12,000 wounded. In effect the entire establishment of the division had become casualties over a year and a half. After such losses it was inevitable that the morale and spirit of the Airborne Division weakened.

Marines

The second elite formation was the Special Landing Force (or "Marine") Division. Beginning with five battalions, the SLF expanded to six battalions (in two brigades) plus a 105mm artillery battalion in 1967. The next year it was accorded division status and given another 105mm battalion. In 1969, the division expanded to three brigades with a total of nine infantry and three artillery battalions. The SLF brigades received their designations based on the original composition of their battalions, thus the 147th Brigade had the 1st, 4th, and 7th Battalions. This became obscured as units shifted between brigades due to tactical requirements. In late 1974 a fourth brigade, the 468th, was formed when the rest of the division was engaged in I Corps. Like the Airborne Division, the SLF was assigned to the General Reserve, liable to serve in any part of South Vietnam. Although the SLF participated in riverine and amphibious operations, it mainly operated as high-quality infantry with airmobile training, deserving an excellent rating.

Rangers

The Special Mobile Corps (so-called "ARVN Rangers") began the 1960s with 86 separate companies. By 1965 these had been consolidated into 20 battalions and an "airborne ranger" battalion (91st, later redesignated 81st) which worked with the US Special Forces Project Delta. Like the airborne and SLF marines, the SMC "ranger"battalions each had four line companies instead of three, as in the ARVN infantry. The SMC battalions were subordinated to Group headquarters, each of which controlled three of four battalions. Originally, the 1st, 2nd, 3rd and 4th Groups were placed under their respective Corps (I, II, III, IV), while the 5th and 6th Groups were under the General Reserve and located near Saigon. By 1972, profound changes had taken place. The 7th Group was formed and assigned to the General Reserve, and 37 border defense battalions were raised to assume the duties of departing US Special Forces and indigenous Civilian Irregular Defense Group border camps.

By January 1974, a blanket reorganization was undertaken to place the veteran "ranger" battalions on a common establishment with the border defense battalions. The number of battalions was reduced to 45, and wholesale redistribution of SMC assets was ordered to account for new realities in the strategic situation. The IV Corps SMC, nine battalions under a headquarters known as 44th Special Tactical Zone, was eliminated and its personnel transferred to units in the north. This was a strange move on the part of the Saigon high command, because it virtually guaranteed a large number of desertions on the part of the men recruited in the Delta. Nevertheless, the resulting SMC structure placed four groups in I Corps, seven groups in II Corps (including two from

EARLY WARNING

High above the Gulf of Tonkin and Laos, venerable four-engined transports described lazy circles for many hours at a time. However, their mission was anything but transport, for they were the highly modified EC-121 variant of the famous Constellation airliner. Although first deployed to South Vietnam as part of the air defenses, the lack of any North Vietnamese airborne threat meant they could be used offensively in strikes against North Vietnam. Equipped with powerful radar they flew as radar pickets, watching all aerial movements across North Vietnam. As strike aircraft headed north, they were warned by the EC-121s of MiG action, and friendly fighters were vectored in to intercept them.

A Lockheed EC-121D 'Big Eye' cruises over Thailand. These aircraft provided radar coverage of South Vietnam during the early years of the war, while also covering strikes against the North.

"College Eye EC-121 airborne early warning aircraft orbiting over the Gulf broadcast the information that eight or more MiG-21s were closing on the F-105Fs fast, in an attempt to make the Weasels drop their ordnance before they could engage the SAM sites. Thanks to the warning, the flight leader could detach two aircraft to tangle with the MiGs while he and his wingman continued their vital defense suppression task"

Above: *An EC-121 'College Eye' is seen from a sister aircraft over northern Thailand. Flying orbits over the Gulf of Tonkin and Laos, the EC-121s remained out of the range of SAMs yet could still provide timely MiG warnings to US aircraft attacking the North. A 'Rivet Top' operational test prototype introduced SAM warning to the repertoire of the 'College Eye', and with these modifications it served until May 1974.*

Left: *An EC-121D lands at a Thai air base. These AEW platforms occasionally operated without the dorsal height-finding radar. The main underfuselage radar remained unable to detect low-flying MiGs, possessing no true look-down capability. Nevertheless, the EC-121Ds were most effective throughout combat operations against the North.*

Below: *All Air Force EC-121Ds were operated by the 552nd Aircraft Early Warning and Control Wing, deploying from McClellan AFB in California to various bases. The South East Asia detachment moved base frequently, beginning at Tainan before moving to Tan Son Nhut, Ubon, Udorn and finally Korat.*

VNAF

While the US Air Force bore the brunt of operations in the south during the early years of the war, a gradual withdrawal of in-country assets allowed the Vietnamese Air Force to increase its importance in the air war, until it was used on all combat operations over the South. Equipment was entirely supplied from US sources, and its structure and mode of operations mirrored the US Air Force closely. During the final invasion from the North in 1975, the VNAF flew constantly in the face of the communists until the last possible moment. Many of the aircraft supplied by the United States fell intact into the hands of the victorious communists.

Above: While some VNAF aircrew fled with their aircraft to Thailand, others fought to the death. This Cessna 0-1 was shot down over Saigon minutes before the surrender.

Left: VNAF assets rested largely on the Douglas A-1 Skyraider for most of the war.

Below: Cessna A-37Bs equipped attack squadrons during the later years of the war.

the General Reserve), three groups in III Corps, and one group in the General Reserve (7th, at Long Binh). IV Corps was left without SMC battalions. Groups were given new two-digit designations with the exceptions of the 4th, 6th, and 7th, which were the nominal reserve. These were intended to form a full division (like the Airborne or SLF), but the resources were never available to implement the plan.

Mike Forces

By the end of 1974, two additional groups (8th and 9th) were hastily organized in the Saigon area, and took part in the final defense. SMC units were, at least until the big reorganization, considered elite light infantry and rated excellent. They provided a steadying influence when operating with the normally lackluster ARVN infantry. Like the SMC were the troops of the Mobile Strike Force Commands (Mike Forces), which worked as multi-battalion reaction forces in support of US Special Forces CIDG camps. Formed between 1965 and 1967, there were four such commands (one per Corps) plus the 5th MSFC, which was a country-wide reaction force. During 1970-71, these units all transferred to the ARVN SMC or were disbanded.

Hue, January 1968. The chairman of the Vietnamese Joint Chiefs and the commanding General of I Corps (ARVN) listen to a presentation of the 1st Division (ARVN) history. Within four weeks, Hue was to become one of the bitterest battlefields of the War.

By 1965 the various South Vietnamese militia-type organizations had been incorporated into the Regional Forces or the Popular Forces (RF/PF or "Ruff Puffs" in American slang). The Popular Forces were static local militia organized into platoons and assigned to their own hamlets and villages under the control of their District Chief. The US Marine Combined Action Program teamed up USMC squads with PF platoons in areas secured by the Marines. The Regional Forces were originally organized in companies as provincial militia. These companies were consolidated into battalions in 1970, and assigned to RF Groups (each of 3 battalions and a 105mm battery) in 1974. At first untrained and ill-armed, RFs and PFs came to represent fully half of the militia strength of South Vietnam. Increasingly they assumed more of the burden of territorial defense from the regular ARVN. Often they were involved in more fire fights and took more casualties than their ARVN counterparts. Always at the bottom of the list for modern equipment and training, the RFs and PFs could vary in effectiveness from a simple body guard for local political figures to very good troops with unrivaled knowledge of the local terrain. One of the "lost opportunities" of the war was the failure of the US to take an early interest in

Above: Many VNAF helicopters escaped to US carriers in the final evacuation. This desperate airman jumps into the sea near a US Navy boat.

Above left: In the latter stages of the war, Lockheed Hercules were provided for in-theatre transport operations.

Right: The most potent warplane fielded by the VNAF was the Northrop F-5A, which had been handed over by the USAF.

Above: Two de Havilland Canada U-6 Beavers, equipped with loudspeakers for psychological warfare are seen over the Delta.

Right: Douglas A-1 Skyraiders head for an attack. They are armed with napalm canisters and cluster bombs.

strengthening the Regional and Popular Forces.

South Vietnamese troops were in high spirits and their officers appeared cocky as Operation Toan Thang (Ultimate Victory) 42 went into its third day in the Parrot's Beak and Operation Toan Thang 43, involving American combat troops, was launched to the north in the Fishhook area.

In Prasaut this morning, Lieut. Gen. Do Cao Tri, the South Vietnamese commander of the operations, instructed his pilot to land his helicopter in the town square where ground troops were preparing to move down Highway One toward Svayrieng after a night in the deserted town.

The general strode up to a battalion commander, took a seat on the hood of a jeep, and lit a cigar.

"Look at this destruction the Vietcong have caused," he said, pointing to the shells of burned out buildings, looted stores and littered streets caused in fighting several weeks ago between the Cambodians and the Vietcong. "It must have been a pleasant place." He put his hand on a small revolver strapped to his side. He was asked what kind it was.

"Smith and Wesson," he said after looking at the nameplate. "but I never use it. If the Vietcong get too close, I use my stick on them." He waved his swagger stick. (7)

ARVN in retrospect

The ARVN have gained an historical reputation as useless soldiers in a sham army. The reputation is not deserved, but there are good reasons for the performance of the ARVN during the war. The typical ARVN soldier was a conscripted rural peasant with little education or aptitude for the complexities of a military system trying to fit the image of the sophisticated United States. For the most part his officers were from the educated urban elite and not of the same religion or class. This often did little to inspire confidence or mutual trust. The soldier and his family could not live on his slim Army pay – a situation which only got worse from 1973 on, with high inflation and a sagging economy. The US Army taught him to fight with lavish expenditures of ammunition, artillery and air support – none of which were available to him in the final years of the war. His enemy was a tireless and determined foe who had outfoxed or outfought well-equipped and supported American units on numerous occasions. Under good leadership the ARVN soldier was capable of a great deal. Under mediocre or poor leadership he still succeeded in defending his country for years. The debacle of 1975 started with the panic of the high command, and filtered down to the soldier only when he had to make a choice of saving his family or trying to save a dying regime.

HUE, South Vietnam, April 13 – The intensified war swirling around Hue and the area north of it near the demilitarized zone is a study in contrasts – placid green rice fields and bloody battles only 20 miles apart – but none are so striking as the difference between the way the Americans fought here and the way the South Vietnamese are fighting now.

Last year, when South Vietnamese troops were on the offensive and were supported by thousands of Americans, they swarmed out of the Quangtri combat base in hundreds of helicopters. Every day that the weather was clear enough to permit them to fly they hit North Vietnamese base areas in western Quangtri Province and, for six weeks, across the border in Laos.

The year the South Vietnamese have taken over all but a few of the American fighting positions, but they get to them by road.

Since suffering initial reverses in the first days of the North Vietnamese offensive at the turn of the month, the Government troops have held stubbornly on to Quangtri city, to Dongha, to the north, and to artillery bases guarding the western defenses of Hue. But they have been slower to counterattack than the Americans used to be and they do it in their own way. (8)

CHAPTER TWELVE

THE END OF THE LINE 1975

Victorious North Vietnamese troops storm the airfield at Ban Me Thuot in April 1975.

By the beginning of 1975, the South Vietnamese forces' supply and maintenance situation was critical. Since the cease-fire, not a single destroyed aircraft or naval vessel had been replaced. Worse, lack of parts and maintenance expertise forced the Air Force to deactivate 10 squadrons and mothball 224 aircraft (including all remaining A-1 attack planes and 31 UH-1 helicopters), while the Navy had to lay up half of its riverine fleet, and 4,000 Army vehicles lay idle. In 1975, close air support and air lift had to be cut to half the 1973-74 level, while navy riverine patrols had to be cut to 28%. Ammunition consumption was limited to 27% of the pre-cease-fire rate. Even with fighting at the 1974 level (i.e., discounting the 1975 offensive), ARVN ammunition would have been totally exhausted by June 1975! In contrast, by the end of 1974 the NVA had amassed enough supplies to continue fighting at the level of the 1972 Offensive for another 18 months.

Manpower problems also plagued the ARVN. With a nominal establishment of 1,100,000 men, a yearly draft intake of 200,000 to 240,000 was necessary to account for deserters and draft dodgers as well as combat casualties. In practice however, conscription was only able to provide 100,000 to 150,000 men annually. The result was that combat infantry battalions were lucky to pull together 60% of their authorized strength.

The beginning of the end for South Vietnam started in a rather unlikely place – the heavily jungled region of Phuoc Long the northernmost province in III Corps. In Phuoc Long, the ARVN garrison consisted initially of only five Regional Forces battalions, four 2-gun 105mm howitzer sections, and 48 Popular Forces platoons. In December of 1974 the Communists massed against the ARVN two NVA Divisions, a separate regiment and a tank regiment, supported by artillery and an air defense regiment and a couple of sapper battalions. The NVA 3rd Phuoc Long Division and 7th Division moved on Phuoc Long City from the south and west respectively, overrunning RF/PF bases. (Note that this NVA "3rd" Division was a new creation, and different from the 3rd Division in Binh Dinh Province – hence "3rd Phuoc Long Division"). All that Saigon could muster in support was the 2nd Battalion of the 7th ARVN Regiment, a 105mm and a 155mm battery. The strategic reserve was already committed in I Corps.

The NVA tanks thoroughly demoralized the outlying RF/PF troops and drove them pell-mell in the direction of the city. The ARVN drew up a perimeter around the city and airfield while the NVA cut Highway 14, the major supply route to the area. III Corps tried to airlift and helilift supplies to the garrison, but was soon forced to use high-level paradrop because of NVA ground fire. In spite of a maximum close air support effort by the South Vietnamese Air Force, the NVA took the heights which commanded Phuoc Long City, and directed 130mm guns to destroy the ARVN artillery. In a desperate last effort to save Phuoc Long, Saigon committed the 81st Airborne Ranger Battalion to the defense. On January 5th the battalion was brought in by helicopter, but by then it was too late. The relentless NVA attack overran the city on the 6th, and the 81st had to exfiltrate from its positions in order to save the half of the battalion which was still alive. Phuoc Long City was the first province capital to permanently fall into Communist hands, and while its strategic position was not critical, its loss was a severe blow to the morale of South Vietnam.

II Corps

The second, and ultimately fatal, NVA offensive was aimed at Ban Me Thuot in the Central Highlands, where the Communists were able to approach nearly undetected, to the surprise of the II Corps commander. ARVN's II Corps had its 22nd Division fighting in coastal Binh Dinh Province and its 23rd Division in the vicinity of Pleiku, where the corps commander expected an attack. To the south, Ban Me Thuot was held only by the 23rd Ranger Group and some RF/PF units. Following intelligence reports, the II Corps commander ordered the 23rd Division to send its 53rd Regiment to Ban Me Thuot in early March. At the same time, NVA elements cut Highway 14 and Highway 21 which linked Ban Me Thuot with the coast, effectively isolating the city. On March 10th the first blow was delivered by the NVA 10th Division (also known as "F-10"), which attacked Ban Me Thuot's southern defenses with armor and artillery support. This initial attack captured an airfield and an ammunition depot and was only halted by the stand of the ARVN 53rd Regiment. The RF/PF units were thrown into disarray and the forward HQ element of the ARVN 23rd Division was threatened. The HQ called for tactical air support which succeeded in knocking out the HQ itself. By evening, the NVA 316th and 320th Divisions moved in from the west and the north respectively to lend their weight to the attack.

The ARVN 23rd Division's 44th and 45th Regiments were ordered south from Pleiku to try to relieve Ban Me Thuot, while the 7th Ranger Group was flown from Bien Hoa to Pleiku to take up defensive positions vacated by the division. By March 13th, Ban Me Thuot had been almost completely overrun by the three-division NVA attack, and the surviving ARVN units streamed northward to meet the relief column. Pockets of resistance were mopped up by March 18th. Many men of the ARVN 23rd Division still had families in Ban Me Thuot, and morale crumbled as it became evident that the city had been given up. A number of troops from the relief column deserted immediately, to search for family members.

Undefendable?

While these events were unfolding in II Corps, President Thieu had already determined that South Vietnam could not be held in the face of increasing pressure. At a meeting with his Prime Minister (Tran Thien Khiem) and the Chairman of the Joint General Staff (Gen. Cao Van Vien) on March 11th, Thieu rationalized that a smaller South Vietnam might be successfully defended and that this meant a strategic redeployment of the ARVN and the evacuation of the northern part of the country. He proposed the abandonment of all of I Corps, and virtually all of II Corps north of Darlac and Khanh Hoa Provinces.

II Corps' situation was not encouraging for an orderly withdrawal. The ARVN 22nd Division, operating from Qui Nhon on the coast, had failed to dislodge the NVA 3rd Binh Dinh Division from its position astride Highway 19 at Binh Khe, where it blocked the way to Pleiku in the interior. From Pleiku, the ARVN 25th Ranger Group and 21st Tank Battalion tried to break through from the opposite direction but were equally unsuccessful. At the same time, the ARVN 3rd Airborne Brigade redeployed from I Corps to Khanh Duong to assist the 22nd Division's 40th Regiment in blocking the NVA 10th Division's advance down Highway 21 toward Nha Trang on the coast. With both of these major routes controlled by the Communists, the remainder of II Corps in the Central Highlands had to attempt to escape along Interprovincial Route 7B, a disused secondary road leading 160 miles toward the coastal town of Tuy Hoa.

NAVY AIR WAR

A standard of excellence has long been a Naval Aviation tradition, and nowhere was it shown more than on the carriers sailing off North and South Vietnam. Operating from carrier decks is a tricky enough business, but during wartime the problems are magnified enormously. That the Navy's aircraft performed as well as any land-based aircraft is a tribute to the excellence of the flight and deck crews in harrowing conditions. From the Tonkin Incident to the final collapse, Naval Aviation was ready for anything.

Above: With arrestor hook down, a VF-96 F-4J Phantom enters the landing pattern of USS Constellation. This squadron scored the first US kill of the war, and went on to notch up eight more, five by the pilot-RIO team of Randall Cunningham and William Driscoll.

Above: Streaming vapour trails, an F-8 of VF-111 based aboard USS Midway dives on VC positions. Crusaders were occasionally employed in the attack role.

Left: Navy Phantoms also saw their fair share of mud-moving, usually as bombers in either dive or medium altitude level attacks. This aircraft is an F-4B from VF-21.

Above: Jack of all trades, and master of many, the Phantom was an excellent bomber. Navy Phantoms were used on air-to-ground sorties over South Vietnam, where their air combat ability was not needed.

Above: Various tactical camouflages were applied to the aircraft of *Kitty Hawk* and *Constellation* during 1966. Deck handlers found the aircraft difficult to work with at night and the schemes were dropped.

Above: Not to be confused with the USAF's 'Wild Weasel' aircraft, this is an F-4G. Flying with VF-114, these were similar to other Navy Phantoms, but had extra datalink equipment.

Right: The greatest Navy tragedy of the war occurred on 29 July 1967, when a Zuni rocket inadvertently exploded on USS *Forrestal*, killing 134 men. 21 aircraft were written off.

Below: Popularly known as the 'Scooter', the Douglas A-4 Skyhawk was flown in large numbers by the Navy during the war. A large bombload for its size was carried, and it possessed good manoeuvrability, although among the disadvantages was a very cramped cockpit. This A-4F is carrying a pair of Bullpup guided missiles for precision attacks, in addition to six Mk 82 500-lb general purpose bombs on the centreline ejector rack.

Converging on Route 7B from Pleiku/Kontum were five Ranger Groups (7th, 21st, 22nd, 24th 25th), three Corps Artillery battalions, 21st Tank Battalion, 1st Bn/44th Regiment, and the 20th Engineer Group. From the debacle around Ban Me Thuot came the remainder of the 23rd Division and the 23rd Ranger Group. The evacuation got under way on the 16th of March after the issue of secret orders, and the surprise move immediately led to civilian panic and flight. The situation was worsened by bad weather and harassment by local VC and eventually the NVA 320th Division. Inaccurate close air support nearly destroyed the leading Ranger battalion. On the 22nd of March, the 7th Ranger Group's 34th Battalion took over the advanced guard position and was remarkably successful in clearing the remaining Communist blocking positions. What was left of the column entered Tuy Hoa on March 27th. Exact casualties are unknown, but the evacuation was a genuine disaster, with perhaps 75% losses. The ill-timed redeployment had been doomed by flawed execution on the part of II Corps. Worse than the military defeat, the rout brought on a fatal crisis in confidence on the part of the South Vietnamese in general.

NVA pressure

At Binh Khe, the ARVN 22nd Division's 41st and 42nd Regiments continued to do battle with the NVA 3rd Binh Dinh Division, reinforced by the NVA 95B Regiment. They held until the end of March. To the north of Bong Son, NVA regiments from Quang Ngai attacked the ARVN 47th Regiment on March 25th and drove it back to the air base at Phu Cat over the next three days. To the south, the NVA 320th Division pressed its attack on Tuy Hoa after having completed the pursuit of the II Corps remnants. It overwhelmed the defenders of Tuy Hoa on the 2nd of April. Still farther south, the NVA 10th Division continued to press the ARVN 3rd Airborne Brigade on Highway 21, finally overcoming the paratroopers with artillery and tanks on April 2nd. Only 300 men of the airborne brigade escaped to Nha Trang.

On March 30th, the ARVN 41st and 42nd Regiments were ordered to retire to Qui Nhon, only to find the city already occupied by infiltrating elements of the NVA 3rd Binh Dinh Division. Along with the survivors of the ARVN 47th Regiment from Phu Cat, they fought their way to a beach south of the city and were evacuated by sea in the early morning darkness of April 1st. Taken to Vung Tau by naval vessels, the three regiments which had constituted the 22nd Division by then numbered only 2,000 men.

In the south of the II Corps area, the ARVN 2nd Airborne Brigade was sent from III Corps in early April to reinforce Phan Rang air base, which was under threat from the NVA 7th Division. Shortly after, the NVA 3rd Binh Dinh Division and 10th Division appeared in Cam Ranh. Because of the worsening situation in III Corps (see below), the paratroopers were withdrawn and replaced by a couple of reorganized I Corps units (a Ranger group and a composite regiment of the 2nd Division). By the 15th of April, the Phan Rang defenders were heavily engaged by the NVA 3rd and 10th Divisions, which subsequently overran them and captured the city. For a second time, the ARVN 2nd Division (or what was left of it) had to retreat by sea. By April 18th the Communists had complete control of the II Corps area.

I Corps – Defeat

By mid-March, the ARVN Airborne Division had been withdrawn from I Corps for redeployment to Saigon. Its 3rd Brigade was diverted to II Corps as mentioned above, and never completed its projected move to the capital. Likewise, the Marine Division (less the 369th Brigade) was repositioned to defend Da Nang. This left the Quang Tri sector (formerly held by two divisions) in the hands of the 369th Marine Brigade, the 1st Armored Brigade and the 14th Ranger Group. Just to the south, the ARVN 1st

NVA IN ACTION

The equipment facing the free world forces in Vietnam varied considerably in quality. In the South, the Viet Cong often had to make do with equipment that had been packed down the Ho Chi Minh Trail. Up near the DMZ however, the North Vietnamese Army could throw fully equipped formations into the fray, leading to disasters such as the Special Forces camp at Lang Vei being overrun by light tanks during the siege of Khe Sanh. By 1975, with American ground forces out of the picture, the North Vietnamese could mount an invasion of the south confident that their Soviet supplied main battle tanks would smash badly led ARVN forces.

Fighting near the Cambodian border in 1965, the nearest NVA soldier is equipped with a Chinese Type 56 rifle, copied from the Soviet SKS.

Below: An NVA anti-tank crew man a B-10 82-mm recoilless gun. The Soviet designed B-10 was also supplied by China as the Type 65.

Soviet supplied T-54/55 series main battle tanks were first used in the 1972 invasion of the South, although they were beaten back. Three years later they led the final assault on Saigon, with tank number 844 squarely in the limelight when it knocked down the gates of the Presidential Palace.

An RPG-2 in action with the NVA. The invasion of 1972 was launched in the belief that without US stiffening the ARVN would crumble. It was to cost the NVA over 100,000 casualties, and half of its artillery and tanks.

"His weapon handling with the AK-47 is often very good. Fortunately his marksmanship is poor; a small man firing full auto will usually shoot high"

VC fighters lie in ambush armed with a Soviet designed RPD light machine-gun, possibly the Chinese-built Type 56 model.

Right: An NVA column crosses a river during the Easter Offensive of 1972. Initial successes were followed by disaster as the ARVN rallied and US air power was deployed.

Division and 15th Ranger Group guarded Hue and Phu Bai respectively. Excluding Da Nang, the ARVN 3rd Division at Hoi An took up positions in Quang Nam Province. The ARVN 2nd Division, based at Chu Lai, supported the 11th and 12th Ranger Groups in the defense of Quang Ngai and Quang Tin Provinces respectively. Against this force, the NVA massed a formidable array, including five divisions (304th, 324B, 325th, 341st & 711th), the 52nd Brigade, nine regiments (4th, 5th, 6th, 27th, 31st, 48th, 51st, 270th & 271st), three sapper regiments (5th, 45th & 126th Naval), and three tank regiments (202nd, 203rd & 573rd) as well as eight field and twelve air defense artillery regiments. Other NVA troops were still north of the DMZ.

Refugees

As news of the debacle in II Corps spread, refugees started to clog Highway 1 on the way south. In addition, NVA units did their best to interdict this major artery at every point possible. On March 19th, Communist pressure against the northernmost defense line proved too much for the emaciated defenses, and the ARVN had to withdraw from the last toehold it retained in Quang Tri Province. Forming a new defense line on the My Chanh River, I Corps hoped to hold Hue, but President Thieu wavered, and instructed the Corps commander to prepare to hold only Da Nang.

Between Hue and Da Nang, the NVA 324B Division and several independent regiments moved to sever Highway 1 at Phu Loc. The ARVN 1st Division's 1st Regiment and the 15th Ranger Group attempted to hold the road open, but they were overwhelmed on March 22nd. ARVN units remaining north of Phu Loc retired toward Hue and prepared to defend, while civilians still in Hue were seized by panic. Two days later, the NVA 711th Division and 52nd Brigade (supported by tanks), struck Tam Ky in Quang Tin Province, and by nightfall had overrun the city. At the same time, another NVA regiment cut Highway 1 between Chu Lai and Quang Ngai. These multiple cuts in the major north-south route had the effect of dividing I Corps into three separate elements, which had fallen back on Hue, Da Nang and Chu Lai by March 25th. Nevertheless, Thieu's directive stood and the Corps was ordered to consolidate at Da Nang.

The ARVN 1st Division and the Marines barely made it to Da Nang. Morale was shot – except for the Marines – and the one-third of the 1st Division that reached Da Nang immediately broke ranks to seek out family members. To the south, the ARVN 2nd Division and dependents were safely evacuated by sea to Cu Lao Re, a nearby island. By March 27th, Da Nang was invested by the NVA 304th, 324B, 325th and 711th Divisions, the hard-pressed ARVN forces trying to regroup and restore order among the frantic civilians in the midst of Communist shelling. Two days later, with fog blanketing the coast, the soldiers of the ARVN 3rd Division and Marine Division embarked on waiting vessels from three beach areas. Unfortunately, a low tide forced the men to wade or swim to the shipping as they were, shelled by NVA artillery. Only 4,000 soldiers and 6,000 marines got out of Da Nang.

Striking at the Vitals

As I and II Corps collapsed, their units were evacuated by sea and a hasty reorganization and re-equipment effort was mounted. Replacement of stocks were low, so reconstituted units had to make do with only half of the normal issue of mortars, grenade launchers, radios and rifle magazines. By the end of the war there were still three artillery, one armored, three ranger and three infantry battalions which were reorganized but useless, due to lack of equipment.

Hard hit II Corps units had gotten out with about a third of their small arms but retained only about 10% of their heavier equipment. Initially, the decimated 23rd Division staged at Dong Ba Thin, near Cam Ranh, where it succeeded in organizing a composite regiment and then was forced to fall back farther south when the NVA moved on Cam Ranh.

HELOS IN ACTION

Helicopters dominated the war against the Viet Cong in South Vietnam, performing a myriad of tasks. Their main role was transport for airmobile operations, a highly important task due to the nature of the terrain and the disposition of the enemy. Indeed, it was the availability of the helicopter which made such air assault tactics possible in the first place. Other tasks performed included heavy lift of outsize objects, gunship fire support, combat rescue, observation, liaison and psychological warfare. In the course of the war, the United States lost 4,869 helicopters, of which 2,382 were downed by the enemy.

Above: The Bell OH-58A Kiowa was used in fair numbers as a light observation helicopter, a role in which it continues today. For suppressive fire the OH-58 carried a forward-firing Minigun mounted on the port side.

"Without a doubt, from the moment the CIA in the form of Air America started using H-34 Choctaws for covert operations, the helicopter came into its own in South East Asia . . . Clearly, airmobile operations dominated the Vietnam battlefield, and Army and Marines alike became skilled at using the helicopter to surprise and outmaneuver the enemy . . . Army helicopters were among the last US combat units to leave Vietnam"

Combat rescue was a major role for the US Air Force, employing armed and armored helicopters to retrieve downed airmen from hostile country. The most capable of these was the Sikorsky HH-53C Super Jolly, which featured good endurance, defensive Miniguns, armor and inflight refuelling capability.

***Right:* Workhorse of the early Marine involvement was the Sikorsky UH-34, ferrying 'grunts' from ship to shore during assaults, and for land-based airmobile operations. Their place was taken by the Boeing Vertol CH-46 Sea Knight.**

Two Army heavy-lifters were the Boeing Vertol CH-47 Chinook (above) and the Sikorsky CH-54 Tarhe (below). Both were used to lift outsize objects, the Tarhe proving particularly adept at this due to its straddling fuselage and secondary pilot station underneath.

***Above:* Initially plagued by slow deliveries and transmission problems, the Boeing Vertol CH-46 Sea Knight proved to be the most important Marine Corps helicopter during the war. First arriving in-country in March 1966, the CH-46 served throughout the war, and is still in widespread use today.**

The 22nd Division at Vung Tau regrouped into two regiments, four 105mm batteries and two M-113 mechanized companies, and was committed to III Corps' defense near Long An late in April.

I Corps' 1st Division was disbanded and its surviving personnel used as replacements, while the 3rd Division refitted a single battalion at the Van Kiep Training Center. It would never function as a division again. The 2nd Division was reorganized at Binh Tuy with two regiments, three 105mm batteries, one 155mm battery and a mechanized company in M-113s. The bulk of the reborn 2nd Division deployed to Phan Rang as mentioned above, where it was reduced to virtual ineffectiveness. The Marine Division gathered its survivors at Vung Tau and was able to field a combat-ready brigade and two 105mm batteries by April 10th. While this unit deployed to III Corps' defenses at Long Thanh, the division organized a second composite brigade. Rangers from I Corps were reorganized into two groups and a supporting 105mm battery at Long Binh. The first group to complete its refit was sent to the Dinh Tuong/Long An area of IV Corps, while the second group continued working up.

The Air Force was in bad shape as well. At its height in December of 1972, the South Vietnamese Air Force (VNAF) had 2,075 aircraft in six Air Divisions (1st in I Corps, 2nd & 6th in II Corps, 3rd & 5th in III Corps, and 4th in IV Corps). By the end of 1974 the inventory had dropped to 1,484 planes, and intense NVA air defenses severely reduced the effectiveness of close air support. At that time the fighter types (F-5 & A-37) had an availability rate of 70%, but with flying time and bomb loads cut in half. In the absence of US air power, particularly the powerful B-52s, the VNAF improvised with its slim resources. C-130s were pressed into service as bombers, dropping pallets of bombs or fuel drums on exposed NVA positions. Sometimes they got lucky. During the last days of the war, a C-130 dropped a US 15,000 pound "daisy cutter" bomb on the NVA 341st Division HQ, destroying it completely.

Target: Saigon

As the ARVN forces in I and II Corps were destroyed, the NVA transferred units south for the final push on Saigon. III Corps had its own 5th, 18th and 25th Divisions, 3rd Armored Brigade, Corps-organic Ranger groups, the reorganized 22nd Division, a composite Ranger Group from I & II Corps survivors, and the Airborne and Marine Divisions (with two effective brigades each). NVA forces included fifteen divisions and a host of non-divisional supporting units.

The ARVN 18th Division, holding the eastern approach to Saigon, was invested at Xuan Loc on April 9th by the NVA 6th, 7th and 341st Divisions. The ARVN 1st Airborne Brigade was helicoptered in to reinforce the defenses, but an armored relief force was turned back about 8km west of the city. An aggressive defense paid off, and initially repulsed the attackers with heavy losses at a cost of 30% of the division, including most of its 52nd Regiment. However, III Corps ordered a withdrawal to Long Binh on April 23rd, and this was achieved professionally by the 18th Division and the paratroopers.

Maneuvering very large military units with great speed, the Communists have closed the road from Saigon to the sea and the road to the south over which food supplies must come. They have driven their way to Ben Luc, 12 miles southwest of Saigon, and have cut the road to Bien Hoa, 12 miles to the northwest.

With an unusual blood-red sunset over Saigon last evening, the Communists were drawing closer to the city by the minute, shelling towns, sealing roads and driving refugees before them from all directions.

INVASION

The complete withdrawal of American forces from Vietnam left the Army of the Republic responsible for the defence of the country. Many of its soldiers had performed well in 1972, and the Paris peace agreement was supposed to have left the South secure. Unfortunately by 1975 corruption and incompetent leadership were rampant, and the North repudiated the peace agreements as soon as the NVA was strong enough. The absence of the protective air umbrella of the US Air Force meant that there was little chance of beating back the overwhelming Northern invasion of 1975, and by May Saigon had fallen.

Above: ***A shattered and abandoned ARVN M41A3 Walker Bulldog tank approached by NVA troops at Duc Lap, April 1975. The attack was co-ordinated with a three-division assault on nearby Ban Me Thuot, the real strategic objective.***

Left: A 105mm howitzer supplied to the ARVN by the US is 'liberated' and turned on its former owners by NVA gunners at Ban Me Thuot. In the 1975 Final Offensive huge quantities of US arms were captured and turned around by the advancing NVA.

Right: At Kontum, NVA troops take cover behind a wrecked ARVN jeep to launch a grenade attack on ARVN defenders. The town was attacked to divert ARVN commanders' attention from the plan to take Ban Me Thuot, whose fall left the Central Highlands entirely in communist hands.

Starting Saturday evening, large Communist infantry units supported by tanks and heavy artillery began their move with a shelling followed by a tank and infantry attack against Phuoc Le. Phuoc Le, 37 miles southeast of Saigon, controls Route 15, the capital's only access to the sea.

By yesterday evening the Communists had broken through local defenses and were in Phuoc Le. Thus the port of Vung Tau, from which many Saigon residents have been hoping to escape the country in boats and ships at the last moment, was cut off.

Swiftly moving up the road to Long Thanh, a district seat, the Communists heavily shelled the area yesterday morning, especially a large refugee camp. This afternoon bodies of many victims were still strewn around the area and on the road itself.

By 9 A.M. yesterday, the situation had become so serious at Bien Hoa that authorities imposed a 24-hour curfew on the town.

Refugees from Bein Hoa and communities along Route 15 had been pouring toward Saigon before the Saigon-Bien Hoa road was cut.

Late yesterday the four-lane road, the countries widest and most modern highway, was so jammed with refugees that movement in the opposite direction, even for army trucks, had become impossible.

Toward evening, army trucks were moving back into Saigon, loaded with ammunition. It was clear that all or most Government troops in the area were being pulled back into the capital. (1)

West of Saigon, the ARVN 25th Division and 3rd Armored Brigade withdrew from Tay Ninh in early March and established a new line based on Cu Chi. Seven NVA regiments continued to exert steady pressure on the Cu Chi front throughout the remainder of March and April. At the same time, the ARVN 5th Division guarded the northern approaches to the capital through Binh Duong. After the battle of Xuan Loc, the NVA 7th Division gave its full attention to the ARVN 5th, but was repulsed by well-executed counterattacks.

In IV Corps the NVA 5th Division moved from Cambodia against the ARVN 9th Division in March, but failed to penetrate the defenses and cut off the ARVN 7th Division as it intended. Late in the month, the newly formed NVA 8th Division attacked ARVN IV Corps HQ at Can Tho, but was thrown back by the ARVN 21st Division and 4th Armored Brigade.

Thieu Resigns

As the military situation worsened, President Thieu resigned on April 21st and left the country. After a transition under Vice President Tran Van Huong, the presidency passed to General Duong Van Minh on April 28th. Minh was a leftist who entertained illusions that the Communists would negotiate with him for a political settlement. Less hopeful, the US Embassy began **Operation Talon Vise** (the evacuation of Vietnam) as early as April 14th. The operation provided passage out of the country for US citizens and their Vietnamese dependents, as well as "high risk" Vietnamese nationals who would be marked for death by the Communists because of their association with the US. Evacuation via Tan Son Nhut airport continued until NVA shelling closed it on the 29th, and continued by helicopter through the 30th.

SAIGON, South Vietnam, Monday, April 28 – As overwhelming Communist forces moved to within barely one mile of Saigon's city limits this morning, South Vietnamese leaders acted at almost the last minute to install Gen. Duong Van Minh as President to end the war on Communist terms.

A ceremony was scheduled for later today, at which out-going President Tran Van Huong will formally hand over the Presidency to his neutralist successor, reliable informants said.

There seemed some possibility that the Vietcong themselves may send a representative to the ceremony.

***Left:* Captured ARVN armor flies a new flag during the Final Offensive, April 1975.**

***Below:* The litter of the battlefield seen during the attack on Duc Lap, March 1975.**

***Above:* The North took some losses. These knocked out NVA tanks are at Tan Son Nhut.**

FALL OF SAIGON

In spite of the peace accords guaranteeing the existence of South Vietnam, Hanoi had only one end in mind: one nation ruled from the north. The overwhelming power of the 1975 invasion and the weakness made the fall of the Saigon government inevitable. By the last week in April, the North Vietnamese Army was battering at the doors to the capital. On April 30 a Soviet supplied T-54 smashed through the gates of the presidential palace, bringing the bloody existence of the Republic of Vietnam to an end.

Above: North Vietnamese troops race past American supplied Hueys at Tan Son Nhut.

Above: North Vietnamese armor heads into Saigon city after the collapse in April 1975.

Left: Officers of the presidential bodyguard surrender to the victorious North Vietnamese outside the presidential palace. Behind them, a PT-76 tank is a reminder that the war was won not by insurrection but by force of arms in a conventional battle.

Late last night, the Hanoi Communist party newspaper Nhan Dan published the text of a resolution passed by the National Assembly here authorizing President Huong to transfer all power to General Minh. The naming of General Minh to power was thought to remove the last obstacle to meeting Communist demands. (2)

On April 27th, the NVA broke through the RF/PF forces guarding Saigon from the west, and the ARVN 18th Division was penetrated at Bien Hoa and forced back to Long Binh. Other sectors held on as long as they could, but NVA tanks and overwhelming numbers made further resistance futile. General Minh announced surrender to the Communists on April 30th, and the Republic of Vietnam passed into history.

SAIGON, South Vietnam, Monday, April 28 -A heavy column of black smoke rose over the edge of Saigon today as advance Communist forces moved close to the city limits.

South Vietnamese Air Force helicopters fired rockets into the Communist positions on the Saigon River at Newport, a former United States port complex on the road to Bien Hoa. The Communists fired back with AK-47 automatic rifles, and the noise was clearly audible inside the city.

Only a few lightly armed South Vietnamese combat policemen and militiamen guarded the road on the northeastern edge of the city. They made no effort to dig in, and several Government officers simply stood around watching the helicopters firing at the Communist forces.

The Communist troops, who had seized the far side of the Newport Bridge over the Saigon River, were believed to be part of major North Vietnamese units moving rapidly toward Saigon from Bien Hoa, 15 miles to the northeast. Another group of Communist troops reportedly had occupied a crossroads two miles beyond the bridge on the way to the biggest South Vietnamese ammunition dump, at Cat Lai. (3)

Elsewhere in the region as well, collapse proved total. The fanatical Khmer Rouge, trained by the Chinese, closed in on Phnom Penh. Lon Nol left the country on April 1st, carrying a considerable amount of gold, and settled in Hawaii. By the 12th, the US Embassy staff departed Cambodia, and the city surrendered to the Communists on the 17th. The new head of state, Pol Pot (born Salot Sar), proved to be the bloodiest leader to emerge from Asia since Attila the Hun. Between May of 1975 and December of 1978 he was responsible for the murder or starvation of up to four million Cambodians. This reign of terror only ceased when the North Vietnamese moved in and took over in late 1978. Pol Pot withdrew to organize an insurgency against the North Vietnamese within Cambodia, an effort which continues to this day.

In Laos, the accommodation which had led to a coalition government with the Communists broke down shortly after the fall of South Vietnam. With NVA assistance the Pathet Lao extended de facto control over the majority of the country and finally ousted the Royalists from the government in December. The new "Peoples Democratic Republic of Laos" was born as a satellite of Hanoi. Thus the "Domino Theory" came to fruition in South East Asia.

THE NORTH VIETNAMESE ARMY

The North Vietnamese and their Viet Cong allies had their work cut out for them during the long fight against South Vietnam and the United States. That they were able not only to endure, but ultimately to prevail, bears careful examination. Basically, while the Americans and the ARVN administered a number of self-inflicted wounds that demonstrated that they were out of touch with the political/military realities of the principles of war, the North Viet-

Left: North Vietnamese soldiers raise the flag after capturing a bunker in Saigon

A North Vietnamese T-54 tank passes a captured M48 in the grounds of Saigon's presidential palace. The Northerners were careful to call themselves the South Vietnam Liberation Army, but could not disguise the fact that it was they and not the Viet Cong who were calling the shots.

Nguyen Trung Kien, later to become a well known Vietnamese actress, rides into Saigon on Liberation Day, 30th April 1975. The vehicle is a Chinese supplied Type 531 APC.

namese made optimum use of their resources, and exerted a crude sort of superiority on several different levels.

At the upper end of this spectrum, the West's foremost scholar in the field, Douglas Pike, attributes victory to Hanoi's organization, doctrine, and singleness of purpose. Americans were "seduced by the trivial" and never grasped the essence of the North Vietnamese war effort. Over the long haul, Pike describes the conflict between the two Vietnams as a battle of social organization, with victory going to the best organized. The North Vietnamese were able to organize, control and manage their population in the middle of a war situation, while the South Vietnamese were never quite able to achieve a government which was efficient, tolerable and rational.

Armed Struggle

The second part of Pike's thesis is the unified doctrine of Hanoi, called **Dau Tranh** (i.e., Struggle). This was an all-embracing concept which involved two major thrusts: 1) The Armed Struggle (military operations and terrorism); and, 2) The Political Struggle (encompassing action among the military, action among the enemy, and action among the people). Much of the social organizational activity mentioned above was accomplished as part of the Political Struggle. With this double program, it is not difficult to see that the US and ARVN could win against the Political Struggle and still not win, while on the other hand they could certainly lose to the Armed Struggle – what actually happened in 1975.

Pike's last major point involves the **spirit** which sustained the North Vietnamese effort. Ever since 1954, the unshakeable goal of the Hanoi regime – and thus the North Vietnamese people – was the reunification of the country. With this single and all-important objective to drive them, there developed a grim determination among the Northerners to bring it about – no matter how long it took and no matter what the cost. The unfortunate South Vietnamese Communists (the Viet Cong) had delusions of two Communist Vietnams – holding power in the south themselves. Steady attrition sapped the strength of the VC, and the Machiavellian NVA strategy for the Tet Offensive just about finished it off. At the hour of victory in 1975, the leadership of the Viet Cong was swept aside as South Vietnam was brought under Hanoi government.

The strategy employed to implement North Vietnam's war aims shifted a good deal throughout the war. The first strategic phase, lasting up until the end of 1964, was a period of revolutionary guerrilla warfare, carried out mainly by the VC and southerners returning to the north. In 1965, the US intervened in strength causing a strategy debate in Hanoi. Within the Politburo two positions emerged, the first being escalation to a "big unit" war, championed by Le Duan, and the second being a continuation of protracted guerrilla war to outlast the opposition, supported by Truong Chinh.

The debate was initially resolved in favor of escalation, leading directly to a regular force strategy period, lasting from 1965 through mid-1968. Overtly, General Giap tried to offset the firepower and mobility advantages of the United States by introducing NVA units and better weapons, including AK-47 assault rifles, air defense machine guns, rocket-propelled grenades (B-40s & B-50s), and later heavy artillery and tanks. The hidden agenda was that the NVA represented a political counterweight to the South Vietnamese Communists in Hanoi's maneuvers to control the war effort.

The regular force strategy brought new dimensions to the war. Organizationally, there were well-defined divisions between the Communist unit types which, as in the case with the South Vietnamese, had

FREQUENT WIND

The collapse of South Vietnam when it came in 1975 was rapid, and emergency plans to evacuate American citizens had to be hurridly put into effect. While a naval task force standing in close to the coast prepared to receive evacuees, the authorities in Saigon had to make the heart rending decision as to which of their loyal Vietnamese employees could be airlifted to safety. Before long, however, Vietnamese helicopters were flying out to the American ships with more refugees. As each was emptied it was ditched to allow more to land.

Above: The US Embassy, Saigon, April 30, 1975. Security men and marines hold former allies at bay.

Below: A Marine CH-53, part of Operation Frequent Wind, picks up refugees in north Saigon as the NVA nears the city.

"At 04.45 Ambassador Martin was on board 'Lady Ace 09'; the last evacuee left at 05.09 and by 07.53 the last of the defending Marines left the rooftop. The Vietnamese mob surged through the building, held back from the top floor and roof by riot control agents. The Marine commander, Major Jim Kean, was on the last helo out of Saigon and by 08.25 was safely with the Task Force. 'Frequent Wind' was over"

little resemblance to what Americans called them. For instance, the term "VC Infrastructure" did not apply in Communist terminology. At the macro level, Hanoi saw things in terms of the "Liberation Army", with two wings: the Main Force, and the Guerrilla Force (subdivided into Regional and Local Guerrillas). The Ho Chi Minh Trail became the center of activity as reinforcements and supplies flowed from the north. The monsoon patterns, which affected mobility, thus regulated the tempo of combat. Between February and June the fighting was heaviest, subsiding in July and intensifying again in August and September. The months of October through January were relatively low in intensity.

Giap's Strategy

Giap's regular force strategy led to up the Tet Offensive in 1968. Tactically he moved in two directions. First was the Coordinated Fighting Method, employing main force units against important targets (e.g. Con Thien and Dak To in 1967), in combat which was not decisive in itself, but drew attention. The second was the Independent Fighting Method, using Viet Cong guerrillas and small units to tie down the enemy in many places, such as was attempted in Tet '68. Giap planned for a decisive campaign to take place during the period of winter 1967 through spring 1968, encompassing both forms of combat in a comprehensive offensive. The first phase took place during the months of October through December of 1967 and involved a number of Coordinated Fighting Method attacks which did pull US troops away from urban areas, but at a very high cost in NVA lives. The second phase incorporated the Independent Fighting Method attacks of the Tet Offensive, which decimated the Viet Cong. The entire campaign cost the Communists perhaps 85,000 of the 195,000 troops they committed.

The physical losses of the Tet Offensive drove Hanoi to revise its strategy and fall back on guerrilla warfare until March of 1972. Over this period the NVA built up its strength and bided its time while the US withdrew its combat forces from Vietnam. From the Spring 1972 Offensive up until the end of 1975, Hanoi resumed the regular force strategy – augmented by heavy weapons and sophisticated logistical support. The premature 1972 Offensive was a definite setback, but after another rebuilding period the NVA was stronger than ever, while the ARVN suffered from decreasing American aid. The army which conquered South Vietnam in 1975 bore little resemblance to the popular image of the guerrilla insurgent army. The NVA was fully integrated in division-size formations with plentiful heavy artillery, tanks, and air defense gun/missile systems. The supporting Ho Chi Minh Trail had developed into a multi-lane highway with accompanying fuel pipeline.

At the lower end of the spectrum, Colonel William D. Henderson offers superior cohesion as an explanation of the effectiveness of NVA combat units throughout the war. Examining a number of indicators of unit cohesion, Henderson ranks the NVA high compared to several of the world's leading armies. In the social area, the basic three-man cell of the NVA was the group which controlled the life of the soldier. It provided mutual support and security, and made defection a risky undertaking. At the platoon level, soldier comments and suggestions were solicited in the formulation of combat plans, giving the individual a feeling of self-worth and a stake in the outcome of battle. His immediate combat leaders suffered the same privations as the soldiers, and earned respect through closeness with the men.

Another motivator, albeit negative, was the NVA soldier's perception that there was no viable way of escaping the army. Service in the NVA was virtually

Left: An ARVN CH-47 goes over the side of USS Hancock.

Above: Fleeing Vietnamese ditch a Huey and await rescue.

Above: Among the last to go, Marines wait to leave the Embassy.

Below: One of 15 RVN choppers pushed from USS Blue Ridge.

for the duration, and the political cadre were charged with keeping discipline strong and preventing desertion. The unit was the center of a man's existence, and group pressure from unit members was used as a tool by the leadership. Any soldier deviating from the NVA's expected norms would be reported to superiors by his fellow soldiers, and could expect to be the object of group pressure.

So important was the concept of the unit, that the NVA did not assign individuals, but rotated whole units for rebuilding when casualties needed replacement. Deliberately stationed away from home areas, NVA units were ethnically homogeneous and their members shared common goals and values. Drugs and racial strife were never problems. The better units in the NVA were professional in every aspect, and were motivated by the same esprit de corps that motivates other armies.

Nationalist or Marxist

Although tied politically to Communism, an idea reinforced by the political officers, the NVA soldier basically fought for his interpretation of nationalism as embodied in Ho Chi Minh. His fight was not for Marxism, but to unify Vietnam and rid it of "American Imperialists and the Saigon Puppets". Aside from Ho Chi Minh, the NVA soldier had little knowledge of the leadership of North Vietnam above the rank of his own company commander. At these lower levels of command, the NVA excelled. Officers held themselves and others to strict account in ethical matters, and believed in leadership by example. They were recognized as competent professionals by their men.

During 1965, the first year of the big American buildup in South Vietnam, the NVA also began serious mobilization. At that time, North Vietnam's regular army had about 300,000 men – two-thirds of them combat troops. These were disposed in 7 divisions, 7 brigades, 35 independent regiments and 10 independent battalions. By the end of the year, 9 NVA regiments were in South Vietnam and 10 battalions were in Laos. By the beginning of the Tet offensive in 1968, the NVA had grown to about 447,000 men, three-quarters of them combat troops. The North Vietnamese population and draft intake permitted about 7,500 men per month to be readied for combat with the field forces. The training base and equipment availability allowed for a theoretical total of 24 to 36 regiments to be formed (or reformed) annually, with the higher figure representing a substantial decrease in quality. There was much debate over whether the US attrition strategy ever reached the "crossover point" at which the NVA lost more men than it could replace. In fact, this point may have been reached at times during the war, but since the NVA controlled the tempo of combat and could adjust the commitment of its troops, the crossover point was irrelevant.

NVA Deployment

Over the entire period of the war, the NVA organized and deployed 23 line infantry divisions (1st, 2nd, 3rd Binh Dinh, 3rd Phuoc Long, 4th, 5th, 6th, 7th, 8th, 9th, 10th, 304th, 308th, 308B, 312th, 316th, 320th, 320B, 324B, 325th, 341st, 711th, and 968th) – though not all existed simultaneously. In addition there were three training divisions (304B, 330th and 350th), as well as a training division (338th) which converted to a line division in 1974. A sapper division (27th) existed, along with a number of artillery and air defense divisions. Using the evaluation system for the other armies discussed thus far, in general the NVA's divisions could be rated good in effectiveness. There were exceptions, of course, for example, the 711th had bad morale and was reformed and redesignated as the 2nd in the summer of 1973 after the 2nd Division had lost half

Tank number 844 bursts into the grounds of the Presidential palace in Saigon, bringing the long Vietnam War to a close.

For all the success of the Hanoi war machine, fifteen years after the war Vietnam remains one of the poorest countries in the world.

its men in the 1972 offensive. The 968th was also known to be low in combat effectiveness.

North Vietnam's allies, the Viet Cong, operated a total of 65,000 full-time regular troops and nearly 100,000 part-time irregular guerrillas and militia in mid-1965. The VC regulars consisted of main force regional units and local force units. At that time, during the first year of the US buildup, there were 64 regular VC battalions and 9 regimental headquarters. In addition, there were 188 separate companies and 114 separate platoons. From that point, the force structure grew and even came to incorporate several divisions. Recruitment however, steadily declined even with forced conscription in Communist-dominated areas. Gradually, NVA troops began to replace VC soldiers in decimated units, and many "Viet Cong" formations became virtually all-NVA. With less effective equipment and training, the Viet Cong units were inferior to the NVA, and would be rated **fair** in comparison with other armies noted in the text. In contrast, the fanatical Khmer Rouge would be rated **excellent**. In combat they would literally die rather than retreat. On the other hand, the Laotians (of both sides) deserved a **poor** rating with the exception of CIA-backed irregulars and mercenaries.

APPENDIX A
UNITED STATES ORDER OF BATTLE VIETNAM – AUGUST 1968

How to read this table: The Order of Battle below is not authoritative and concentrates only on major combat formations. Within each brigade or group, subordinate units are considered to be located in the vicinity of the brigade or group location unless otherwise noted. Battalion and company units are normally listed by an abbreviated designation with the number of the battalion followed by a dash and the historical regimental designation, and any amplifying information in parentheses. For example: **1-5 FA (155T)**=1st Battalion, 5th Artillery (using 155mm towed howitzers). "Cavalry" units are of three types: airmobile infantry battalions [e.g., **1-8 Cav (Ambl)],** armored cavalry squadrons [e.g., **1-1 Cav (Armd)],** and air cavalry squadrons [e.g., **1-9 Cav (Air)].** Non-"regimental" battalions (i.e., engineers, aviation) have a designating number followed by **Bn** for battalion. Company-size units (not included in the list unless part of an independent brigade) are either separately numbered or have a letter designation followed by a parent battalion designation. Company-size units are listed as **Co** (company), **Trp** (troop), or **Bty** (battery).
Unit type abbreviations are:
(Abn)=Airborne; **(Abn ATk)**=Airborne Anti-Tank; **ACR**=Armored Cavalry Regiment; **ADA**=Air Defense Artillery; **(Air)** =Air Cavalry; **Arm**=Armor; **Avn**=Aviation; **AWSP**=Automatic Weapons, Self-Propelled; **Cav**=Cavalry; **Eng**=Engineer; **FA**=Field Artillery; **Inf**=Infantry.
Supplementary designations are:
(Ambl)=Airmobile; **(Arm)**=Armored Cavalry; **(Aslt Hel)**=Assault Helicopter; **(Aslt Spt Hel)**=Assault Support Helicopter; **(Cmbt)**=Combat Support; **(Const)**=Construction; **(Hawk)**="Hawk" SAM; **(Lt)**=Light; **(M-48A3)**=M-48A3 Medium Tank (90mm gun); **(Mech)**=Mechanised; **(Riv)**=Riverine; **(40mmSP)**=M-42 "Duster" Twin 40mm Self-propelled Anti-Aircraft Gun; **(105T)**=M-101 or M-102 Towed 105mm Howitzer; **(105SP)**=M-108 Self- propelled 105mm Howitzer; **(155T)**=M-114 Towed 155mm Howitzer; **(155SP)**=M-109 Self-propelled 155mm Howitzer; **(8"SP)**=M-110 Self-propelled 8-inch Howitzer; **(175SP)**=M-107 Self-propelled 175mm Gun; **(155T/8"SP)**=mixed battalion with M-114 and M-110 pieces; **(175SP/8"SP)**=mixed battalion with M-107 and M-110 pieces.

US MILITARY ASSISTANCE COMMAND VIETNAM
HQ – Saigon, Tan Son Nhut
5th Special Forces Group – Nha Trang
97th Artillery Group (Air Defense) – Tan Son Nhut
6-56 ADA (Hawk) – Chu Lai
6-71 ADA (Hawk) – Cam Ranh Bay

I FIELD FORCE VIETNAM
HQ – Nha Trang

4th INFANTRY DIVISION
HQ & Division Troops – Pleiku
5-16 FA (155T/8"SP)
1-69 Arm (M-48A3)
1-10 Cav (Arm)
4th Avn Bn (Cmbt)
4th Eng Bn (Cmbt)
attached:
2-1 Cav (Arm)
1st Brigade – Dak To
1-8 Inf
3-8 Inf
3-12 Inf
6-29 FA (105T)
2nd Brigade – Ban Me Thuot
2-8 Inf (Mech)
1-12 Inf
1-22 Inf
4-42 FA (105T)
3rd Brigade – Pleiku
1-14 Inf
1-35 Inf
2-35 Inf
2-9 FA (105T)

173rd AIRBORNE BRIGADE – Bon Son
1-503 Inf (Abn)
2-503 Inf (Abn)
4-503 Inf (Abn)
3-319 FA (105T)
Co D/16 Arm (Abn ATk)
Trp E/17 Cav (Arm)
173rd Eng Co
335th Avn Co
attached:
1-50 Inf (Mech)

17th AVIATION GROUP – Nha Trang
10th Avn Bn (Cmbt) – Dong Ba Thin
52nd Avn Bn (Cmbt) – Pleiku
223rd Avn Bn (Cmbt Spt) – Qui Nhon
268th Avn Bn (Cmbt) – Phu Hiep
7-17 Cav (Air) – Pleiku

I FIELD FORCE ARTILLERY
41st Artillery Group – Phu Cat
7-13 FA (105T) – Bong Son
7-15 FA (8"SP) – Phu Cat
5-22 FA (175SP) – An Khe
5-27 FA (105T) – Phan Rang
6-32 FA (8"SP) – Tuy Hoa
4-60 AWSP (40mmSP) – An Khe
6-84 FA (155T) – An Khe
52nd Artillery Group – Pleiku
3-6 FA (105SP)
6-14 FA (175SP/8"SP)
1-92 FA (155T)

18th ENGINEER BRIGADE – Dong Ba Thin
87th Eng Bn (Const)
35th Engineer Group (Constrution) – Qui Nhon
19th Eng Bn (Cmbt) – Bong Son
62nd Eng Bn (Const) – Phan Rang
70th Eng Bn (Cmbt) – Ban Me Thuot
84th Eng Bn (Const) – Qui Nhon
577th Eng Bn (Const) – Tuy Hoa
589th Eng Bn (Const) – Phan Rang
864th Eng Bn (Const) – Nha Trang
[Note: In September, 116th Eng Bn (Cmbt) of the Idaho National Guard deployed to the 35th Group]
45th Engineer Group (Construction) – Phu Bai
14th Eng Bn (Cmbt) – Thon Me Thuy
27th Eng Bn (Cmbt) – Gia Le
35th Eng Bn (Cmbt) – Da Nang
86th Eng Bn (Cmbt) – My Tho
937th Engineer Group (Combat) – Pleiku
20th Eng Bn (Cmbt)
299th Eng Bn (Cmbt) – Dak To
815th Eng Bn (Const)

TASK FORCE SOUTH – Dalat
3-503 Inf (Abn) – Bao Loc
3-506 Inf (Abn) – Phan Thiet

II FIELD FORCE VIETNAM
HQ – Long Binh

1st INFANTRY DIVISION
HQ & Division Troops – Lai Khe
8-6 FA (155T/8"SP)
1-4 Cav (Arm)
1st Avn Bn (Cmbt)
1st Eng Bn (Cmbt)
1st Brigade – Quan Loi
1-2 Inf
1-26 Inf
1-28 Inf
1-5 FA (105T)
2nd Brigade – Di An
2-16 Inf
1-18 Inf
2-18 Inf
1-7 FA (105T)
3rd Brigade – Lai Khe
2-2 Inf (Mech)
1-16 Inf (Mech)
2-28 Inf
2-33 FA (105T)

9th INFANTRY DIVISION
HQ & Division Troops – Dong Tam
1-84 FA (155T/8"SP)
3-5 Cav (Arm)
9th Avn Bn (Cmbt)
15th Eng Bn (Cmbt)
attached:
6-77 FA (105T) – Can Tho
1st Brigade – Tan An
6-31 Inf – Nha Be
2-39 Inf
2-60 Inf – My Phuoc Tuy
1-11 FA (105T)
2nd Brigade (Mobile Riverine Force) – Dong Tam
3-47 Inf (Riv)
4-47 Inf (Riv)
3-60 Inf (Riv) – Mo Cay
3-34 FA (105T)
3rd Brigade – Can Giuoc
3-39 Inf
4-39 Inf – Nha Be
2-47 Inf (Mech) – Binh Phuoc
5-60 Inf (Mech)
2-4 FA (105T)

25th INFANTRY DIVISION
HQ & Division Troops – Cu Chi
3-13 FA (155T/8"SP)
2-34 Arm (M-48A3)
3-4 Cav (Arm)
25th Avn Bn (Cmbt)
65th Eng Bn (Cmbt)
1st Brigade – Tay Ninh
4-9 Inf
2-14 Inf
4-23 Inf (Mech)
7-11 FA (105T)
2nd Brigade – Cu Chi
1-5 Inf (Mech)
1-27 Inf
2-27 Inf
1-8 FA (105T)
3rd Brigade – Dau Tieng
2-12 Inf
2-22 Inf (Mech)
3-22 Inf
2-77 FA (105T)

3rd BRIGADE/101st AIRBORNE DIVISION – Cu Chi
3-187 Inf (Ambl)
1-506 Inf (Ambl)
2-506 Inf (Ambl)
2-319 FA (105T)

199th LIGHT INFANTRY BRIGADE – Long Binh
2-3 Inf (Lt)
3-7 Inf (Lt)
4-12 Inf (Lt)
5-12 Inf (Lt)
2-40 FA (105T)
Trp D/17 Cav (Arm)
87th Eng Co

1st AVIATION BRIGADE – Long Binh
12th Aviation Group – Long Binh
11th Avn Bn (Cmbt) – Phu Loi
145th Avn Bn (Cmbt) – Bien Hoa
210th Avn Bn (Cmbt) – Long Thanh
214th Avn Bn (Cmbt) – Bear Cat
222nd Avn Bn (Cmbt Spt) – Vung Tau
269th Avn Bn (Cmbt) – Cu Chi
3-17 Cav (Air) – Di An
164th Aviation Group – Can Tho
13th Avn Bn (Cmbt)
307th Avn Bn (Cmbt)
7-1 Cav (Air) – Vinh Long

II FIELD FORCE ARTILLERY
5-2 AWSP (40mmSP) – Long Binh
23rd Artillery Group – Phu Loi
2-12 FA (105T) – Phu Loi
6-15 FA (105T) – Tan Son Nhut
1-27 FA (155SP) – Dau Tieng
6-27 FA (175SP/8"SP) – Quan Loi
2-32 FA (175SP) – Tay Ninh
[Note: 3-197 FA (155T) and 2-12 FA (155T) joined the group in Sep '68 and Sep '69 respectively]
54th Artillery Group – Xuan Loc
7-8 FA (8"SP) – Bien Hoa
7-9 FA (105T) – Bear Cat
2-35 FA (155SP) – Xuan Loc
5-42 FA (155T) – Bear Cat

20th ENGINEER BRIGADE – Bien Hoa
34th Engineer Group (Construction) – Vung Tau
36th Eng Bn (Const) – Vung Tau
69th Eng Bn (Const) – Can Tho
93rd Eng Bn (Const) – Dong Tam
79th Engineer Group (Construction) – Long Binh
34th Eng Bn (Const) – Phu Loi
168th Eng Bn (Cmbt) – Di An
554th Eng Bn (Const) – Cu Chi
588th Eng Bn (Cmbt) – Tay Ninh
159th Engineer Group (Construction) – Long Binh
31st Eng Bn (Cmbt) – Phuoc Vinh
46th Eng Bn (Const)
92nd Eng Bn (Const)
169th Eng Bn (Const)

11th ARMORED CAVALRY REGIMENT – Long Binh
1st Sqdn/11 ACR
2nd Sqdn/11 ACR
3rd Sqdn/11 ACR
Air Cav Trp/11 ACR

XXIV CORPS
HQ – Phu Bai

1st CAVALRY DIVISION (AIRMOBILE)
HQ & Division Troops – Phong Dien
2-20 Aerial Rocket Artillery
1-30 FA (155T) – Phu Bai
1-9 Cav (Air)
8th Eng Bn (Cmbt)
attached:
2-17 FA (105T)
1st Brigade – Phong Dien
2-5 Cav (Ambl)
1-8 Cav (Ambl)
1-12 Cav (Ambl)
2-19 FA (105T)
2nd Brigade – Phong Dien
1-5 Cav (Ambl)
2-7 Cav (Ambl)
2-8 Cav (Ambl)
1-77 FA (105T)
3rd Brigade – Phong Dien
1-7 Cav (Ambl)
5-7 Cav (Ambl)
2-12 Cav (Ambl)
2-21 FA (105T)
11th Aviation Group
227 Avn Bn (Aslt Hel)
228 Avn Bn (Aslt Spt Hel)
229 Avn Bn (Aslt Hel)

AMERICAL DIVISION
HQ & Division Troops – Chu Lai
1-82 FA (155T/8"SP)
1-1 Cav (Arm)
26th Eng Bn (Cmbt)
attached:
3-16 FA (155T)
3-18 FA (175SP/8"SP)
39th Eng Bn (Cmbt)
11th Light Infantry Brigade – Duc Pho
3-1 Inf (Lt)
4-3 Inf (Lt)
1-20 Inf (Lt)
4-21 Inf (Lt)
6-11 FA (105T)
196th Light Infantry Brigade – Tam Ky
2-1 Inf (Lt)
3-21 Inf (Lt)
4-31 Inf (Lt)
3-82 FA (105T)
198th Light Infantry Brigade – Chu Lai
1-6 Inf (Lt)
1-46 Inf (Lt)
5-46 Inf (Lt)
1-52 Inf (Lt)
1-14 FA (105T)
16th Aviation Group
14th Avn Bn (Cmbt)
123rd Avn Bn (Cmbt)
212th Avn Bn (Cmbt)

101st AIRBORNE DIVISION (AIRMOBILE)
HQ & Division Troops – Phu Bai
2-11 FA (155T)
2-17 Cav (Arm)
326 Eng Bn (Cmbt)
1st Brigade – Phu Bai
1-327 Inf (Ambl)
2-327 Inf (Ambl)
2-502 Inf (Ambl)
2-320 FA (105T)
2nd Brigade – Phu Bai
1-501 Inf (Ambl)
2-501 Inf (Ambl)
1-502 Inf (Ambl)
1-321 FA (105T)
160th Aviation Group – Phu Bai
101st Avn Bn (Cmbt)
159th Avn Bn (Aslt Hel)
[Note: At this time the division was converting to the airmobile organization. Further changes included: addition of the 158th Avn Bn (Aslt Hel) to the aviation group in Feb '69, and the group's redesignation to **101st Aviation Group;** conversion of 2-17 Cav to air cavalry in Jul '69; and addition of the 4-77 Aerial Rocket Artillery in Oct '68.]

1st BRIGADE/5th INFANTRY DIVISION (MECHANIZED) – Quang Tri
1-77 Arm (M-48A3)
1-11 Inf – Cam Lo
1-61 Inf (Mech) – Cam Lo
5-4 FA (155SP)
Trp A/4-12 Cav (Arm)
Co A/7 Eng Bn (Cmbt)

3rd BRIGADE/82nd AIRBORNE DIVISION – Phu Bai
1-505 Inf (Abn)
2-505 Inf (Abn)
1-508 Inf (Abn)
2-321 FA (105T)
Trp B/17 Cav (Arm)
Co A/82nd Avn Bn (Cmbt)
Co C/307 Eng Bn (Cmbt)

XXIV CORPS ARTILLERY
108th Artillery Group – Dong Ha
8-4 FA (175SP)
6-33 FA (105T) – Quang Tri
1-40 FA (105SP)
1-44 AWSP (40mmSP)
1-83 FA (175SP/8"SP) – Phu Bai
2-94 FA (175SP)
[Note: 2-138 FA and 1-39 FA, both 155SP, joined XXIV Corps Artillery in Oct '68 and Oct '69 respectively]

III MARINE AMPHIBIOUS FORCE
HQ – Da Nang

Note: Rifle battalions are designated with battalion and regiment numbers separated by a slash (e.g., **1/7 Marines**=1st Battalion, 7th Marine Regiment). Artillery battalions are designated similarly but with primary weapon type in parentheses following the unit. Marine regiments often traded rifle battalions with other Marine regiments, depending on the tactical situation. Shown below are the normal regiment compositions without task organization.

1st MARINE DIVISION
HQ & Division Troops – Da Nang
4/11 Marines (155T)
1st Tank Bn
1st Amphibian Tractor Bn
1st Recon Bn
1st Eng Bn
1st Marines – Gio Linh
1/1 Marines
2/1 Marines
3/1 Marines
1/11 Marines (105T)
5th Marines – Da Nang
1/5 Marines
2/5 Marines
3/5 Marines
2/11 Marines (105T)
7th Marines – Da Nang
1/7 Marines
2/7 Marines
3/7 Marines
3/11 Marines (105T)

Appendix A (continued)

3rd MARINE DIVISION
HQ & Division Troops – Dong Ha
4/12 Marines (155SP)
3rd Tank Bn
3rd Amphibian Tractor Bn
3rd Recon Bn
3rd Eng Bn
3rd Marines – Cam Lo
1/3 Marines
2/3 Marines
3/3 Marines
1/12 Marines (105T)
4th Marines – Khe Sanh
1/4 Marines
2/4 Marines
3/4 Marines
3/12 Marines (105T)
9th Marines – Cam Lo
1/9 Marines
2/9 Marines
3/9 Marines
2/12 Marines (105T)

REGIMENTAL LANDING TEAM 26 – Phu Loc
1/26 Marines
2/26 Marines
3/26 Marines
1/13 Marines (105T)
REGIMENTAL LANDING TEAM 27 – Da Nang
1/27 Marines
2/27 Marines
3/27 Marines
2/13 Marines (105T)
1st FIELD ARTILLERY GROUP
two 8″SP batteries
two 155T batteries
one 155SP battery
ENGINEER BATTALIONS:
7th, 9th, 11th
COMBINED ACTION BATTALIONS:
1st, 3nd, 3rd, 4th

APPENDIX B
MAJOR USAF UNITS SOUTHEAST ASIA 1964-1973

Unit	Initial Aircraft	Dates of Service	Base
Tactical Fighter Wings:			
3rd TFW	F-100	7/65-3/70	Bien Hoa (1)
4th TFW	F-4	4/72-10/72	Udorn, Thai (2)
8th TFW	F-4	12/65-1/73	Ubon, Thai
12th TFW	F-4	11/65-3/70	Cam Ranh Bay
		4/70-11/71	Phu Cat
31st TFW	F-100	1/67-10/70	Tuy Hoa
35th TFW	F-4	7/65-9/66	Da Nang (3)
		10/66-6/71	Phan Rang
37th TFW	F-100	3/67-3/70	Phu Cat
49th TFW	F-4	5/72-10/72	Takhli, Thai (2)
355th TFW	F-105	11/65-11/70	Takhli, Thai
366th TFW	F-4	4/66-9/66	Phan Rang
		10/66-6/72	Da Nang
		7/72-10/72	Takhli, Thai
388th TFW	F-105	4/65-3/73	Korat, Thai (4)
Tactical Reconnaissance Wings:			
432nd TRW	RF-4	9/66-post	Udorn, Thai
460th TRW	RF-4	2/66-8/71	Tan Son Nhut
553rd RW	RF-4	11/67-12/70	Korat, Thai
Special Operations Wings ("Air Commando Wings" until 8/68):			
14th SOW	AC-47/119	3/66-9/69	Nha Trang
		10/69-9/71	Phan Rang
56th SOW	AC-119	4/67-6/74	Nakhon Phanom, Thai
315th SOW	C-123	3/66-6/67	Tan Son Nhut (5)
		7/67-3/72	Phan Rang
633rd SOW	AC-119	7/68-3/70	Nakhon Phanom, Thai
Tactical Airlift Wings ("Troop Carrier Wings" until 8/67):			
314th TAW	C-130	pre-3/66	Clark, Philippines
		4/66-6/71	C.C.K., Taiwan (6)
374th TAW	C-130	8/66-5/71	Naha, Okinawa (7)
		6/71-post	C.C.K.
463rd TAW	C-130	12/65-12/71	Clark, Philippines
483rd TAW	C-7	1/66-4/72	Cam Ranh Bay (8)
Rotational squadrons from the US were attached to the following:			
315 Air Div.	C-130	2/68-4/69	Tachikawa, Japan (9)
834 Air Div.	C-130	11/66-11/70	Tan Son Nhut (9)
Strategic Air Command ("Bombardment" or "Strategic" Wings):			
307th SW	B-52	6/66-post	U-Tapao, Thai (10)
4133rd BW	B-52	2/66-6/70	Andersen, Guam (11)
4252nd SW	B-52	1/65-3/70	Kadena, Okinawa

Notes:
1. Designated 6251st TFW until 11/65.
2. Emergency reinforcement during NVA Spring 1972 Offensive.
3. Designated 6252nd TFW until 4/66.
4. Designated 6234th TFW until 4/66.
5. The 315th SOW, used for defoliant spray operations, was redesignated as 315th Tactical Airlift Wing on 1/1/70.
6. "C.C.K." is Ching Chuan Kang in Taiwan.
7. Since early '65, 3 × independent squadrons were at Naha.
8. Formed from six US Army aviation companies which had arrived in Vietnam between 7/63 and 1/66.
9. These Air Divisions had C-130s in wing strength during the periods noted.
10. Designated 4258th SW until 4/70. Under command of 17th Air Division (Provisional) from 6/72.
11. Conducted operations under 3rd Air Division until that formation was inactivated 31/3/70. Thereafter, bombing operations from Guam were controlled by 8th Air Force, which replaced 3rd Air Division. During the NVA Spring '72 Offensive, 57th Air Division (Provisional) was formed to handle increased bombing operations (6/72).

General Notes:
A. Several smaller units also operated in Vietnam during the period, including: 3rd Aero Rescue & Recovery Group; 504th Tactical Air Support Group; and 505th Tactical Control Group.
B. Operations in South Vietnam were controlled by 2nd Air Division (formed 10/62) until that formation was replaced by Seventh Air Force (4/66). Thirteenth Air Force, located at Clark Air Base in the Philippines, controlled other elements, while a subsidiary command, 7th/13th Air Force, operated from Thailand.

APPENDIX C
The B-52 EFFORT IN SOUTHEAST ASIA

Representative Date	Sortie Rate (Monthly)
Jul 65	300
Nov 66	600
Feb 67	800
Feb 68	1,200
Apr 68	1,800
Jul 69	1,600
Oct 69	1,400
Jun 71	1,000
Feb 72	1,200
Mar 72	1,500
Apr 72	1,800
Jun 72	3,150

Notes: The B-52 effort, which numbered over 200 aircraft at its peak, ultimately delivered 5,898,000,000 pounds of bombs in 124,532 sorties, only 6% of which were conducted against North Vietnam itself. Over half (55%) were flown in support of operations within South Vietnam, and the remainder were part of the interdiction campaigns in Laos (27%) and Cambodia (12%).

APPENDIX D
TASK FORCE 77 – MAY 1964 TO MAY 1975

The following table presents US Navy aircraft carriers which served with Task Force 77 during the war years. Information is organized by class, with information on type, carrier name and hull number, deployment dates and Carrier Air Wing (CVW) embarked.

MODIFIED "ESSEX" CLASS

Completion Dates – 1943-1950
Full Load Displacement – 41,000 tons
Flight Deck – 899 ft. × 172 to 195 ft.; 2 × catapults
Complement – 3,200 personnel and 70-80 aircraft

Ship	Deployments	Embarked
Bon Homme Richard (CVA 31)	24/2/64-20/11/64	CVW 19
	12/5/65-4/1/66	CVW 19
	10/2/67-17/8/67	CVW 21
	9/2/68-29/9/68	CVW 5
	6/4/69-19/10/69	CVW 5
	21/4/70-3/11/70	CVW 5
Hancock (CVA 19)	16/11/64-11/5/65	CVW 21
	6/12/65-24/7/66	CVW 21
	20/1/67-14/7/67	CVW 5
	6/8/68-23/2/69	CVW 21
	21/8/69-6/4/70	CVW 21
	7/11/70-19/5/71	CVW 21
	28/1/72-25/9/72	CVW 21
	19/5/73-24/12/73	CVW 21
	6/4/75-31/5/75	CVW 21
Intrepid (CVS 11)	1/5/66-30/10/66	CVW 10
	9/6/67-9/12/67	CVW 10
	6/7/68-16/1/69	CVW 10
Notes: Employed in limited attack role. First deployment was to Dixie Station.		
Oriskany (CVA 34)	27/4/65-6/12/65	CVW 16
	11/6/66-8/11/66	CVW 16
	26/6/67-23/1/68	CVW 16
	5/5/69-10/11/69	CVW 19
	1/6/70-29/11/70	CVW 19
	4/6/71-8/12/71	CVW 19
	21/6/72-20/3/73	CVW 19
	30/10/73-17/5/74	CVW 19
Note: Major fire on board during second deployment.		
Shangri-La (CVS 38)	30/3/70-24/11/70	CVW 8
Ticonderoga (CVA 14)	11/5/64-10/12/64	CVW 5
	25/10/65-7/5/66	CVW 5
	27/10/66-22/5/67	CVW 19
	13/1/68-9/8/68	CVW 19
	18/2/69-10/9/69	CVW 16

"MIDWAY" CLASS

Completion Dates – 1945-1947
Ful Load Displacement – 64,000 tons
Flight Deck – 979 ft. × 238 ft.; 2 × Catapults (3 on Coral Sea)
Complement – 4,500 personnel and 75 aircraft

Coral Sea (CVA 43)	23/1/65-23/10/65	CVW 15
	11/8/66-16/2/67	CVW 2
	10/8/67-29/3/68	CVW 15
	23/9/68-11/4/69	CVW 15
	14/10/69-18/6/70	CVW 15
	8/12/71-11/7/72	CVW 15
	20/3/73-30/10/73	CVW 15
	29/12/74-24/5/75	CVW 15
Franklin D. Roosevelt (CVA 42)	25/7/66-29/1/67	CVW 1
Midway (CVA 41)	22/3/65-14/11/65	CVW 2
	7/5/71-24/10/71	CVW 5
	21/4/72-23/2/73	CVW 5
	2/10/73-27/2/74	CVW 5
	25/10/74-1/5/75	CVW 5

"FORRESTAL" CLASS

Completion Dates – 1955-1959
Full Load Displacement – 76,000 to 79,000 tons
Flight Deck – 1,063 to 1,086 ft. × 252 ft.; 4 × catapults
Complement – 5,000 personnel and 90-100 aircraft (70 for CVA 59)

Forrestal (CVA 59)	8/7/67-22/8/67	CVW 17
Note: Catastrophic fire curtailed deployment.		
Independence (CVA 62)	5/6/65-21/11/65	CVW 7
Note: Deployed first A-6 all-weather bombers.		
Ranger (CVA 61)	17/8/64-24/4/65	CVW 9
	3/1/66-18/8/66	CVW 14
	20/11/67-18/5/68	CVW 2
	12/11/68-10/5/69	CVW 2
	4/11/69-23/5/70	CVW 2
	11/11/70-9/6/71	CVW 2
	28/11/72-14/6/73	CVW 2
	24/5/74-27/9/74	CVW 2
Note: Embarked first A-7 bombers on third deployment.		
Saratoga (CVA 60)	8/5/72-16/1/73	CVW 3

"KITTY HAWK" CLASS

Completion Dates – 1961-1965
Full Load Displacement – 79,000-81,000 tons
Flight Deck – 1,047 ft. × 252 ft.; 4 × catapults
Complement – 5,000 personnel and 85 aircraft

America (CVA 66)	12/5/68-20/11/68	CVW 6
	12/5/70-23/11/70	CVW 9
	1/7/72-4/3/73	CVW 8
Constellation (CVA 64)	11/6/64-14/1/65	CVW 14
	29/5/66-24/11/66	CVW 15
	15/5/67-26/11/67	CVW 14
	14/6/68-23/1/69	CVW 14
	1/9/69-29/4/70	CVW 14
	27/10/71-24/6/72	CVW 9
	16/1/73-2/10/73	CVW 9
	11/7/74-29/10/74	CVW 15
Kitty Hawk (CVA 63)	15/11/65-6/6/66	CVW 11
	17/11/66-12/6/67	CVW 11
	6/12/67-20/6/68	CVW 11
	15/1/69-27/8/69	CVW 11
	27/11/70-6/7/71	CVW 11
	1/3/72-17/11/72	CVW 11
	1/1/74-19/6/74	CVW 11

"ENTERPRISE" CLASS

Completion Date – 1961
Full Load Displacement – 90,000 tons
Flight Deck – 1,102 ft. × 252 ft.; 4 × catapults
Complement – 5,500 personnel and 85+ aircraft

Enterprise (CVAN 65)	21/11/65-14/6/66	CVW 9
	3/12/66-30/6/67	CVW 9
	14/1/68-12/7/68	CVW 9
	15/3/69-26/6/69	CVW 9
	27/6/71-2/2/72	CVW 14
	19/9/72-3/6/73	CVW 14
	16/10/74-24/12/74	CVW 14
	26/2/75-4/5/75	CVW 14

Note: First nuclear-powered ship in combat.

APPENDIX E
ARMY OF THE REPUBLIC OF VIETNAM ORDER OF BATTLE – LATE 1974

How ro read this table: The Order of Battle below is not authoritative and concentrates only on major combat formations. With exception of corps and division headquarters (or operating areas), unit locations are not provided. Unit designations are read in a similar manner to the US Order of Battle appendix, with the battalion number followed by a slash and the regiment number. Although ARVN units are presented in their "Americanized" form in the text, a more literal translation of the Vietnamese designations is provided here. For example, the US terms "ranger" and "armored cavalry" have no direct equivalents in Vietnamese. These were terms the US Army used to refer to ARVN units of similar capabilities, which the Vietnamese called "special mobile corps" and "armored vehicle units" respectively. When different from the US Order of Battle, equivalents and abbreviations are: **Armored Vehicle Bn**="armored cavalry squadron" in US terms, these units each had 1 × company of old US M-41 tanks and 2 × companies of 22 × M-113 APCs each, plus 81mm SP mortars and a platoon of V-100 armored cars at Bn HQ; **Division Airborne**=Airborne Department more than "airborne division", it included the entire airborne establishment of the ARVN and not just a tactical HQ; **Regional Forces** or **RF**=Provincial militia which assumed a more regular role as the war went on; **Sapper/Labor Bn**="combat engineer" in US terms, but incorporating what Europeans would call "assault pioneers", and laborers; **Special Landing Force** or **SLF**="marines" in US terms; **Special Mobile Corps** or **SMC**="ranger" in US terms, but incorporates border defense units, elite light infantry units, and some special warfare units; **Tank Bn**="armored bn" in US terms, with about 50 × US M-48A3 medium tanks (90mm gun) in 3× companies.

The table depicts normal unit subordination, but in practice a lot of cross-attachment of battalions occurred. Some field artillery and other battalion designations were not available at the time the list was compiled. Not shown are 17 × labor construction battalions, 4 × anti-aircraft battalions (40mm M-42 and .50-cal.), and a host of Regional Forces battalions. The ARVN had plans to raise 27 × Regional Forces groups (3 × bns each) by June of 1975. Not depicted in the list are 174 artillery sections (eqach of 2 × 105mm howitzers) which were spread throughout the country in support of Regional Forces. A number of these had been consolidated to provide one battery for each Regional Forces Group.

ARMY OF THE REPUBLIC OF VIETNAM
HQ – Saigon

Capital Security Group
Joint General Staff Honor Guard Bn
Special Mission Service (i.e., special forces)

I CORPS
HQ – Da Nang

DIVISION AIRBORNE
- **HQ & Division Troops** – Quang Tri vicinity
- **1st Airborne Brigade**
  - 1st Abn Inf Bn
  - 8th Abn Inf Bn
  - 9th Abn Inf Bn
  - 1st Abn FA Bn (105T)
- **2nd Airborne Brigade**
  - 5th Abn Inf Bn
  - 7th Abn Inf Bn
  - 11th Abn Inf Bn
  - 2nd Abn FA Bn (105T)
- **3rd Airborne Brigade**
  - 2nd Abn Inf Bn
  - 3rd Abn Inf Bn
  - 6th Abn Inf Bn
  - 3rd Abn FA Bn (105T)

SPECIAL LANDING FORCE DIVISION
- **HQ & Division Troops** – Quang Tri
- **147th Brigade**
  - 1st SLF Bn
  - 4th SLF Bn
  - 7th SLF Bn
  - 2nd SLF FA Bn (105T)
- **258th Brigade**
  - 2nd SLF Bn
  - 5th SLF Bn
  - 8th SLF Bn
  - 3rd SLF FA Bn (105T)
- **369th Brigade**
  - 3rd SLF Bn
  - 6th SLF Bn
  - 9th SLF Bn
  - 1st SLF FA Bn (105T)

1st DIVISION
- **HQ & Division Troops** – Hue
  - 10th FA Bn (155T)
  - 11th FA Bn (105T)
  - 12th FA Bn (105T)
  - 13th FA Bn (105T)
  - 1st Sapper/Labor Bn
- **1st Regiment**
  - 1/1 Inf Bn
  - 2/1 Inf Bn
  - 3/1 Inf Bn
  - 4/1 Inf Bn
- **3rd Regiment**
  - 1/3 Inf Bn
  - 2/3 Inf Bn
  - 3/3 Inf Bn
  - 4/3 Inf Bn
- **51st Regiment**
  - 1/51 Inf Bn
  - 2/51 Inf Bn
  - 3/51 Inf Bn
  - 4/51 Inf Bn
- **54th Regiment**
  - 1/54 Inf Bn
  - 2/54 Inf Bn
  - 3/54 Inf Bn
  - 4/54 Inf Bn

2nd DIVISION
- **HQ & Division Troops** – Quang Ngai
  - 20th FA Bn (155T)
  - 21st FA Bn (105T)
  - 22nd FA Bn (105T)
  - 23rd FA Bn (105T)
  - 2nd sapper/Labor Bn
- **4th Regiment**
  - 1/4 Inf Bn
  - 2/4 Inf Bn
  - 3/4 Inf Bn
  - 4/4 Inf Bn
- **5th Regiment**
  - 1/5 Inf Bn
  - 2/5 Inf Bn
  - 3/5 Inf Bn
  - 4/5 Inf Bn
- **6th Regiment**
  - 1/6 Inf Bn
  - 2/6 Inf Bn
  - 3/6 Inf Bn
  - 4/6 Inf Bn

3rd DIVISION
- **HQ & Division Troops** – Da Nang
  - 30th FA Bn (155T)
  - 31st FA Bn (105T)
  - 32nd FA Bn (105T)
  - 33rd FA Bn (105T)
  - 3rd Sapper/Labor Bn
- **2nd Regiment**
  - 1/2 Inf Bn
  - 2/2 Inf Bn
  - 3/2 Inf Bn
- **56th Regiment**
  - 1/56 Inf Bn
  - 2/56 Inf Bn
  - 3/56 Inf Bn
- **57th Regiment**
  - 1/57 Inf Bn
  - 2/57 Inf Bn
  - 3/57 Inf Bn

1st SPECIAL MOBILE CORPS COMMAND
- **11th Special Mobile Corps Group**
  - 68th SMC Bn
  - 69th SMC Bn
  - 70th SMC Bn
- **12th Special Mobile Corps Group**
  - 21st SMC Bn
  - 37th SMC Bn
  - 39th SMC Bn
- **14th Special Mobile Corps Group**
  - 77th SMC Bn
  - 78th SMC Bn
  - 79th SMC Bn
- **15th Special Mobile Corps Group**
  - 60th SMC Bn
  - 61st SMC Bn
  - 94th SMC Bn

1st ARMORED BRIGADE
- 4th Armored Vehicle Bn
- 7th Armored Vehicle Bn
- 11th Armored Vehicle Bn
- 17th Armored Vehicle Bn
- 20th Tank Bn (M-48A3)

I CORPS ARTILLERY
- 101st FA Bn (175SP)
- 104th FA Bn (175SP)
- 105th FA Bn (175SP)

10th SAPPER/LABOR GROUP
- 101st Sapper/Labor Bn
- 102nd Saper/Labor Bn
- 103rd Sapper/Labor Bn

REGIONAL FORCES (MOBILE GROUPS)
- **913th Regional Forces Group**
  - (3 × RF Bns)
- **914th Regional Forces Group**
  - (3 × RF Bns)
- **Regional Forces Group**
  - (3 × RF Bns)

II CORPS
HQ – Pleiku

22nd DIVISION
- **HQ & Division Troops** – Binh Dinh Province
  - 220th FA Bn (155T)
  - 221st FA Bn (105T)
  - 222nd FA Bn (105T)
  - 223rd FA Bn (105T)
  - 224th FA Bn (105T)
  - 22nd Sapper/Labor Bn
- **40th Regiment**
  - 1/40 Inf Bn
  - 2/40 Inf Bn
  - 3/40 Inf Bn
- **41st Regiment**
  - 1/41 Inf Bn
  - 2/41 Inf Bn
  - 3/41 Inf Bn
- **42nd Regiment**
  - 1/42 Inf Bn
  - 2/42 Inf Bn
  - 3/42 Inf Bn
- **47th Regiment**
  - 1/47 Inf Bn
  - 2/47 Inf Bn
  - 3/47 Inf Bn

23rd DIVISION
- **HQ & Division Troops** – Ban Me Thuot
  - 230th FA Bn (155T)
  - 231st FA Bn (105T)
  - 232nd FA Bn (105T)
  - 233rd FA Bn (105T)
  - 23rd Sapper/Labor Bn
- **44th Regiment**
  - 1/44 Inf Bn
  - 2/44 Inf Bn
  - 3/44 Inf Bn
- **45th Regiment**
  - 1/45 Inf Bn
  - 2/45 Inf Bn
  - 3/45 Inf Bn
- **53rd Regiment**
  - 1/53 Inf Bn
  - 2/53 Inf Bn
  - 3/53 Inf Bn

2nd SPECIAL MOBILE CORPS COMMAND
4th Special Mobile Corps Group
42nd SMC Bn
43rd SMC Bn
44th SMC Bn
6th Special Mobile Corps Group
35th SMC Bn
36th SMC Bn
51st SMC Bn
21st Special Mobile Corps Group
72nd SMC Bn
89th SMC Bn
96th SMC Bn
22nd Special Mobile Corps Group
62nd SMC Bn
88th SMC Bn
95th SMC Bn
23rd Special Mobile Corps Group
11th SMC Bn
22nd SMC Bn
23rd SMC Bn
24th Special Mobile Corps Group
63rd SMC Bn
81st SMC Bn
82nd SMC Bn
25th Special Mobile Corps Group
67th SMC Bn
76th SMC Bn
90th SMC Bn

2nd ARMORED BRIGADE
3rd Armored Vehicle Bn
8th Armored Vehicle Bn
19th Armored Vehicle Bn
22nd Armored Vehicle Bn
21st Tank Bn (M-48A3)

II CORPS ARTILLERY
102nd FA Bn (175SP)
37th FA Bn (155T)
(1 other 155T FA Bn)

20th SAPPER/LABOR GROUP
(3 × Sapper/Labour Bns)

REGIONAL FORCES (MOBILE GROUPS)
927th Regional Forces Group
(3 × RF Bns)

III CORPS
HQ – Bien Hoa

5th DIVISION
HQ & Division Troops – Lai Khe
50th FA Bn (105T)
51st FA Bn (105T)
52nd FA Bn (105T)
53rd FA Bn (105T)
5th Sapper/Labor Bn
7th Regiment
1/7 Inf Bn
2/ Inf Bn
3/7 Inf Bn
8th Regiment
1/8 Inf Bn
2/8 Inf Bn
3/8 Inf Bn
9th Regiment
1/9 Inf Bn
2/9 Inf Bn
3/9 Inf Bn

18th DIVISION
HQ & Division Troops – Xuan Loc
180th FA Bn (155T)
181st FA Bn (105T)
182nd FA Bn (105T)
183rd FA Bn (105T)
18th Sapper/Labor Bn
43rd Regiment
1/43 Inf Bn
2/43 Inf Bn
3/43 Inf Bn
48th Regiment
1/48 Inf Bn
2/48 Inf Bn
3/48 Inf Bn
52nd Regiment
1/52 Inf Bn
2/52 Inf Bn
3/52 Inf Bn

25th DIVISION
HQ & Division Troops – Cu Chi
250th FA Bn (155T)
251st FA Bn (105T)
252nd FA Bn (105T)
253rd FA Bn (105T)
25th Sapper/Labor Bn
46th Regiment
1/46 Inf Bn
2/46 Inf Bn
3/46 Inf Bn
49th Regiment
1/49 Inf Bn
2/49 Inf Bn
3/49 Inf Bn
50th Regiment
1/50 Inf Bn
2/50 Inf Bn
3/50 Inf Bn

3rd SPECIAL MOBILE CORPS COMMAND
7th Special Mobile Corps Group
32nd SMC Bn
33rd SMC Bn
34th SMC Bn
31st, 32nd, 33rd Special Mobile Corps Groups
consisting of:
30th, 31st, 38th, 41st,
52nd, 64th, 83rd, 92nd SMC Bns, and
81st Airborne SMC Battalion Group
8th Special Mobile Corps Group (newly formed)
(3 × SMC Bns – total 1,600 personnel)
9th Special Mobile Corps Group (newly formed)
(3 × SMC Bns – total 1,900 personnel)

4th AIRBORNE BRIGADE (brigade HQ newly formed)
4th Abn Inf Bn
10th Abn Inf Bn

468th SPECIAL LANDING FORCE BRIGADE (newly formed battalions)
14th SLF Bn
16th SLF Bn
18th SLF Bn

3rd ARMORED BRIGADE
1st Armored Vehicle Bn
5th Armored Vehicle Bn
10th Armored Vehicle Bn
15th Armored Vehicle Bn
18th Armored Vehicle Bn
22nd Tank Bn (M-48A3)

III CORPS ARTILLERY
103rd FA Bn (175SP)
(2 or 3 × 155T or 105T FA Bns)

30th SAPPER/LABOR GROUP
(3 × Sapper/Labor Bns)

REGIONAL FORCES (MOBILE GROUPS)
(several groups of RF Bns)

SCHOOL UNITS
(2 × Composite Armored Bns)
each: 1 × Co of M-41 Tanks
1 × Co of M-113 APCs
1 × Co of M-42 twin SP AA Guns
(1 × Composite FA Bn 155T7105T)

IV CORPS
HQ – Can Tho

7th DIVISION
HQ & Division Troops – My Tho
70th FA Bn (155T)
71st FA Bn (105T)
72nd FA Bn (105T)
73rd FA Bn (105T)
7th Sapper/Labor Bn
10th Regiment
1/10 Inf Bn
2/10 Inf Bn
3/10 Inf Bn
11th Regiment
1/11 Inf Bn
2/11 Inf Bn
3/11 Inf Bn
12th Regiment
1/12 Inf Bn
2/12 Inf Bn
3/12 Inf Bn

9th DIVISION
HQ & Division Troops – Sa Dec
90th FA Bn (155T)
91st FA Bn (105T)
92nd FA Bn (105T)
93rd FA Bn (105T)
9th Sapper/Labor Bn
14th Regiment
1/14 Inf Bn
2/14 Inf Bn
3/14 Inf Bn
15th Regiment
1/15 Inf Bn
2/15 Inf Bn
3/15 Inf Bn
16th Regiment
1/16 Inf Bn
2/16 Inf Bn
3/16 Inf Bn

21st DIVISION
HQ & Division Troops – Bac Lieu
210th FA Bn (155T)
211th FA Bn (105T)
212th FA Bn (105T)
213th FA Bn (105T)
21st Sapper/Labor Bn
31st Regiment
1/31 Inf Bn
2/31 Inf Bn
3/31 Inf Bn
32nd Regiment
1/32 Inf Bn
2/32 Inf Bn
3/32 Inf Bn
33rd Regiment
1/33 Inf Bn
2/33 Inf Bn
3/33 Inf Bn

4th ARMORED BRIGADE
2nd Armored Vehicle Bn
6th Armored Vehicle Bn
12th Armored Vehicle Bn
16th Armored Vehicle Bn

IV CORPS ARTILLERY
(3 or 4 × 155T or 105T FA Bns)

40th SAPPER/LABOR GROUP
(3 × Sapper/Labor Bns)

REGIONAL FORCES (MOBILE GROUPS)
(several groups of RF Bns)

APPENDIX F
SOUTH VIETNAMESE AIR FORCE ORDER OF BATTLE – 1975

1st AIR DIVISION (Da Nang, Hue, Quang Ngai)
2 × F-5E fighter sqdns
4 × A-37B ground attack sqdns
1 × A-1H ground attack sqdn
2 × O-1, O-2, U-17 spotter sqdns
5 × UH-1 assault helicopter sqdns
1 × CH-47 transport helicopter sqdn

2nd AIR DIVISION (Nha Trang, Phan Rang)
2 × A-37 ground attack sqdns
1 × O-1, O-2, U-17 spotter sqdns
1 × UH-1 assault helicopter sqdn
1 × T-37 training sqdn
1 × T-41 training sqdn

3rd AIR DIVISION (Bien Hoa)
4 × F-5A fighter sqdns
2 × A-37B ground attack sqdns
2 × O-1, O-2, U-17 spotter sqdns
5 × UH-1 assault helicopter sqdns
1 × CH-47 transport helicopter sqdn

4th AIR DIVISION (Binh Thuy, Soc Trang)
3 × A-37B ground attack sqdns
2 × O-1, O-2, U-17 spotter sqdns
5 × UH-1 assault helicopter sqdns
1 × CH-47 transport helicopter sqdn

5th AIR DIVISION (Tan Son Nhut)
2 × AC-119 gunship sqdns
1 × EC-47 electronic recon sqdn
1 × RC-47 photo recon sqdn
1 × C-47/UH-1 special transport sqdn
1 × C-47 transport sqdn
3 × C-7 transport sqdns
1 × C-119 transport sqdn
2 × C-123 transport sqdns
2 × C-130 transport sqdns
1 × UH-1 assault helicopter sqdn

6th AIR DIVISION (Pleiku, Phu Cat)
1 × F-5E fighter sqdn
1 × A-1H ground attack sqdn
1 × AC-119 gunship sqdn
1 × O-1, O-2, U-17 spotter sqdn
3 × UH-1 assault helicopter sqdns
1 × CH-47 transport helicopter sqdn

APPENDIX G
FORCES ARMEES NATIONALES KHMERS
(Cambodian Army Order of Battle – late 1974)

1e DIVISION D'INFANTERIE
1 Brigade
48 Brigade
81 Brigade

2e DIVISION D'INFANTERIE
2 Brigade
24 Brigade
43 Brigade

3e DIVISION D'INFANTERIE
13 Brigade
47 Brigade
51 Brigade

7e DIVISION D'INFANTERIE
7 Brigade
45 Brigade
72 Brigade

9e DIVISION D'INFANTERIE
36 Brigade
69 Brigade
83 Brigade

Brigade des Fusiliers Marines

Brigade d'Infanterie Parachutistes

BRIGADES D'INFANTERIE AUTONOMES:
5 Brigade
12 Brigade
20 Brigade
23 Brigade
28 Brigade
78 Brigade
79 Brigade
80 Brigade

Notes: After Lon Nol's coup in 1970, the Cambodian Army's 35 × infantry battalions were organized into 12 × brigades (exclusive of special troops like marines and airborne). These formed the nucleus for later expansion to the structure shown above. Additionally there was a brigade's worth of armored assets. By late 1974, a number of the original brigades had been destroyed or otherwise disbanded (1st, 3rd, 4th, 6th, 8th, 10th, 11th and 14th). Each brigade had a normal complement of three infantry battalions. The Cambodian Air Force and Navy were strictly auxiliary arms with little combat potential.

APPENDIX H
NORTH VIETNAMESE ORDER OF BATTLE – JANUARY 1973 (WITH ADDITIONS THROUGH 1975)

How to read this table: Any attempt to set out an NVA/VC order of battle involves the use of scant, and often contradictory, sources. In addition, myriads of small independent units, and units which existed prior to 1973, could not be included here. The table is broken down by location of units within the four South Vietnamese Corps areas, and further subdivided by the NVA hierarchy within these areas. The base-line order of battle is that which existed in January of 1973, with an additional section devoted to units which appeared (or reappeared) thereafter, or remained in North Vietnam. Within each formation (division etc.) a notation is given in parentheses following any unit which subsequently left the formation during the war. Similarly, a unit title enclosed in parentheses indicates that it joined the formation after January of 1973. Abbreviations used are: **aka**=also known as; **Arty**=Artillery; **Bn**=Battalion; **Inf**=Infantry; **NVA**=North Vietnamese Army; **Rgt**=Regiment; **VC**=Viet Cong. A "(*)" symbol indicates that the numerical designation of the unit is found more than once in the order of battle. The NVA perpetuated famous units by replacing them when destroyed or raising duplicates. There were no less than three **141st NVA** infantry regiments extant in different formations at the same time! No attempt has been made to identify battalions within regiments. There were normally three battalions per regiment, but these were not necessarily sequenced "1", "2" and "3" as with most armies. For example, the 2nd NVA Regiment had the 94th and 95th Battalions in 1965.

UNITS IN SOUTH VIETNAM'S I CORPS ZONE:

NVA B-5 FRONT (Quang Tri Province)
325th NVA Division (to NVA 2nd Corps in 1974)
18th NVA Inf Rgt
95th NVA Inf Rgt (*)
101st NVA Inf Rgt (*)
84th NVA Arty Rgt (85mm/130mm gun, direct support)
320B NVA Division (to NVA 1st Corps in 1973)
48B NVA Inf Rgt
64B NVA Inf Rgt
312th NVA Division (to NVA 1st Corps in 1973)
141st NVA Inf Rgt (*)
165th NVA Inf Rgt (*)
209th NVA Inf Rgt (*)
304th NVA Division (to NVA 2nd Corps in 1974)
9th NVA Inf Rgt
24B NVA Inf Rgt
66th NVA Inf Rgt (*)
68th NVA Arty Rgt
Independent Regiments:
27B NVA Inf Rgt
31st NVA Inf Rgt (*)
126th Naval Sapper Group
246th NVA Inf Rgt
270B NVA Inf Rgt
DMZ Sapper Group (5 × battalions)
202nd NVA Tank Rgt
203rd NVA Tank Rgt
38th NVA Arty Rgt
45th NVA Arty Rgt
58th NVA Arty Rgt
164th NVA Arty Rgt (130mm gun)
166th NVA Arty Rgt
Independent Battalions:
15th NVA Sapper Bn
47th NVA Inf Bn
75th NVA Air Defense Gun Bn

NVA TRI-THIEN MILITARY REGION
324B NVA Division (to NVA 2nd Corps in 1974)
29th NVA Inf Rgt (to NVA MR5 in 1974)
803rd NVA Inf Rgt
812th NVA Inf Rgt (to 6th Div in 1974)
78th NVA Arty Rgt
(5th NVA Inf Rgt from MRTT in 1974)
(6th NVA Inf Rgt from MRTT in 1974)
Independent Regiments:
4th NVA Inf Rgt
5th NVA Inf Rgt (to 324B Div in 1974)
6th NVA Inf Rgt (to 324B Div in 1974)
675B NVA Arty Rgt
Independent Battalions:
7th NVA Sapper Bn
11th NVA Recon Bn
35th NVA Rocket Bn
582nd NVA Inf Bn
Phu Loc NVA Inf Bn

NVA FRONT 7 (Quang Tri Province)
Independent Battalions:
808th NVA Inf Bn
810th NVA Sapper Bn
814th NVA Inf Bn

NVA MILITARY REGION 5 (Quang Nam & Quang Tin Provinces)
711th NVA Division (units to 2nd Div in 1974)
31st NVA Inf Rgt (*) (to 2nd Div in 1974)
38th NVA Inf Rgt (to 2nd Div in 1974)
270th NVA Inf Rgt (to NVA MR 5 in 1974)
12th NVA Arty Bn
2nd NVA Division (absorbed 711th Div personnel in 1974; ARVN continued to call this amalgamated division the 711th, so it is noted as such in the text for 1974-75)
1st NVA Inf Rgt (disbanded in 1974)
141st NVA Inf Rgt (*) (to 3rd Binh Dinh Div in 1974)
52nd VC Inf Rgt (*) (NVA from 12/72; disbanded 1974)
(31st NVA Inf Rgt (*) from 711th Div in 1974)
(38th NVA Inf Rgt from 711th Div in 1974)
Independent Regiments:
5th NVA Sapper Rgt
45th NVA Sapper Rgt
(270th NVA Inf Rgt from 711th Div in 1974)
572nd Tank/Arty Group
Independent Battalions:
32nd NVA Recon Bn
120th VC Montagnard Inf Bn

NVA FRONT 4
Independent Battalions (Quang Nam Province):
1st NVA Inf Bn (*)
2nd NVA Inf Bn (*)
42nd VC Recon Bn
80th NVA Inf Bn
83rd NVA Inf Bn
86th NVA Inf Bn
89th NVA Sapper Bn
91st NVA Sapper Bn
471st NVA Sapper Bn
575th NVA Arty Bn (Rocket)
577th NVA Arty Bn
Independent Battalions (Quang Tin Province):
11th NVA Inf Bn
70th NVA Inf Bn
72nd NVA Inf Bn
74th VC Inf Bn
Independent Battalions (Quang Ngai Province):
38th NVA Inf Bn
48th NVA Inf Bn
70th VC Sapper Bn
107th NVA Rocket Bn
145th VC Inf Bn

UNITS IN SOUTH VIETNAM'S II CORPS ZONE:

NVA B-3 FRONT
320th NVA Division
48th NVA Inf Rgt (to B-3 Front in 1974)
64th NVA Inf Rgt
54th NVA Arty Rgt
(9th NVA Inf Rgt from 968th Div in 1974)
[note: also 52nd VC Inf Rgt until Aug '72 when it transferred to 2nd Div)
10th NVA Division (aka "F-10")
28th NVA Inf Rgt
66th NVA Inf Rgt (*)
95B NVA Inf Rgt
40th NVA Arty Rgt (130mm gun/122mm Rocket)
Independent Regiments:
24C NVA Inf Rgt
400th NVA Sapper Rgt
(48th NVA Inf Rgt from 320th Div in 1974)
Independent Battalions:
2nd NVA Inf Bn (*)
5th NVA Inf Bn
28th NVA Recon Bn
297B NVA Tank Bn
631st NVA Inf Bn
Unidentified NVA Arty Bn
Independent Battalions (Kontum Province):
304th NVA Inf Bn
406th NVA Sapper Bn
Independent Battalions (Gia Lai):
2nd NVA Inf Ben (*)
45th VC Inf Bn
67th VC Inf Bn
408th VC Sapper Bn
Independent Battalions (Darlac Province):
301st NVA Inf Bn
401st NVA Sapper Bn

under **NVA MILITARY REGION 5**
3rd (Binh Dinh) **Division** (NVA, formerly VC)
2nd NVA Inf Rgt (formerly VC)
12th NVA Inf Rgt
21st NVA Inf Rgt (to COSVN in 1974)
(141st NVA Inf Rgt (*) from 2nd Div in 1974)
(Note: also 18th & 22nd VC Rgts in 1960s., replaced by 12th & 21st NVA)
Independent Battalions:
405th NVA Sapper Bn
Independent Battalions (Binh Dinh Province):
50th NVA Inf Bn
52nd NVA Inf Bn
53rd NVA Inf Bn
54th NVA Inf Bn
55th NVA Inf Bn
56th NVA Inf Bn
Independent Battalions (Phu Yen Province):
9th NVA Inf Bn
13th NVA Inf Bn
14th NVA Sapper Bn
96th NVA Inf Bn
Independent Battalions (Khanh Hoa Province):
7th NVA Sapper Bn
12th NVA Inf Bn
407th NVA Sapper Bn
460th NVA Inf Bn
470th NVA Inf Bn
480th NVA Inf Bn
Khanh Hoa VC Sapper Bn

VC MILITARY REGION 6
Independent Battalions:
130th NVA Arty Bn
186th NVA Inf Bn
240th NVA Inf Bn
481st VC Inf Bn
482nd VC Inf Bn
810th NVA Inf Bn
840th NVA Inf Bn

VC MILITARY REGION 10
Independent Battalion:
251st VC Inf Bn

UNITS IN SOUTH VIETNAM'S III CORPS ZONE:

CENTRAL OFFICE FOR SOUTH VIETNAM
7th VC/NVA Division
141st NVA Inf Rgt (*)
165th NVA Inf Rgt (*)
209th NVA Inf Rgt (*)
75th NVA Arty Rgt
22nd NVA Arty Bn
28th NVA Sapper Bn
9th VC Division (all NVA personnel by December 1972)
95C NVA Inf Rgt
271st VC Inf Rgt (*)
272nd VC Inf Rgt
(42nd NVA Arty Rgt (122mm/85mm gun) from 1974 on)
429th Sapper Command
29th NVA Sapper Rgt
7th NVA Sapper Bn
8th NVA Sapper Bn
9th NVA Sapper Bn
10th NVA Sapper Bn
11th NVA Sapper Bn
12th NVA Sapper Bn
16th NVA Sapper Bn
Independent Regiments:
33rd NVA Inf Rgt (to 3rd Phuoc Long Div in 1974)
101st NVA Inf Rgt (*)
201st NVA Inf Rgt (to 3rd Phuoc Long Div in 1974)
205th NVA Inf Rgt (*)
271st NVA Inf Rgt (*)
274th VC Inf Rgt (to 3rd Phuoc Long Div in 1974)
Independent Battalions:
4th NVA Sapper Bn
6th NVA Sapper Bn
7th NVA Sapper Bn
89th NVA Sapper Bn
211th NVA Sapper Bn
268th NVA Sapper Bn
10th VC Sapper Bn
12th VC Sapper Bn
3rd NVA Tank Bn
5th NVA Tank Bn
2nd NVA Arty Bn
3rd NVA Arty Bn
8th VC Arty Bn
35th NVA Arty Bn (from 96th Arty Rgt)
74A NVA Rocket Bn
74B NVA Rocket Bn
1st NVA Inf Bn (*)
2nd NVA Inf Bn (*)
4th NVA Inf Bn
14th NVA Inf Bn
267th NVA Inf Bn
506th NVA Inf Bn
1st Tay Ninh VC Inf Bn
6th VC Inf Bn
9th VC Inf Bn
20th VC Inf Bn
168th VC Inf Bn
269th VC Inf Bn
368th VC Inf Bn
445th VC Inf Bn
508th VC Inf Bn

UNITS IN SOUTH VIETNAM'S IV CORPS ZONE:

also under **CENTRAL OFFICE FOR SOUTH VIETNAM**
1st Division (disbanded in September 1973)
44th NVA Sapper Rgt
52nd NVA Inf Rgt (*)
101D NVA Inf Rgt (became separate brigade in 1973)
5th VC Division (composition changed to all NVA during war)
6th VC/NVA Inf Rgt (aka "E-6")
174th VC/NVA Inf Rgt
275th VC/NVA Inf Rgt
25th VC/NVA Sapper Bn
(367th NVA Sapper Rgt attached in 1975)
6th Division (disbanded late 1973; reformed 1974)
24th NVA Inf Rgt (to 8th Div in 1974)
207th NVA Inf Rgt
320th NVA Inf Rgt (to COSVN in 1974)
(812th NVA Inf Rgt from 324B Div in 1974)
(DT-1 – VC Inf Rgt from COSVN in 1974)
Independent Regiments:
Z-15 NVA Inf Rgt (to 8th Div in 1974)
Z-18 NVA Inf Rgt (to 8th Div in 1974)
(320th NVA Inf Rgt from 6th Div in 1974)
Independent Battalions:
1 × Bn of 96th NVA Arty Rgt
1 × Bn of 208th NVA Arty Rgt

VC MILITARY REGION 2
Independent Regiment:
DT-1 VC Inf Rgt ("Dong Thap"; to 6th Div in 1974)
Independent Battalions:
207th VC Sapper Bn
267B NVA Sapper Bn
281st NVA Sapper Bn
309th VC Arty Bn
209th VC Inf Bn
268C VC Inf Bn
271st VC Inf Bn
278th VC Inf Bn
279th VC Inf Bn
295th VC Inf Bn
310th VC Inf Bn
502nd VC Inf Bn
512th VC Inf Bn
514C VC Inf Bn
516A VC Inf Bn
516B VC Inf Bn
590th VC Inf Bn
504th NVA Inf Bn

VC MILITARY REGION 3
Independent Regiments:
D-1 VC Inf Rgt
D-2 NVA Inf Rgt (to 4th Div in 1974)
D-3 VC Inf Rgt
18B NVA Inf Rgt (to 4th Div in 1974)
95A NVA Sapper Rgt (to 4th Div in 1974)
Independent Battalions:
2012th VC Sapper Bn
2014th VC Sapper Bn
2311th VC Arty Bn
2315th VC Arty Bn
Tay Do VC Inf Bn
2nd U Minh VC Inf Bn
10th U Minh VC Inf Bn
501st VC Inf Bn
764th VC Inf Bn
857th VC Inf Bn
962nd NVA Inf Bn

HO CHI MINH TRAIL ORGANIZATION

MILITARY REGION 559
Logistical Group 470
Tri-border area and adjacent South Vietnam
Logistical Group 471
Tri-border area north to the A Shau Valley
Logistical Group 472
Southern Laos
Logistical Group 473
A Shau Valley north to Khe Sanh
Logistical Group 571
Southern North Vietnam and passes to Laos

UNITS FORMED AND OR DEPLOYED/REDEPLOYED AFTER JANUARY 1973

1st NVA Corps Headquarters
Formed October 1973 for 308th, 312th and 320B Divisions
2nd NVA Corps Headquarters
Formed May 1974 for 304th, 324B and 325th Divisions
3rd NVA Corps Headquarters
Formed in June 1974 for 2nd and 711th Divisions
301st NVA Corps Headquarters (aka "4th Corps")
Formed July 1974 for 3rd Phuoc Long, 7th and 9th Divisions
3rd Phuoc Long Division (formed 1974)
33rd NVA Inf Rgt (from COSVN in 1974)
201st NVA Inf Rgt (from COSVN in 1974)
274th VC Inf Rgt (from COSVN in 1974)

4th NVA Division (formed 1974)
D-2 NVA Inf Rgt (from VC MR 3 in 1974)
18B NVA Inf Rgt (from VC MR 3 in 1974)
95 NVA Sapper Rgt (from VC MR 3 in 1974)
8th NVA Division (formed 1974)
Z-15 NVA Inf Rgt (from COSVN in 1974)
Z-18 NVA Inf Rgt (from COSVN in 1974)
24th NVA Inf Rgt (from 6th Div in 1974)
27th NVA Sapper Division (formed late 1974 or 1975)
115th NVA Sapper Rgt (formed 1974/75)
(Other elements not known, but probably a consolidation of existing sapper assets.)
308th NVA Division (in 1972 Offensive; redeployed south in 1973)
36th NVA Inf Rgt (*)
88th NVA Inf Rgt
102nd NVA Inf Rgt (aka "162nd")
308B NVA Division (Hanoi Garrison; to NVA 1st Corps in late 1973)
Units unknown, but presumably:
(36B NVA Inf Rgt)
(88B NVA Inf Rgt)
(102B NVA Inf Rgt)
316th NVA Division (Laos & North Vietnam; to South Vietnam late 1974)
98th NVA Inf Rgt
174th NVA Inf Rgt
176th NVA Inf Rgt
341st NVA Division (DMZ defense 1973; to South Vietnam in 1975)
273rd NVA Inf Rgt attached from NVN's MR 4
Other subordinate units unknown

968th NVA Division (Trail defense in Laos; to South Vietnam in 1974)
9th NVA Inf Rgt (to 320th Div in 1974)
19th NVA Inf Rgt
39th NVA Inf Rgt
75th NVA Artillery Division (To South Vietnam in 1975 as cotrolling headquarters for five artillery regiments)
377th NVA Air Defense Division (deployed 1973-74) fifteen air defense gun battalions
671st NVA Air Defense Division (deployed 1973-74)
673rd NVA Air Defense Division (deployed 1973-74)
675th NVA Air Defense Division (deployed 1973-74)
679th NVA Air Defense Division (deployed 1973-74)
5th NVA Engineer Division (formed 1974)
26th NVA Armor Group (aka "M-26"; to COSVN in late 1973)
20th Tank Bn & two other tank battalions
46th Recon Bn
52nd NVA Brigade (to NVA MR 5 in 1974)
15th NVA Sapper Bn
four infantry batallions
one artillery battalion
101D NVA Brigade (formed September 1973 from remnants of 1st Div)
69th NVA Artillery Group (to COSVN in 1973)
208th NVA Arty Rgt
Other artillery units as attached
71st NVA Air Defense Brigade (in South Vietnam in 1975)

Independent Units:
E-1 VC Inf Rgt (in Delta area in 1973)
21st NVA Inf Rgt (to COSVN from 3rd Binh Dinh Div in 1974)
E-24 NVA Inf Rgt (to Delta area in 1973)
25th NVA Inf Rgt (in South Vietnam by March 1975)
26th NVA Inf Rgt (to B3 Front in September 1973)
27th NVA Inf Rgt (to northern provinces in late 1974)
(32nd NVA Inf Rgt in Ia Drang campaign 1965, probably disbanded subsequently)
36th NVA Inf Rgt (*) (formed spring 1974, with two infantry battalions, AAA Co, & light artillery)
41st NVA Inf Rgt (to Quang Nam in December 1974)
51st NVA Inf Rgt (to northern provinces in late 1974)
74th NVA Arty Rgt (to NVA MR 7 in early 1973)
86th NVA Inf Rgt (to Central Highlands early 1973)
98th NVA Arty Rgt (supported 325th Div in March 1975)
205th NVA Tank Rgt (?) (possibly in 1972 Offensive)
210th NVA Arty Rgt (supported 7th Div in 1975)
262nd NVA Air Defense Rgt (in South Vietnam, 1975)
305th NVA Airborne Bde (aka 405th; presumed formed in 1965 at Hanoi and subsequently converted to sappers)
367th NVA Sapper Rgt (Cambodia late 1973; attached to 5th Div in 1975)
573rd NVA Tank Rgt (to northern provinces in late 1974)
D-14 NVA Inf Bn (to COSVN prior to 1975)
D-16 NVA Inf Bn (to COSVN prior to 1975)
D-18 NVA Inf Bn (to COSVN prior to 1975)
33rd NVA Sapper Bn (to northern provinces in 1974)
200th NVA Inf Bn (to COSVN in 1973)

OTHER NVA MILITARY UNITS

304B NVA Division (Training in North Vietnam)
330th NVA Division (Training in North Vietnam)
350th NVA Division (Training in North Vietnam)
338th NVA Division (Converted from Training Division to line infantry division in 1973; to South Vietnam in 1975; subordinate units unknown.)
Home Defense:
There were seventeen provincial regiments in North Vietnam.

APPENDIX I
AUSTRALIAN ORDER OF BATTLE IN VIETNAM – AUGUST 1968

1st AUSTRALIAN TASK FORCE – Nui Dat
1st Bn, Royal Australian Regiment
3rd Bn, Royal Australian Regiment
4th Bn, Royal Australian Regiment
12th Field Regiment, Royal Australian Artillery (105T)
"C" Squadron, 1st Armoured Regiment (Centurion tanks)
"A" Squadron, 3rd Cavalry Regiment (M-113 APCs)
1st Field Squadron, Royal Australian Engineers
2nd Squadron, Australian Special Air Service Regiment
No. 9 Squadron, Royal Australian Air Force (UH-1 helicopters)

Notes: The first Australian units in South Vietnam were attached to the US 173rd Airborne Brigade. They brought their own equipment, such as 7.62mm FN rifles. As troop strength grew, an Australian brigade ("task force") was formed, and units (not individuals as in the US Army) rotated through it on one-year tours of duty. All nine battalions of the Royal Australian Regiment served in Vietnam, eventually equipped with US weapons such as the M-16 rifle, M-79 grenade launcher, and M-60 machinegun. Supporting arms (tanks, APCs, engineers, etc.) were deployed in squadron (i.e. company) size units. The RAAF also operated a squadron of Caribou light transports and a squadron of Canberra jet bombers, while the Royal Australian Navy contributed a ship to the "gun line" (relieved every six month). New Zealand provided one or two infantry companies, an artillery battery, and an SAS troop, which rotated service with the Australian Task Force. Compared to other troops in Vietnam, the Australians would be rated *excellent*.

APPENDIX J
SOUTH KOREAN ORDER OF BATTLE IN VIETNAM – AUGUST 1968
REPUBLIC OF KOREA FIELD COMMAND
HQ – Nha Trang

CAPITAL "TIGER" DIVISION
HQ & Division Troops – Qui Nhon
Cap Div Eng Bn
Cap Div Tank Co
Cap Div Recon Co
Cavalry Regiment
1/Cav Inf Bn
2/Cav Inf Bn
3/Cav Inf Bn
1st Regiment
1/1 Inf Bn
2/1 Inf Bn
3/1 Inf Bn
26th Regiment
1/26 Inf Bn
2/26 Inf Bn
3/26 Inf Bn
Capital Division Artillery
10th FA Bn (105T)
60th FA Bn (105T)
61st FA Bn (105T)
628th FA Bn (155T)

9th "WHITE HORSE" DIVISION
HQ & Division Troops – Ninh Hoa
9th Div Eng Bn
9th Div Tank Co
9th Div Recon Co
28th Regiment
1/28 Inf Bn
2/28 Inf Bn
3/28 Inf Bn
29th Regiment
1/29 Inf Bn
2/29 Inf Bn
3/29 Inf Bn
30th Regiment
1/30 Inf Bn
2/30 Inf Bn
3/30 Inf Bn
9th Division Artillery
30th FA Bn (105T)
51st FA Bn (105T)
52nd FA Bn (105T)
966th FA Bn (155T)

2nd "BLUE DRAGON" MARINE BRIGADE – Hoi An
1st Marine Bn
2nd Marine Bn
3rd Marine Bn
5th Marine Bn

Notes: The South Koreans originally deployed with weaponry that was little better than that of the South Vietnamese. They gradually rearmed with more modern US weapons. In comparison with other troops, the ROK infantry would be rated as *good*, and the marines *excellent*. Problems existed mainly with the ROK high command.

APPENDIX K
ROYAL THAI ARMY ORDER OF BATTLE IN VIETNAM

The following Thai units served in Vietnam:
The Queen's Cobras Regiment (Sep '67-Aug '68)
3 × infantry battalions
1st Brigade, Royal Thai Expeditionary Division (Jul '68-Aug '69)
3 × infantry battalions
2nd Brigade, Royal Thai Expeditionary Division (Jan '69-Jan '72)
3 × infantry battalions
3rd Brigade, Royal Thai Expeditionary Division (Jul '69-Aug '70)
3 × infantry battalions
Division Troops (various periods of service)
3 × 105mm towed howitzer battalions
1 × 155mm towed howitzer battalion
1 × armored reconnaissance battalion
1 × engineer battalion (–)

Notes: A relatively small portion of Thailand's considerable army was committed to combat in Vietnam. The Queen's Cobra Regiment, which would be rated *excellent* in comparison with other units in country, was replaced by the Royal Thai Army "Black Panther" Expeditionary Division, which would be rated as *good*. The Queen's Cobras left Vietnam as the 1st Brigade arrived for a one-year tour in July of 1968. The 2nd Brigade arrived in January of 1969 and stayed on until January of 1972. The 3rd Brigade replaced the 1st in July of 1969, and remained for only one year also. Thus, the "division" only operated two brigades at its peak of strength, between February of 1969 and August of 1970. After the latter date, the headquarters was reduced to the "Royal Thai Army Volunteer Force." The Thais operated from Bear Cat near Saigon. Aside from the official Thai participation, there were approximately five brigades of CIA-sponsored mercenaries which made up the 014 That Division serving covertly in Laos.

APPENDIX L
LAOTIAN FORCES

There were a number of different military organizations operating in Laos throughout the period. These included the government's regular army (Forces Armees Royales), irregular forces, neutralist forces (Forces Armees Neutralistes), and CIA-sponsored units. Brigade-level units ("Groupements Mobiles, or GMs" of about 3,000 men in 3 or 4 battalions) are presented below by component and Laotian Military Regions.

FORCES ARMEES ROYALES
Military Region I
GM 11
GM 25
Military Region III
GM 12
GM 15 (airborne)
GM 18
GM 21 (airborne)
Military Region IV
GM 16
GM 17
GM 19

LAOTIAN IRREGULAR FORCES
Military Region III
GM 30
GM 31
GM 32
GM 33
Military Region IV
GM 41
GM 42
GM 43

FORCES ARMEES NEUTRALISTES
GM 801
GM 802

CIA-SPONSORED LAOTIAN UNITS
Military Region IV
4001
4002
4003
4004

Notes: Military Regions III and IV were adjacent to the panhandle of North Vietnam and the northern provinces of South Vietnam respectively. In general, the FAR units were *poor* with the exceptions of GM 15 (*fair*) and GM 21 (*good*). Irregular forces were *good* and the CIA-sponsored units were *excellent*. The FAN neturalists were *bad*, and could not be counted on for anything. On the other side, the Communists had similar strengths and quality ratings. The Neo Lao Hak Xat, better known as the Pathet Lao, were roughly equivalent to the FAR, or slightly better, with about eight brigades/regiment equivalents (one of which was airborne qualified). The NVA did not let the Pathet Lao operate near the Ho Chi Minh Trail. NVA also fielded regular units in Laos for security purposes, including the 968th Division and the 39th and 101st Independent Regiments, which provided a counterweight to the CIA units. The Communists also had to put up with their own Dissident Neutralist Laotian units, which were about as unreliable as those on the government side.

INDEX

Page numbers in **bold** refer to an illustration

Picture Credits

The majority of the photographs used in this book were supplied by the United States Department of Defense. Others who provided photographs include the Associated Press, Bell Helicopters, The Robert Hunt Library, Lockheed, The McClancy Collection, Pilot Press Ltd, Robert F. Dorr and the Socialist Republic of Vietnam

Extract Credits:

Chapter 1
1. Newsweek, Dec 14 1965; 2. Robert F. Dorr; 3. USAF in SE Asia
Chapter 2
1. Robert F. Dorr; 2. Newsweek Feb 22 1965; 3. Newsweek August 1965
Chapter 3
1. Time March 19 1965; New York Times May 7 1966; 3. Newsweek 1966; 4. Newsweek August 30 1965; 5. Time November 26 1965; 6. Time November 26 1965; 7. Newsweek October 25 1965
Chapter 4
1. Newsweek February 28 1966; 2. Newsweek February 11 1966; 3. Newsweek February 14 1966; 4. Newsweek May 30 1966; 5. Newsweek August 8 1966; 6. Newsweek August 15 1966; 7. Time February 11 1966; 8. Time November 4 1966; 9. New York Times July 12 1966; 10. Newsweek July 3 1967; 11. Newsweek January 1967; 12. Time
Chapter 5
1. Time April 1967; 2. Newsweek July 17 1967; 3. Newsweek January 23 1967; 4. Mounted Combat in Vietnam, US Army
Chapter 6
1. Time June 28 1968; 2. New York Times; 3. US Marine Corps History; 4. US Marine Corps History; 5. Time Feb 16 1968; 6. Time; 7. USMC History; 8. Robert F. Dorr; 9. Robert F. Dorr; 10. Time February 9 1968
Chapter 7
1. New York Times February 2 1970; 2. New York Times May 3 1970; 3. New York Times June 29 1970; 4. New York Times August 10 1970; 5. Time Jan 12 1970; 6. Time June 22 1970
Chapter 8
1. Time Feb 2 1970; 2. New York Times May 3 1970; 3. New York Times August 10 1970; 5. Time January 12 1970; 6. Time June 22 1970
Chapter 9
1. Newsweek January 4 1971; 2. Newsweek April 12 1971; 3. Newsweek 15 March 1971; 4. Newsweek March 29 1971; 5. Time January 21 1966; 6. New York Times March 20 1972
Chapter 10
1. New York Times March 20 1972; 2. Robert F. Dorr; 3. New York Times April 4 1972; 4. Time May 8 1972; 5. The View from the Rock, USAF; 6. The View from the rock, USAF.
Chapter 11
1. New York Times Jan 23 1973; 2. New York Times Jan 25 1973; 3. New York Times Feb 14 1973; 4. New York Times March 29 1973; 5. New York Times April 23 1973; 6. New York Times April 9 1973; 7. New York Times May 3 1970; 8. New York Times April 15 1973
Chapter 12
1. New York Times April 28 1975; 2. New York Times April 28 1975; 3. New York Times April 28 1975